The Complete
Canadian Book Editor

The Complete Canadian Book Editor

LESLIE VERMEER

Brush Education Inc.

www.brusheducation.ca

contact@brusheducation.ca

Design and layout: Carol Dragich, Dragich Design; Cover image: iStock: Dominik Pabis.

Proofreading: Shauna Babiuk.

Figure credits: Photos used courtesy Bruce Timothy Keith: 1.1–1.5, 2.1, 8.3, 8.8, 8.9. Image of proof page (7.4) courtesy Bruce Peel Special Collections & Archives, University of Alberta. istock/focusstock: 8.15. Courtesy Webcom: 8.16. Illustrations by Chao Yu, Vancouver: 8.10, 8.12, 8.18–8.22.

Library and Archives Canada Cataloguing in Publication

Vermeer, Leslie, 1969-, author   The complete Canadian book editor / Leslie Vermeer.

Includes bibliographical references and index. Issued in print and electronic formats. ISBN 978-1-55059-677-9 (paperback).--ISBN 978-1-55059-678-6 (pdf).-- ISBN 978-1-55059-679-3 (mobi).--ISBN 978-1-55059-680-9 (epub)

1. Editing. 2. Publishers and publishing--Canada. 3. Book industries and trade--Canada. I. Title.

PN162.V47 2016   070.5'1   C2016-903926-9   C2016-903927-7

We acknowledge the support of the Government of Canada | Canadä
Nous reconnaissons l'appui du gouvernement du Canada

*This book is dedicated to Bruce,
the best kind of editor,
with love.*

Contents

Acknowledgements

My thanks to Brush Education for their enthusiasm about this book. In particular, warm thank-yous to Glenn Rollans for his enormous patience while the manuscript developed and to Lauri Seidlitz for her discerning queries and sharp editorial eyes.

I would also like to thank the creative people who contributed their personal observations and experiences to this project: Cathie Crooks, Carol Dragich Bishop, Lisa Guenther, Rick Lauber, and Ruth Linka. And thank-you to Don Watt for allowing me to use and build on his punctuation exercise.

My gratitude to the Central Branch of the Greater Victoria Public Library for being an incubator and writing space. Also, I acknowledge Grant MacEwan University for sabbatical funding that enabled me to finish the manuscript.

Most importantly, thank you to my personal support system: Gigi Meade Jabs, for her encouragement and kindness; Carmen Hrynchuk, for her amazing and absolutely not invisible support; and Bruce Keith, for reading, listening to, and living through this project with me.

Introduction

You're holding in your hands a book. Maybe it's a paper book—a codex—the form the West has used for nearly two thousand years. Maybe it's an ebook, carried on a dedicated reading device or read from a smartphone, jostling for your attention alongside numerous apps, images, games, and other texts. Regardless of its container, a book is notable for its content: the sustained transmission of knowledge and thought, the creation of an authoritative voice that delights, admonishes, encourages, inspires. A book is always greater than the sum of its parts, more than the words and images on its pages, more than its physical shape. A book is an experience. And book editors are integral to creating that experience, for building the bond between writers and readers, every day.

A book editor's success in building that bond depends on the act of publishing. At its foundation, *publishing* refers to the process of making writing public, enabling it to circulate widely, without restriction. Over the course of several centuries, the work of printers and booksellers overlapped and diverged to create the distinctions in the industry we recognize today.

One of my industry colleagues defines book publishing as the process of turning money into books and then turning books back into money. On the surface, this explanation of the business isn't particularly profound: all industries, in one form or another, turn capital into a product and expect the product to sell, earn a profit, and return capital to continue the production cycle. The cultural industries—like book publishing—are different, though. No one asks an author to write a book, no one asks a publisher to publish a book (other than an author, of course),

1

and people don't need books in quite the same way they need food, shelter, clothing, power, and heat. (I know, for serious readers, books can feel like life necessities. Like many of you, I have, on occasion, chosen books over food.) And every book is, in some sense, unique, intended for a specific audience and requiring an original, carefully tailored marketing plan. Turning books back into money is in fact very difficult, and book editors have the broadest involvement of anyone in the process. They first try to find the authors and the manuscripts of books that will feel like needs, not wants, to their potential readers. Then they work deep inside the text—often in conjunction with authors and designers—to create a physical object that will fulfill readers' expectations. Eventually they work with marketing staff to discover the unique sales points to make a book fascinating and appealing to its intended audiences. While all of these processes are in motion, editors are also nurturing the next book, the next author, and the next. And they do all of this work for a tiny fraction of the cover price of each copy of the book sold.

Writer, editor, and publisher Marshall Lee defines book EDITING as "The preparation of the content of a book, and sometimes its conception and planning, in cooperation with the author and designer." While this is a factually accurate definition, it barely touches the specifics of the hour-by-hour, day-by-day processes of acquiring and editing manuscripts and working with authors, publishers, designers, marketing staff, and other editors, and it also misses the all-important human element of the work. This book seeks to fill in those details.

What This Book Is and Is Not

The Complete Canadian Book Editor has been written to teach aspiring and working editors how to succeed in the field of book editing. As you read the chapters and work through the activities and exercises, you will learn about the tasks a contemporary book editor performs, from contracting new manuscripts to producing back cover copy, from going through the slush pile to congratulating the author at a book launch. Textual editing is a fairly common activity, performed in all areas of publishing as well as in other types of business. This book explains how the conventions and processes of book publishing differ from those in other fields of publishing, and defines and contextualizes a large number of industry-specific terms. It surveys the various sectors within the book-publishing industry and explores the regional, national, and international structure of the business. It gives you background and insight into specific processes and activities, such as editorial meetings and sales conferences, so that you will be well prepared to step into an editorial or marketing role with an established firm or to provide writers with effective and appropriate consultation and coaching as a freelance editor. The book is situated in the Canadian context but necessarily refers to the broader context of international publishing.

In covering so much ground, I must inevitably make some generalizations. My general comments about certain activities may not reflect your specific experience, although they are informed by my experiences, those of my friends and colleagues in the business, and the perspectives of industry experts I've quoted. There are differences in processes, practices, and even basic working assumptions between, say, trade publishing and scholarly publishing, or between literary publishing and textbook publishing. As much as possible, I have tried to note distinctions between sectors, and of course every publishing house has its own idiosyncrasies and peculiarities. I've written in broad strokes; I hope your experiences and your discussions with colleagues and peers will add further detail.

What you won't learn from this book is how to edit per se. There are, however, various exercises to help you practise and refine your copyediting and proofreading skills, as well as a variety of activities that invite you to reflect on the significance of editorial tasks. Very little of a book editor's day-to-day job involves working with text. Instead, most of it involves working with other people in the publishing cycle, especially sales and marketing staff. In fact, the jump from sales and marketing into editing is fairly common today. If you want to be a book editor, don't turn down a job in sales, marketing, or publicity: right now, this may be one of the best ways to break into the business.

On January 2, 2013, Mike Shatzkin published the following comment on his highly influential book-publishing industry blog:

> *I think the clearest indication that marketing is reaching its proper 21st century position in publishing will be its increasing importance in driving title selection. As publishers become more audience-centric, it is the people who are communicating with the audience (the marketers, but also the editors, and the line between them will get fuzzier, not that it hasn't sometimes previously been blurred) who will see what's needed that isn't in the market yet. In a way, that's always happened. But in another year or three, it will be a formal expectation in some structures, and will have a defined workflow.*

This quotation is talking about you, the aspiring book editor. You may be less likely to get a job in contemporary book publishing without a sound sense of book marketing and its related issues. Marketing—at least for major publishers—is becoming a crucial part of the in-house editor's required skill set. In turn, freelance editors may be increasingly responsible for the mechanical and, to a lesser extent, substantive editing of manuscripts. In-house editors may be fewer (at least at very large firms), and their jobs will be more financially driven.

Does this mean there are no jobs to be had? Not at all. It simply means that to get one of those jobs, you need to be as well prepared as possible. Knowing what book editors do, knowing what's expected of publishing interns and editorial assistants, knowing the language of publishing and the makeup of an editor's interests ... all of this knowledge will help you compete more effectively and insightfully for a book-publishing job. It will help you be a more effective and resourceful colleague if you join a small, independent book-publishing firm—and there are many such firms across Canada. It will also help you be a more informed and valuable consultant if, as a freelance editor, you work with authors looking to self-publish.

This book aims to prepare editors of books for commercial sale. I've worked in the world of academic publishing, where selling a few hundred copies of a book is a significant accomplishment, and with small, independent Canadian publishers whose print runs are modest compared to the publishers whose books are routinely featured on the *New York Times* bestsellers list. As I said above, the historical purpose of publishing has been to make books for selling. For some writers and editors, the idea of financial success—in fact, the idea of relating artistic production to money in any way—suggests compromising one's artistic vision or pandering to common tastes and expectations. If this is your outlook, you might question some of the information in this book—and such questioning is appropriate. I think we need to ask whether commercial publishing has over-commodified the book, whether economics has in fact created the *anti-book*, as scholar Sherman Young describes certain texts (books ghostwritten for a celebrity as part of her public relations program, for instance). According to Young, anti-books are "cynical creations, manufactured for marketing reasons only"; they derail our social conversation and mock our intellectual curiosity. Yet these books do circulate, and do generate social conversation (at least for some audiences), alongside books written with very different purposes, books perceived to be more socially valuable. Does that make some forms of publishing less legitimate or less important than others? Asking these kinds of questions and assessing the larger values of our business are necessary processes if we are to keep our discipline vibrant and relevant. Editing and publishing are intellectual labours; success demands that we think critically, that we question everything. That said, for most people, publishing *is* a business, and most jobs in the industry depend on the successful marketing and selling of a substantial proportion of the books a firm publishes in any given season, so it's that perspective I adopt in my discussion and advice throughout this book.

EXAMINE THE APPEAL
The reasons people want to get into editing and publishing vary widely. What appeals to you about books? About working as a book editor? In a few sentences, explain your views.

Chapter Overview

Now that you've done some thinking about the profession and about your motivations for becoming a book editor, here's an overview of what *this* book will provide to support your goals.

Chapter 1 discusses the history and significance of books in Western culture. It looks at the emergence of the book editor—a relatively new figure on the publishing scene—and what value editors contribute to the process of making books for the commercial market. It then invites you to connect yourself as a prospective editor to the traditions of book culture and to reflect on the way you perceive and understand the work that book editors do.

Chapter 2 moves from the broad reach of book history to a brief survey of publishing in Canada, in particular its roots in nationalism and regionalism. I discuss the structure of the Canadian market, its various publishing sectors, and their composition. This section also looks briefly at the economics of the business and introduces important concepts—such as royalties, discount structures, and subsidies—that affect editors' acquisition choices and publishers' programs and lists. The general survey of publishing in this chapter may be useful to anyone entering the industry in any capacity, including hopeful writers.

Chapter 3 deals with the numerous details associated with the acquisitions process. I look at the processes of commissioning books and handling submissions, and discuss how editors assess the manuscripts they read. This chapter explains and provides examples of various documents editors use in editorial evaluation and communication, such as query letters, proposals, editorial reports, and rejection letters. It also investigates the construction of taste, why certain editors and certain publishers make the choices they do, and how the commodification of books creates opportunities for some authors—and silence and invisibility for others.

Chapter 4 looks specifically at contracts. This chapter discusses the first principles of book contracting, the major clauses of a standard contract, typical subsidiary rights, and the relationship between acquisitions and house economics, as well as a number of other, smaller details of contracts. This chapter is intended to teach you how to walk an author through a standard book contract and how to read and understand the specific points in the contracts offered by the firms you will work with.

Chapters 5, 6, and 7 focus on elements of editing a manuscript. First, I look at the relationship between the book editor and the author and how the editor can support the author when various problems emerge. Next, I look at aspects of manuscript preparation. I present the book as a constructed object, engaged in genre and audience expectations and supported by a publisher-built apparatus. This chapter also looks at specific structures that become the responsibility of the editor and the publisher, such as the title, the cover, and the cover copy, as well as various aspects of the front and back matters. Then I turn to textual editing. I review some key ideas in stylistic editing and copyediting, and revisit proofreading. Throughout these chapters, I refer to resources that support book editing and closely consider the book editor's sensibility and the elusive concept of style.

Chapter 8 looks at the design, production, and manufacture of the book as a material object. I start with some basic processes, terms, and concepts in design and layout. Then I look at printing and binding. Finally I introduce the notion of production editing, including issues such as budgeting, costing, schedules, and administration. This chapter also examines processes involved with a digital workflow and considerations for the future of both physical and digital books.

Chapter 9 considers in turn the strands of sales, marketing, and promotions. It looks at several tasks—such as preparing a title information sheet or a catalogue description and attending a sales conference—specific to editors supporting manuscripts prior to publication. It then discusses tasks generally handled by the marketing team, such as social-media marketing, publicity, book trailers, book tours, readings, and reviews. This chapter also looks at the larger context in which book marketing occurs, the place of book reviewing in contemporary culture, and the problem of discoverability.

Chapter 10 considers the future for book editors and book editing. While the purchasing of books is fairly stable, amid ever-increasing entertainment and information alternatives, larger global trends are having an effect on the job of the editor. Here I look at the shift to digital publishing, the rise of self-publishing, the economics of the industry at large, and other matters. Since 2010 the upsurge in ebooks has led to a revival of interest in paper books, and recently sales of ebooks have appeared to stabilize. The business of making books is indeed changing, but the industry needs knowledgeable, versatile book editors more than ever. This chapter brings all of the preceding chapters together to discuss the iterative, and generative, process of publication.

Chapter 11 presents an array of stand-alone exercises for you to practise specific editorial skills. Supporting this chapter is a series of appendixes, intended to reinforce and extend your understanding of specific editorial tasks. You'll find a list of publishing terms, a checklist for editorial project management, and a marketing planner. You'll also find an annotated list of books useful in building a comprehensive editing library and a grammar and punctuation primer.

There is a glamour associated with book editors. The legend—or is it a shadow?—of Golden Age book editor Maxwell Perkins hangs over us, inspiring us, sometimes intimidating us. It's my hope that *The Complete Canadian Book Editor*, which draws from the knowledge and experiences of veteran editors as well as a diverse literature about writing, editing, and publishing, will help you find your inner Max: to be an inspiring, leading book editor in whatever role or sector you find yourself working in. Let's get started.

1

Why Edit Books?

"When you read a book, you hold another's mind in your hands."—James Burke

Why do you want to be a book editor? One of the reasons many people are attracted to book editing is the allure of authors. What editor wouldn't want to meet the next J.K. Rowling, an up-and-coming Margaret Atwood, a Joyce Carol Oates in the making? Another attraction is the physicality of books themselves and what they contain. Around the globe, humans have invested books with a special significance, both for the ideas they present and for the cultural values they represent.

What Is a Book?

Simply put, books are storehouses for information and narratives of various kinds—whatever a culture deems to be valuable. Books as objects have existed for several thousand years, although not always in forms that people today would recognize as "books." For our purposes today, a *book* is a gathering of sheets bound together in some manner (such as by sewing or with glue) and protected by a COVER, possibly including a spine; this definition of book reflects the codex, which dates from the early Common Era. The codex is what most people think of when they visualize a book, and it is to the codex that most people refer when we contemplate the concept of "bookness," or an object's likeness to a generic book structure.

Prior to the development of the codex, and for centuries after it, too, books were produced in the form of scrolls. The significance, and

Figure 1.1 A Japanese scroll book, ca. 1125, showing detail from *The Secrets of the Nine Luminaries*, a text that explains aspects of the sun, moons, and planets

Figure 1.2 A twelfth-century Japanese handscroll from the *Lotus Sutra*

advantage, of moving toward the codex and away from the scroll is that the codex made documents more durable (because the covers protected the contents), made them easier to store and transport (because flat is more convenient geometry than round), and allowed greater ease of use (because a codex can be opened at any point randomly, while a scroll must be rolled from beginning to end to be useful). Prior to the scroll, we might look to collected and numbered clay tablets such as the Sumerians made—but perhaps that stretches our modern sense of "book" too far.

Yet whether we consider a collection of clay tablets a "book" or not *is* relevant today, when many commentators argue that the experience of consuming text from a screen is qualitatively different from consuming text from bound paper—that is, that an ebook isn't a "book" because of how it is used, regardless of the text it contains. For many people, the physical object of the book—the paper, glue, and ink—is what matters, not the structure of the text or its provision of information or story. People who read ebooks often respond to the evocation of the paper book with a strongly defensive tone; ebook readers are frequently accused of disliking books, or of not being "real" readers, whatever that may mean. And we might look to the way in which dedicated ereading devices have been manufactured to emulate the experience of conventional book-in-hand reading—a clear evocation of bookness. What a book is—and relatedly, what kinds of reading are valuable and what kinds are not—is a highly contentious question at this moment in our society, as we stand ready to embrace, or reject, the transformation of the book in a digital world.

Questions of what is and is not a book—much like questions of what is and is not publishable—depend on privilege and authority: who gets to decide? That notion is something you should keep in mind as you work through this text: books are a technology of privilege. For most of human history, most people could not write or read; and until the last few decades, the ownership of multiple books was restricted to a relatively small group of people. Even today, many millions of people in Canada, the United States, the United Kingdom, and other Western nations cannot afford to own books. That there are books in so many formats that we can argue about them—that there are books to edit at all—is an outcome of our society's tremendous privilege, something we ought not to take for granted.

A book is both a physical and an abstract thing. Many writers are encouraged by the notion that they have a book in them—in which case we are obviously not talking about a physical glue-and-paper object. And most of us would distinguish "our" books—the books we personally own and cherish—from the masses of other people's books, as well as from the unpurchased books stocked in bookstores. Digital books add a new dimension to our mutable sense of the book—although some people would say digital books also erase elements of the book. Since the late nineteenth century, scholars have been studying books as objects that transmit specific information about a culture and its meanings, examining the process of manufacturing, circulating, reading, and preserving both books in general and specific EDITIONS and specific copies of individual titles. For instance, reading a cheap "student" edition of a book versus a fine limited edition may, perhaps, change our experience of the text it contains—or perhaps not. Our preferences as readers should never be cast as "wrong" or "better," but they deserve to be investigated because they tell us important things about ourselves as individuals and as a society. If all the elements of publication are successful, readers should ideally lose themselves in the book's content, experiencing the physical book almost invisibly, yet the physical book is still there. Our preferences and judgements for and against various editions precede and emerge from our actual experiences of reading and using text. As book editors, we have these experiences of text ourselves and in turn produce them for others.

My purpose in this text is more practical than academic, but you should keep these points in mind. The book as the West has known it for some five hundred years is changing, and these changes are pushing Western society to ask important questions about who we are, how we communicate, and what we value. Books represent a portable visual record of information and narrative for future generations—but somehow that's not all they are, either, even from the most crassly commercial point of view.

Why a Book?

Books have history. From the earliest days of cuneiform (an ancient system of writing) to the monks copying pages in scriptoria, through the advent of moveable type to today's digital formats, books have formed a significant part of human culture. The reception of books changes over time, and some ages of human society have been less friendly to books and writing than others; still, written texts have endured over centuries, even over millennia. In the Western world, books engage and inform our legal, political, and moral organization—and of course are informed by these forces in turn.

Books also have permanence. Unlike newspapers or magazines, which are intended to be disposable, most books are intended to be lasting physical forms. Medieval books, constructed prior to the rise of moveable type, were often precious objects, written on fine vellum, ornamented with illumination, and decorated with ivory, gems, and other luxury materials. (Medieval textbooks, by the way, were not ornamented or decorated; in fact, according to book history scholar Erik Kwakkel, their proportions and page design were similar to those found in contemporary textbooks, but they were much less colourful.) As books and other printed objects became more common in the early modern era, the cost of books dropped; by the nineteenth century, books were often produced in inexpensive, if inelegant, editions affordable to almost anyone. In the twentieth century, shelves displaying rows and rows of books became a standard feature of the middle-class home, and continue to be a fixture of today's interior design. The shift from physical to digital formats, however, is affecting our idea of a book's permanence and even changing how we "own" books.

Figure 1.3 A book from the twelfth century with gemstones and ivory plates (showing the Annunciation)

Figure 1.4 The highly decorated cover of a medieval book

THE ROLE OF LIBRARIANS

As we think about books' history and permanence, we should consider the role of libraries and librarians. For thousands of years, specialized workers have collected, catalogued, maintained, and circulated written text and other information cultures value, and it is through this work that we now have copies of some of humanity's most ancient texts. Libraries play an important role—sometimes unintentionally—in determining the books that are preserved and those that are forgotten. In the late nineteenth century, alongside the rise of public schooling, public libraries were founded with the express intent of offering people the opportunity to better themselves through almost unlimited access to information. By the early twentieth century, many librarians had become champions of books and the freedom to read, and libraries became the physical representation of this belief. Today, libraries continue to collect, organize, and circulate books, as well as periodicals, DVDs, video games, toys, and even seeds; and increasingly, libraries provide portals to digital texts, including ebooks and streaming music.

While you may not think of libraries when you think of the role of the book editor, libraries remain an important—and sometimes challenging—SALES CHANNEL for most publishers. Some book editors, particularly those publishing materials for children and teens, think carefully about libraries' values and technical practices as the editors make their acquisitions decisions. For instance, if a manuscript contained subject matter or language that might discourage in-school or community librarians from buying the finished book, some editors would be wary of acquiring that manuscript.

Authority

Books have authority. In the hierarchy of perception, books are seen to be more authoritative than newspapers, magazines, journals, and the Internet, although that perception may be shifting. The trust people invest in books has certainly changed over time. In the early days of print, many people distrusted books and warned others not to believe what they learned from books, echoing concerns that reach back to the origins of writing. (Socrates, for instance, argued that writing would destroy people's memories and weaken people's minds.) In the last couple of centuries, however, books have ascended to a more authoritative cultural position. Consider, for instance, how many candidates for political office produce books to undergird their campaigns. But recent scandals have rocked at least some people's sense of books' authority. The notorious example of James Frey's *A Million Little Pieces* (an alleged memoir of the author's extreme experiences as consequences of drug and alcohol addiction; the website The Smoking Gun subsequently showed the book to be largely fictitious) is only one of several examples of fraud that have revealed weakness in the systems of contemporary publishing. Others have included falsified Holocaust memoirs acquired by major publishers and the much-publicized YA novel *How Opal Mehta Got Kissed, Got Wild and Got a Life*, which contained passages plagiarized from other novels. More examples of literary fraud are, regrettably, discovered every year or two.

Another challenge to the authority of books is that posed by technological change. The availability of free reference material on the Internet has damaged or destroyed entire segments of the traditional publishing industry. Scholarly publishing and reference publishing have been dramatically affected by the open access movement and crowd-sourced online references such as Wikipedia. General-purpose dictionaries, general encyclopedias, and atlases have all suffered with the rise of online information. Several world-famous encyclopedias have ceased operations, for instance, and the high-profile *Oxford English Dictionary* has cancelled plans to produce a third edition in print and instead dedicated itself to being the authoritative online compiler of English vocabulary and usage. Similarly, open access and online publication have allowed highly specialized academic information to be shared more widely, more rapidly, and at less cost than traditional print publication have allowed. Still, at least some scholars continue to buy print editions despite the availability of free or inexpensive digital editions of texts.

WHAT IS OPEN ACCESS?

Open access is a movement led by scholars, researchers, and academic librarians to prevent knowledge and information from being controlled by private corporations. It is complementary to larger issues of digital rights and information flow, such as Creative Commons licences (creativecommons.org) and open source software.

A great deal of scholarly and professional research is published in journals, and access to most journals is through database subscriptions. Libraries may spend millions of dollars annually subscribing to these databases, particularly in the fields of science, medicine, engineering, and high technology; some university and college libraries—particularly those in developing economies—simply cannot afford the subscription fees, and thus their faculty and students lose access to the emerging scholarship in their disciplines.

Open access allows scholars and researchers to publish their work freely, outside of databases and paywalls. At the time an article (or a book) becomes available through a database, or after a reasonable period (generally three to six months), the author or journal publisher posts the content online in a manner that is readily available, such as in an open access repository or on the author's institutional website.

The open access movement strives to balance respect for COPYRIGHT and for scholars' and researchers' intellectual labour against the global need for information to move freely and the recognition that database publishers are making large sums simply from owning digital assets. For more information, contact your local university library or google "open access."

We know the online availability of information formerly confined to printed books is changing the shape of learning, expertise, and scholarship. The accelerated speed of publication and the loss of the reference editor's expertise mean there is no gatekeeper on information—both a strength and a weakness in our data-saturated world. We also know the widespread adoption of online resources, and their ease of access and use, is changing the economics of writing and publishing. Writers, in particular, have lost income with the rise of social media and the shift to digital publication. Finally, we can observe how quickly online resources have become mainstream, ordinary, and even expected— if you're attending or have attended post-secondary education in the last ten years, you likely recognize the omnipresence of digital journal databases, Wikipedia, and blogs in your research. At present, although incomplete and still controversial (because it potentially violates copyright), the Google Books project represents one vision of a fused print/ digital future. Still, it's very early to imagine that we can understand the full consequences of this technological shift, particularly as the digital environment itself continues to evolve.

YOUR BOOK CONNECTIONS

Think about some of the books that have been important to you, whether you currently own physical copies of these books or not. What made or makes these books important to you? What books have you borrowed (from a library or from other people) instead of buying? What books did you once own but have now sold, given away, or recycled? Think critically, reflectively, and personally about the books you've named and their significance. Do these various books communicate the same values to others?

Figure 1.5 Shelves of books in Shakespeare and Company bookstore in Paris, France, waiting for readers to buy them

To extend this exercise, talk to other people about their important books. What do your shared reading experiences, if any, signal to you about the significance of the book? What kind of culture or society does it reflect and project? What kinds of reader does it signal as intended or ideal? What social values or messages do you see being transmitted in this book?

Finally, books have value. As I touched on briefly above, books reflect certain cultural values, such as the significance of spirituality captured in religious and philosophical texts; the importance of education communicated through textbooks; respect for social institutions such as government and law in the publication of government and legal records and decisions; and the artistic value of literature. Book collectors and book artists remind us of the aesthetic value of books, whether as art objects in themselves or as materials incorporated into art. As scholar Janice Radway discusses in her study of the Book-of-the-Month Club, the ownership of books communicates social values and speaks to others about our individual backgrounds and aspirations. And of course, we also invest books with personal value when we give or receive them as gifts and to mark events and accomplishments. At the University of Alberta, for example, an artist's book is selected in honour of every individual granted an honourary doctorate, and these works become part of the university's special collections library. If you think of the books you own and cherish, you can likely identify their significance in your life's story, whether because of the giver, the occasion, or the content.

The Commodification of Books

The competing argument, of course, is that books have been so thoroughly commodified, particularly in the last decade or two, that they can no longer command the social and cultural value they once had. This argument looks to the rise of big-box chains, the preponderance of celebrity biographies and other expressly commercial titles, and the emergence of self-published ebooks, which arrive in the marketplace with variable quality. Perhaps one of the most significant unintended consequences of Johannes Gutenberg's invention of moveable type—which marks the beginning of mass media—has been the phenomenon of the bestseller, epitomized by Scholastic's print order for *Harry Potter and the Deathly Hallows*, the seventh and final book in the series (twelve million copies for the United States market alone). We might also consider how several publishing news stories from the summer of 2015 feature the book as a commodity: the enormous print order for *What Pet Should I Get?*, the newly discovered Dr. Seuss book; the record-setting publication of E.L. James's *Grey* (sequel to *Fifty Shades of Grey*, itself one of the best-selling books of all time); and the first week sales for *Go Set a Watchman*, Harper Lee's "rediscovered" novel. Such books became media events in themselves, not for their content or their artistic achievement but for their ability to set sales records and to signal consumer behaviour—not values traditionally associated with books and literature.

Books do, undeniably, have an economic value. A copy of a rare book, such as a Gutenberg Bible, might sell for many millions of dollars, while an old, used paperback might sell for a dollar or less—or might even be free at a Free Wee Library or a community book exchange. Under these obvious differences in economic value, though, we see other cultural and social values lurking, such as rarity and exclusivity, or the ephemeral nature of genre publishing versus the perceived persistence of "taste." Beyond the exchange value of the books themselves is the economic significance of the work done by writers, editors, publishers, booksellers, and others involved in the manufacturing and selling of books. This too is substantial and should not be overlooked. But the multinational, corporate context in which many books are published and sold today—particularly within our increasingly stratified global economy—complicates this work, with the consequence that some voices are less amplified by publication than others, and some voices aren't heard at all.

From a society in which very few people owned very few books, and those who did own books read them again and again, and even committed them to memory, the West has evolved into a culture in which most people own at least a few books and many people own many books. Even more significantly, many, many people have often read the same book, sometimes with the attitude that the book is a consumable, interchangeable, and entirely replaceable object. Think, for example, of Oprah's Book Club selections or the rush to consume the latest "It" book. Yet for others, books remain ineffably irreplaceable.

Making a Book Editor

The book editor operates as a gateway to the book community for both the publisher and the author, albeit in very different ways. I believe that *all* writers need editors, whether the writer publishes with international houses or produces chapbooks to sell at story slams. A book editor's wider knowledge of the book community and the industry can be invaluable to any author, and editors bring objectivity—and also passion—to projects that authors themselves cannot possess. So again, consider why you want to be a book editor. What about books and authors draws you?

If you plan to work as a book editor, you should be reading and buying books all the time. If you are not a serious reader (reading fifty-plus books a year—some editors suggest a hundred books a year or more), you may not want to be a book editor. Remember, most book editors spend a major portion of their work lives reading book manuscripts, as well as many other documents. Buying books is also important, since you're in the business of encouraging others to buy books. Many editors have "friend of house" relationships with other publishers that ensure they can buy books at a discount, but it's important for an editor to get into bookstores and buy books in the retail environment regularly so that she has the same experiences other book buyers are having—including, of course, buying online.

One of the joyful aspects of working as a book editor is that you are *expected* to spend time in bookstores and libraries, attending book launches, and reading industry-related publications. When you go to bookstores and libraries, pay attention to what's on the shelves and how it's being promoted to readers—even the books outside your personal interests and your firm's interests. It's always important to consider the wider industry. In the United States, PUBLISHERS WEEKLY is the go-to magazine; in Canada, QUILL AND QUIRE is the book-industry monthly. You need to know and read these publications, and others, to advance in the business. You also cannot ignore what other sectors are publishing— in the academic world, in the world of children's books, in newspapers and magazines—because trends tend to echo.

But your engagement with reading and text must extend beyond print. You must also watch television and movies, attend cultural events, and be aware of cultural life in general—particularly popular culture. Book editors are problem solvers at heart, and the world bombards us with narrative problems, in the form of stories, daily. Engaging with media and culture also keeps an editor on trend and alert to potential book ideas in what our friends, families, and social media networks are discussing. This awareness is particularly valuable during both ACQUISITION and COMMISSIONING of books.

A good book editor is intensely aware of larger cultural movements and constantly thinking about how these movements affect the house in terms of acquisition, threats/opportunities, marketing tactics, PRODUC-TION decisions, and economic well-being. It is reasonable and defensible—practically speaking, it's essential—to spend a few working hours each week in libraries and bookstores, at books launches, readings, and literary festivals, in coffee shops, music stores, and comic shops: any place books and other cultural texts are sold, circulated, discussed, and valued. Robert McCullough, formerly of Whitecap Books and currently publisher of the Appetite IMPRINT of Penguin Random House Canada, often talks about working in a bookstore prior to getting into publishing, and about keeping his bookstore job even after he was promoted at Whitecap. He has attributed part of his professional success to his hours in the bookstore, examining books closely and talking with diverse book buyers.

YOUR BOOK-BUYING HABITS
How would you answer the following questions? How do you think your habits compare to those of people you know?

1. What are your book-buying habits? How much time in a typical month do you spend in brick-and-mortar bookstores or visiting online bookstores? What kinds of stores do you usually shop in? What area of the store do you tend to visit?
2. What are your media-consuming habits (beyond social media)? In a typical day, what media do you read or listen to?
3. What is something of current interest to you in media (TV/radio, newspapers/magazines, Internet, other)?

When I hire editorial staff, I look for a demonstrated interest in reading, writing, and book culture (the idea that books are relevant and meaningful to society). A bachelor's degree is great, but you don't need to study English or comparative literature to be a book editor; a degree in communications, library science, sociology, or history can provide similar awareness of language, research skills, and attention to detail. A work history that reflects a commitment to writing and publishing is valuable: writing for the high school or college/university newspaper, writing professionally—even working in a bookstore! But being a reader is mandatory. I have asked potential staffers what they had read lately, what they'd recommend to others. I was generally less interested in the specific titles than in the facility of the answer: if you're not reading, I'm curious why you want to be a book editor.

There is an indisputable tension—suspicion, animosity—between some writers and editors. T.S. Eliot famously remarked, "Some editors are failed writers, but so are most writers." On the contrary, however, evidence shows that many editors go on to write later in their careers— Diana Athill, Susan Juby, Michael Korda, and Michael Redhill to name just a few examples. Eliot himself was an editor at Faber and Faber. Perhaps it would be fairer to say that good book editors are not content to be merely readers—not content to remain passive in making communication happen. It's true that many editors didn't *plan* to be editors and rather hoped to be writers, but through a variety of circumstances found themselves working as editors—such as Betsy Lerner, formerly a book editor and currently an AGENT and author. The belief that editors are jealous of writers leads to many misunderstandings between authors and editors. The fact that editors enjoy reading, enjoy writing—and perhaps want to write themselves—should make them sympathetic to writers; but what writers and editors want from their work together may be very different things. Do you really want to be a book editor, or is editing just a job until you publish your masterwork? If the latter, perhaps book editing isn't your best fit.

The reason reading is so important to book editors is our need for textual fluency—for an immersion in words, if you will. From reading we learn about language at a variety of levels: the mechanics of spelling and punctuation, the tensile strength of grammar, the colour and shimmer of diction, a sense of the fresh and the staid. This is a crucial part of an editor's preparation, far beyond a basic sense of order and accuracy. Attentive reading helps editors hone their editorial senses, what editors Leslie Sharpe and Irene Gunther call the editorial eye, ear, and nose.

The ability to read analytically—to break a text down to its component parts and then reassemble it successfully, strongly—is referred to in literary criticism as *close reading*. It is the primary editorial skill. As they read, editors accumulate editorial memory, a sense of how to solve various kinds of problems in prose through observing how authors and editors before them have made texts work. From analytical reading, the editor collects a set of tools for working with words and ideas. And having understood how other texts operate, she has clues about how the project she's currently considering *could* work.

Working as a Book Editor

Many would-be editors are drawn to book editing by the idea of working in solitude, lovingly polishing an author's fine prose. While this is an admirable idea, it's far from reality. One of the shocking discoveries for most editorial interns and assistants is that very little of a book editor's day-to-day work involves working with text, and almost no solitude. Instead, most of the day involves working with other people in the publishing cycle, especially sales and marketing staff. It involves numerous meetings, a great deal of email, and masses of non-book paperwork. Reflecting on her typical workday, Ruth Linka, associate publisher at Orca Books and editor of the Rapid Reads series, commented, "I had to work from home today to get some editing done. For me, not much editing gets done in the office."

Another shocking discovery for most people drawn to editing and publishing is the pay: it is frankly low, particularly relative to positions in other fields that require similar education and responsibility. According to *Quill and Quire*'s most recent salary survey (2013), entry-level in-house positions paid $25,000 to $30,000 annually, on average. For some people, total compensation—such as having considerable independence, doing cultural work, and holding a fascinating job—makes up for the low pay and limited benefits. Others move on. The skills of language use and judgement that make a book editor a valued professional are in high demand in non-publishing positions, and good editors can move readily in and out of a variety of communications fields.

Think about the kind of book editing you want to do. Chances are you want to be a fiction editor. It's important to realize that while fiction is front and centre in our culture—witness all our awards, our literary idols, and the literary canon itself—fiction forms only a small segment of the overall publishing market. That is, the great majority of book publishing is nonfiction. Think of any bookstores you've ever visited. While the fiction and literature section is prominent, the shelves of self-help, current affairs, business primers, language references, and travel guides—not to mention textbooks for students in K–12 and in college and university—take up much more of the retail space. Of the fiction that is published, literary publishing (which includes poetry and drama) is a very small segment within the category. Fiction tends to accumulate the strongest social and aesthetic admiration (think of the writers readers identify with most, the books we read in literature courses, the books that win the most glamorous awards); but for a variety of reasons, nonfiction is often much more interesting and challenging to publish.

In-house book editors tend to specialize in certain segments of the industry. For instance, scholarly editors, who work for scholarly and university presses, tend to have advanced degrees and often concentrate in a field or a band of related fields, such as the humanities, the social sciences, or health sciences. Similarly, fiction editors often don't edit much nonfiction, nor nonfiction editors much fiction. Freelance editors, however, tend to be generalists. It has been to the advantage of freelance editors that increasingly more editorial work—including high-level DEVELOPMENTAL EDITING and SUBSTANTIVE EDITING—is being outsourced as financial pressures on publishers increase.

I've mentioned before that working in sales and marketing is a way to break into book editing. Another way in is by working as an agent. Book editors and book agents perform some similar tasks, such as evaluating manuscripts, recommending changes, and building supportive relationships with authors; moving from one role to the other could be a sensible step along your career path. Working as an agent, you'll gain insight into publishing houses and cultures across Canada as well as internationally—invaluable experience for any book editor. The example of Nicole Winstanley of Penguin Random House Canada—a relatively young Canadian woman who currently holds one of the top jobs in publishing—is excellent if you're looking for inspiration. Equally, some editors—such as Betsy Lerner—go on to work as agents, taking their textual skills, networks, and insider knowledge with them to the benefit of writers.

If you're thinking of becoming an agent, be aware that presently there are only a limited number of agents working in Canada. The reason for the small number is that for many kinds of publishing, authors do not need agents. For instance, most academics do not have agents, nor do many of the writers who publish with small independent presses. Also, many Canadian publishers, outside of the major international firms, don't require authors to have agents to submit manuscripts (and some authors don't bother using an agent even when working with the largest firms: unless an author is generating enough income to be willing to give up fifteen percent of it to someone else, he or she is unlikely to need an agent). These comments are not meant to discourage you but rather to help you plan a suitable career path. Of course, if you're willing and able to work outside of Canada, you may have many more opportunities.

WHAT DO YOU THINK ABOUT EDITORS?
Make a list of words you would use to describe an editor from your current knowledge of what editors do. When you have completed your list, share it with someone else—ideally a writer or another editor. Then, make a list of the personal qualities, background knowledge, and specialized training a book editor may need. Do you see yourself in this list?

My aim in this chapter has not been to discourage you from becoming a book editor—quite the opposite! I do want you to have a clear sense of the qualities that make an effective editor, however. If you've worked through the activity above, which invites you to check your perceptions about editors, you're already evaluating whether you see yourself working in this field. In my experience, most book editors are hard-working and dedicated to their jobs—sometimes to a fault. They are highly self-motivated, because editing can be lonely work. As I've said before, most book editors are voracious, wide-ranging readers. They usually love language (although I can think of a few who don't) and possess a tremendous facility with and enjoyment of various aspects of English, encompassing grammar, punctuation, homophones and homonyms, rhymes, word play, puns, and more. Most books editors also possess diplomacy, tact, compromise, grace, and wisdom, qualities needed because they work with such a range of personalities and interests. Here, building on a list presented in the Editors' Association of Canada's document *So You Want to Be an Editor,* are some other skills and qualities typical of a book editor:

- a commitment to lifelong learning
- strongly self-directed and capable of working independently
- able to work with a wide variety of roles and personalities
- able to make knowledgeable decisions and provide appropriate direction or guidance
- able to solve problems, to admit ignorance, and to ask for help, and aware of resources for finding solutions and support
- attuned to coherence and consistency, with a strong awareness of patterns, categories, and organization
- able to ask incisive questions that get to the heart of a matter
- willing to critique, question, and rethink
- capable of recognizing what's missing from a text as well as perceiving what has been repeated, intentionally (for emphasis) and unnecessarily (by mistake)
- slightly (but functionally) obsessive-compulsive
- willing to build order out of chaos
- capable of leadership (perhaps burnished by formal training)
- able to adhere to a deadline
- able to balance the goals of striving for perfection and aiming for excellence within the real limitations of a given project or author and the industry as a whole

Most importantly, effective book editors know when to stop. That is, they must be able to evaluate the difference between what is correct and what is good and to know which quality is more important when. As the saying goes, perfection is the enemy of the good, but also of the finished.

I hope you see yourself in this list—and if you don't yet, perhaps the next few chapters will help you identify qualities and skills you didn't recognize you have.

EDITORS MAKING CULTURE

Research one—or several—of the following book editors. Why, in your opinion, is this editor notable? How is the publishing milieu of the editor you've chosen different from yours? How is it similar? How do you evaluate the contribution of this editor to contemporary book publishing—and to English-speaking literary culture? Why should today's book editors know about this editor—if you feel they should?

Diana Athill	Robert Gottlieb	Ursula Nordstrom
Phyllis Bruce	Michael Korda	Maxwell Perkins
Jason Epstein	Daniel Menaker	M. Lincoln Schuster
Douglas Gibson	John Metcalf	Nan Talese

Editors are the products of books, just as books are the products of editors (and authors, of course!). A book editor may also be called a senior editor, an acquisitions editor, or a title editor; but regardless of the role identified on her business card, the work she does with books is particular and important, and is informed by the many texts she has encountered in the world at large. Betsy Lerner says, "editors are still the world's readers. And thus the eyes of the world." We know the joy of reading a truly astonishing book, and most of us are motivated by the idea of creating a truly astonishing book for other readers. In chapter 2 we'll look at how the world's readers work within the commercial space of publishing.

2

The Book Industry
in Canada and North America

"Being medium-sized in the field of trade
publishing is in some ways the most difficult
place to be."—John B. Thompson

It is difficult to talk seriously about book editing without talking about book publishing generally. Serious talk about book editing also often leads to talking about bookstores and the retail environment in which many books circulate. Whatever our ideals, in our current world, book editing is inextricably tied to larger economic forces.

You must understand that, as a book editor, you do not work in isolation. Your work takes place in the context of a fragile ecosystem of retail consumption and reading culture. One of the most recent struggles in this ecosystem involved the pricing of ebooks and the distribution of income derived from their sales; just a few years ago, we saw struggles over greatly discounted book pricing. Although retailers and publishers have been struggling in various ways for decades, the industry as a whole has experienced particular anxiety around the emergence of ebooks, as their sale and circulation could dramatically change the larger context of book culture—authors' livelihoods, bookselling, book distribution, and ultimately reading. This is a fight in which book editors definitely have a stake. One of the regrettable consequences of these struggles, from a book editor's perspective, is that it has amplified a sense of "us" and "them," particularly dividing writers who are conventionally published from writers who self-publish.

Book publishing has changed considerably since its so-called Golden Age in the early twentieth century. Publishing has long been referred to as a gentlemen's game; historically, publishing was, and remains, a largely white, male, middle-class profession, although many women now work in the industry and there has been a strong push to make the industry more diverse and inclusive. Until the 1960s, most book publishing was done by a large number of private firms, many of them fairly small, most of them independent. Penguin Books, for example, was founded in 1935 by Allen Lane with the express purpose of publishing inexpensive but good-quality editions of important books; Simon and Schuster was founded in 1924 by Richard L. Simon and M. Lincoln Schuster; Random House was founded in 1927 by Bennett Cerf and Donald Klopfer. The independent, privately owned firms began to disappear in the 1960s alongside larger international shifts in corporate structure, and soon publishing became much more corporate. Traditional firms were integrated into imprints (specialized publishing units) of other firms, and publishers came to be owned by larger corporations—sometimes media companies, but sometimes organizations that had nothing to do with printing or communications.

Penguin Books makes an outstanding example of the changing landscape of ownership. From the 1960s to the 2010s, various configurations of Penguin Books in different regions were bought and sold, and in turn bought and sold other publishers, repeatedly. Then in 2013, the Penguin Group, co-owned by Pearson and Bertelsmann (a German media company), merged with Random House in a historic deal to become Penguin Random House, an extremely large publisher with exceptional market clout and span. According to *Shelf Awareness,* a newsletter for publishers, "Penguin Random House had 261 *New York Times* bestsellers in its first six months as a newly merged company, has nearly 12,000 employees and sold more than 100 million e-books worldwide." And of course, the company continues to evolve, just as other firms do.

In North American publishing today, we refer to the *Big Five*: Penguin Random House, Hachette, Harper Collins, MacMillan, and Simon and Schuster. With their extensive international reach, these firms control the majority of the bookselling market, jointly representing more than three-quarters of books sold in Canada and the United States. Corporate integration, such as the Random House–Penguin merger, and evolving digital media are changing the way books are published and sold, from submission to the level of individual bookstores; this statement applies to publishing in the United Kingdom, Europe, and Australia, as well as in Canada and the United States.

The shift to digital has changed publishing in many ways, but two particular trends we can examine immediately emerge from the relative ease of creating and distributing digital texts: self-publishing and PRINT ON DEMAND (POD).

Self-Publishing and Print on Demand

Self-publishing in itself is nothing new. Authors have been self-publishing for centuries; until recently it was often referred to as *vanity publishing* or *subsidy publishing*. The rise of desktop publishing software, along with computer-based innovations in printing and manufacturing, lowered the cost of book production markedly: authors can now design, lay out, and print their books easily and affordably. Print-on-demand providers such as Blurb and Blitzprint made the process easier still. The arrival of ereaders and ebook stores, such as Sony, the Nook (Barnes and Noble), and especially the Kindle (Amazon), removed the need for print publication, warehousing, and physical shipping. Suddenly a big portion of self-publishing authors' costs disappeared.

An infrastructure for authors to publish their digital texts already existed in online fanfiction communities and writing sites, and sales interfaces were emerging through online retailers. Then in early 2012, one particular breakthrough—the conventional publication of the previously self-published novel *Fifty Shades of Grey*—dramatically changed the relationship dynamics between traditionally published and self-published authors. Other self-published authors, such as Amanda Hocking (and long before her James Redfield, author of *The Celestine Prophecy*), had previously caught the attention of major publishers and the media, but the arrival of *Fifty Shades* was qualitatively different. Self-publishing gained a large degree of credibility—and economic success. Arguably, 2015's movie hit *The Martian*, which had its roots as a self-published text, has helped, too.

Meanwhile, corporate publishers were facing considerable pressure to remain economically viable. The global economic collapse of 2008 reduced consumer spending and drew new attention to book prices and book sales. Authors from many sectors of publishing who were perceived to be underperforming—not selling enough books to recover production costs, not earning out their ADVANCES—discovered that their contracts for future books were being cancelled. It seemed a quietly successful book was no longer "successful."

Some of these authors, and many others, tried to recover the rights to their older books that were no longer available in bookstores, only to discover that publishers were unwilling to revert their rights. Instead, many publishers opted to manage their inventory by converting slow-selling titles to print-on-demand format, reducing warehousing costs without giving up their rights to the book as an asset—because technically a print-on-demand book is never OUT OF PRINT.

Many authors have since successfully recovered their rights and are self-publishing new editions of their older works (and new work, too) as print-on-demand volumes and as ebooks. As far as generating a reliable income goes, their success is mixed. But this collision of rights and opportunities has led to sharp debate about how authors should be compensated and whether conventional publishing operates to authors' benefit. For many emerging and established writers, self-publishing appears a likelier route to finding an audience, if limited profit.

Ebooks

And of course, there is the question of ebooks. Quite apart from their popularity with self-published authors, ebooks are increasingly important to traditional publishers, who now recognize the ease of producing an ebook from an already digital workflow. Ebook and print editions often arrive simultaneously. Pricing remains an issue, however. Digital books require no printing, no shipping, no warehousing, and limited DISTRIBUTION costs—points the buying public understands and that have translated into resistance to ebook prices above $9.99. Initially, sales figures seemed to suggest that ebooks would cannibalize print income—a problem because low-priced ebooks return small revenue. Recently, however, ebook sales seem to have stabilized, and pricing looks to be stabilizing, too. Digital sales are currently poised to make up a relatively small but consistent portion of many publishers' income, but print remains stalwart. Still, publishers must continue to invest in digital development, as well as try to anticipate what's coming next.

IMPRINTS AND EMBLEMS

Take a moment to reflect. Do you notice the publisher's emblem on the books you buy? Can you identify specific publishers or their imprints— do you buy books based on the publisher or imprint? For example, some readers of science fiction and fantasy look to Tor books because of positive prior reading experiences from this publisher's "brand"— but many readers don't notice this detail. If you have books close to hand, look at the various publishers and imprints represented. What do you notice?

Go further. Do you notice where the books you read were originally published—in Canada, the United States, the United Kingdom, Australia, or elsewhere? Would knowing this kind of information influence your buying decision? Why or why not?

The Canadian Industry

The business of publishing in North America is changing. Big-box and online retailers—particularly Amazon.com—have an increasingly strong influence on large-scale corporate publishing, while independent bookstores are allying themselves with local writers and publishers to produce stronger regional book cultures. This change is creating opportunities for independent publishers as well as self-publishing and author-directed publishing—and therefore more need for well-trained, forward-thinking book editors in both in-house and freelance roles.

The publishing industry in Canada is similar to that in the United States and the United Kingdom. Four of the Big Five publishers have Canadian operations, and several major independent publishers boast national reach. There is also substantial small-scale independent publishing in Canada, some of exceptionally high quality. In 2015, for instance, three of the five books on the Giller Prize short list were published by independents, including two from Windsor, Ontario-based Biblioasis; the winner, *Fifteen Dogs* by André Alexis, was published by Coach House Books, a house that publishes sixteen to eighteen titles per year. Basic publishing operations are similar regardless of scale, but at a small firm, a book editor's job is likely to be much wider, whereas at a Big Five imprint, the editor's job is likely to be more specialized. Similarly, for large publishers, large sales and power deals may be the ultimate measure of an editor's success, while for editors at small independents, other features of the editorial role may be at least as important.

In the last decade, publishing houses internationally have seen major layoffs, particularly among editors; Canada is no exception to this trend. And even with the rise of ebook purchasing, statistical research is showing an overall decline in people's book buying, a decline attributable to many factors, both cultural and economic. Since the turmoil of the Chapters collapse in 2001 and the General Distribution Services bankruptcy in 2002, the Canadian book industry has generally been shaky. The industry faced a pricing crisis in 2007 when the Canadian dollar was trading on par with the US dollar, then struggled with reduced sales after 2008. As government policy has shifted, Canadian publishers have also faced threats to various funding programs and tax credits, as well as increased competition from international publishers. Viable grant programs and tax credits are a major concern for Canadian publishers, as is increasing international penetration into the formerly protected Canadian market.

CHAPTERS, GENERAL DISTRIBUTION SERVICES, AND CANADIAN BOOKSELLING

In 2001 and 2002, the Canadian publishing industry was rocked by two entwined crises. First was the near bankruptcy of Chapters, then owned by Larry Stevenson. Second was the bankruptcy of General Distribution Services (as well as Stoddart Publishing), owned by Jack Stoddart. Combined, these business failures dramatically changed the Canadian publishing landscape, particularly for small presses.

In the late 1990s, Chapters introduced the big-box bookstore to Canada, modelled on the Barnes and Noble superstores in the United States. To fulfill Chapters' orders, which tended to be quite large, publishers began ordering markedly larger print runs of their new titles and offering bigger discounts to retailers placing large orders. Chapters' arrival in the marketplace, alongside other cultural changes such as the rise of the Internet, upset the already precarious state of independent bookselling, and many indie bookstores went out of business. Meanwhile, to take advantage of the apparent strengths of Chapters' numerous stores, Stoddart rapidly expanded General Distribution Services (GDS) and took on a large roster of clients, many of them small regional and literary publishers whose traditional allies were their local booksellers. At the time, these presses believed that getting into the Chapters system would bring them a much wider, national readership, which had long been difficult for them to attract.

By 2001, Chapters was failing to pay invoices and held large volumes of publishers' inventory, which might be returned at any moment. Based on Chapters' orders, publishers had paid ROYALTIES to authors on titles that were subsequently returned in monstrous quantities, leaving both authors and publishers cash strapped. Chapters was on the verge of bankruptcy. After complex, protracted, and sometimes acrimonious wrangling with various federal government departments and external business partners, Heather Reisman bought Chapters, now consolidated into Chapters/Indigo, with the promise to downsize operations and correct imbalances that had emerged in Canadian publishing.

Then in late 2001, GDS lost its line of credit, which a distributor needs to stay solvent. GDS was heavily dependent on Chapters/Indigo, which continued to experience financial turmoil for several years after its consolidation. By the middle of 2002, GDS was bankrupt and its warehouse was locked. This meant not only that its client publishers were unpaid, but also, and more importantly, that they were unable to retrieve their inventory, leaving them with massive printing bills, no books to sell, and little or no income to pay for future titles. Amid a frenzy of lawsuits, GDS was shuttered. Its closure took months to resolve and again left publishers with large volumes of unsold inventory and numerous costs—as well as the problem of finding a new distributor so they could get their books to retailers and readers.

Many small presses went out of business after this prolonged economic disruption. Some were able to survive by significantly curtailing their

operations; others by being bought by rival publishers, becoming imprints, or otherwise integrating their operations. Most large publishers
survived—in some cases because of foreign ownership—but they too were
weakened by these crises. More than a decade later, we can identify the
dozens of casualties of these events—and feel the genuine anxiety of those
left standing.

Until 2014, Canada's largest book publisher was Harlequin Enter-
prises, owned by Torstar Corporation; it was then sold to News Corp and,
although it continues to operate in Canada, is no longer Canadian owned.
One of Canada's most respected and celebrated publishers, McClelland
and Stewart, is no longer Canadian owned but rather exists as an imprint
of Penguin Random House Canada. Another Canadian publishing
stalwart, Douglas & MacIntyre, filed for bankruptcy in 2012—but the
imprint survived with the help of other firms. Meanwhile, in 2013 Simon
and Schuster set up a Canadian acquisitions office, expanding publishing
opportunities for Canadian authors—to no small controversy regarding
foreign ownership and Canadian cultural policy.

Canadian Books and Government Policy

Commercial book publishing exists in a tense relationship with larger
society. It may be understood as part of what social theorists Adorno
and Horkheimer call the *culture industry*, but this labelling is somewhat problematic. Adorno and Horkheimer argue that popular culture
is like a factory that produces standardized cultural goods (genre novels, movies, popular music, and so on) that function to control mass
society—that is, that keep the workforce docile and pliable. The theory goes that messages and images in mass communication products
encourage people to participate in consumer culture by buying objects
to quell their sense of personal and social dissatisfaction. The problem
with consuming these products, Adorno and Horkheimer argue, is that
in doing so, people falsely inoculate themselves against the problems of
capitalism. They believe that they are happy and successful because they
can consume, but they are actually suffering, too distracted by easy-to-
consume, pleasant media products to recognize their reality or to be
motivated to change it.

Today, the view of people who work in the industry of making books
and other products of mass communication reflects the notion of *cultural industries*—book publishing as well as magazine publishing, live
and recorded music, theatre, dance, film, museums, galleries—which
exist in a tension between obvious commodities and "cultural" products.
As scholar Sherman Young explains, "A book is not just 200 paper pages,
with ink-printed words and an appealing cover. It is a combination of

ideas, cultural practices and industrial processes. Whilst books share an apparently similar material form, the reasons for their existence and the cultures they inhabit may be poles apart." Inarguably, some book publishers produce "mass culture" products; this accusation is most often levelled at publishers of GENRE FICTION, but do consider that one of America's revered publishers, Simon and Schuster, started out publishing books of crossword puzzles and only later was heralded for its PROGRAM of outstanding nonfiction (as well as blockbuster fiction). Other publishers—particularly small literary houses—make it their mission to capture and promote examples of the literary fine arts, or high culture: "literature."

Canada was historically a dumping ground for other nations' cultural products: first from the United Kingdom—particularly Edinburgh— and then from the United States. Starting in the late 1950s and 1960s, in the lead-up to the 1967 centennial, the Canadian government began to take Canadian-originated cultural production seriously and introduced protectionist policies to encourage domestic music, film, and publishing. (If you're aware of so-called CanCon rules, you are at least tacitly familiar with these policies.) By the era of the Free Trade Agreement in the late 1980s, culture and cultural industries were officially protected in Canada by policy. Subsequent trade deals have weakened cultural protections, but the concept of a distinct "Canadian culture" yoked to culture makers is entrenched in both policy and funding.

Canada is very large geographically, its population is relatively small and far-flung, and books are heavy and difficult to ship. For all of these reasons, Canada, like many European nations, has fairly robust government funding for publishing. Unlike European nations, however, Canadian publishers receive funding directly from various levels of government. Publishing policy scholar Rowland Lorimer observes that "this direct support turns out to be often substantially less than the indirect support provided by valued-added tax (VAT) reductions in European countries." In these countries, VAT reductions make the retail price of books much lower, encouraging more purchasing. Other policy mechanisms are also at work, in these countries and elsewhere, to support national book publishing and protect local publishers from the might of multinational publishing corporations.

These policy mechanisms, however, point to another tension in the cultural industries. Historically, cultural workers have been subsidized by wealthy individuals or by the state—the phrase *patron of the arts* reflects this history. Yet the *industry* element of cultural industries suggests that this sector should be able to pay its own way. People tend to hold strong opinions about whether today's writers, artists, actors, and other "creatives" should be subsidized to do their work.

At the federal level, the Canada Council for the Arts and the Canada Book Fund provide the major funding. The Canada Council is highly cultural in its orientation. Its funding guidelines emphasize artistic value, Canadian nationalist topics, a sense of writing and community, and a clear contribution to Canadian cultural fabric—that is, not the obviously commercial or the arcanely academic. The Canada Book Fund, on the other hand, recognizes business success. Its grants are based on income, and a publisher's sales-to-inventory ratio is considered. Eligibility for funding is capped so that publishers who outgrow the need for support do not gain an advantage over smaller firms still trying to grow. Content is generally not considered for industry-support funding, but is closely scrutinized for Canada Council funding—necessarily, given the Council's cultural mandate. In both cases, Canadian ownership regulations and authors' nationality affect a firm's funding eligibility.

Federal funding is also available through the Foreign Rights Marketing Assistance Program (FRMAP). Grants from this program are intended to support sales of books and rights outside of Canada and help Canadian publishers find CO-PUBLICATION opportunities. FRMAP funds travel to rights fairs, participation in international sales events, and other kinds of trade development, particularly in Africa and Asia.

Provincial programs vary widely and are subject to change with regime change. In some provinces, funding is available through culture departments; in other provinces, publishers have access to tax credits. Within provinces, individual municipalities may offer support to the arts, which may include funding for regional publishing. In some cases, funding is directed to authors, not to publishers, however.

From the mid-2000s until late 2015, Canada's federal government threatened federal grants to publishers and other cultural industries and made trade decisions that put the Canadian book industry in peril, particularly with respect to competition from foreign-owned firms. In this way, the Canadian political situation is quite unlike that in some European nations. France, for instance, has passed protectionist legislation that is explicitly anti-Amazon and more generally anti-American, and many European countries have fixed-price legislation specific to book publishing to ensure an economically healthy supply chain.

ARE YOU FOR OR AGAINST GOVERNMENT SUPPORT?

Do you believe various levels of government should offer support to publishers through grants or other measures? Why or why not? What about support to writers? Do you think of publishing as a cultural activity or as an industry? How so?

People adopt a variety of perspectives on subsidies to cultural industries. Some argue that it is the government's responsibility to enable people to participate in cultural activities and discourse. In particular, the government may be expected to create opportunities for its citizens to learn about Canadian cultural heritage. From this view, publishers who create books that portray and celebrate Canadian history, regional distinctiveness, and local storytelling deserve to be supported (whereas more overtly "commercial" publishers do not). Others perceive government grants as a kind of public service aimed at producing and preserving a Canadian identity and creating a strong citizenry. From this view, support to publishers encourages general literacy and allows Canadians to read Canadian writers from across the country.

On the other hand, some people argue that only the market is an appropriate mechanism with which to deal with culture. From this perspective, the culture that is "good" and valuable endures because the invisible hand of market success ensures its survival. In much recent Canadian political discourse, this view has been dominant. However, the public will to invest in arts and culture is generally high, particularly in Canada's major cities, and investment in cultural industries is economically valuable.

Statistics show that jobs in the cultural industries contribute significantly to Canada's national prosperity. Using figures from 2010, the Cultural Human Resources Council found that "The arts, culture and heritage industry in Canada was larger than the accommodation and food services industry ($30.6 billion) and twice as big as the agriculture, forestry, fishing and hunting industry ($23.9 billion)." Writing and publishing contributed more than 10 billion dollars to the Canadian economy in 2010 and accounted for some 146,000 jobs. However, as large corporate publishers outsource more of their editing, LAYOUT, and printing beyond Canada's borders, this economic picture will change.

The Publication Sequence

Even if you already work as an editor, you may not be familiar with the publication sequence in book editing. Importantly, this is a *recursive sequence* from author through publisher to reader, in the sense that every time an author produces a text that reaches an audience, a reader may be inspired to create something herself in response to that text, thereby setting the sequence in motion again. Feedback from readers, including critics and scholars, may also influence what a writer creates subsequently. Many people are usually involved at every stage of publication, so although writing often feels like a lonely business, it's rarely so for long.

The stages are roughly as follows.

1. **Creation**

   The process begins with an author who creates a manuscript. That manuscript may be a work of fiction or nonfiction, poetry or technical prose, searingly personal or sternly objective. When the manuscript has been completely written (a process that generally involves substantial revision and rewriting) and the author is satisfied to let it be read by others, the acquisition stage can begin. (The "author," as I will explain in chapter 5, may refer to a single writer or to a collaboration between two or more writers.)

2. **Acquisition**

   Acquisition is the process of assigning a monetary value to a manuscript. A manuscript is circulated to acquisitions editors, either by the author or by an agent. Ideally, the author has already contacted the publisher she feels offers the best home for the manuscript. Editors read manuscripts, both solicited and unsolicited, looking for content that suits the strengths of the publishing house. Editors defend, or champion, promising manuscripts by describing their potential to other editors and to in-house staff. When a manuscript looks like a fit, the editor contacts the author or agent, and the book is (ideally) put under contract. At this stage, the manuscript may be referred to as a PROPERTY, a description that sometimes offends novice authors because they feel it reduces their creative expression to an exchange value. But whether we like it or not, commercial publishing is a business, and manuscripts represent monetary value for both the author and the publisher. Just the same, editors do fall in love with manuscripts and fight to acquire them simply because they believe in them.

   Authors often wonder why publishers may be slow to respond to submissions. It's important for authors (and editors) to understand that review processes take time to be done well. Unfortunately, many book editors don't have enough time to do all that their jobs require, and reviewing manuscripts is sometimes a low priority. As we'll discuss, authors can help the process by ensuring their manuscripts are solicited submissions.

   Once the manuscript is under contract, the author's hard work is effectively over, but for the book editor, the hard work is just beginning. This difference in perspectives often leads to tension in the author–editor relationship. As a book editor, your best tools for defusing tension are regular communication and well-managed expectations. If you can tell the author about the publishing process, the timelines involved, and your expectations at each step, your relationships will be much happier.

3. **Substantive edit**

Substantive editing deals with what Canadian editor Douglas Gibson calls "the editing of ideas": the substance and structure of the manuscript. During the substantive edit, the editor asks questions about the length and sequence of a book argument, content to add or remove, the needs and expectations of the audience, the vocabulary level for the book's intended readers, and other features of presentation. In some cases, the substantively edited manuscript is returned to the author to address rewrites, queries, and other changes to fit the text to its intended audience.

Regrettably, with the leaner staffs in publishing houses and the increased responsibilities most book editors carry, some writers report that substantive editing is becoming rarer.

4. **Copyediting**

COPYEDITING is performed by an editor who works through the manuscript closely, at the level of individual words and phrases, but with an eye to correctness, consistency, and clarity. The copyedit may be strictly mechanical or may include stylistic changes. (STYLISTIC EDITING, sometimes called LINE EDITING, works at a higher level of language than copyediting and tends to be more rigorous. It should be a separate step in the process, but today it's commonly rolled into the copyedit.) Most copyeditors in book publishing are not responsible for fact checking beyond common knowledge, but at some firms, fact checking is included in the copyedit. Most copyediting is done out of house by freelance editors.

After the copyedit has been completed, the manuscript may be returned to the author to review, in order to address any questions and to ensure the editor has not altered the author's ideas or voice. The author signals acceptance of the edit through a *signoff*; this is normally the last chance the author has to make any significant changes to the text prior to publication.

5. **Design and layout**

Although I've positioned design after editing in this sequence, in practice, this step normally begins earlier. DESIGN refers to a set of decisions applied to the visual presentation of the text: the cover, the page size, the type used for the body, the treatment of illustrative matter, and similar decisions. LAYOUT refers to the technical process of applying design styles to the copyedited text and necessarily begins after the copyedit is complete. Cover design often happens long before the manuscript has been edited—sometimes almost immediately after a manuscript has been accepted—and in an XML workflow, the text may be roughly laid out and tagged prior to the copyedit.

6. **Proofreading**

   PROOFREADING is done by both an editor and the author (and perhaps additional readers), who work through the laid-out pages slowly to catch any errors introduced in the layout, any errors missed in the copyedit, and any other errors or problems with the text. At this stage, time is tight because publication is imminent. Once again, the author normally provides a signoff.

WHICH EDIT IS WHICH?

In this chapter, I discuss several types of editing using a variety of names, which you may already know or may hear in your future work life. All this vocabulary may get overwhelming, so here's a quick crib-list.

- **Developmental editing**: editing done to guide the research and writing of a manuscript; also editing undertaken to rework an underdeveloped or ineffective manuscript to bring it to publishable standards; a specialized area of book editing

- **Substantive editing**: editing of a document's content, structure, and organization in the interests of a particular audience or use; a high-level edit that occurs early in the publication sequence; also known as *structural editing*

- **Stylistic editing**: editing of a document's language to improve its clarity and sound and to eliminate awkwardness, repetition, and bias; also known as *line editing*

- **Copyediting**: editing of a document's correctness and consistency at the level of grammar, spelling, punctuation, and mechanics; also known as MECHANICAL EDITING

- **Proofreading**: editing of a document to catch any remaining textual or visual errors; a limited edit that occurs late in the publication sequence

- **Textual editing**: a broad term that encompasses both stylistic editing and copyediting, as well as proofreading

- **Manuscript editing**: a loose synonym for substantive editing, this term is closely associated with the work of book editors

It's particularly important for freelance editors to understand these terms and to be able to explain them to clients, who may not understand the distinction between copyediting and proofreading, or between a substantive edit and a copyedit.

7. **Production**

This is the manufacturing step. The designed manuscript, including the verbal text, any illustrative materials, any ancillary materials, and the cover, is printed (in the case of a physical book) or encoded (in the case of an ebook). For printed books, production usually includes the time needed to ship the books to the centre from which they will be distributed, generally a warehouse. Digital books need little more than uploading to a secure server for distribution.

8. **Distribution**

This is the process whereby books reach individual readers through the work of the publisher's sales force, distributors (who store and ship books to sales channels), and retailers, primarily bookstores.

Thus, the idealized process is as follows: author→manuscript→ acquisition→substantive editing→copyediting→design and layout→proofreading→production→distribution→readers. This cycle typically takes nine to twelve months, but can of course be considerably sped up or slowed down, depending on the needs of the project and the publisher. You'll note that this book follows a similar sequence, with a sharp turn to sales and marketing before the conclusion. Sales and marketing, though, is not so much part of the sequence as wrapped around it, ideally promoting a book from the moment it is acquired.

Key Terms and Concepts

As you've likely noticed, in the last few pages I've started introducing some of the commonplace terms of publishing. Here are a few more terms and concepts relevant to what we're discussing in this chapter and throughout the rest of the book. You'll find these terms and others explained in the glossary (pages 365 to 374).

A publisher's *program* refers to the publisher's areas of interest. After all, no publisher can publish everything, just as no book is written for every reader. As an example, a publisher's program might encompass literature and literary criticism, biography and memoir, political science and philosophy, history, and natural history, with an emphasis on western Canadian topics and themes. A publisher's LIST refers to the books the publisher has published previously and plans to publish in the future. The FRONTLIST refers to a publisher's most current books—that is, the books that have been published within the last few months or that will be published in the next few months. The BACKLIST refers to the perennial sellers, books that have sold consistently and have remained in print for years (often in new editions or with new packaging). Backlist titles provide an important source of income for many publishers. MIDLIST is a murkier category, though: it refers to the majority of books, books that will sell moderately well for a year or two but are unlikely to become classics. As I mentioned a few pages ago, some major publishers have recently been trying to rid their programs of so-called midlist authors, and so the term has grown negatively charged among authors and agents.

Books may be published throughout the year, but many publishers try to coordinate the arrival of books to take advantage of shared resources and opportunities. A SEASON refers to the period in which a large number of books are published; it may also be used to refer to a group of books planned for release within that period. Many publishers have two seasons, a fall season (which tends to be bigger) and a spring season (which tends to be smaller). The season is rarely visible to consumers directly but is very important to booksellers and SALES REPS. You'll notice that the fall season—and holiday marketing—coincides with the major awards season in Canada, with the Governor General's Literary Awards, the Giller Prize, and the Writers' Trust Awards being announced in October and early November. (Interestingly, the ReLit Awards, which the *Globe and Mail* called Canada's "pre-eminent literary prize recognizing independent presses," are awarded in February. Only independent Canadian publishers may submit books for consideration, and self-published books are explicitly excluded.) Many awards are also announced in spring, as people begin to think about their summer reading—for instance, the Arthur Ellis Awards for crime writing and the Nebula Awards for science fiction and fantasy writing—and as scholars' season of conferences and annual meetings begins.

KEY PUBLISHING TERMS

Publishing insiders, like people in every profession, use a distinct vocabulary to discuss tasks, operations, and outcomes. Because we work with people at so many stages of the process, editors tend to have an especially large vocabulary of publishing terms.

Review the Glossary: Publishing Lingo on pages 365–374. Which terms or concepts catch your attention? Which ones do you want to know more about? Why? Which ones do you recognize from other settings?

How income is derived from books sold is complicated. From an author's perspective, royalties and DERIVATIVE RIGHTS are the income source—we'll discuss them in chapter 4. But for publishers, income is derived from the differential between the cost to manufacture a book and the price at which it is sold into the supply chain. This differential is referred to as the DISCOUNT.

Discounts are in flux right now due to changes in the retail landscape at large.

- In general, what is called a TRADE DISCOUNT—a discount for books sold to general audiences—starts at forty percent off the cover price of the book, and may be as high as fifty percent (for the purchase of a large number of books).

- There is also a SHORT DISCOUNT—twenty percent—for books sold to more or less captive audiences, such as textbooks sold to students or academic books sold to university libraries. The short discount is based on the assumption that the market comes to the bookseller with little or no advertising, which is increasingly a risky assumption for university bookstores because many students buy their textbooks online or don't buy them at all.

- Finally, there is a WHOLESALE DISCOUNT—sixty percent—which obviously applies to wholesalers. WHOLESALERS distribute books to the supply chain on behalf of publishers; they make their money from fulfilling a large number of transactions with little overhead. A publisher receives less income from the wholesaler than from a retailer, but in exchange is relieved of some distribution costs.

Publishers may also grant discounts for other kinds of sales, as I will explain in a few pages.

The retail, or cover, cost of a book is roughly five to six times the unit cost to manufacture the book, subject to what the market for the book will accept. So, if a book costs $4.75 to print and bind, the cover price of that book might be $24.95.

- The trade discount on a book that costs $24.95 is $9.98 (assuming a 40% discount); the bookseller pays the publisher $14.97 for the book.

- The short discount on the same book is $4.99; the bookseller pays the publisher $19.96 for the book, so there's more of a contribution to the publisher's overhead but less money for the retailer.

- The wholesale discount is $14.97; the wholesaler pays $9.98 for the book, leaving only a slender $5.22 above the cost of manufacturing to cover the publisher's other costs.

What I'm trying to illustrate is that the proceeds from publishing are minimal at best. Let's walk through another example to illustrate my point, using round numbers to make the math clear.

- Let's assume that the cover price of a book is $20.00.
- If we use forty-five percent—$9.00—as a standard trade discount, the publisher receives $11.00 for each copy sold to booksellers.

- If we use a standard royalty rate, the author receives $2.00 for the sale of each copy.
- After the publisher pays the author her royalties, $9.00 remains to cover the cost of editorial, design and production, printing and binding, sales and marketing, warehousing, distribution, and overhead—plus profit, if there is any!

There's rarely much profit, at least not for most small publishers. The small profit margin is a compelling reason for publishers to find other income streams, such as exploiting derivative rights, and it also explains why grant funding is so important to many small presses. Note that increasing the cover price of the book doesn't help: you can make the pie bigger, but the pieces remain proportionately the same.

A publishing house has several structural areas, all of which must be paid for by the proceeds received from the sale of books. Many functions may be performed within these areas, particularly as technologies create new products and opportunities. In this text, we're concentrating on the editorial area, which obviously performs a variety of editorial functions. There is also a design and production area, often called the *art department*, which is responsible for visual communication and the format decisions for both print editions and ebooks. The sales and marketing area ensures that books find their readers. This area includes not just marketing staff but also the staff and systems required to move books into the supply chain: sales representatives, warehousing, and distribution services. The administrative area is responsible for keeping the firm operating: answering telephones, handling correspondence, chasing payments, and keeping the accounts. And of course there is the publisher's area, responsible for vision, direction, and management of the firm. Overhead—the physical plant of the firm and its furnishings—must also be covered by book revenues.

Self-publishing authors may be nimbler because their overhead is generally less than that of a conventional publisher and the functional areas are considerably streamlined. Self-publishers can't eliminate every cost, however. They must think about editing (audiences are volubly unhappy about error-filled books) and design, as well as sales and marketing. It is frankly *much* easier to create a book than to sell one.

Structure of the Industry

The publishing industry—indeed, book publishing itself—is not a monolithic enterprise, but rather is made up of several sectors that perform similar kinds of work following similar processes to produce objects that look superficially similar. The sectors are trade, or general, publishing;

educational publishing; scholarly publishing (also called academic or university press publishing); children's publishing; reference publishing; and specialty publishing. The sectors are not absolute; a scholarly publisher, for instance, might publish textbooks and books for general readers, and a trade publisher might publish books for children and teens. Here's a quick description of each sector.

- **Trade:** TRADE PUBLISHING refers to commercial publishing generally: the HARDCOVER fiction and nonfiction (and increasingly PAPERBACK) books that make up most of what we see in bookstores. Trade publishers publish for "the book trade": adult general readers.
- **Educational:** Educational publishing refers to textbooks and books produced for use in schools. This sector may be further divided into K–12 and college/university publishing.
- **Scholarly:** Scholarly publishing helps scholars disseminate their thinking and research. This sector publishes mainly highly specialized, expert-level texts for scholars, graduate students, and academic libraries.
- **Children's:** Children's publishing refers to picture books, books for early readers, "chapter books," books for middle-grade readers (grades four to seven), and young-adult publishing. Some firms are dedicated to publishing for these age groups, while others publish through an imprint. (For instance, HMH Books for Young Readers is an imprint of Houghton Mifflin Harcourt.)
- **Reference:** Reference publishing encompasses instructional texts like the For Dummies series, technical self-help manuals such as software and car buyer's guides, and cookbook publishing, as well as specialized encyclopedias, dictionaries, and other reference materials. Reference publishers may also produce books for highly specialized professional and technical audiences.
- **Specialty:** Specialty publishing refers to firms with narrow lists and a tight subject focus such as religious, legal, and paranormal publishing. As with children's publishing, some firms publish in these areas through an imprint. (For instance, Zondervan, which produces bibles and Christian books, is an imprint of Harper Collins US.) Some specialty publishers also produce books packaged with non-book items such as toys or gifts.

Regional and national publishing

Beyond the sectors, there is also a significant difference between regional publishing and national publishing. Regional publishers, unsurprisingly, concentrate on a particular area of the country, publishing books about the area and creating opportunities for local writers—though of course regional books can have national and even international audiences. Some well-known regional publishers in Canada include Flanker Press (in Newfoundland and Labrador), Great Plains Publications (in Manitoba), Coteau Books (in Saskatchewan), and Harbour Publishing (in British Columbia). Regional publishers usually have diverse programs, encompassing literary fiction, genre fiction, books for children and teens, poetry, drama, memoirs and biographies of high-profile local figures, regional history, natural history, cookbooks, guidebooks, and more. They tend to have small seasons (ten to twenty books, for instance) but may have large backlists. While they may not have the reach of national publishers, many regional presses offer boutique-style publishing, emphasizing quality and craft, such as Coach House Books in Toronto and Gaspereau Books in Kentville, Nova Scotia. Regional publishers are often important to fostering emerging writers, who may publish with regional firms or small literary presses before they move on to national and international publishers.

National publishers, on the other hand, tend to produce books with less emphasis on regional interests and more emphasis on broad audiences and topicality. Importantly, though, what makes a publisher national is its reach and operations. National publishers have well-developed infrastructure for sales, distribution, and marketing; they are substantial businesses, unlike many regional publishers, which have fairly lean staffs.

The tumult in book publishing in the last two decades has changed the shape of Canadian national publishing. We have lost several of our best-known national publishers—some to bankruptcy, such as Key Porter, and some to corporate purchase, such as McClelland and Stewart. Many of our apparently "national" publishers are actually branch plants of multinational publishing corporations, such as Penguin Random House Canada and Pearson Canada. Still, a few large independents are still standing, such as House of Anansi and Fitzhenry & Whiteside.

Book packaging

Another sector of the business is book packaging. BOOK PACKAGERS develop books much as conventional publishers do—that is, they work up a concept, hire a writer, and then edit, design, and lay out the text. Instead of publishing under its own imprint, however, a book packager sells the developed package to a publisher as ready-made content. The book is then published under the publisher's imprint. Book packagers sell licences by territory and can sell the same package or similar packages into multiple regions with limited adaptation, thereby keeping costs relatively low. Dorling Kindersley, for instance, now a multinational publisher of illustrated information books, gained market clout in the 1990s as a book packager. Book packaging is a surprisingly common practice, but one the buying public barely recognizes.

It's important to understand that no publishers publish in every area. Even the largest publishing corporations divide their interests into imprints, each with a particular focus, personality, and style. This idea is especially important to book editors when we're considering which authors to woo and which manuscripts to acquire. An effective book editor focuses on what her firm does well, be it literary publishing, regional publishing, genre publishing, or otherwise.

Sales Channels

A discussion of the publishing sequence and the structure of the industry brings us to a consideration of *sales channels*: the routes through which books get to readers.

For most publishers, bookstores remain the most important sales channel, but bookselling has also gone through tremendous changes in the last decade. Bookstores may be chain based (e.g., Chapters/Indigo) or independent (e.g., Munro's Books in Victoria). Currently the biggest distinction in bookselling is that between online and physical bookselling. Online and chain-based retailers are important for the Big Five, but physical bookstores remain important for independent publishers, particularly regional publishers who often foster relationships with their local booksellers. Bookstores also may be general or specialized. In particular, college and university bookstores are the main retailers for college/university textbooks, many scholarly books, and certain serious trade nonfiction. There are also dedicated bookstores for children's books, cookbooks, mystery novels, and other specialized interests.

Big-box non-book retailers have become another important sales channel for publishers. These are stores such as Home Depot, Costco, Staples, and Walmart. Such stores buy in large quantities (hundreds or even thousands of copies at a time), and their orders are usually non-returnable (in exchange for a larger discount). Big-box retailers are great for certain kinds of publishers and certain kinds of books, but are simply unavailable to many small independents.

Libraries remain an important sales channel for most publishers, although library budgets have been greatly reduced over the last twenty years. Libraries tend to collect books appropriate to their audiences, so you'll find primarily scholarly books in an academic library and primarily TRADE BOOKS in a public library—with some degree of crossover, of course. Specialized libraries, such as law libraries and government libraries, will tend to buy from a range of publishers, often drawing

Figure 2.1 A visitor to Black Sheep Books on Salt Spring Island, British Columbia, which sells both new and used books

on the advice and expertise of wholesalers, such as Library Bound or Baker & Taylor.

A growing channel for some publishers, though not all, is NON-TRADITIONAL outlets such as gas stations, gift shops, and non-book retailers (e.g., Anthropologie). Working in this channel can be challenging, however, because publishing's discount structure and return systems don't always mesh well with other retail settings. Closely related to this channel is the opportunity for SPECIAL SALES, or BULK SALES. Special sales involve a company or organization buying a large number of books (normally hundreds or thousands of copies) direct from the publisher at a discount and distributing them to a closed group, such as members of a society or all the employees of a company. The key idea of special sales is that it bypasses the retail channels by selling directly into an organization. When arranging special sales, publishers must ensure they are not simultaneously wiping out potential retail sales.

From the 1920s onward, mail-order BOOK CLUBS were a vital sales channel for certain publishers—so important that some publishers created their own clubs (e.g., the Doubleday Book Club, Scholastic Reading Club). You've likely heard of the Book-of-the-Month Club or perhaps even been a member of the Quality Paperback Book Club. These are two of the most popular mail-order book clubs that continue to operate, and there are others. While mail-order book clubs have diminished since the late 1990s with the rise in online purchasing, BOOK GROUPS—smaller groups of readers who meet regularly to read and discuss selected books—have grown increasingly important. (Throughout this text I'll use the term *book group* to differentiate from mail-order book clubs.)

Remainder buyers may be an important sales channel later in a book's life. Although publishers try not to print more copies of a book than the market will take up, sometimes our estimates are overly generous—we get the number wrong. Remainder buyers purchase REMAINDERS— excess book inventory—at very low prices (20%–30% of the cover price or less) and sell them through discount outlets and warehouses, as well as on the discount tables of local bookstores.

What It All Means

At this point you may be wondering what all this information about industry structure and sales channels means for the day-to-day work of a book editor. It means a lot!

First of all, as I noted earlier, editors tend to specialize in certain sectors or segments of the industry—there are scholarly editors, fiction editors, reference editors, medical editors, and so on. While it's certainly not impossible to move from editing literary fiction to editing children's books or trade nonfiction, such a move is not common either. If you start work in one area of the business, you may end up spending a substantial part of your career there gaining breadth and depth of experience. Of course, freelance editors are often generalists, so their client bases and career paths may be quite different.

Second, book editors acquire manuscripts that suit their publisher's program and complement the list. Few editors can champion a book that doesn't fit the program or list, unless the publisher is list building, refining or refocusing the program, or supporting an author already in the publisher's stable. So in addition to watching trends and being attuned to culture, book editors must keep a close eye on their firm's interests. They also need to monitor their primary sales channels and acquire to support those markets. In chapter 9, we'll discover that it's increasingly difficult for both editors and marketing staff to navigate sales channels easily. To be commercially successful today, books editors must be aware of changes in the supply chain and the effects these changes have on the larger economics of the business.

Further, editors tend to acquire for seasons, and the work of subsequent editors (such as copyeditors) is affected by the acquiring editor's intentions for the book. It doesn't take much of a delay to upset plans down the line in the publishing sequence—and the original book editor may not be present to mop up. Though most of the Canadian publishing industry is less rapidly mobile than it appears in Toronto and Vancouver, there is regular movement within firms. If the acquiring editor leaves the firm while a book is in process, or if the priorities of the firm change, a book may become an orphan, and orphaned books often struggle in the marketplace. A book needs a champion. If you know you're planning to leave your firm, or if you know your firm is about to make a significant change to its program or mandate, consider the ethics of acquiring manuscripts that may lose their champion or their resonance. Is it fair to saddle the publisher with a book you are no longer able to support?

Finally, very little of a book editor's day-to-day work involves working with text; most of it involves working with other people in the publishing cycle, especially sales and marketing staff. The kind of thinking involved in working closely with text complements but is also distinct from the "soft" skills required to maintain numerous positive interpersonal relationships, not to mention the kind of knowledge and skills needed to work productively with staff from diverse disciplines. Book editors must be versatile and adaptable, and must adopt a broad view of the overall publishing process, not just the text work. As such, we must be committed to regular professional development and further training.

These considerations don't mean that today's book editors don't value authors and writing, don't value literature, or have reduced books to interchangeable products like turnips or bars of soap. They do mean, however, that for most editors, what delights us is tempered by business considerations.

A book editor has the responsibility—the opportunity—to make the decisions that shape a publisher's list, program, and reputation. Acquisition—selecting texts to publish and moving them into the publishing sequence—is the main work that distinguishes a book editor from other kinds of editors. Acquisition is the focus of the next chapter.

3

Acquisition

"In literature, as in love, we are astonished at
what is chosen by others."—André Maurois

Acquisition—discovering a manuscript and putting it under contract—
remains the core work of an in-house book editor. For most book editors,
acquiring a project involves a series of steps and a range of documents.
This chapter will walk you through the acquisition process, including
the process of finding projects and writers; how to evaluate a QUERY
LETTER, a book PROPOSAL, and a completed manuscript; and the various forms of editorial communication used in assessment and decision
making.

Wherever a project might originate, book editors go through similar
steps to decide whether or not to take a risk on it, a process of informed
evaluation. Many factors inform an editor's acquisition decision: the
publisher's overall program, the current list, the season, the author
offering the project, what competing firms are publishing, and the project budget, to name only a few. Of these, the most important factor is
usually program fit. Orphans on your list—books that don't fit the program and are outside of your firm's expertise—aren't good for you or
the house; they generally aren't good for the author, either. Booksellers
won't be used to looking to your firm as a source for this kind of book
and so may not order it. Without related titles on the list, a book has
no chance for cross-promotion, and the sales and marketing staff may
struggle to generate interest in it. Reviewers may ignore it. Overall, the
book may not perform as well as it should, meaning less income for both

author and publisher. Even if you love a manuscript, if your house can't support it, you should turn it down so a firm that can publish it well and support it effectively may do it justice.

Fit is arguably the most important criterion; without an obvious program fit, the manuscript is likely to be rejected. This means writers must do their research when they propose books: a manuscript is much more likely to be acquired if it suits the firm it is pitched to.

Before we discuss acquisition, however, let's briefly examine the idea of commissioning books, often described as *developmental editing*. (Note that developmental editing may also be involved in a book acquired by submission, as I will explain in coming chapters.)

Commissioning Books

One way to acquire a book is to commission it. In most publishing houses, commissioning manuscripts is uncommon, but for some publishers, it's a regular part of the business. Book packagers, who work alongside book publishers, regularly commission books for international markets, and national publishers may commission books of cultural significance whose development costs may be too great for an author to take on without secure funding.

Generally, when a book is commissioned, publishing staff identify a project and a likely author, develop a budget and a schedule, prepare a project brief or assignment sheet, and then assign the work. The author is often a seasoned professional writer, experienced in researching, synthesizing, and presenting information quickly, but may also be a subject-matter expert (perhaps with the assistance of a collaborating writer or ghost writer) who may lend authority and credibility to the project. An in-house editor is normally responsible for the project development and may provide a detailed—often inflexible—outline of the content and presentation. If the project will involve extensive supportive materials—such as photography, original artwork, or archival research—the in-house editor will be responsible for staffing each role and overseeing the completion of the work.

The author of a commissioned book is generally paid a flat fee for service. Such a work-for-hire arrangement is typical, and the author may retain few, if any, rights to the manuscript. Commemorative volumes and highly topical, short-lived books are often created this way. For example, the author who contributes the text to an art exhibition catalogue would likely be paid a one-time fee; the book is unlikely to be printed more than once and will probably have a limited circulation. Authors of commissioned books may be offered a royalty-based contract, although this is uncommon. In the case of a high-profile author or a cause-based book, the royalties may be dedicated to a relevant agency or cause. For example, the author of a commissioned book about the whales of British Columbia's Broughton Archipelago might donate her royalties to an environmental organization dedicated to conserving and rehabilitating ocean habitats. Ideally, this book will remain in print for years and continue to generate funds for the cause.

If you are the in-house editor responsible for a commissioned book, ensure that the contract your author and other contributors sign is extremely clear about payment and rights. You do not want to fight with an author after the fact about a contract misunderstanding, nor to develop a reputation as a firm that exploits or abuses writers.

The more usual process of acquiring books, however, is through submission: authors sending their work, directly or through an agent, for evaluation and potential publication. If the editor decides to acquire the manuscript, the author is offered a contract and often paid an advance (against future royalties).

Submissions

There are two kinds of submitted manuscripts: solicited and unsolicited. A solicited manuscript may come to the house as an element of an author's contract (through RIGHT OF FIRST REFUSAL); from an author already in the stable who has written or is writing something new; as the result of an earlier conversation between an editor and an author; through the work of an agent; or because the author has been asked to submit the completed manuscript as the result of earlier submission processes (a query letter or a proposal, which I will explain below). The key idea here is that solicited means *requested*: a solicited manuscript has been invited and should be received warmly and reviewed promptly.

Unsolicited manuscripts may be referred to, often unkindly, as the SLUSH PILE or as OVER-THE-TRANSOM SUBMISSIONS. The task of reviewing the accumulation of unsolicited manuscripts, referred to as *reading the slush pile*, is typically given to editorial interns or assistants at those firms that accept unsolicited submissions. While the Big Five publishers, and many other large publishers, do not normally accept unsolicited submissions now, most regional and independent publishers still do. At these firms, reviewing unsolicited manuscripts is a semi-regular task for every editor. By the way, when agents send blanket submissions lacking the name of a specific editor, editors consider them slush, too—it's not only novice authors who end up in this pile.

Most firms have submission guidelines on their websites. The in-house editors must know what the guidelines dictate, and ideally, prospective authors should follow them, although many optimistic or ambitious writers don't. If you are an aspiring author, pay attention to the guide-lines; while it's certainly possible to circumvent the guidelines in some cases, in general editors will ignore—or may even feel hostile toward—aggressive attempts to get their attention.

As I touched on above, books acquired by submission may be offered in one of three ways: as a query letter, as a proposal, or as a completed manuscript. To move us toward an examination of editorial assessment, let's look at query letters and proposals, and how editors act on them. (Note: query letters are distinct from QUERIES, which are questions and notes editors add to a manuscript during the editing process.)

Query letters

A query letter is most authors' initial approach—it's akin to a pitch in the magazine world. It is a brief letter, normally generated by an author (not an agent) and usually one page long (to a maximum of three pages long). A query letter outlines the general idea of the book, the specific angle or treatment, the anticipated audience, and the author's basic credentials for writing; it is also an opportunity for the author to show off her writing style, her research ability, and her marketing sense. Query letters are most commonly sent in broadcast form—that is, to multiple publishers at once—to determine publishers' overall interest in a project; they are almost always unsolicited. Because of the large number of projects under development and the constant strain on editorial resources, many houses prefer to receive a query letter first (often by email) and will then request a proposal or a complete manuscript if they are interested.

The most important quality of query letters and proposals is that they be appealing for book editors to read, because we read so many of them. Even novice writers should have sufficient understanding of the publishing process to recognize why it's in their best interests to make their query letters difficult to resist.

EVALUATING QUERY LETTERS
In Figure 3.1 you see a sample query letter. Imagine it's one of twenty or thirty you have to read today. What does the author do well in this letter? What does the author do poorly? How do you judge the potential of this project based on the query letter?

For more information on writing and evaluating query letters, you may want to read the chapters "The Annotated Query Letter from Hell" and "An Annotated Query Letter That Does It Right" in Cheryl B. Klein's book *Second Sight: An Editor's Talk on Writing, Revising, and Publishing Books for Children and Young Adults*. Although intended for writers, these chapters offer excellent analysis of typical problems and strengths in query letters—valuable insight for novice book editors.

23 August 2016

Dear Editor:

Living with an obsessively busy English teacher, I understand the agonies and the ecstasies teachers who assign compositions go through when marking. It was from watching my boyfriend mark more than 140 essays in one week that I came upon the idea for my new manuscript, *Piles to Go Before I Sleep: A Guide to Marking Papers for Teachers of English Composition and Other Writing-Intensive Subjects*. I hope you'll be interested in publishing this innovative and important book.

Piles to Go Before I Sleep helps today's overburdened secondary and post-secondary teachers plan, organize, consolidate, execute, and manage their composition-based marking. Part One surveys the history of composition in curricula and the curricular expectations of composition-based assignments and then discusses the value of written feedback from student and parent perspectives. Part Two provides clear and well-organized plans and directions for assigning useful composition activities; developing thoughtful rubrics that help students learn from their efforts; organizing assignment dates and planning marking schedules; managing marking piles and marking efficiently, accountably, and quickly; and providing useful written feedback that reinforces student learning. Part Three includes a variety of forms, charts, planners, sample rubrics, and checklists that teachers can use and adapt to manage their particular teaching and marking loads.

The complete manuscript is approximately 61,000 words long. I have also compiled a bibliography and an annotated list of resources for further reading. All of the Part Three materials are my own and have been reviewed by professional educators for accuracy and appropriateness.

According to Statistics Canada, there were approximately 756,900 teachers and professors in Canada as of June 2014. That's a huge potential audience for my book. And according to my research, this group is easy to market to. We could reach them through provincial teachers' associations, faculty associations, teachers' convention book fairs, annual academic meetings, and national publications directed at English, social studies, and related disciplines. Teachers buy books—have you ever known a teacher who didn't buy books? This book comes with its own compelling call to action, making it a must-have on practically every teacher's bookshelf.

I have previously published two books: *The Earnest Gaze: A Romance* (self-published, 2011) and *A Hiker's Guide to Clear-Cuts* (Coastal Pines Publishing, 2013). I have also published an assortment of magazine articles (copies available on request), and some of my poems were published in an anthology of prairie poets in 2009. In my day job, I am a technical communicator for Direct Energy.

I hope you would like to read my manuscript. If so, please contact me at <aloveleeauthor@yahoo.ca> or call me at 250-555-1212 to request it. If I don't hear from you within thirty days, I will propose to another publisher.

Yours truly,
Lovelee Author

Lovelee Author
123 Anywhere Avenue
Victoria, British Columbia V8W 6N4

Figure 3.1 Sample query letter

Proposals

Unlike a query letter, a proposal is a major undertaking. It is a well-developed treatment—perhaps thirty or forty pages long or longer—that includes information about the project, the author, the author's previous publishing credits, and the book's marketing potential, as well as a substantial writing sample. Proposals may be submitted unsolicited, but they're usually better received after a response to a good query letter. The job of the proposal is to demonstrate that the concept possesses a well-developed architecture and the author has the ability to realize it. A proposal is a sell piece, so the author should have invested considerable time in grooming the prose and organizing the content; a sloppy proposal is generally a very bad sign. If the author has an agent, the agent is likely to submit the proposal, which has been developed in concert with the author. Most editors know most agents who pitch to them, so agents' proposals tend to get quicker and more serious consideration.

As an editor, you must understand what a good proposal contains and how it helps you with editorial assessment and acquisitions. A good proposal starts with a developed pitch as a cover letter; this document will usually run to at least three pages but should be no more than five. The cover letter should thoroughly establish the author's credentials, especially highlighting any insider knowledge that lends the project authority and any past publishing experience that makes the author marketable. It should also present some sense of the potential readership and related markets, and should communicate that the author knows where the book fits in a wider context. (If you're interested, you can use the Internet or a library to research how to prepare an effective book proposal.)

The Process of Editorial Assessment Begins

From the query letter or book proposal, a book editor starts a process of decision making that I've referred to as editorial assessment. From just a few lines in a cover letter, an experienced editor can judge whether or not a project suits the house's list on the basis of program fit, project quality, and professional response.

- **Program fit**: Do you publish in this area? Do you *want* to publish in this area? Does the project suit your list or program? What expertise can your firm bring to the project? How difficult will it be to find titles to support this one and round out the list? No publisher can do everything well, so think about whether the project complements the larger interests of your house or the larger goals of your program. Consider too whether retailers will think of your house as a likely publisher for this type of title.

- **Project quality**: Can the author express the essence of the book in a few sentences? Are those few sentences sufficiently compelling to encourage you to read more? Is the query letter/proposal well written and cleanly composed? Does the author appear to have the ability to execute the proposed book? Does the idea sound big enough to sustain a book-length treatment? How familiar is the subject matter? Is the market already saturated? Is the trend already passing? (This question applies to fiction as well as to nonfiction—think of current and passing trends in fiction such as vampires or steampunk.) Does the author have the credentials to bring this book to market effectively? Does your press have the credentials to bring this book to market effectively?

- **Your professional response**: What do your editorial senses tell you? Does this project suit your professional (not personal) taste? What editorial memories does it evoke? What feeling do you get from the query letter/proposal? Experienced book editors say that they can often tell from a query letter whether a manuscript is likely to be publishable or not. That claim may sound arrogant, but after a few years, an editor's sense of what is publishable and what is not—and what the process of getting to publishable will involve—becomes quite keen. (There are, of course, many, many stories about famous, important books that have been rejected numerous times, and also many, many stories of editors taking a risk on an unknown, first-time author and winning big, so perhaps it's the exceptions that prove the rule.)

Some editors also evaluate the cultural value—and consequences—of a project. In their examination of how to make publishing more sustainable, Jessicah Carver and Natalie Guidry suggest acquisition editors take a holistic view of the process, not thinking only of the economic bottom line, but also of environmental and social outcomes: "What is the societal value of the potential book? Is it worth the environmental and social costs?"

Some editors have the authority to buy projects from proposals, particularly if the project comes from a well-known, experienced author. Other editors must have a complete manuscript, as well as the agreement of an editorial board, in order to offer a contract. As a *very* broad generalization, fiction, poetry, drama, and other literary forms tend to be bought from finished manuscripts, while trade nonfiction tends to be bought from proposal. There are exceptions either way, of course. In university press publishing, for example, everything is acquired from finished manuscripts because the evaluation process involves reviews by other academics; and for some name-brand authors, even a sketch of a novel might elicit a contract. Most authors, however, will go through the ordeal of submitting and waiting while their submission is read and evaluated by any number of editors prior to being offered a book contract.

Perhaps this is a good place to interject that both editors and writers must recognize that a publishing hierarchy—or pecking order, if you prefer—exists. Editors tend to take a chance on writers other editors have already taken a chance on; for an aspiring author, having relevant publication credits can make a manuscript more attractive. Most authors go through something of an apprenticeship, starting with publication in journals, periodicals, or blogs, then advancing to publication with regional firms, then on to large independents or national firms, and perhaps to the Big Five. Of course, some authors' first novels are published by Big Five imprints—though certainly not as many as novice writers might imagine. And anyway, it's not every author's goal to be published by a very large commercial firm; the goal depends on the author and the project. Some authors intentionally move from house to house. Thomas Wharton, for example, published his first novel, *Icefields*, with NeWest Press in Edmonton; his second novel, *Salamander*, with McClelland and Stewart; his third novel, *The Logogryph*, with Gaspereau Press in Kentville, Nova Scotia; and three novels for children with Doubleday. Editors must also recognize that there is a widening gap in the interests and practices of smaller, independent publishing and the Big Five. This divergence shapes which authors are published where.

If a query letter hooks your interest, you invite the author to submit a book proposal (or the finished manuscript, if it's available). You are not making a commitment to the author by requesting the proposal, but do respect that developing a proposal package takes time. Don't request a proposal for a book that you aren't genuinely interested in. Also, keep in mind that if you request the proposal, it is now solicited. You have given at least minor encouragement to the author, so you must behave appropriately when the proposal arrives. That means you are undertaking to read it thoroughly and fairly, and to communicate promptly with the author once you have done so.

Sometimes, you'll discover that the author has already submitted a proposal (or the completed manuscript) to another publisher. This fact tells you something about the author's knowledge of the industry and the author's manners. Authors often use MULTIPLE SUBMISSION (sometimes called *simultaneous submission*) as a way to reduce the length of their wait before a publisher shows interest in a project; authors may wait months in the slush pile, and the waiting can be frustrating. That said, simultaneous submission is generally done with query letters, not with proposals. If the author is submitting to multiple publishers simultaneously, or if the proposal is being reviewed by multiple publishers, it's good form for the author to declare that information in her cover letter. Not doing so can lead to unpleasant surprises for all the parties involved.

WHAT IS AN AUCTION?

An AUCTION refers to the process of circulating a proposal or manuscript to multiple editors simultaneously, within a time limit, in order to push the editors to compete with one another to bid for the project. Auctions may go to multiple rounds, the bids increasing each time. An agent auctions a book when the author has power or cachet, and the agent anticipates the project will appeal to several editors and wants to get the best offer quickly. This is a situation where simultaneous submission is declared openly; it's up to the interested editor to respond with a bid to win the project.

One thing an editor is looking for in the proposal is a preliminary sense of a hook or SALES HANDLE. A sales handle is an extremely compressed, expressive articulation of the book's content, summing up the key to the book in a single sentence (e.g., "The Canadian *What to Expect When You're Expecting*" or "The one guide to the Edmonton Oilers, written by Canada's foremost hockey journalist" or "What happens when Emily Brontë meets *Gone Girl*"). While the actual sales handle may not be in the proposal right now, you should be able to form some clear ideas about what the handle could or should be.

The other thing an editor is looking for in the proposal is whether the proposal delivers on the promises of the query letter (if one was received). After reviewing the proposal, you should know clearly whether you want to see the full manuscript (if it exists and if its evaluation is required for acquisition) and whether you want to offer a contract. You should also have a rough sense of how much the property is worth.

For a nonfiction project, the proposal should contain a clear, well-developed outline. You should be able to see the structure of the finished book, and gain a secure sense of its ultimate length, from this outline. It should identify the intended number of chapters and the overall organization of the manuscript; should provide a clear sense of the content of each chapter and how the chapters collectively build to present a cohesive story about the topic; should demonstrate the resources the author is using to develop the discussion; and should identify any special features of the treatment (such as images, maps, glossary, self-quizzes, foreword by an esteemed and relevant figure). If the outline seems underdeveloped, vague, or uneven, be suspicious. Outlines provide a very limited sense of creative work, so proposals for fiction generally skip this step, unless the proposal is for a series. Sample chapters are much more important to the sale of creative writing.

The proposal should be supported by at least two complete chapters of the book; many fiction editors prefer to receive three. The presentation of these chapters should be tactical on the author's part. Ideally, the author will not submit sequential chapters, but rather a very early chapter (or the introduction) and a mid-book chapter; on some projects, though, sending sequential chapters is a good idea—the author needs to consider which presentation will show the book off best. If a manuscript is so new that no complete chapters yet exist, this may be a stopper for the editor: why are there no complete chapters, and how quickly can the author complete the manuscript? The other elements of the package must suggest that the author can execute the promised manuscript on her own. The sample chapters should give the editor a secure sense of the author's style and ability. Can she structure and tell an interesting story? Does she have an appropriate sense of argumentation and evidence? Is there something original and accessible in the presentation?

If the author has prior publication credits, you may want to see some of these writing samples as well (e.g., magazine clips). Keep in mind, of course, that clips have probably been professionally edited. Works published in literary journals tend to reflect the author's own voice and style with less external editing. If the author has published prior books, you can of course check their quality for yourself. You may also be able to get prior sales figures and, through your network, a sense of the author's reliability.

From all of this, you should have a clear idea whether you want to read the finished manuscript and whether it could be a plausible project. It's important to realize that arriving at that clear idea is not easy. In fact, one of the toughest things for new book editors to develop is a sense of a manuscript's *potential*—for good and for bad.

A book editor quickly learns to read a manuscript not for what it is, but for what it could be. Editor and author Arthur Plotnik puts it plainly: "Truth is, an editor doesn't always think a raw manuscript is worth very much. What attracts an editor to it in the selection process often is its potential for being shaped into a successful product." One problem involves seeing potential in a manuscript without also seeing its limitations, such as the small size of its audience or its being too late to market. Book editors must balance being an author's champion against being hard-headed and taking bad risks. Yet with experience, balance arrives; potential announces itself. In 2010, Dan Franklin, publisher at Jonathan Cape, remarked, "The thing that really really turns me on—and I've now been doing it for 40 years, and it still works in exactly the same way—is this: you are sitting at home reading a manuscript and your hair stands on end and you think, 'I know how to publish this and, with a bit of luck, it could really work.'" That, or something like that, is the feeling you are looking for.

Does the proposal have genuine potential? If so, it's time to request the finished manuscript. But before we discuss how to evaluate a finished manuscript, let's pause to talk about taste—in particular, *your* taste.

Taste and Editorial Assessment

De gustibus non est disputandum—there is no arguing about taste—or so goes the claim. Editors are described in communications theory as gate-keepers; that role means that, on behalf of their houses, editors uphold certain standards, values, and tastes. And indeed, most editors assess submissions from an informed perspective beyond their own personal tastes—although their individual tastes are also important—on behalf of potential readers, reflecting interests and currents in the wider society.

Book editors read manuscripts and proposals in a thoughtful, informed manner because of their training and experience in a particular critical milieu. We believe that we know quality when we see it, and equally that we know when something doesn't merit publication; but these beliefs defy the fact that book editing involves a great deal of professional subjectivity. Not every editor is reading for the same tastes, and as a book editor, you cannot afford to be indifferent to either the interests of your firm or the interests of the culture at large. Former literary editor Daniel Menaker puts it well: "When you are trying to acquire books that hundreds of thousands of people will buy, read, and like, you have to have some of the eclectic and demotic taste of the reading public." While your personal tastes and your house tastes may not entirely coincide, you cannot let your personal tastes excessively influence your professional tastes. A manuscript may not be a title that you particularly want, but if it's a good property for your list or house, you should be considering it seriously. You might not like the Kardashians, but you cannot ignore their significance in the cultural moment. Equally, even if your personal tastes run to mystery novels, you may have to read and acquire high-concept literary fiction if that's what your firm produces.

It's important to read the kinds of books that you acquire at work—perhaps not as an exclusive diet, but at least some of the time. You cannot expect to develop a feel for the genre and its conventions without regular contact with similar books, written by writers other than yours and edited by editors other than yourself. If you're editing serious nonfiction, you must read serious nonfiction; if you're acquiring YA novels, you must read broadly and deeply in the genre; if you're acquiring for a scholarly publisher, you must be aware of your general disciplines and how they're changing. Regardless of what sector you work in, you must also recognize how the area you acquire in is changing and growing—or contracting.

EXAMINING YOUR TASTES

Every person who works with text—and in the creative industries generally—has widely divergent tastes; this point is a strength, not a weakness.

Consider what you like to read. What do you dislike reading? Do you prefer story to style, or vice versa? Do you want to meet likeable characters and personalities, or do you prefer challenging, gritty, difficult people and topics? Do you think your tastes are wide or highly selective? How do you think others would describe your taste— not only in reading materials but also in movies, television, games, food, fashion, and so on? How will your tastes help you as someone who needs to read and evaluate other people's words and ideas?

Write roughly eight to ten sentences (or more, if you wish) about what you recognize about your tastes. Be honest with yourself: you're the only one reading what you write.

As the activity above suggests, it's important for book editors to recognize both our tastes and our professional ethos, and to understand how personal taste plays into our acquisition decisions. I believe that taste is constructed and not absolute, natural, or innate, even though some cultural authorities argue the opposite. Rather, taste is acquired over time and through exposure to a variety of texts—often because the purported possessor of taste has been rewarded for developing or demonstrating particular responses valued by others. We need to think about taste because book editors in particular, and cultural workers generally, tend to have a somewhat difficult relationship with taste—in the sense that it's easy for us to assume that we (and our colleagues, and our preferred authors and readers) have it and most other people lack it. The same critical apparatus that makes a good book editor, however, should enable us to look at ourselves and recognize how false this assumption is, how self-interested, and class-interested, it is.

Questions of taste and our acquisition practices are important because they *underpin* the enterprise of publishing, but they are not the entirety of it. As Richard Nash observes, "We have come to believe that the taste-making, genius-discerning editorial activity attached to the selection, packaging, printing, and distribution of books to retailers is central to the value of literature"—but publishing is much more than "literature," whatever we take that term to mean; and literature itself is a constructed, value-laded category. We'll come back to some of these questions later in this book, particularly in chapter 10, when we look at emerging issues in publishing. For now, however, recognize that through evaluation processes—and by communicating with one another and with others involved in the publishing process—book editors constantly develop and refine their tastes and judgement.

Evaluating a Manuscript

In most firms, the initial assessment of a query letter, proposal, or manuscript is fairly superficial. As distressing as it may be to authors to hear this news, many publishers receive too many unsolicited manuscripts, and far too many poor-quality manuscripts, for the initial evaluation process to be fine-grained or nuanced. Rather, at this stage, the editor's general stance is to look for reasons to reject the submission—reasons to say *no*. The aim is to cull out obviously unsuitable manuscripts so more attention can be paid to the stronger prospects.

I noted above that for experienced editors, the query letter itself may be all that is necessary to decide whether or not to proceed to the next step. What the editor's sense of the query letter means for emerging authors is that the letter must be impeccable: attention grabbing, well researched, self-aware, and well composed. A proposal or finished manuscript must be equally captivating and well written. Authors must be strategic: they should never give the editor a reason to say no easily, whether through a silly factual error, because of poor research, or from a lack of patience.

Once the editor has found a project that looks plausible, a pragmatic—and ideally tough—process of assessment begins. For our purposes here, I'll discuss the evaluation process based on a completed manuscript prior to acquisition. You should recognize that similar evaluation processes may apply to a proposal, and may occur on a manuscript after acquisition as well.

In trade publishing, most acquisition decisions are organized around the answers to several questions, as Susan Rabiner and Alfred Fortunato explain in their excellent book *Thinking Like Your Editor: How to Write Great Serious Nonfiction and Get It Published*. Rabiner and Fortunato's discussion focuses on nonfiction, and for the next few paragraphs, so will I. Increasingly, similar questions pertain to fiction, particularly series fiction.

First, does the project have a self-identifying audience? If so, does that audience buy books? If so, what compelling message does this book contain for this audience? To Rabiner and Fortunato's original questions, I'd add one more: will audience members buy this book once they are aware of it? This question, of course, leads to yet another, a marketing problem that editors themselves increasingly must consider: how do we make the audience aware of the book?

To answer whether the project has a self-identifying audience, we must be able both to identify that audience *and* to demonstrate that the audience sees itself as such. For example, let's imagine that a Canadian author is pitching a book about hockey violence, masculinity, and racism. It's easy to say that the audience for this manuscript is Canadian hockey fans—but that's also very simplistic and wrongheaded. How many Canadian hockey fans buy critical books about the culture of hockey? Would a potential buyer, standing in a bookstore, see the cover of the book and identify himself as someone to whom the book speaks? As Rabiner and Fortunato observe, "the people interested in your subject have to include, first, people who buy books, and, second, people receptive to your treatment and conclusions." The book editor must ensure that both author and editor have identified the audience correctly—*and* that the audience is one that buys books.

Today, the question of whether those self-identified audience members buy books is increasingly tied to the question of whether the concept is big enough to support a book. Rabiner and Fortunato observe that writers often have an inflated sense of their topic, imagining it to require book-length treatment when it really could be explored in a few thousand thoughtful words as a magazine article. Most book editors—and regrettably many readers—have had the negative experience of reading a manuscript or published book that ends up being unnecessarily repetitive because the content was simply too thin for the author to stretch to 160 or 200 pages. We also need to consider the proliferation of blogs and recycled content, which certainly have the potential to overlap a book's topic, argument, and relevance. With the omnipresence of the Internet and smartphones, a book must offer something that can't easily be retrieved from a website—particularly for free. Perhaps all that distinguishes a book from web content is its consolidation and ease of reading; for some audiences, that's enough. Consider, as an example, the multivolume publications of the web comic *Questionable Content,* one of many print books spawned by a strong Internet fan base. But increasingly, a book must offer a greater value proposition.

Don't make the mistake of either underestimating or overestimating the tastes of the buying public. If you have a hunch that the market currently finds a certain kind of book, angle, or author appealing, do the research to prove it. Go to a bookstore, go to a library, look at the ads and reviews in industry publications, and ask readers beyond your colleagues and your social circle. If you can find several books on the topic or with this treatment, ask yourself whether the market may already be saturated. In the nine to twelve months required to bring a new property to market, how many more books will exploit this topic or angle? But if you can find only a small number of books on the topic or with this treatment, look closer. Who is the author of these books? Who is the publisher? These two ideas can give you important clues about what prior publishers have been able to identify about the market—and whether a new manuscript has any hope of entering the market successfully. And remember the question I raised a few paragraphs ago: is the message of the manuscript compelling for its intended audience? You may have a good sense of who reads books similar to the one you're considering, but would that same readership read *this* one? Why?

Be careful if you can find no similar books already in print: that's a huge red flag. Either the project you're considering is so innovative that no one else has published in the area—and considering the scope of human knowledge and endeavour in the early twenty-first century, there's very, very little that's unprecedented—or the project is so unusual that other commercial publishers have been unable to find a place for similar books. Your firm may or may not be the one to take the risk.

In chapter 1, I raised the issue of books' authority. In our media-saturated society, authority is another key consideration in the acquisition decision, as Rabiner and Fortunato observe. If the author is not an expert in the subject area, the book may be difficult to sell: the Internet is loaded with text produced by non-expert writers. When readers turn to books, they often do so because they want *the* answer to a question or *the* solution to a problem. The author's credentials matter; if the author has a master's degree in the discipline, has worked at the top levels of a field, has coached world-class figures, or has been recognized by her peers as an authority, that qualification must be part of the book editor's decision-making process because it will ultimately be used to sell the book to consumers.

You might object that these points obviously pertain to general trade nonfiction and popular fiction, but aren't as applicable to literary fiction, academic manuscripts, and highly specialized technical and professional manuscripts, which don't have general-interest audiences. Yes, but the issues of pertinence and value still matter. Do not deceive yourself that literary, academic, and professional publishing don't follow and react to trends. They do. Particularly for highly specialized materials, you must be sure that the audience is big enough to warrant the effort and expense of a book-length publication. Of course, in some situations, there may be other options for such materials, such as an ebook-only edition or a dedicated website.

In short, the factors a book editor must weigh in making an acquisition decision involve content, trends, market fit, and credibility. A further consideration for the book editor involves the standards of prose. In reviewing a manuscript submission, the book editor must consider how much time she (or her company) has to invest to make the manuscript publication ready, or publishable. *Publishable* means the manuscript is sufficiently well written that it can be published within the means and usual mechanisms of the publisher. Importantly, however, what is publishable for the editor of educational books will be very different from what is publishable for the editor at a literary house or for the editor who specializes in children's books, because these editors' processes, outcomes, and audiences are so different. Some publishers have been champions of non-standard composition, creating opportunities for writers who might not otherwise break into print. But most publishers tend to publish writing that is clearly composed using standard grammar, punctuation, and diction. Remember what I said earlier about editors looking for reasons to say no to manuscripts. At the Communication Convergence conference in Vancouver, British Columbia, in October 2015, a speaker observed that North American publishers are accepting only well-polished manuscripts because they have less time and money to spend on editing.

Many books, particularly novels and books of serious nonfiction, will go through a substantive edit, meaning that their "substance" will be edited: their structure, length, pacing, development, vocabulary, level of interest, support apparatus, and so on. Not all books go through a substantive edit, however. Regrettably, this kind of editing is becoming a luxury, at least at some presses. (You may have read a book that felt like it took too long to get going, or that contained annoyingly redundant information, or that was pitched too high or too low for your background knowledge. A lack of substantive editing can lead to these kinds of problems.) The resources required to make a book ready for its readers represent a critical factor in acquisition decisions.

A related factor is budget. I'll defer a discussion of how to prepare a book budget, or COSTING SHEET, until chapter 8, but as a basic practice, a book editor cannot acquire a book that will not at least in theory recover its costs of manufacturing within its first year of publication. That means the advance paid to the author (if any) cannot be more than the royalties the book is likely to earn between sales of copies and licences for derivative rights. It also means that the book editor—at least, at most firms— must be thinking about audience and POSITIONING, that question I raised a few pages ago: will the audience buy this book once they are aware of it? What kind of investment is the editor proposing, for what kind of return?

In commercial publishing, editor Pat Walsh observes, "How an editor's book sells is the final number. You do not get judged on how the book was reviewed, or how smoothly it went through production, or how happy the author is. It has to sell." For those of you interested in literary and less-commercial publishing, though, it may be valuable to remember that in Canada's grant landscape, sales success *is* important, but artistic success—measured in reviews, awards, course adoptions, and a book's presence in literary discourse—is also valuable, perhaps even more so. Nevertheless, the decision to publish is still economic.

In most publishing houses, once the editor has found a project and evaluated its potential, she must make a case for acquiring the project. The editor will develop a simple P&L STATEMENT for support, breaking out costs and projected sales income (plus derivative rights income, if relevant). A P&L statement is a balance sheet that breaks out profits and losses, hence P and L. Some editors have the authority to make an offer without consulting with their colleagues or the publisher. Other editors will make their case in front of a publishing board or an editorial committee of colleagues, which gives its assent to the potential acquisition. In scholarly publishing, the process is protracted by PEER REVIEW, in which a manuscript is read and evaluated by two or three scholars; after peer review, a press committee decides whether the manuscript deserves publication. Finally, if the manuscript is a fit with the program and falls within the editor's or firm's budget, then the editor may offer the author a contract. Then, depending on whether the contract was offered on a proposal or a finished manuscript, there may be a pause in the process until the final manuscript is submitted and accepted and editorial work resumes.

Book Fairs and Rights Catalogues

So far, we've concentrated on the submission of manuscripts from an author or agent as a mechanism for finding books to publish, but an editor has other ways to acquire books: by attending BOOK FAIRS and by finding titles in rights catalogues.

Book fairs, or rights fairs, are held annually around the world. The FRANKFURT BOOK FAIR, the London Book Fair, the Guadalajara International Book Fair, and the Bologna Children's Book Fair are a few of the most notable, but many smaller, specialized rights fairs also exist. The main focus of a book fair is to bring editors, publishers, and rights managers together to buy and sell derivative rights, which are sold based on regions or territories, and languages. For instance, an editor might acquire the Canadian publication rights to a book that has been previously published in another English-speaking country, or she might acquire the English-language rights to a book that has been previously published in French, German, or another language. Book fairs often have a professional development component for attendees, and some fair activities may be open to the public at large. Attending a book fair is an expensive proposition, however, and many small publishers simply cannot afford the cost. In this case, rights catalogues may be an answer.

Rights catalogues provide opportunities for publishers to advertise books with rights available to license, without the need for editors to travel long distances to discuss a deal. An excellent example is *Rights Canada*, published by Livres Canada Books, which you can find online. *Rights Canada* is a collective rights catalogue—that is, it includes offerings from publishers across Canada, and any publisher who wishes to advertise therein may do so. Agencies also produce rights catalogues featuring licences from the authors their agents represent. Rights catalogues and book fairs overlap: you'll find these catalogues at book fairs. Depending on the author's contract, the rights to a property may be *shopped* (advertised as being available), either by the author's publisher or by the author's agent, if she has one.

An editor interested in buying the rights to a property at a fair or through a catalogue will evaluate it using the assessment criteria I've discussed above. That is, she'll review the proposal, manuscript, or finished book for program fit, project quality, and her professional response, tempered by the cost of the licence and her budget.

Editorial Communication

As part of their assessment and acquisition processes, editors produce a variety of documents. We'll now look at three types of editorial communication in detail: reader's reports, peer review reports, and editorial letters. We'll also necessarily look at rejection letters. As you might expect, beyond reading and preparing such documents, editors also spend a lot of time in meetings, on the telephone, and on emails communicating with authors, agents, and other editors.

Reader's reports

A reader's report is a basic form of editorial communication and likely the first thing an editorial intern will be asked to prepare. It is a brief report (a page or two) about a finished manuscript, prepared to assist editors and editorial boards in deciding what to publish. It is written prior to an acquisition decision. The report normally summarizes the manuscript, evaluates its strengths and weaknesses, and discusses the manuscript's market and potential. In some cases, the reader may comment on the work required to bring the manuscript to publication (substantive edit, rewrites, depth of copyedit), may suggest complementary materials (e.g., photography, LINE ART, maps, appendixes), and may offer marketing or positioning ideas.

Reader's reports may be written by either in-house or contract staff. Every house has its preferred format, content, and length, but the model reports in Figures 3.2 and 3.3 are fairly typical. The point of a reader's report is to weigh a manuscript's strengths against its weaknesses. Then it's up to the book editor to determine how the weaknesses might be turned into strengths with the application of resources such as time, money, specialized editorial skill, or subject-matter experts' help.

From time to time, a manuscript will be acquired with limited editorial evaluation and limited communication underpinning the acquisition process. In such cases, an external editor (or an in-house editor not involved with the acquisition) may be asked to prepare something

FANTASTIC PUBLISHING READER'S REPORT

Title of work: A Bridge to Build a Dream On

Author: Georgia Nicholson

Genre: Fiction

Reader: Merry O. Contraire

At its heart, this is a romance novel, but with a sad ending rather than a happy ending. It details the experiences of a woman and her extended family in pre– and post–World War II Europe, and her story after arriving in Central Canada. It explores some familiar terrain—surviving the war, the difficulties of the European reconstruction, and the long-term consequences of war—and the narrative style suggests that the manuscript has its roots in biography or family stories.

There is nothing wrong with this rather lengthy manuscript, but there is nothing compelling about it either. The trajectory of the story is predictable, the resolution trite and unsatisfying. There is a great deal of telling rather than showing. Although some writers are able to make that style work, I'm not convinced it's successful here. The pacing is quite slow, particularly in the middle section; many of the very detailed scenes could be cut without harming the integrity of the story. There is drama, but it's muted and predictable. Rarely does the writer surprise us. The dialogue is mostly stock and sometimes stilted. Most of the characters are nothing more than props for the action; they are underdeveloped and bland. Even the protagonist's children seem interchangeable: I could not tell the two sons from one another, and the daughter seems to have no distinguishing personality traits whatsoever. The most consistent weakness of the manuscript, however, is that the writer does most of the work for readers. We get into characters' heads in a direct and didactic way; the writer tells us exactly what characters are thinking and feeling, and what their reactions mean to the situation. There is limited readerly pleasure to be found in this text.

If we pursue it, this manuscript will require extensive reworking to speed pacing, develop characters, rework dialogue, and strengthen the telling. There are also some inconsistencies in period diction and facts, particularly some questions of continuity of timing. We would also need to confirm usage with the various European languages, particularly the Yiddish expressions.

This is a competent treatment but not literary or innovative. I'm not convinced it is the right book for us right now. I would not buy this book and do not recommend publication.

Figure 3.2 Sample reader's report 1

similar to a reader's report, but concentrating on the editorial work required to bring the manuscript to publication. This communication may be referred to as an *editorial report*. An editorial report provides a substantive assessment of the manuscript and is generally used for the purposes of planning: costing and scheduling the work to be done.

Peer review reports

Peer review is normally done at scholarly or university presses. Two or more independent scholars from the same field as the author (or from a related, relevant field) read and evaluate the manuscript and prepare a written response—the peer review report—about the manuscript and its presentation. As with reader's reports, peer reviews are gathered before the author is offered a contract; these reports help the book editor assess the manuscript—and defend it, if necessary.

Peer review reports are often substantial, running from four to eight pages or longer, and they take time to collect; an editor may spend three months or more getting peer reviews for a manuscript. The reports are sent to the author for response and revision to the manuscript as

---

FANTASTIC PUBLISHING READER'S REPORT

FANTASTIC PUBLISHING
WWW.FANTASTICPUB.CA

Title of work: Prosperity and Disaster: Mining Vancouver Island

Author: Donnatella Maas

Genre: Nonfiction (history)

Reader: Archie Leach

I found this manuscript fairly interesting and readable, if somewhat dry. It's chock full of facts! I would like someone with more background in history to read it for accuracy. It seems well researched and reasonably balanced, but I can't vouch for its accuracy. As popular history goes, though, it's a solid representative of the genre.

The writer has a good sense of structure and organization, and a competent style. The presentation is secure overall. The manuscript is publishable at present but would be improved by a judicious substantive edit to trim and tighten the presentation. Some fact-checking will be necessary, too, either by the substantive editor asking the author to back up some of her claims or by the copyeditor confirming some details with sources. There are some details in the telling that likely don't need to be included at all. The manuscript will need an attentive copyedit; there are minor stylistic and mechanical errors on virtually every page. A map (or maybe several maps) is crucial for readers to understand this text. Can the author supply one? Also, images have been included inconsistently. Can the author supply others? Have publication rights for the images been acquired? Is the author willing to do more photo research?

This manuscript complements the regional titles we've been publishing recently and should draw an audience from both local history buffs and tourists. We might want to consider a co-publication with Coastal Pines Publishing, however, to get access to their rack system, where the book may have better pickup and sales.

Figure 3.3 Sample reader's report 2

necessary. When the editor feels the author has addressed the concerns raised in the reports, the reports, the author's response, and the editor's recommendation are presented to a press committee for a publication decision. (A press committee is a body of scholars responsible for the integrity of the press—the members may be referred to as the *guardians of the imprint.*) Of course, if the author is unable or unwilling to change the manuscript in response to the reports, he is free to withdraw it and seek publication elsewhere, as the manuscript is not yet under contract. Positive reader reports are often a condition for grant funding of academic books in Canada.

Figure 3.4 models the kinds of questions typically asked in a peer review report, while Figure 3.5 provides a sample response using a somewhat different report form.

THE UNIVERSITY OF KAMLOOPS PRESS

Academic Reader's Report Form

Manuscript title:

Author name:

1. What is the core subject of the manuscript?

2. What are the objectives of the manuscript?

3. Is the manuscript intended for scholars, researchers, graduate students, undergraduates, or the general public? How effectively does it speak to this audience?

4. Does the manuscript as you read it make an important and innovative contribution to its field?

5. Is the research sound? Is the research current?

6. Describe the organization, style, and tone of the manuscript. Is the presentation appropriate for the intended audience? Is anything missing?

7. Is the manuscript as you read it ready for publication (apart from mechanical editing)?

8. List any general suggestions for improvements to this manuscript that you have not already identified.

9. Is it important to the discipline that this manuscript be published? That is, will the manuscript appeal to most readers in this field, some readers in the field, or few readers in the field?

10. Would you personally want to own a copy of this manuscript as a finished book? Would you recommend that your institution's library buy a copy of the book?

11. If we decide to publish this manuscript, may we reveal your name to the author?

12. May we use your comments in this report for our marketing and promotion?

Reviewer name:

Institutional affiliation:

Date:

The University of Kamloops Press thanks you for completing this report. Please return your report, along with your current CV, by 31 March 2016.

Figure 3.4 Sample peer review report form

ACADEMIC READER'S REPORT FORM

Title: Let's Be Careful Out There

Author: Janice Wlodarczyk, ed.

WHAT IS THE OBJECTIVE OF THE MANUSCRIPT? DOES THE CONTENT SUPPORT THIS OBJECTIVE?

Over the past decade or two, injury and fatality statistics have shown remarkable resistance to public health policies intended to lower them. Traditional methods of tackling home-based injuries and accidents are obviously failing or ineffective. A new approach is needed. This book is an attempt to expand thinking about the wide umbrella of domestic and public safety. This is a critical need. The book explores the foundations of such an approach by focusing on the knowledge and expertise of a variety of experts from varied disciplines. Bridging the communication gap between academic disciplines, practitioners, and policy makers is an essential part of this effort and that is where the book can play a major role.

DOES THE MANUSCRIPT AS IT STANDS MAKE A SIGNIFICANT ORIGINAL CONTRIBUTION TO ITS FIELD?

Yes, it does. By offering the perspectives of experts from such areas as law, sociology, economics, and engineering to applications of public health and safety, the book provides researchers in all of these areas with an expanded perception of safety challenges and policy problems. In particular, it provides practitioners, especially educators, law enforcement, and civil engineering, with important, mind-expanding reading material. By placing the phenomenon of "the accident" within a wider matrix of concern, encompassing sociological and cultural factors, including long-range economics, the book will help enormously in the effort to draw contributions from all the disciplines concerned into a single pool of ideas.

TO WHAT AUDIENCE IS THE WORK DIRECTED?

I see this work as being directed toward specialists in the field of public health and safety, particularly researchers. In its writing style, it is obviously aimed more at the scholar or researcher than at the practitioner. Any polishing of the writing style, or perhaps rephrasing of some difficult sentences, would expand its usefulness in the direction of a broader readership.

IS THE SCHOLARSHIP SOUND?

This volume editor is well known in the field and has previously published many significant texts. The various contributors she has assembled in this book are respected in their fields, and I am personally familiar with the work of several of these scholars. The diversity of methodologies leads to some fascinating epistemological collisions in the articles, but these are a benefit and not a boon, in my opinion. However, I do take issue with Lisa MacLaren's second-wave feminist analysis of safety at home as symptomatic of international public safety issues. It seems dated and out of place in this book.

Figure 3.5 Sample peer review report (page 1 of 2)

IS THE ORGANIZATION OF THE WORK APPROPRIATE?

Overall, yes, but perhaps Janice could write overviews for each section to help non-specialist readers understand the focus of the section and the key points. I think section six should appear between sections two and three. Chapter 12 should logically come after chapter 13, not before.

DOES THE MANUSCRIPT HAVE A READABLE STYLE?

With the density of theory in some chapters, this book will probably be challenging reading for most practitioners. It's clearly beyond most lay readers. However, for the market niche it is aimed at, it is acceptable. A work such as this could bridge gaps between a wide variety of readers, from researchers to practitioners and policymakers, if some thought was given to the language level. I believe this kind of investment would pay off, but perhaps that's beyond the scope of this book.

COULD THIS WORK BE SHORTENED WITHOUT HARM OR LOSS?

Yes. I think most chapters could be shortened. In a book of this type, I do not find literature reviews necessary. Get to the meat of the chapters quickly.

ARE THE AUTHOR'S TECHNIQUES FOR HANDLING CITATIONS AND WORKS CITED APPROPRIATE?

Overall, yes, but there are some inconsistencies. Most chapters use APA, but some of the authors seem to be following other styles. This could be addressed in the copyedit, though. It was not a problem for me as a reader.

IN YOUR OPINION, DOES THIS MANUSCRIPT NEED TO BE PUBLISHED? DOES IT DUPLICATE WORK ALREADY IN PRINT?

Yes, this manuscript deserves to be published. The only truly similar work I can name is *Public Safety and Public Policy*. It was also edited by Janice Wlodarczyk and has a similar presentation style. However, *Let's Be Careful Out There* is more up-to-date and has some different slants on the problem. It's likely to make a significant contribution to discussions about domestic and public safety.

YOUR SUGGESTIONS FOR IMPROVING THE MANUSCRIPT

Apart from the copyediting that needs to be done, I suggest that there are many paragraphs that could be rewritten for clarity and sentences that could be revised. Since this work is aimed at bridging communication gaps between disparate fields of expertise and groups of stakeholders, I believe it would benefit greatly from someone polishing the writing, sharpening the phraseology, and perhaps even rewriting some parts in a more down-to-earth style. Pare out the discursive notes. If the content is important enough to mention, it belongs in the chapter; if not, leave it out. The author's current introduction reads badly. I think she needs to look at it again and tease out more connections among the chapters and with the larger theoretical discourse around harm and injury reduction and public health. If you're serious about reaching practitioners, you might want to consider including a glossary and a list of additional resources in addition to the chapter bibliographies.

Figure 3.5 Sample peer review report (page 2 of 2)

Editorial letters

Reader's reports are generally unsigned; peer reviews are always anonymous (although a canny scholar can usually figure out who her reviewers are). Knowing that the author should not learn who the reader is may
encourage readers to be more direct and less opaque in their manuscript
assessments. However, if a manuscript is likely to be acquired, the editor
will send the author the peer reviews or the early readers' reactions and
suggestions. That's the work of editorial letters.

An EDITORIAL LETTER is an adapted version of the reader's report(s)
or peer review(s), intended for the author to read and respond to. It
typically amalgamates repeated comments into single observations and
softens some of the assessment language to make the commentators'
directions more palatable to the author. One of the book editor's jobs is
to manage communications between publisher and author to keep the
author's attention on their mutual goal. An editorial letter is generally
prepared by the acquiring or substantive editor, and may be sent prior
to the contract being offered or immediately after the contract has been
signed, depending on house practice. Figure 3.6 provides a sample.

The editorial letter does a lot of work beyond its specific textual
recommendations: it forms the underpinnings of the author–editor
relationship. The tone and structure of the letter should position the editor as the author's champion. In the sample letter, for instance, the editor
provides specific direction about the work to be done and the schedule
for doing it, but because the language is friendly and collaborative, the
author should receive this information positively, ideally responding
in kind.

Other editorial communication

Two other forms of editorial communication are common: *vetting reports*
and *legal reads*. Although both vetting and legal reads are normally done
on a final, copyedited manuscript, they form part of the larger web of
editorial communication, so I'll mention them here.

VETTING is similar to a peer review, but the reader is normally a practical expert in the field, rather than an academic, reading for obvious
gaps or errors in the text. Vetting is normally undertaken only on works
with substantial technical or professional content, particularly when
there is potential for harm if the content is wrong. A vetting report is
generally not anonymous, and the reader is normally paid a flat fee or
honorarium for reviewing the manuscript.

A LEGAL READ (sometimes called *lawyering*) may be requested for a
project in which the editor or publisher believes the author may be at

Lovelee Author
123 Anywhere Avenue
Victoria, British Columbia
V8W 6N4

1 April 2016

Dear Lovelee:

A few of us have now read the manuscript of *Transparent as a Glass Eye*. I've amalgamated our comments so you can get started with revisions while your agent and I work through the details of your contract. Let me say again how much we like your manuscript, particularly the comedy of the narrative and the oddness of Rory's situation. We think your book's a winner!

Our readers particularly like Rory and Sandi as characters. They feel real and well developed. One reader says her best friend is exactly like Sandi. But we all agree with your feeling that you could develop some of the other characters. As you know, the manuscript as it stands is short, so you should plan to add about 14,000 to 16,000 words in new scenes and rewrites. Perhaps you can provide back story for some of the other characters and help them come fully to life like Rory and Sandi.

In our phone conversation last week, you asked me to zero in on two other things: whether the title is doing its job and whether the descriptions provide enough pegs for readers to follow the action. I've made some specific notes, plus notes and comments from other readers, on a copy of the manuscript that I'll mail to you tomorrow. Please let me know if you have any questions about our suggestions.

Will it be possible for you to turn over a revised version of the manuscript by Labour Day? We'll need the final manuscript by the first week of December to have advance reading copies for the sales reps and reviewers early in the new year. The copyedit shouldn't take long, but I can't speak for how much time design and production may need. If you have any concerns with the timelines, just let me know.

Remember, all of our suggestions *are* suggestions. You don't have to take any of the edits you don't like. I'm also happy to discuss your ideas for the rewrites or to chat if you're having problems with the story or want to bounce a concept around. In that case, it might be best for us to set up a phone meeting. Fridays and Mondays are best for me, but I will try to work with your schedule.

Looking forward to seeing the next pass on the manuscript soon.

Cheers!

Darl Yu
Acquisitions Editor

Figure 3.6 Sample editorial letter

risk of defaming someone, in contempt of legal process, or in any other way on legally shaky ground. Legal reading is generally expensive and may have to be done repeatedly, depending on the degree of risk and the author's/editor's solution to problems. Given the habit of some high-profile personalities to sue when they encounter text they don't like, a legal read can be sensible; at the same time, much like chill in news reporting (i.e., the decision not to report on a person or event out of fear of legal repercussions or a nuisance lawsuit), legal reads can inhibit the author's expression and diminish the quality of public knowledge.

Rejection

In any discussion of acquisition hovers the spectre of the other option: rejection. Rejection is part of being a book editor, simply because you cannot say yes to every project. You cannot say yes even to every project you like and want to champion. So you must get used to saying no.

There's no reason to be cruel or offensive when you reject a manuscript, however. There are several published books about crushing and mean-spirited rejections editors have sent, in some cases to authors whose subsequent work went on to be triumphant. How would you like to be one of the editors who rejected J.K. Rowling's Harry Potter manuscript? Keep in mind, too, that the book industry in Canada is small, and you could quite plausibly run into the author or someone he knows at some point. For all these reasons, and many more, it is a BAD idea to write rude, insulting, or derogatory rejection letters—and bad karma, too! Figure 3.7 provides a model rejection letter that should do the trick for most editors.

There are a few specific points about Figure 3.7 I'd draw to your attention. First, if you do not want to see a manuscript (or a proposal) again, ensure that your rejection letter is clear. You do not need to be hurtful, but don't waffle either. I've found that an effective strategy is not to reject the author or the project, but rather to encourage the author to find a more appropriate fit for the project (e.g., a press with a different program or a different market) if your press is not the right one. If your press might have published the manuscript had you not recently published a similar one, you can (gently) observe this point as well; perhaps with a little more research, the author can find another publisher with similar interests. If the manuscript is clearly not publishable as a commercial book, either because of its content, its style, or its intended audience, you may want to redirect the author to his reasons for publishing (e.g., sharing this manuscript with family and friends). Walt Crawford refers to publishing texts with sharply limited audiences as

19 April 2016

Lovelee Author
123 Anywhere Avenue
Victoria, British Columbia
V8W 6N4

Dear Ms. Author:

Thank you for submitting your manuscript *The Earnest Gaze* for consideration by Fantastic Publishing. We reviewed your manuscript with interest and enjoyed the passionate story of Romeo and Ethel, the pirate's daughter.

I regret to tell you, however, that Fantastic will not offer to publish your manuscript. Romantic fiction falls outside our program, and your manuscript would be better supported by a publisher whose list emphasizes genre fiction.

I wish you every success in placing your manuscript elsewhere. Thank you for considering our house.

Yours truly,

A. Lowlee Editor
Acquisitions and Development

Figure 3.7 Sample rejection letter

micropublishing and suggests that public libraries may be resources for authors to get these kinds of manuscripts into circulation. Encouraging an author to self-publish can be a gracious (and guiltless) way to redirect an author whose work just doesn't suit commercial publication. Keep the letter brief and upbeat; ensure that it demonstrates you have read at least some of the manuscript; and refrain from criticizing either the author or the talent on display. (If you want to see an author's comedic response to receiving a rejection letter, search YouTube for Bernard Black Rejection.)

Some editors, almost always at small, independent presses, offer more or less extensive notes on the manuscript in their rejection letters. This is done as a courtesy, out of respect for the author and the industry's collective commitment to fostering talent and a diversity of voices. But there are risks to offering notes, too. Most importantly, the author may interpret your notes as encouragement that you would publish the manuscript if it were revised according to the notes. If you would genuinely be interested in reading a revised version of the manuscript, say so. But do not encourage revisions on a manuscript that you do not intend to acquire. Why would you invest time in a manuscript that isn't ultimately going to become your property?

Do note, however, that if you have asked for a book proposal and then reject the project based on the proposal, it is not unreasonable—and in fact is good practice—to offer a detailed rejection. Again, be clear that you do not want to see the manuscript again if that is in fact the case. Editors must recognize that a well-developed book proposal involves a substantial commitment of effort and time, and it is unprofessional to reject something you've solicited with a boilerplate rejection letter. If the author has submitted a printed proposal, it is also appropriate to return it at your cost with the rejection letter, unless the author has indicated that you may destroy it.

Do *not* recommend the author approach other publishers or editors by name unless you have discussed the project with the house or the editor first. If you break this rule, you will regret it. Most editors and publishers are overwhelmed by unsolicited proposals and manuscripts—even firms that do not accept unsolicited projects receive hundreds of "hopefuls" every week. If you add to your colleague's workload, you'll see the decision come back at you—likely in spades. That said, reaching out to a colleague when you receive a likely project that your firm simply cannot take on, for whatever reason, can be wise. If you can connect a viable project to an interested house, both your colleague and the author will appreciate the favour.

One more point: if you're going to reject a proposal or manuscript, do so promptly. Authors will not dislike rejection less if it arrives slowly; in fact, waiting a long time to be rejected frustrates authors. Former book editor Betsy Lerner suggests that "part of the reason why editors take so long to decline on projects, apart from never having enough time to consider them, is how uncomfortable they are rejecting and disappointing people." I have observed this discomfort first-hand with colleagues and peers, and can confirm that it's real. Most editors aren't jerks, but we may come off as jerks because we don't like saying no, yet saying no is integral to our job. For the sake of authors and relationships, do not procrastinate when you must reject a project.

REFLECTING ON EDITORIAL COMMUNICATION
Now that you've read examples of typical editorial documents and thought about how they are used, take a moment to connect editorial communication to the image of a book editor you considered in chapter 1 or to the larger context of a book editor discussed in chapter 2. How do you think these documents fit into the book editor's day-to-day work? How do these documents fit with what you already knew about acquisitions? Does anything about editorial communication surprise you? How does this type of communication change your perspective on the author–editor relationship?

Now that you've decided that a manuscript is worth a commitment of risk—time and money—let's look at putting the manuscript under contract and turning it into a literary property.

4

Contracts

*"The ... task for book people of this time in history
is to find the appropriate balance between author
and publisher reward, on the one hand, and public
access, on the other."—Rowland Lorimer*

So you've worked your way through a pile of manuscripts, completed
the process of evaluation, and selected a text that looks like a winner.
Now you're ready to acquire the manuscript formally by putting it under
contract. That's where this chapter comes in. Here, I discuss the basics
of a publishing contract, but also a great deal of other information you
need to know related to contracts in general and how a contract affects
your relationship with your author.

Most publishing firms have a so-called boilerplate contract, with
standard clauses and terms, that editors use to open the contract conversation with authors. You may also see distinctive elements in a contract
particular to one firm. As a book editor, you must understand the essential elements of a book contract so you can knowledgeably present a
contract to a potential author. Model contracts provide a good basis for
your understanding of contracts and their components. However, you
may find yourself having to draw up a new contract (if you're starting
your own publishing firm, for instance) or having to customize clauses

(if the boilerplate contract isn't sufficient—and sometimes it's not), so it's important to understand what each clause means and why it exists. You need to recognize where contracts may deviate, how to walk an author through the contract, and where the conflicts tend to reside in contract discussions. And Canadian book editors, in particular, need to understand and be able to explain the concept of MORAL RIGHTS in our country.

You do not need to be a lawyer to prepare or offer a contract. (That said, it's vital to have a lawyer who is experienced in publishing law review a new contract if you're starting a new publishing firm.) People can enter into agreements without legal representation and in fact do so all the time. But if you're representing the interests of a party other than yourself—for instance, the publishing house for which you work—then you may need a little backup from time to time. Senior staff in your firm and experienced editors in your network may be valuable resources when you have questions. There are also some excellent print and online resources available; see appendix E for more details. Also, if your contract is fair and well drawn, and your contractual explanation is clear, your author should not need to visit a lawyer prior to signing the book contract.

CHECK YOUR KNOWLEDGE ABOUT CONTRACTS

What do you know about contracts? Most of us think we know about contracts because of what we've seen or read about in popular media— option clauses, six-figure advances, and assignment of copyright, for example. But as a book editor, you need to understand contracts inside and out. Briefly identify and, if necessary, explain three concepts you think you know about book contracts.

Contract Basics

At its heart a contract is an agreement, but it's an agreement that produces a legal relationship, and that's where things get complicated. Let's start by looking at the basic principles of contracts.

First, both parties to a contract must intend that the act of negotiating is likely to lead to an agreement. It's possible that an agreement won't occur, but when the discussion begins, the intention to form an agreement should be the goal that binds the parties. This is the principle of *bargaining in good faith*. Time is also a factor in contracts. An offer may be revoked or may lapse if it is not acted on in a reasonable period. This is where we get the idea that *time is of the essence*.

To become binding, a contract must first make an offer, which must contain all the terms of the agreement, explicit or implicit. The offer must be communicated clearly; it cannot be suggested or implied. The offer then must be clearly accepted by the other party. Like the offer, the acceptance cannot be suggested or implied, and it must be unconditional and unequivocal. Finally, there must be *consideration*. Consideration refers to the benefit exchanged in return for the promise—an exchange of value for value—and must be appropriate to the scope of the contract.

Importantly, a contract must be legal to be valid. This is a very simple principle: if a contract is not legal, it's not valid. This means a legal contract cannot, for instance, contradict public policy. It's also important to know that only people competent to make an informed decision may form a contract. This principle protects people who may be vulnerable or easy to exploit from being harmed by people who would try to take advantage of them.

So, in short, here is the essence of a contract:

- a contract is an agreement that is enforceable through legal standing;
- the parties to the contract must intend to form an agreement;
- the purpose of the contract must be legal;
- one party must communicate an offer, and the other party must accept the offer; and
- the agreement must include consideration, the exchange of something of value between the parties.

A book contract, also known as an *agreement to publish*, meets all of these requirements. It is an agreement between the publisher and the author to exploit the primary right of the manuscript: to publish a book, an activity both parties have voluntarily sought to engage in. The offer is the offer to publish; it is communicated in the text of the contract and is always explicit. The acceptance is indicated by the author's signature, usually witnessed by someone who is not a party to the contract. A royalty payment or fee (and the advance, if one is offered) is the consideration given in exchange for the completed manuscript.

The contract represents the shift of the manuscript into a text with exchange value. At this point, the manuscript may be referred to as a *property*. In the context of a contract, though, it's more likely to be referred to as "the work," reflecting its still-abstract existence.

The Major Clauses

All legally valid book contracts have a few things in common. They all contain an explicit offer to publish, an acceptance of the offer (including the author's signature), and a statement of consideration. They also bear a date on which the agreement comes into effect. They must identify the author by the author's legal name, even if the author will be publishing under a pseudonym, and the title of the work (or at least a working title), as well as the publisher or imprint name.

Beyond these elements, most contracts also contain the same basic clauses, some in accessible language and some in highly legalistic jargon. These clauses tend to be presented in similar order, but firms do vary their presentation. The major clauses in a Canadian book contract are the *grant of rights;* a *waiver of moral rights; delivery, acceptance, and publication;* the *author's warranty;* the *publisher's indemnity;* and *termination.* Beyond identifying the royalty percentage and payment structure (including the advance, if one is to be paid), most contracts also contain some details around how derivative rights will be managed. Let's look at these clauses in detail.

Grant of rights

Most contracts begin with a grant of rights, referring to the primary right—the right to publish. Rights may be granted in two ways: through *assignment,* which involves transferring control of the primary right, or through LICENSING, which permits rights to be exploited in a limited way. A book contract grants, or assigns, the primary right to the publisher. Here is a sample grant of rights:

> *The Author hereby grants to the Publisher the sole and exclusive right to produce, publish, distribute, and sell, or cause to be produced, published, distributed, and sold throughout the world in book form and in the forms set forth below, the Work currently titled* Transparent as a Glass Eye *and hereinafter referred to as "the Work."*

Within the grant of rights clause, the copyright (which protects the author's expression and is distinct from the right to publish) may be assigned to the publisher or may be retained by the author. This point produces immense conflict with authors and agents. There is no need for the publisher to hold the copyright to a work in order publish it, but until recently many publishers have simply assumed the copyright of works—and sometimes been reluctant to revert the copyright when books have gone out of print. (The issue becomes much more complicated today, when print-on-demand technology raises the question of whether a book is ever truly out of print.) Many university presses continue to assume copyright to a work with the grant of rights. Be sure you know and can explain your house policy on this issue.

Let's digress for just a moment to discuss copyright further. As I noted above, at one level the concept of copyright is extremely easy: you either have it or you don't. The law makes limited provisions within copyright. For instance, you can legally copy portions of this book, but you cannot legally make multiple copies of this book to sell to other people without negotiating with the rights holder. But at another level, copyright is tremendously complex; some commentators even argue that it has lost its relevance in this century because of how complex rights management and protection of intellectual property have become. The protection of copyright is vital for writers and editors, however, because copyright—the protection of intellectual property—is vitally tied to the protection of physical property, that is, our income.

Three concepts emerge to limit the scope of rights: the *term*, the *territory*, and the *language*. The term of the contract refers to how long it will endure before it expires; the term is normally the same as the copyright protection, unless the publisher reverts the primary right to the author. The term begins when the contract comes into effect. The term of a licence is much more limited and lasts for a fixed number of years, with a provision for renewal. The *territory* refers to the parts of the world encompassed by the grant of rights; many publishers ask for world rights (or increasingly, universe rights, enabling the potential for publication beyond the surface of Earth), but not all authors and agents are willing to grant world rights. The *language* refers to the original language of the manuscript (e.g., English, French, Japanese). Translations of the work are normally published by licence unless the publisher has the capacity to publish in multiple languages.

Before we go on, however, let me clarify one concept that emerged in the last paragraph. REVERSION OF RIGHTS occurs when a publisher formally returns the primary right (the right to publish) to the author. This step occurs when a work has been declared out of print and the publisher does not intend to produce a new edition or otherwise keep the work available. When the rights revert to the author, the author may try to sell the work to a new publisher or may self-publish. The original publisher has no further claim on the work.

Waiver of moral rights

Moral rights refer to a bundle of rights with a long history. The three issues bundled into the moral rights clause are the right to identification/anonymity, the right to the integrity of the work, and the right to control the association of the work. A waiver of moral rights may appear in contracts offered in Canada, the United Kingdom, Australia, and other Commonwealth countries, but importantly will not appear in contracts offered in the United States. The clause acknowledges in a sentence or two that the author has moral rights in the work, that these rights may be affected by the publishing process (particularly editorial and marketing), and that the author's moral rights need to be waived only to the degree required for the author to fulfill the terms of the contract and for the publisher to publish the book.

In the early days of moveable type, printing—and artistic expression generally—was closely controlled by the crown and/or the church. Writers and printers (the nearest things to publishers at the time) were accountable for the ideas and opinions they published. If those ideas or opinions were treasonous or blasphemous, the work could be seized and destroyed, and the writers and printers themselves could be fined, imprisoned, or potentially even executed. Publishing was a serious undertaking.

Out of this history emerged two related rights: the right to be identified as the author of a work and, equally, the right to publish work anonymously or under a pseudonym. Another right allowed the author to protect the integrity of the work, so that a publisher or editor could not alter the text to distort or misrepresent the author or his ideas. Yet another right allowed the author to control what the work might be associated with, so that a publisher could not align the text with a cause or philosophy prejudicial or harmful to the author's character or status in the community.

Today, a writer can write under her own name, under a pseudonym, or anonymously. Writers normally approve the text after each editorial process (for instance, after the copyedit and after proofreading), and no one can legally mash up the author's work and re-present it as his own. And writers usually have considerable say in how their books are promoted in the marketplace, so a vegan author should never see her culinary writing appearing to endorse animal abuse, or a pacifist author should never see his work used to promote militarism or fascism. Should such things occur, legal remedies are available. In short, moral rights allow artists to protect the representation and circulation of their words. Importantly, though, unlike the primary or derivative rights, moral rights cannot be assigned to another party; they endure with the author because they are in effect an extension of the author's reputation.

Delivery, acceptance, and publication

In this clause, or series of clauses, the publisher agrees to publish the author's book. The delivery clause stipulates the details of the work to be delivered, including the parameters of the topic, how the text is to be submitted, and what additional materials must be included (such as illustrations, photographs, or maps); an approximate word count may also be stipulated. This clause normally includes a due date or deadline, which is tied to the agreement to publish. If the author fails to deliver the manuscript, the agreement may be terminated, although the due date may also be extended.

The real significance of the delivery clause rests with acceptance, however. Even if the author submits a manuscript by the due date in the form and with the content required, the delivery clause states that the manuscript must be satisfactory to the publisher in order to be accepted. If the publisher (practically speaking, the acquiring editor) determines that the manuscript is not satisfactory, it is returned to the author with instructions for correcting its deficiencies. Deficiencies might include a manuscript that is significantly shorter or longer than the length specified or on a topic that deviates substantially from what was agreed to. The author has a reasonable period to correct the deficiencies, usually a matter of weeks. If the manuscript is not corrected and resubmitted (and a manuscript might go through several iterations before it is finally accepted), the publisher may terminate the agreement. Technically, if an advance was paid, it must be returned to the publisher; but in practice, writers are rarely able to repay their advances, so few publishers pursue this course.

If the author submits the manuscript by the due date in the form required *and* it is accepted, the process of publication begins. In the publication clause, the publisher agrees to publish the work by a given date. In some contracts, this date refers to a month or season; in others, it is within a year or eighteen months of receipt of an acceptable manuscript. This clause usually contains language to allow the publisher to delay publication if market conditions are not favourable when the specified date arrives, and the publisher normally reserves the right to determine the format (hardcover versus paperback), the number of copies to print, and the retail price of the book. The publication clause normally also details the editorial work the publisher will undertake, the author's obligations for reviewing editorial changes, and who determines the look of the cover. All these clauses are based on print publication, but the same ideas pertain to digital publishing.

Cover approval is almost always a sore spot with authors and agents, but equally it is one place where publishers tend to stand firm. Few authors have the clout to actually approve their book covers; at best, most are entitled to see the cover before the book is published. The publisher assumes financial risk in publishing the book and has expertise in bringing other books to market with a particular style or identity, so publishers rarely bend to the author's whims. For book editors, it is valuable to show the author the planned cover as early as possible and to listen to the author's feedback. While the author/agent may not have the right to approve the book cover, you don't want your author to hate the cover. The author may also know his audience better than you do and may be well positioned to suggest the cover's most appealing form. Your job may be to negotiate with the art department to find a compromise everyone can accept.

Author's warranty

The author's warranty (or warranty by author) requires the author to confirm that the manuscript is the author's own creation and that the author has the legal ability to grant the primary right. The author must agree that the work does not plagiarize another work, published or unpublished; that the work has not been published in any form in the territory of the contract; that the work does not violate any legal boundaries (such as patents, trademarks, confidentiality agreements, trade secrets, or privacy rights); and that the work does not contain anything defamatory or obscene. This warranty extends to ancillary materials included with the manuscript, such as photographs, illustrations, charts, and maps. All of these points are vital.

Plagiarism is an issue in academic and corporate life because of intellectual integrity, and publishers certainly care about this point. But for publishers, plagiarism is also potentially a violation of copyright and thus has potential financial and legal consequences. If, in the manuscript, an author uses words or images that are protected by someone else's copyright, the author must acknowledge this use fairly and appropriately. For

WHAT IS PLAGIARISM?

Plagiarism is the act of using another person's words and ideas as one's own. Obviously, the wholesale copying of material from an unattributed source into a manuscript is plagiarism, but plagiarism can also be subtler. When an author fails to acknowledge where a specific idea or passage came from, that's plagiarism. When an author copies the ideas and structure of a published text, changing a few words here and there, that's plagiarism. When an author uses a piece of information that is not part of the common knowledge of a field and does not refer to its source, that's plagiarism. When an author incorporates an already published table, figure, or illustration into a manuscript without written permission from the copyright holder to do so, that's plagiarism.

Authors who do not write as a major element of their profession may find the concept of plagiarism difficult to understand, but even academic authors and professional writers have been guilty of plagiarism. Lack of understanding is not a defence. The best advice for authors is this: if the idea and its expression aren't yours, cite a source. An editor will happily remove an excess of citations; a publisher will be very unhappy to discover your research processes have been "sloppy" and "inadequate" (which is how one accused plagiarist attempted to explain the failure to cite sources).

small samples of text, such as brief quotations from other texts, standard citation (such as notes or inline academic citations) is generally all that's required. For larger passages, for quotations of lyrics, and for reproduction of figures and graphics, formal permission may need to be sought. This is the author's work, although the publisher *may* be able to help with it. Regrettably, in the last two decades, several authors have acknowledged that significant portions of their books were plagiarized, causing at least embarrassment, at worst financial loss, for their editors and publishers.

In Canadian contracts, the warranties regarding defamation and obscenity deserve attention. Under Canadian law, the writer must prove herself innocent of defamation; in other jurisdictions, the defamed party must prove the intent to defame. Because Canadian defamation law is fairly wide reaching, many Canadian publishers insist on a legal read prior to the publication of controversial books.

Canada's obscenity laws are fairly liberal, having been modernized in response to the British challenge to *Lady Chatterley's Lover* by D.H. Lawrence in the 1960s, and books that contain coarse language, sex scenes, and other "dirty" bits are not in peril. Two areas of concern do exist, however: graphic representations of sexuality and violence, and sexualized representations of children. In many cases, freedom of expression and artistic value will provide sufficient defence; but again, some Canadian publishers will seek a legal read prior to publishing a book that may be controversial, particularly since community standards (i.e., what reasonable people in the area would accept) are often engaged when obscenity charges are considered.

The purpose of the author's warranty is to assure the publisher that the author is not *knowingly* leading both parties into legal jeopardy. This assurance ties clearly into the publisher's indemnity.

BANNED AND CHALLENGED BOOKS: SHOULD EDITORS CARE?

The seizure of books by government officials, books' removal from school and public libraries, and challenges to freedom of expression, both at home and abroad, are important issues for book editors and publishers. Recently, anyone who is paying attention to our culture at large has become all too aware of how our freedom of speech and our privacy may be compromised—through digital surveillance and aggressive anti-terrorism legislation, for instance. But the history of banned and censored texts reaches back to the earliest days of writing. Consider the line penned by British writer Evelyn Beatrice Hall (a line often misattributed to Voltaire): "I disapprove of what you say, but I will defend to the death your right to say it." For people in the business of making words and ideas public, this idea should be acutely relevant.

In Canada, Freedom to Read Week is celebrated annually in late February. In the United States, Banned Books Week is recognized annually in late September. Events drawing attention to censorship and the free circulation of books are often sponsored by library organizations, such as the American Library Association, which since the early twentieth century have taken freedom of intellectual inquiry ("freedom to read") as a first principle. Complementary organizations, such as Canada's Book and Periodical Council, have increasingly gotten involved, with the recognition that it is authors and publishers who bear most of the burden when a book is challenged, censored, or banned. Book editors must be aware of the issues surrounding banned and challenged books, if not as champions of intellectual freedom then because of the fiscal consequences of a challenge.

Books that have been challenged in Canada—and that in some cases have been removed from classrooms, libraries, or curricula—include *The Handmaid's Tale* by Margaret Atwood; *The Wars* by Timothy Findley; *A Jest of God* and *The Diviners* by Margaret Laurence; *Barometer Rising* by Hugh MacLennan; *Of Mice and Men* by John Steinbeck; the Harry Potter series by J.K. Rowling; the His Dark Materials series by Phillip Pullman; *The Giver* by Lois Lowry; and *Bridge to Terabithia* by Katherine Paterson, among others. You may also have heard about several high-profile banned or challenged books in the United States, including *The Bluest Eye* and *Beloved* by Toni Morrison; *The Kite Runner* by Khaled Hosseini; *To Kill a Mockingbird* by Harper Lee; *The Adventures of Huckleberry Finn* by Mark Twain; and *The Absolutely True Diary of a Part-Time Indian* by Sherman Alexie, among many others. On these lists you'll notice some classics of CanLit, as well as books you might have read as a child and books you might have studied in school. Banned and challenged books can have positive outcomes, such as the upturn in sales for Sherman Alexie every time *The Absolutely True Diary* is challenged; but the social harm from book challenges and bans may be far-reaching.

Banned and censored books are an issue for book editors because of editors' role as gatekeepers. Editors decide what is suitable for publishing, from the perspective of both socially sanctioned topics and socially uncomfortable perspectives. Indeed, like librarians and writers, editors are in a position to control what circulates and what does not—a position that some people claim is itself a form of censorship and that at the least depends on the construction of taste informed by powerful social forces. As we have seen in the last few years, it doesn't take much pressure to silence certain points of view. Keeping up with which books are being challenged and removed from libraries and classrooms is an important part of being aware of our larger literary culture. And remember that writing and publishing are iterative processes. A writer and her text encourage a social conversation, and a reader of the text may become a writer in turn. When books are challenged, banned, and censored, these processes are damaged, sometimes irreparably.

Publisher's indemnity

This clause exists to indemnify—that is, protect or compensate—the publisher if the author and publisher find themselves in legal jeopardy for some reason. It means the author may not sue the publisher for third-party problems arising from the publication of the author's book—for instance, if the author has plagiarized content in her book, she cannot sue her publisher for publishing the plagiarized material. This clause does not stop the author from suing the publisher for other issues, such as failure to pay royalties or breach of contract, however.

Many publishing contracts also contain a clause that outlines how legal action will be handled, should the need arise. Author and publisher normally stand together as defendants or plaintiffs in these situations.

Termination

While most people don't like to think about a break-up just as a new relationship is getting started, book editors must, if only because contracts require us to. All contracts must have a termination clause: language that details how to bring the relationship to an end. A relationship is organic and changes over time. If the relationship changes in a way that the parties no longer desire, they need an organized way to end the relationship. They can't just walk away: the contract remains in effect until the parties agree to end it. That's why termination clauses are important.

A contract may be terminated if one party fails to meet the terms of the agreement—that is, if the agreement is breached. One reason for termination, as I noted above, might be the author's failure to deliver an acceptable manuscript. Another reason might be the publisher's failure to produce a ROYALTY STATEMENT and pay outstanding royalties. Most contracts include some requirement for notice that one party intends to terminate the agreement, so that the other party has an opportunity to correct the fault within a reasonable period (usually two to four weeks). Most contracts also include some discussion of how the inventory (if the book is in print) or the property (if the manuscript has not yet been published) will be managed after the dissolution of the agreement.

Other Clauses

Other clauses you may find in a contract will further refine the relationship between publisher and author, ideally so that termination is not necessary. For instance, you will likely find a clause obligating the author to perform some degree of promotion on behalf of the newly published book. There may also be a clause that speaks to how cash awards will be handled—will the publisher have the right to claim some of the award, and if so, how much?

Most contracts contain a clause to explain how new editions of a title will be managed if a book is successful over a long period, and another for dealing with remainders (and the royalties to be paid on remainders) if excess inventory becomes an issue. Most contracts also contain a clause for taking the book out of print and reverting the rights to the author. Some contracts contain provisions for multiple authors (beyond those already named in the contract itself), which may be invoked in the case of a book that continues to sell after the original author's death, or that requires a new edition that the author is unable to complete on her own.

WHAT DOES "OUT OF PRINT" MEAN?

You may hear the term *out of print* tossed around casually, as if it were synonymous with "out of stock" or "out of inventory," but it's not. For authors and publishers, taking a book out of print is a serious decision.

When a book goes formally out of print, the publisher makes a conscious decision not to replenish inventory and fulfill retail orders. No copies are available for retail sale and the book is effectively out of circulation, and therefore neither publisher nor author is earning income from the title. After a book has been formally out of print for at least a year (or longer, depending on the details of the contract), the author may request in writing that the publisher REPRINT the book and bring it back into print. The publisher must decide whether to do so within a reasonable period, such as three or four months. If the publisher chooses not to reprint the book, the author may terminate the publishing agreement and ask that her rights revert.

Taking a book out of print is a process that depends on time and communication; it is not arbitrary, and it is not the same as a book being BACK-ORDERED or temporarily unavailable. In trade publishing, most publishers will have to order hundreds, perhaps even thousands, of copies to make conventionally reprinting a book affordable. The risk of printing more books than will sell in a reasonable period influences the decision to reprint or keep the book out of print. Print-on-demand (POD) technology allows the publisher to keep a book available without having to invest in ordering hundreds or thousands of copies, although not all books can be easily or effectively reprinted using POD.

When a book is available through POD, the question of whether it remains "in print" is tricky. Because a customer *could* buy a copy at any time, the book is still in circulation, whether it is actively selling or not. Some authors want their books to remain available, even if sales slow to a trickle. Other authors want their rights back and do not want their books available through POD; they may prefer to try placing the book with a new publisher in a new edition or to self-publish. As with other points in the contract, be sure you know your house policy.

Finally, in a Canadian contract, you may see a reprography collective licence, which creates a relationship between the contract parties and Access Copyright, Canada's rights management collective. Not all Canadian publishers and authors are affiliated with Access Copyright, but the relationship is valuable for those who are. More information about this licence may be found at www.accesscopyright.ca.

Royalties

One of the most fraught areas of the publishing relationship is the author's income, referred to as *royalties*. (For the moment, we will defer the discussion of derivative income and concentrate on income earned by the book itself in its first publication.) Royalties are calculated as a percentage of the income earned from the sale of the book. How they are calculated, when they are paid, and when authors get a bigger portion of the profits are all contentious issues in the publishing relationship. Note that this discussion is based in print publication; we will look at digital royalties separately below.

Let's start with the royalty rate and how it is calculated. A typical royalty rate is ten percent. Most authors assume this means ten percent of the *retail*, or cover, price of the book, but as a book editor, you must know what your contract says. An increasing number of publishers are calculating royalties based on NET income; the difference for authors' income may be significant. Let's work through an example.

If an author's royalty rate is ten percent of retail, the royalty calculation is fairly straightforward. The publisher counts the number of copies sold, multiplies that number by the retail price of the book, and sends the author ten percent of that figure. So, for example, if the publisher sold 1,500 copies of the book with a $19.95 retail price, the author's royalties are $2,992.50 (10% of 1,500 × 19.95).

If an author's royalty rate is ten percent of net income, however, the royalty calculation is considerably more complex. The publisher counts the number of copies sold, but must calculate the income based on the discounted price of the book (i.e., the price at which the book was sold to the retailer, not to the consumer). Retail discounts today range from forty to fifty-five percent; many publishers calculate an average discount figure—say forty-three or forty-seven percent—and use it to determine royalties. (In some contracts, the net income also factors in bad debt, so if a publisher doesn't get paid by a bookstore, neither does the author.) The author then receives ten percent of the net income. Based on the example in the previous paragraph, if the publisher sold 1,500 copies of the book with a $19.95 retail price, at an average retail discount of forty-three percent, the publisher's net income is $17,057.25 and the author's royalties are $1,705.73 (10% of 1,500 × 0.57 × 19.95)—a difference of almost $1,300.00.

If a book is very successful for a long period of time and through repeated printings, the author may want a bigger portion of the overall income. The publisher controls the costs of manufacturing and sets the retail price of the book; once the initial investment in the book has been recovered (i.e., the costs sunk into editorial and design), the publisher is less exposed to risk and thus, many authors feel, should share more income with the author. An ESCALATING ROYALTY allows the author to gain a greater share of the income if a book remains successful over time.

Every publisher has different breaks for escalating royalties, but a model for a small independent might look something like this: ten percent of retail for the first 10,000 copies sold; twelve percent of retail for the next 15,000 copies sold; fourteen percent of retail for all subsequent copies sold. To figure out appropriate breaks, if your firm offers escalating royalties, you must consider your initial unit costing (how many copies will be produced in the first printing), your market conditions (how many copies you can afford to hold in inventory in a given period), the book's potential audience (for instance, a textbook has a larger potential audience than a volume of poetry has), and the book's long-term viability (does the book contain information that requires updating regularly, or is its content timeless?). Consider, too, that in Canada, sales of 5,000 copies of a book (equivalent to sales of 50,000 copies in the United States) are considered substantial—for many firms, you're into bestseller territory at that point.

Be aware that the contract may stipulate the number of GRATIS COPIES to be given to the author on the book's PUBLICATION DATE (typically ten copies, sometimes twenty). Most contracts specify that royalties are not payable on gratis copies, review or desk copies, and inventory that is pulped or destroyed. The contract may also make provision for the author to buy additional copies of her book at a discount (typically 40%); these copies are also normally exempt from royalties, but not always. A reduced royalty (generally half or less of the basic royalty rate) may be paid on remaindered books, although some publishers do not pay any royalties at all on remaindered copies. A reduced royalty may also be paid on books sold through special-sales deals.

The ROYALTY PERIOD refers to the span of time over which the publisher calculates royalties, usually a year (sometimes six months—some publishers pay royalties twice a year). The publisher calculates the inventory sold, returned, and damaged within this period and prepares a royalty statement that is sent to the author (or agent) along with the royalty payment for the period. Note, however, that many publishers retain a percentage of the author's first royalty payment against RETURNS, copies of the book returned unsold by bookstores; the RESERVE AGAINST RETURNS may enable up to thirty percent of the first royalty payment to be withheld. (It is, of course, released at the next royalty payment if the returns are less than the sum retained.) This practice became common in the late 1990s when the advent of big-box retailing saw publishers ship many thousands of copies of their books to stores, pay large royalty payments to authors based on these shipments, and then receive many thousands of returns within the publication year. While authors dislike the practice, it helps to stabilize a publisher's cash flow and prevents authors from receiving repeated negative royalty statements (i.e., a royalty statement that shows a loss due to returns).

One more point: authors who receive an *advance* for the manuscript are receiving that advance against royalties (and derivative income). Until a book has EARNED OUT—that is, sold enough copies, or raised enough derivative income, to cover the amount of the advance—the author is not paid royalties. The advance is normally divided: typically one-third at contract signing, one-third on delivery of an acceptable manuscript, and one-third on publication date (or half on contract signing and half on publication—as with so many other matters, different houses have different practices). Many books never earn out, so the author receives no further money after the advance is paid.

As you see, there's plenty of room for conflict in royalties. There's even more room for conflict in the discussion of derivative rights.

Derivative Rights

Again, in book publishing, the primary right is the copyright: the right to make and circulate copies of a text. We understand this as the right to publish. There are all kinds of rights that arise from the primary right, however, and they are all protected. The term *derivative rights*—also referred to as *secondary rights* or *subsidiary rights*—refers to the several ways in which the book as a property may be exploited. Many authors dislike the term *exploited* in this setting, as it suggests that the publisher intends to take advantage of the author; be assured that the term is just legal language and does not mean anyone is being treated unfairly. Two issues emerge in derivative rights: who holds the rights, and how is the income split when an opportunity arises? Going into a contract negotiation, most publishers try to acquire as many rights as possible, as the rights add to the overall value of the property. Meanwhile, many authors try to retain as many rights as possible, in hope of controlling their income to their best advantage.

Here's the advice I've heard again and again in book publishing: derivative rights should reside with the party best able to exploit them. Authors often find this stance offensive, yet it's sensible and practical. Most authors do not have the ability to exploit their own derivative rights; and even if they had, their talents might be better applied to writing new books rather than selling the rights to their existing work. This is one reason authors retain agents—to sell rights on their behalf—but many, many authors, particularly those publishing with scholarly presses and regional presses, don't have agents. While some publishers are notably better at exploiting derivative rights than others, any publisher is generally better positioned, through relationships in the community and through the supply chain, to exploit a property's rights than the author alone is. My advice is that writers and their agents should control a book's derivative rights when they have the ability to take advantage of the subsidiary opportunities that exist; if the publisher is better poised to do this work, then it is generally to the author's advantage to allow the publisher to do it. If the publisher fails to exploit the rights, the author can take them back through legal channels. Derivative income may be paid to the author/agent at the time of the licence is sold, or it may be held until the end of the current royalty period. Derivative income, like royalties, is not paid until the author's advance has earned out.

The derivative rights generally encompass dramatic rights, English-language licences, translation licences, anthology rights, commercial licences, mass-market rights, and book club rights. Contracts may also contain clauses to control income received for prizes and awards, and for revenues not otherwise stipulated in the agreement. Bear in mind that anything not explicitly controlled by the contract represents a point for dispute, and you'll understand why contracts tend to be so wide-reaching and why the phrase *without limitation* occurs so often.

Dramatic rights refer to the adaptation of the book's text to a non-book verbal form, such as an audiobook, a stage play, a film, a television program, or a segment broadcast on radio. The dramatic rights may be licensed repeatedly by different parties for different iterations of the text, and the value of each iteration could vary significantly. For instance, a broadcaster might pay twenty-five dollars to read a poem at the end of a radio program, while a film company might pay several thousand dollars to OPTION (have the exclusive right to read) a manuscript for potential development.

In the early days of ebooks, some publishers assumed they held digital rights, or ebook rights, within the dramatic rights; this assumption was eventually overturned. Today, most publishers insist on acquiring digital rights, and these rights are set out in a distinct clause. Because of the dynamic nature of these rights, and because the agreements ebook retailers sign with publishers are proprietary, I will say no more here about digital rights other than to observe that they remain contentious and that authors, as well as book editors and agents, should make a point of being aware of the terms of the licensing agreements under which their books are distributed digitally.

English-language publishing licences involve the notion of territory I raised earlier. A book may be acquired with world rights, or may be acquired for a particular territory, such as Canada, the United States, the United Kingdom, or Australia and New Zealand. If we assume that a Canadian publisher operates primarily in Canada and has limited international reach, these licences allow a book to be published in English in another part of the world, on the understanding that the Canadian publisher will not distribute a competing edition in that territory. (The English-language publishing licences and translation rights, below, are sometimes referred to jointly as FOREIGN RIGHTS, recognizing the normal extent of a publisher's operations.) Consumers may circumvent these agreements, however, by buying books from online retailers that fulfill orders from the site host's country rather than the consumer's country. For instance, a Canadian who buys a book from Amazon.co.uk will receive the UK edition of that book, even if a Canadian-licensed edition exists in Canada. The Canadian publisher obviously loses on this transaction, so publishers tend to dislike the practice of buying around.

Translation licences involve the issue of language. Such licences permit non-English-language publishing based on the English-language edition—for example, a Canadian novel in English might be translated into German. Non-English-language licences may be tied to territory, too, but they need not be; for example, a book might be translated into French and sold in both France and Quebec. Translation rights are important yet often overlooked within Canada, where many English readers miss important books by francophone writers because their work is not translated into English.

Anthology or excerpt licences refer to the publication of a portion of a book outside of the book itself—for instance, as an excerpt in a magazine or in an anthology. Two issues are important here. The first issue arises when a portion of a book is published in a magazine or newspaper, often referred to as *serial publication*; serial publication is managed through a SERIAL RIGHTS clause. If the material is published in the magazine/newspaper prior to the book's publication, this is called *first serial publication*; by convention, the author receives the entire payment (if there is any) for this publication. If the material is published in the magazine/newspaper on or after the book's publication, this is called *second serial publication*;

the proceeds (if any) are split between author and publisher. Payment for second serial publication is less common today than it once was, but marketing staff still seek these opportunities because of the potentially large readership of periodicals—from tens of thousands to millions.

A second issue arises when a portion of a book is published as a component of another book—when a publisher seeks permission to use an excerpt. PERMISSIONS represent a substantial income stream for some writers—for instance, those whose short stories are anthologized again and again; but publishers are notoriously inconsistent with permission fees, sometimes drastically overcharging for permission (leading to the exclusion of the intended excerpt) and sometimes far undervaluing an excerpt (meaning the author and publisher both lose potential income). Permissions departments and publishers in general could stand to be more conscientious with permissions, with regard to both the consistency of fees assigned to permission requests and the timeliness of responding to such requests, a point you may experience first-hand as a book editor when you or your author must seek permission for material to be included in a manuscript.

Commercial licences, also known as *exploitation licences*, refer to the exploitation of non-textual materials derived from a book. When an author's characters are transformed into action figures or stuffed toys, it happens under a commercial licence. As with dramatic rights, commercial licences may be exploited repeatedly by different parties for different products, depending on the reach of the text.

The MASS-MARKET EDITION clause is relevant for only a small number of authors today as so much publishing is now in paperback originals. However, for authors whose book will be published first in hardcover and then in a TRADE EDITION, a licence to publish the mass-market edition may be available. Think of brand-new fiction from authors such as Stephen King or Nora Roberts, or of highly trendy nonfiction such as diets or self-help books, which are reprinted in cheap editions and sold in drugstores, convenience stores, and grocery stores: these books are produced under mass-market paperback licences. Mass-market editions have low margins and are treated disposably in the supply chain, so authors usually receive markedly lower royalty percentages than on other editions. Today, many of the publishers dedicated to mass-market publishing are now imprints of multinational publishing firms.

The *book clubs* clause is also relevant for only a small number of authors today, as the number of book clubs has decreased markedly. Still, a few remain, such as the Literary Guild and the Book-of-the-Month Club. Book clubs buy in two ways: through a bulk purchase of your edition or through a reprint licence to create a club edition.

Finally, some contracts contain a general clause to account for opportunities and income not identified in one of the already existing categories. Such a clause provides a safeguard for both publisher and author because new technologies and opportunities may emerge quickly. However, these clauses tend to irritate agents exactly because of their vague, undefined nature.

As I noted above, points of conflict may emerge not only from who holds the rights but also from how the income derived from the exploitation of the rights is divided. As a working principle, a 50/50 split between publisher and author is a solid place to start. You must know your firm's strengths in derivative rights development and the likelihood of exploiting some rights over others, so you know when to stand firm on a split and when to be generous. Perhaps in your setting, a 75/25 split (75% of income to the author, 25% to the publisher) makes more sense. What matters is that you can explain to your authors why you are offering the contract and the percentages.

Many authors wonder why derivative income is split between author and publisher at all: why doesn't the author earn all the income? There are two reasons. First, publishers add value to a manuscript by publishing it—that is, by making a manuscript into a text that can circulate effectively in the public sphere. Second, publishers assume risk in the act of publishing, because not every book is financially successful. In order to keep taking such a risk, publishers need some of the proceeds from those books that do succeed.

Publishers demonstrably bring value to the manuscript through their work in developing it. Various editors help to groom and improve the narrative or the argument; they also ensure that the text is clear, accurate, and as close to error free as possible. Designers and art directors make the cover, the type, and any images attractive and clear, and make manufacturing decisions to enhance a book's physical existence. Sales and marketing staff, as well as book editors, ensure that the book is read, reviewed, and recognized, creating interest for subsidiary rights opportunities. The move to self-publishing has created opportunities for authors to assume more of these roles, and more of this expertise, themselves, but many authors do not want or are unable to do this work on their own. When authors understand that the publisher has expertise, reach, and systems that add value to the manuscript, they tend to accept and acknowledge that the publisher deserves to share the income the manuscript earns. Some authors embrace self-publishing as a rejection of what they perceive about international publishing—that it perpetuates a narrative of exploitation—but that perception is certainly not the whole story.

Ethical considerations

Now, think back to chapter 3, when we discussed costing. One of the considerations in costing a book is its potential for rights development. You must keep your rough costing in mind as you negotiate the contract: what can you afford to offer as an advance, and what can you afford to lose? For instance, you may want to offer an author a large advance because you think the book has legs and you should be able to sell translation rights and dramatic rights—but does your firm have a solid track record of selling translation rights, of having books adapted into movies? If not, can you afford the risk? There are costs associated with rights development (the book editor is not usually responsible for selling rights), and the author remains under contract with the firm even if you leave and are no longer a champion for the project. Is it ethical to expose your firm to risk by offering an advance that may not earn out? How much of an error is too much?

As I mentioned in chapter 2, book editors leave positions in pursuit of better opportunities (including better pay) regularly; they may also retire, take leaves of absence, and even lose their jobs due to downsizing and mergers. Projects under contract and rights negotiations may be affected, even halted, by staffing changes. Scott MacDonald explains in his article "Lost in the Shuffle" that orphaned authors feel abandoned, and their projects may falter without a champion. An editor's departure may have consequences both in and beyond the house, and I encourage you to think about consequences and ethics in every aspect of your editorial work, both project by project and throughout your career.

Legal Recourse

Before we leave the topic of contracts, we should discuss the idea of legal remedies. Publishers and authors have contracts to manage their relationships; the contract lends structure and direction to what can be a complex process, particularly when financial questions arise. But whenever a contract exists, the possibility of legal action—suing—also exists.

A remedy in law should be a last strategy, not a first strategy. That is, your first impulse to correct a wrong should not be "sue, sue, sue!" Going to court is expensive, takes a lot of time, and rarely ends satisfactorily for anyone but the lawyers. That doesn't mean suing someone isn't the right answer sometimes. But it's not necessarily the right *first* answer. Most book contracts contain language that obligates both parties to communicate before certain actions are taken, and a wise book editor recognizes that communication forms the heart of the relationship with her author. With that idea in mind, let's move on to a detailed discussion of the editor–author relationship in chapter 5.

5

The Substantive Edit:
Building Trust

"... what most editors truly want
is a book they love."—Betsy Lerner

So, the book is under contract. Now what?

According to the publication sequence sketched out in chapter 2, the next step in the process is the substantive edit, in which the book editor edits the manuscript critically for structure and content. It's a process that requires trust and goodwill on the part of both editor and author.

"Trust is a huge part of the acquisitions process," says Dan Wells, editor and publisher at Biblioasis, and trust is also a huge part of every stage after acquisition, too. This chapter looks at the relationship between book editor and author as it emerges during the substantive edit. Like every relationship, its strength depends on communication and honesty.

Once a book is under contract, part of the book editor's job involves managing the author's expectations. Another major part involves communicating regularly with all the other people involved in manufacturing and selling the book, as well as with the author. After the author submits an acceptable version of the manuscript, most of his work is over, while most of the editor's work is still ahead of her, in the specific jobs of the substantive edit (which may mean further work for the author) and the development of a preliminary book design (in conjunction with the art department), and then in various mechanical processes such as copyediting, layout, and proofreading.

96

As Marshall Lee explains, a book poses three distinct kinds of problems: editorial problems (in ensuring that the book expresses its author's message appropriately), commercial problems (in becoming a book that fits its audience), and mechanical problems (in becoming an affordable, well-manufactured physical object). In this chapter and the next, we tackle the first two problems explicitly, with a few pointers toward the final problem, which we will tackle in detail in chapter 8.

Mechanical Matters: Handling the Manuscript

Someone in the publishing house must be responsible for handling the manuscript the author has submitted after contract and, if applicable, after the substantive edit. For our purposes, I'm going to assume this someone is the book's editor, although in some firms a PROJECT EDITOR or managing editor may be responsible for the manuscript and its supporting components. Whoever it is, this person ensures that the firm retains a complete, unedited version of the author's manuscript, regardless of whether it is submitted electronically, on paper, or both. Custody of the original manuscript is related to version control, as we will discuss later. Holding a complete copy of the accepted manuscript is not a casual matter, so be sure that responsibility for this step (and backups) is clear and consistent for every project. Before the manuscript is released for mechanical editing, someone in the firm must confirm possession of the final manuscript and ensure all subsequent work occurs only on this version. Make a backup copy of the digital file and, if necessary, print a paper copy for your house archive.

The author's manuscript file should be as plain as possible. Although it may seem counterintuitive from the outside, a clean, plain file ensures greater accuracy during the edit and saves the layout technician work later in the process. Only necessary CHARACTER styling (e.g., italics and bold) should be applied. Levels of subheads within chapters should be differentiated by format, and the text should be set flush left. All tracked changes from previous editorial work must be resolved—that is, changes either accepted or rejected and any comments deleted. If tracked changes are still in place, you may not in fact have the final version of the author's submitted manuscript.

It should not need to be said, but today manuscripts are normally accepted only as standard word-processing files (e.g., Microsoft Word .doc or .docx files). Circumstances would have to be peculiar for a publisher to accept a handwritten or typed manuscript—and the file would ultimately end up being word-processed anyway. In the case that a manuscript has been prepared from an existing printed work (e.g., a new edition of an old book), the submission manuscript *must* be read word for word against the original text, a process called *paired proofreading*, which is slow, meticulous work. When the text is proofread later in the process, the proofreaders may have to refer again to the original text for verification, and records of changes (for instance, if changes are intentionally being introduced to correct errors in the original text) may be required for some kinds of publishing.

The publishing contract usually specifies how the manuscript should be formatted when it is turned over (e.g., double spaced, one-inch margins, with a print copy as well as the digital file), and many publishers also post clear guidelines for manuscript preparation on their websites. If your house does, you must know your guidelines, including the default style manuals and file formats. The book's editor may have to return a manuscript for further work if an author hasn't prepared the manuscript accordingly—for instance, if an academic manuscript lacks correctly formatted citations and a bibliography. Sometimes book editors will let these matters slide—often it's easier for an editor to do manuscript preparation than it is for the author to do it—but if extensive work will be required to make over the file, or if a makeover could produce liability, it's best to return the manuscript to the author.

For the purpose of illustrating my point, let me give you a brief example from my work experience. As a freelance editor, I once received a book manuscript formatted as a PowerPoint document. This file included low-RESOLUTION photographs and illustrations, image CAPTIONS, slide titles intended as chapter subheads, foreign-language characters, and the running text of the book. It had been submitted to the publisher late, and my editing timeline was already short, so I could not return it to the publisher or the author to be reformatted into a word-processing document. Instead, I had to extract the manuscript line by line from the PowerPoint document, comparing files closely to ensure I did not miss or overwrite any of the text. This was finicky work that added pressure to an already challenging edit. And because only the designer received the images at a reasonable resolution, I had to cross-reference text to very small images, some of which were later eliminated, replaced, and renumbered. Because of a breakdown in the publisher's process, I received an inappropriately formatted manuscript, which should have been returned to the author for correction. Not doing so introduced unnecessary risk—including increased cost and potential delays—to the project.

Depending on the size of firm you work for and your editorial role, you may read a manuscript three to five times or more over its production lifetime, from initial acquisition to acceptance through substantive edit, as well as possibly the copyedit and possibly the PROOFS (but ideally not both the copyedit and the proofs). Be aware that no single editor should be the only reader of a manuscript; editors need distance from the manuscript to be able to do their best work. After a while, you will become blind to errors in a text you have worked on intensively.

As the book's editor, you must make mechanical decisions about the book, such as which dictionary to refer to, which style manual to refer to, and when to deviate from house style. When you do your read-through of the manuscript you accept post-contract, keep an informal list of issues you want fixed in subsequent edits, such as inconsistencies in character details, the structure of different levels of headings, the use or absence of Canadian spellings, other distinctive spellings, the use of metric versus imperial measurements, particular hyphenation practices, treatment of typographical elements, and so on. You may not remember these points by the time the manuscript gets to copyediting, and you might not be the copyeditor. If you keep a list, you can pass it forward to the person doing the work, and that person can add to it. Consistency matters in book publishing, and you can start building consistency during the substantive edit and as you assemble the manuscript for copyediting. As *The Chicago Manual of Style* observes, "even minor errors reflect badly on publishers and authors alike."

What Is Substantive Editing?

According to the Editors' Association of Canada, substantive or structural editing includes "Clarifying and/or reorganizing a manuscript for content and structure. Changes may be suggested to or drafted for the author." It involves a close examination of how ideas are presented: their logic and development, and the rigour of their investigation; in the case of fiction, it looks at how the story is told—voice, point of view, characters. Beyond how an argument or a narrative is built, the substantive edit examines what evidence is marshalled for claims, how information is ordered and revealed, the pacing of narrative and exposition, and the consistency of presentation (including tense and sequence in fiction). It looks for patterns and irregularities, with the aim of creating an appropriate and secure structure for a given text, and requires the editor be able to see both the whole manuscript and its parts at once. To use a rough analogy, a developmental edit works from an outline—a skeleton. A copyedit deals with the surface presentation—the skin. A substantive edit focuses on the musculature atop the skeleton, underlying the skin, and the key to a successful edit is not to produce Frankenstein's creature.

The substantive editor works through complicated explanations and ensures they make sense, teases out assumptions and ensures the author is aware of them, finds the author's tics and ensures they do not irritate or distract from the larger project, connects dots, and fits the presentation to the audience. Could information be presented more effectively as a chart or table, or could pages of tables be summarized in a few sentences or paragraphs? Do the photographs included with the text help readers understand the subject better, or are they merely decorative? Other considerations in substantive editing may include examining the author's language for appropriateness to audience and presence of bias, and evaluating the text for its potential adaptation to another territory or another language (think *licensing*). (Note that in the United Kingdom, the term *sub editor* refers not to a substantive editor but to a mechanical editor—what we call a stylistic editor or copyeditor in Canada and the United States. Be careful you don't confuse overseas colleagues by misusing the term.)

The task of the substantive editor is problem solving: finding a way to produce meaning for readers while meeting the goals of the genre or the publication design, such as the available space, the physical format, and the conventions of the genre. Substantive editors tend to be highly experienced editors, but not absolutely. An editor's overall good sense of texts and reading can sometimes fill in for a lack of specific book experience. Over time, some substantive editors come to specialize in a discipline or a range of topics, such as academic editors, medical editors, and science editors. Their deep knowledge and range of problem-solving skills make them immensely valuable to the authors and firms they serve.

As you might imagine from these descriptions, substantive editing is slow, intensive work. Expect to get through no more than two to five pages per hour—and maybe even less if the project is particularly complicated. Long-time book editor Michael Korda describes how slow manuscript editing can be: "In editing, time becomes meaningless. A single page can sometimes absorb hours, like the most infuriating kind of puzzle." Many substantive edits involve the author rewriting passages, chapters, or even the bulk of the manuscript in response to the editor's queries and directions. That last point should suggest the reason the substantive edit requires a trusting relationship between author and editor: a substantive edit usually involves a substantial amount of work for both sides.

There are significant differences in the way editors in different sectors approach a substantive edit. Fiction editing tends to adopt a light hand stylistically and is highly suggestion based. Poetry editing tends to exhibit a similar respect for the author, as does the editing of memoir and other forms of creative nonfiction. Other nonfiction editing is still respectful but may reflect less concern with artistry and more concern with fact, organization, and communication. The editor may do much more rewriting and recasting in nonfiction, particularly in certain genres that are less invested in style and more interested in information.

Textbook editing also tends to involve extensive EDITORIAL DESIGN and a heavy editorial hand, the authors being primarily subject-matter experts and not instructional designers.

If you're editing a genre of book that's new for you, look at and read some examples of the type, and seek advice from experienced editors in the area. Here are a few resources I'd recommend:

- If you're editing a graphic novel for the first time, Neil Bailey's short article "The Right Approach for Editing the Graphic Novel" is a great place to start.
- The editors in Gerald Gross's old but apt collection *Editors on Editing* (1985, 1996) offer advice from numerous areas of publishing.
- Thomas McCormack's insightful book *The Fiction Editor, the Novel, and the Novelist* (2006) provides a smart and sensitive perspective on how to edit fiction.

Regardless of genre, the purpose behind substantive editing is the same: to point out trouble spots and to work (usually in conjunction with the author) to fix them.

All documents have a purpose, or reason for being. In nonfiction, that "reason" is often made explicit in a thesis or controlling idea. The confines in which this controlling idea operates are often set out in the book's title or subtitle. Look, for instance, at the recent bestseller *I Am Malala: The Girl Who Stood Up for Education and Was Shot by the Taliban*. The core of this text is autobiographical, as the "I" in the main title announces (and as signalled to readers by the subject's photograph on the book cover); but the purpose and the shape are clear from the subtitle, highlighting resistance, education, violence, and a religious context. If you as editor can't quickly identify the controlling idea, the boundaries of that idea, and the architecture of the idea within a manuscript, neither will a general reader. The purpose of the substantive edit is to ensure that the manuscript establishes boundaries and appropriate structures for its genre, and that the book is editorially designed to make these structures clear to readers.

The "reason" in fiction is different, yet boundaries still exist. Every effective narrative has a beginning, a middle, and an end, for instance, if not always in that order. Fiction editors may be looking for signs of style and voice, an unusual way of seeing the world, and an unexpected way of telling a story; or they may be looking for a fresh take on a straightforward formula. While the style and shape may be signalled to readers differently in fiction than in nonfiction, the editor must still be able to identify the key features of plot, character, setting, and theme quickly, must still be able to recognize the genre and its conventions (and deviations), as well as appropriate mechanisms for revealing the narrative.

In substantive editing, it's the book editor's job to remember the reader's ignorance relative to the author. Whether the manuscript is fiction or nonfiction, the reader knows less than the author does about the content; the author necessarily knows more. The editor must ensure the reader will understand the author's ideas clearly. Thus, although editors work with authors, editors work on behalf of the readers of the finished book. What will it say to these readers?

BETA READING

You may have heard of BETA READING as a stage in or form of editing, and indeed, it is a type of PEER EDITING. Beta reading often elicits substantive feedback, involving readers' immediate emotional and intellectual reactions to a text. It is a process almost exclusively used with fiction, although some authors writing creative nonfiction will also approach beta readers.

Beta readers may be editors, but more often they are writers and appreciative readers; and while their comments are often valuable to authors, the feedback may lack the coherence and focus that a single, trained editor can bring to the task. This observation is not intended to knock beta reading during the writing process, but rather to provide a reminder that beta reading is best used during an author's revision and rewriting stage, prior to submitting a manuscript for publication. Beta reading cannot replace the work of an experienced, professional editor. Similarly, WORKSHOPPING and other forms of peer editing must occur before an author circulates a manuscript to publishers, never after, unless the manuscript has been rejected repeatedly and the author is looking for help with revising.

Why Do a Substantive Edit?

The purpose of substantive editing is to shape the text so it best realizes both its author's and the publisher's goals. What is the goal of the text? To inform, to teach, to explain, to record, to criticize, to persuade, to promote, to delight? What is the expected response to the text? That is, if the book does its work effectively, how will the reader respond? As an editor, you must have a sense of the audience—as does the author—but as a book editor, your sense of audience is simultaneously broader and more nuanced. An author may have a very particular reader in mind; as the book editor, you must have a broader image of potential readership, the potential use of the book, and how the book must be constructed to be best used. The shaping you do as the book's editor may take many forms, depending on the genre of the text, its likely audience, the resources of your publishing house, and the ability of the author. But remember what author and long-time editor Arthur Plotnik says: "An editor's job is to shape the *expression* of an author's thoughts, not the thoughts themselves" (emphasis added).

As an editor, you're in the business of manipulating readers. I don't mean that an exploitive or inappropriate way: all rhetoric is about some kind of manipulation. But a book is an amazing tool that, when it is well built, teaches its users how best to use it. As an editor, you direct how the reader reads; you train the reader's response. Your manipulation is in aid of balancing the needs and assumptions of the author against the needs and expectations of the reader.

If you've been reading closely over the last few pages, you've likely noticed that the book editor forms a complex web of loyalties. The book editor works for a publisher, with an author, alongside other members of the publishing process, on behalf of a wide body of readers, and is constantly informed by her often-dynamic personal sense of the best way to achieve various goals. Managing this web of loyalties requires communication, good faith, self-awareness, and confidence. The work of substantive editing is rarely easy, and the author may not appreciate it, at least, not initially. (I've had authors tell me how much they hated being edited, even when they're thrilled with the published book.) The interests of author and editor obviously intersect—we both want to share ideas and stories with other people—but we come at the work from different directions with different outcomes in mind.

A few pages ago, I evoked the image of Frankenstein's creature. The following description of the experience of being edited, from first-time memoir writer Ruth Rakoff, suggests how an author may see the editor's work:

> *Being edited is like giving someone your favourite, most cherished toy or doll to play with ... and begging they treat it with the same love and respect you feel toward it. When they return your doll, you see with horror that they have pulled off the head and stuffed it up the bum and rearranged all the limbs, creating a mutant, all the while assuring you that you'll like it better this way.*

You can hear the author's agony plainly in this quotation. Yet this is exactly why substantive editing is important: because for many authors, the manuscript becomes a cherished toy. The author cannot see its flaws and does not recognize that someone else will have different wants or needs from the experience of playing with—that is, reading—it. At some point, the author may simply be too close to make the book everything it could be. This is why the editor gets involved in the substance of the book. Her involvement must be underpinned by trust. As former editor Betsy Lerner puts it, "The editor says, *I will catch you.*" To build a trusting relationship, editor and author must work together and must both fulfill their mutual responsibilities.

Some editors are idea editors. That is, they read argumentation incisively, recognize and detangle logical snarls, and bring clarity to the author's discussion. Some editors are story editors (which may apply to narratives of nonfiction as well as fiction). They see the world as story, recognize how to pace a telling, know when a digression works and when it is intrusive, and can grasp and draw out the authenticity of a story's characters, dialogue, motivation, and action. Some editors are language editors, some of whom respond to the writing, some of whom respond to the structure. You *must* know what kind of editor you are. You must also be aware of your own tastes and know your limits—resources, including your time and energy, are ultimately finite. When you commit to a book, you must commit to it fully: there is nothing more dispiriting for an author than for her editor-champion to lose interest partway through a project or to treat the process like an afterthought.

All of the foregoing being said, not every book will go through a substantive edit. Some publishers don't have the resources—it's simply not part of their publishing operations. Many self-published books don't go through substantive editing because the author has intentionally chosen to avoid external editorial involvement. Some authors turn to self-publishing as a mechanism for circumventing what they view as the editor's and the publisher's control over authors through substantive editing, such as calling for certain kinds of changes, limiting the length of the manuscript, or requiring a story to be more commercial than literary. And of course, some books don't need substantive editing—the authors have such a clear command of audience, purpose, and style that there is nothing an editor can add but polish—but these are rare books indeed!

Do Book Editors Really Edit?

If there's one thing you can find in the literature on editing and publishing, it's book editors' thoughts about substantive and structural editing. This is unsurprising, really, because it is this expertise that makes a good book editor so valuable. You can also find authors' thoughts about the process—particularly about what works and what doesn't. It is in the aftermath of the substantive edit—or the lack of one—that conflict between author and editor may emerge.

In 2009, former Random House executive editor-in-chief Daniel Menaker remarked,

> *The sheer book-length nature of books combined with the seemingly inexorable reductions in editorial staffs and the number of submissions most editors receive, to say nothing of the welter of non-editorial tasks that most editors have to perform, including holding the hands of intensely self-absorbed and insecure writers, fielding frequently irate calls from agents, attending endless and vapid and ritualistic meetings, having one largely empty ceremonial lunch after another, supplementing publicity efforts, writing or revising flap copy, ditto catalog copy, refereeing jacket-design disputes, and so on—all these conditions taken together make the job of a trade-book acquisitions editor these days fundamentally impossible. The shrift given to actual close and considered editing almost has to be short and is growing shorter, another very old and evergreen publishing story but truer now than ever before.*

Menaker is talking about books intended for adult general readers, but similar pressures exist for book editors in all sectors. His remarks struck a sombre chord with many writers. In the debate that has emerged, about whether book editors do or do not actually *edit* books, authors and editors alike have struggled with the consequences of the "impossibility" of the book editor's job.

Some authors bemoan the idea that editors have little time for substantive editing; these authors depend on their editor's advice, on the collaborative art that is editing, and perceive a lack of "close and considered editing" in the books they have published. Other authors are more cynical and feel that editors' priorities have always been more commercial than artistic, that the "impossibility" is just an honest reckoning of what really matters in commercial publishing. Some critics and many everyday readers have picked up the debate and blame book editors' lack of editing for both unabashedly commercial books and for spectacular flops. And some book editors have battled back and asserted strongly that yes, book editors edit, no matter how "impossible" their job may be.

Canadian editor and publisher Douglas Gibson's somewhat tongue-in-cheek comments from more than twenty years before Menaker's suggest it was ever thus, however:

> *Unless the author is willing to stand up for his rights, the editor will routinely cheapen and distort the author's manuscript. The*

editor's cynical aim will be to make the book as "commercial" as possible—and she will treat the author's artistic aspirations with weary contempt. The author will have to fight her at every stage if his manuscript is to be treated decently and published with care.

And so the cycle continues. If you read interviews with and memoirs of writers, editors, and publishers, you'll discover a great deal of animosity and finger pointing on both sides when relationships go bad or books fail. Editors blame authors for "bad" books and resistance to editorial suggestions. Writers in turn blame editors for their perceived crass pursuit of formulaic text and commercial success.

What everyone in this conversation is really discussing is substantive editing (as well as stylistic editing, although to a lesser degree), which is perhaps the most secret and certainly the least understood part of the publishing process. After all, as Betsy Lerner says,

It is finally the writer who knows whether his editor has a gift for language, an understanding of structure, a grasp of the dynamics of plot, pacing, tension, and resolution. Only the writer knows if his editor edits. ... Only the writer know for sure whether an editor is making a serious contribution to and improvement of his work. Only the writer really knows how good an editor is on the page.

If successful, the book editor's work is invisible: only the author's best words and thoughts remain. While it's possible for the book editor to blame some of a book's foibles or failures on the people later in the process—the copyeditor, the designer, the proofreader, the marketing department—it's only the writer who knows the truth about the work the book editor did or did not do. And often that work goes unacknowledged.

So let's assume that, claims to the contrary notwithstanding, book editors *do* edit books substantively as well as stylistically and mechanically. What may go wrong with the process?

One of the big problems is about perceptions and expectation management. The writer is invested in what she's accomplished—particularly if that accomplishment has been rewarded with a healthy advance. While editors don't ignore accomplishment, they also see the distance the manuscript still needs to go to achieve the firm's goals for it. But many authors cringe at the idea of compromising their artistic integrity or capitulating to a publisher's desires.

Arthur Plotnik says, "A manuscript's *content*, most editors will agree, is the author's province; the author knows the subject or would not have made the sale. But the *form* of the final product—its organization, pace, packaging—is what editors like to think is their specialty." Problems may emerge if an author doesn't understand that what has caught the editor's eye is a puzzle, a problem to solve: the potential of the manuscript. It's the book editor's job to realize that potential, and authors need to understand the editor's motivation from the moment contract negotiations begin, or else both parties are likely to be unhappy with the finished book.

Marshall Lee's observations are helpful here:

> *Who determines whether extensive revision is needed? Answer: The editor. Next question: Does the author agree with this judgment? Sometimes yes, sometimes no, often both. This is the most critical point in the relationship of author and publisher.*

Having a plan, with clearly articulated editing objectives, to communicate either in person or as part of an editorial letter, can help salve the relationship. So many complicated aspects of person and personality are tied up in writing and publishing a book. The act of publication in itself is significantly more complex than the already complicated task of writing the manuscript because it introduces so many factors the author controls only minimally, if at all. Your plan for step-by-step revision should affirm the value and importance of the manuscript and focus on what you and the author can accomplish jointly, together. A supportive, open, respectful editorial process will go a long way to assuring the writer that his efforts have been given every chance of success.

All editing is mindful, but substantive editing is often emotionally engaging, sometimes exhausting. You may feel more connected to the text in this kind of work than in other kinds of editing. Sharpe and Gunther say that an editor works with her senses: her editorial eye, ear, nose, and touch, and I would add that an editor works with her head and her heart in varying measure. But frankly, editors also edit with their egos. A book editor believes that she uniquely sees the solution to a book, that she knows how to amplify the music of the text, that she can cut, fold, and stitch the manuscript into a compelling argument or story unlike anyone else, including the author. Consider what Michael Korda, who was editor-in-chief at Simon and Schuster for more than thirty years, has to say on this point. According to him, book editors

> *are a curious combination of cheerleader and story doctor, fixers-up of lame prose, inventors of the dramatic ending to a scene (instead of the one that fizzles out), ruthless cutters, the kind of people who don't hesitate to challenge everything the author has done in the attempt to make the book work the way it could, or the way it was supposed to, and who can sometimes guess what the author was trying to do and show him or her how to get there.*

Korda continues:

> *To a real editor, cutting a manuscript from seven hundred pages*
> *to four hundred, inventing a new title, reshuffling chapters to*
> *give the book a drop-dead beginning and a surprise ending, is*
> *all in a day's work, a bravado challenge, like a difficult operation*
> *for a surgeon. Real editors, if they're any good, also know—more*
> *important still—when to leave well enough alone. "If it's good,*
> *don't touch it" might be the first rule of our oath, if we had one.*

Such bravado takes ego. Not every manuscript requires the work Korda describes here, but many manuscripts do need an editor who is confident enough to call for difficult, and even sweeping, changes. Editing like this is called being a *hard editor*. While the term sounds unattractive to novice editors, it's actually a title of praise. Hard editing can produce teachable moments for authors, enabling writers to learn to edit themselves.

Of course, there is ego on both sides of the desk. Publishing is an endeavour in which egos leap forward more strongly than in many other businesses. Some authors want a lot of editing; others won't take many edits. Editing makes some authors feel vulnerable because writing exposes them to another mind in an intimate way: not only *what* they think, but *how* they think. For other authors, the editor and the process of editing are merely vectors to realizing the author's larger goals, such as gaining tenure or securing a political platform. The key for the book editor is to respect the author, and the author's ego, but not to take the author's ego needs personally. In her discussion of the editor–author relationship, children's book editor Cheryl Klein notes humbly, "my work doesn't exist without the work these authors do." But this comment expresses only part of the book editor's obligation. Although on the surface, editors seem to serve writers, what editors really do is serve the work: the manuscript.

WHAT DO YOU THINK ABOUT SUBSTANTIVE EDITING?
What is your opinion about substantive editing? Do you feel it's necessary, or is it a mechanism publishers use to control authors' voices and ideas? Consider the kinds of books you read most often. Could the need for substantive editing be different in different sectors?

Editorial sensibility: The underpinnings of the relationship
An editor develops over time, and part of that development is the emergence of a quality I and many other editors refer to as EDITORIAL SENSIBILITY. Editorial sensibility, to me, refers to a subjective set of traits the editor brings to the task of the edit, both at the substantive stage and at the mechanical stage: perceptiveness, diplomacy, intelligence, problem

solving, patience, sensitivity, carefulness, and method. This sensibility is not already present in the novice editor, although its roots are there. As Leslie Sharpe and Irene Gunther affirm in their book *Editing Fact and Fiction*, "The editor's instinct—how, when, and to what degree to intervene in a text—is developed and honed through practice." It comes from being immersed in both the art and the craft of editing, from reading deeply and widely, from encountering a range of dialects and registers, and from dealing with many kinds of people in many circumstances. It is enhanced by self-reflection and engagement with the larger professional discourse of editing.

You can learn to edit only by editing. A book can train you, but only working with a live, responsive writer will really *teach* you. Don't be afraid to start. We are all beginners as our careers get underway. Don't give up if your suggestions meet resistance; that can be a good sign—and remember that you may be right even if the author is struggling to admit it. *Pay attention* to what the author is resisting, though—that's important. Remember that editing, especially book editing, is still largely a mentored profession, so ask for help if you need it. Also look for resources that can help you with specific elements of editing—you'll find a starter list in appendix E. Above all, be prepared to *listen*—to the prose itself, to your author's natural voice, to your more senior colleagues, and to the feedback you receive after every process. Listen, reflect, learn, then try again; and repeat. Editing is a language *art*.

The inverse of the editor's unique sensibility is the fact that every book is also unique, as Sharpe and Gunther observe: "There is no pat formula, no one way of approaching each different text. Each book has its own problems; each feels like starting from scratch." All the changes you call for in the substantive edit, regardless of your editorial sensibility, must make sense in the context of the author and the project.

You can be passionate about the potential of a manuscript without having to endorse the position it takes. But when we work with a manuscript, the manuscript may become a foil for the author. The problems editors may experience with authors—failures to meet deadlines, failures to resolve problems in the text, emotional issues, financial troubles—have relatively little to do with the book-as-object and a great deal to do with the writer as a human being. If things are going badly in the human relationship, the editor must recognize the risk of sublimating the author into the text; if she doesn't, the text may end up receiving a harsh and difficult edit that satisfies no one. The editor is not the author; it is the author's name that goes on the book, and the editor does not own the work. But it's easy for an editor to invest so much effort in a text that the distinction between these roles becomes fuzzy.

Communication: The Key to a Good Relationship

The months of waiting between signing the contract and holding the finished book can be frustrating for writers, as well as detrimental to their continued productivity. As with any relationship, communication can keep the relationship positive and productive.

When you accept a manuscript and put it under contract, you are (or your firm is) inherently accepting two obligations. First, you undertake to share information with your author promptly and responsively. For some editors, this means sharing personal information, such as a home telephone number for late-night meetings and crises of confidence. (But be assured that not every editor takes this step.) Second, you undertake to be the author's in-house champion—and equally to be the publisher's ambassador to the author. The author (or her agent) should never have to resort to contacting the publisher over your head to get something done or to learn about the status of the project. Editors and publishers alike respond negatively to this kind of move, yet it happens sometimes when communication goes astray.

Just as your friends don't want to hear about the fun you're having with other friends, no author wants to hear how busy you are with other authors' books. Having made the decision to publish with your firm, an author wants your firm's support, and the book editor is usually the most visible face of the publishing house. Writing is an extraordinarily lonely art, even if publishing is not; most authors need to know their editor is available and interested. And many authors enjoy the illusion of exclusivity in their relationship with the editor, even when they recognize it cannot possibly be true.

One important aspect of communication is to ensure that your author receives regular updates about the progress of her project. Updates should include internal processes (such as preparing catalogue copy, generating a cover, taking the book to a SALES CONFERENCE, and determining the ON-SALE DATE) as well as delays. (That said, many writers don't want to hear about *your* editorial process—there's that ego issue again.) Your regular communication signals that the manuscript is receiving appropriate care and attention as it moves toward publication. Many authors—particularly first-time authors—don't understand the production cycle, so reviewing the cycle with your author, with an emphasis on the budget and costs, and the increasingly important role of sales and marketing, is a valuable use of your time. Also be sure your author understands the significance of deadlines at all stages of production: pre-publication is not the time for the author to take a long voyage and go silent!

Another important aspect of communication is follow-through. As I noted earlier, some writers feel incredibly vulnerable when their books are being edited, and that feeling may linger during production and even after publication. Some writers take harsh reviews—and worse, an absence of reviews—badly and deeply personally. The book editor must be present to provide reassurance and to ensure the firm does everything it can to support the success of book *and* author. Authors rarely realize that, while editing processes are about the author, marketing processes are about the book. Authors are often shaken by being left behind once the book is published: marketing promotes books more often than it promotes authors, and publishers sell books, not authors. Coach, mentor, therapist, cheerleader, *in loco parentis*: the editor fills numerous roles for every author, often over many years.

Your relationship with your authors should matter to you. Even if you don't become lifelong friends with an author, during the time you are working together, your job as editor is to be ready to help the author with *all* book-related problems. Communicate regularly. It never hurts to pick up the phone or send a quick email just to check in. Never let an author feel abandoned. In chapter 4, I mentioned Scott MacDonald's article "Lost in the Shuffle," which discusses authors' experiences of being lost when editors and publicists leave; it's pertinent here. Feeling abandoned is traumatic, and both author and publisher lose when a relationships ends prematurely.

Regrettably, sometimes things do go wrong. Betsy Lerner reminds us, "Rejecting a project is easy; taking on a project is complex." In an ideal world, a book editor would never acquire a manuscript without being confident she has the resources necessary at all stages to publish it successfully. The world is rarely ideal, however, and book editors do acquire unwieldy and demanding books and authors. An editor's personal resources are finite, and so are a publishing company's. Sometimes an editor is called on to pick up the pieces when another editor cannot or will not complete a project. And sometimes, despite their best efforts, editor and author simply don't get along. The book needn't suffer, though. Douglas Gibson affirms, "as long as both parties treat the editing process as a procedure in which nobody loses and the book wins, the likelihood of an intractable dispute is extremely slim."

Let's give a last word about successful working relationships to legendary editor Robert Gottlieb:

> *I don't believe there is such a thing as "the editor–author relationship." Of the hundreds of writers with whom I have dealt as a book publisher, there were really no two cases that were the same. Different writers need different things. The editor's job is to intuit, somehow, what those things are.*

Process in Substantive Editing

In chapter 3, I explained that book editors looking for manuscripts to acquire read in a particular, evaluative way. During the substantive edit, the editor also reads to evaluate, but the work is often done in multiple passes through the manuscript. (I am referring now to the author's submitted and accepted post-contract manuscript.) Some editors read with a pencil in hand, making notes as they go. Others don't, feeling the impulse to annotate is unnatural, not typical of most readers and most reading situations. Regardless, the book editor reads the manuscript as a reader first, as an editor second.

Your first pass through the manuscript should be impressionistic. If you can, read the manuscript in a single sitting with as few distractions as possible, the way the reader of the finished book might experience the text. Pay attention to your gut reaction, your emotional response, your mind's sparking to argue with the text. Where did you feel you couldn't put the manuscript down? Were there passages you couldn't wait to be finished (the *my-eyes-glaze-over* feeling)? How did you feel at the conclusion of the manuscript—and did it feel like a "book" as you read it? If not, why not? What's missing? Note the author's strengths and weaknesses. What is the most this author is capable of at this point in her writing life? You will never again have the experience of reading the manuscript for the first time, so it's important to pay attention to your impressions. If you read the manuscript prior to contract, try to recall your impressions, if you didn't keep notes at that time.

During your second pass through the manuscript, move into analytical mode. A book editor measures a manuscript both on its own terms and within the larger context of publishing. This is why reading widely and deeply is so important; it is also why knowing what is going on in other sectors of publishing matters. Evaluate what the author has accomplished against the expectations for similar texts. Has the author given what she promised readers to deliver? How effectively has she accomplished her own goals for the text? Again, remember that you are reading to develop the manuscript's *potential*, the qualities that drew you to acquire the project in the first place. Toronto-based editor and editing instructor Jennifer Glossop puts the point beautifully: "Can this manuscript become a remarkable book?" This time, keep detailed notes as you read. These notes will form the basis of your directions to the author, either embedded in the manuscript itself or summarized in an editorial letter (or both, for many editors). Don't, however, worry about correcting mechanical issues at this stage. You may end up cutting sentences, paragraphs, pages, even entire chapters, so there's no need to invest in the perfection of the words now. Some editors also start an outline or a book map. It's much easier to trace the writer's digressions and unexpected turns—and bring the text back on track—if you have a clear sense of the intended destination.

A substantive edit involves analysis but also planning. In many cases, this edit will involve multiple iterations of a document the author felt was finished. Therefore, the process is potentially fraught with conflict. Start by discussing the strengths of the manuscript, then move on to the areas that need work. As you develop notes and queries and write your editorial letter, think carefully about how you will direct the author to fix the weaknesses—and what you might have to do if the author does not or cannot do so. As Alana Wilcox of Coach House Books suggests, "Ask a lot of questions instead of offering answers. Your job is to make the author fully interrogate the text, not rewrite it for them. But have answers ready, just in case."

Use praise to instruct. If the author does something well, point it out to direct changes in weak areas (e.g., "I like the way you've built out the image of Chief Colombo in chapter 2. Can you do something similar with Frank here?"). That said, be cautious. If your praise is too generous or glib, the author may distrust it. In particular, don't praise the parts of the manuscript the author doesn't like, the places where he's struggled and isn't yet satisfied. If the author doesn't believe your reading is as rigorous as his, he won't trust that you've given the manuscript the attention it needs and deserves. Never give false praise. No one likes the Polyanna editor: editors are supposed to be tough! If you're doing your job well, the author shouldn't like everything you suggest.

You've probably encountered the notion of "the shit sandwich" somewhere in your life. If you haven't, it's the concept of packing a criticism between two positive comments in order to soften the negative between them: praise—problem—praise. Authors know the shit sandwich for the tool it is, but they also want to create successful books. Praise—particularly thoughtful praise—can be an effective technique to get authors to do what they need to do to be successful. Praise coupled with specific examples of what the author has done well, what you want more of, is even more effective.

If one rule of the editor's oath might be Korda's "If it's good, don't touch it," another might be *Do no harm*, as Sharpe and Gunther observe: "Editors can do harm primarily in two ways: when they alter an author's individual style—her voice—or when they change the content or meaning of her prose." Beyond these points, there is relatively little specific advice I can give you on how to edit a manuscript substantively: your process depends on the manuscript in question. The goal is to make the prose the best that it can be, within reason; and to weigh "the best it can be" against "within reason," you must recognize when to stop editing as well as when to push harder.

Even if you sit down in person with the author to discuss the substantive edit, an editorial letter or TRANSMITTAL LETTER is likely to underpin your comments. This letter is vital to the successful, trust-based relationship you're trying to develop with your author. Enthusiasm isn't all you need to make the manuscript the best it can be, but the editor's enthusiasm rarely hurts and almost always helps the writer. Written enthusiasm (alongside written feedback) has the advantage of being permanent, a record the author can refer to repeatedly and specifically, especially when a publishing process is prolonged or revisions are difficult. But recognize that the author is not obligated to accept every comment and change slavishly. As Alana Wilcox says, "Fight for what's best for the book, with fisticuffs if necessary, but let the author make the decision in the end. It's his/her name on the front cover." (If you've read Max Perkins's letters to his authors in John Hall Wheelock's *Editor to Author: The Letters of Maxwell E. Perkins*, you'll recognize that this point is where Perkins excelled.)

To recap, I have outlined a model substantive edit like this:

1. Read the manuscript impressionistically.
2. Read the manuscript analytically.
3. Plan your commentary and make any changes to the manuscript that are yours to make.
4. Praise and instruct the author to undertake any changes to the manuscript that are hers to make. Be sure to give a due date.
5. Review the author's revisions, and repeat steps 2 through 4 as necessary.

Writer Susan Bell observes, "While we write into a void, we edit into a universe." It's easy to forget that the writer has created the manuscript from the resources of her self, while the editor has the manuscript on which to work. The editor has by far the easier job in this transaction. Be compassionate, be engaged, and be fair.

Queries in substantive editing

A *query* is a bit of conversation with the author in which the editor makes a comment or asks a question. Editor Cheryl Klein characterizes substantive queries as the work of the "reader's advocate," helping the author adapt the manuscript in both the author's and the reader's interests. Editors tend to write different kinds of queries depending on the stage of editing. In substantive and structural editing, queries tend to be fairly developed and often directive. Here are some examples:

> *In this paragraph the speaker seems much older than in the previous paragraphs. How immediate is the telling? Are we more or less in the speaker's head, or is she looking back through time? I will identify a few other places where I find the questions of the narrator's immediacy a little jarring.*

> *Please review the next few paragraphs carefully regarding narration and consistency: what is the point of view? Can a six-year-old get into other people's heads? Her thoughts sometimes seem very sophisticated for six. Again, think about how immediate you intend the narration to feel.*

> *This sentence repeats the sentence above under the list of chapter strategies. Could you rework this sentence, please? Extend the idea, or add a different list, or explain the purpose in another way.*

But a query doesn't need to be detailed. Here's an example: "Author: This sentence was a little circular; I tried to build out what I think you mean. Have I understood you correctly here? Please confirm." Here's another: "Author: Here, I've embedded the idea from your original last sentence earlier in the paragraph, and added a sentence based on other ideas you've introduced elsewhere. OK with you?" You'd be surprised how often a quick comment followed by "OK?" is the right tactic.

The point of querying is not to show off or to prove how smart you are: the point is to make the book better. If you catch a narrative inconsistency, a logical fault, or an error in basic facts, point it out to the author, unless you are absolutely sure of *your* facts or unless you have the authority to work very deep in the manuscript (for instance, in the editing of a textbook or field guide).

If an author is missing a step in a process, requires a transitional sentence, or lacks a conclusion, you can point out this omission and query rather than attempt to write the copy yourself. If you must write or rewrite, be sure to call at least some of the work to the author's attention. (The one exception to this advice arises when you're working in educational publishing, where, as I've noted earlier, extensive rewriting and restructuring of the author's submitted text is ordinary fare.) As Sharpe and Gunther say, "The key to fixing a sentence is to know exactly what the author is trying to say. If there is any doubt as to the author's meaning, the editor should simply query."

One of my favourite descriptions of the role of the editor is the designated idiot. In this view, the editor's job is to be the author's most ardent supporter (other than perhaps a partner or spouse) and smartest reader. Simultaneously, it's the editor's job not to "get it" when elements of the text aren't working, to ask silly and sometimes annoying questions. The editor's goal as designated idiot is to prevent the author from being embarrassed. Authors die a little when other people—friends, reviewers, readers—point out problems post-publication.

DO-IT-YOURSELF MASTER CLASS

Read a book that gives practical advice about writing and editing. Here are some suggestions to get you started.

- Joni Cole, *Toxic Feedback: Helping Writers Survive and Thrive*
- Betsy Lerner, *The Forest for the Trees: An Editor's Advice to Writers*
- Susan Bell, *The Artful Edit: On the Practice of Editing Yourself*
- Arthur Plotnik, *Spunk and Bite: A Writer's Guide to Bold, Contemporary Style*
- William Zinsser, *On Writing Well*

Select four or five passages in the book that particularly stand out for you. Perhaps they speak to your sense of your strengths or weaknesses as a writer or editor, your confidence or anxiety about editing or being edited, your concerns about working in this field. Or perhaps they are strictly sensible and useful for your intended work as a book editor. Now write a few paragraphs about these passages, tying them together with your own observations about why they strike you as important, how they spoke to you, how they may guide you in the future, or why they resonated with your editing experiences to date. Re-read and reflect on what you have written. What do you understand about yourself as an editor now? Are you able to synthesize the advice you've received?

The best advice I can leave you with is this: edit as you would wish to be edited. For what it's worth, I strongly believe that every editor should write and be edited regularly, simply to be reminded of what it's like to be on the receiving end of the relationship. Look for opportunities to write and be critiqued, whether it's on a blog, in an industry periodical, or in creative settings. You may be surprised at how humbling sitting on the other side of the desk can be.

In chapter 6 we move away from the relationship with the author and look instead at some of the specific work a book editor does to turn a manuscript into a finished book. The author is never far removed from this work, however, so the relationship lessons you've learned in this chapter are vital to your success with the technical editing of the manuscript.

6

Editing the Manuscript 1: Technical Editing

"The editor is the only one who cannot say,
'That's not my problem,' when the inevitable
screw-up happens."—Pat Walsh

Now that the substantive edit is complete and you and your author have developed a secure, trusting relationship, the manuscript moves on to a series of largely mechanical processes. If you work for a large firm, your connection with the manuscript may be effectively finished. The next time you're likely to think about the book is close to its publication date, although you'll likely be in touch with your author fairly regularly. If you work for a small firm, your role as book editor may be shifting to project editor, in which you are responsible for ensuring that various mechanical processes are completed (although you may not be carrying them out yourself), that staff is assigned to these processes, and that schedules are met. Mechanical processes, staff, and schedules are the major interests of this chapter, as well as the next two.

This chapter examines the book as a physical, constructed object. Here we consider the process of handling a manuscript once it has gone through acceptance and substantive editing in preparation for copyediting, layout, and proofreading. In particular, we look closely at the PARATEXT, which refers to the elements a publisher wraps around the manuscript to make the book a book. It is in the paratext that publishers add value to the manuscript, in part by making the book accessible to

WHICH EDITOR IS WHICH?

In this chapter and in chapter 7, you'll notice that the discussion refers to many editors. It's likely to get a little confusing, so here's a quick crib-list.

- **Book editor**: the editor who acquires a manuscript (sometimes called an *acquiring editor*)
- **Project editor**: an editor responsible for shepherding a manuscript through various processes after it is accepted by the book editor (may also be called a *managing editor*)
- **Substantive editor**: an editor responsible for the substance and structure of a book's presentation; often the book editor, but in some cases an experienced in-house staffer or freelancer
- **Stylistic editor**: an editor responsible for the language and style of a manuscript at the level of sentences and paragraphs (thus, also known as a *line editor*); today this work is often completed during the copyedit; possibly an in-house staffer but more commonly a freelancer
- **Copyeditor**: an editor responsible for mechanical editing of a manuscript (e.g., grammar, punctuation, spelling); often a freelancer, but possibly an in-house staffer
- **Proofreader**: an editor whose responsibility is to bring a book's textual and visual presentation as near to perfect as possible
- **Assigning editor**: an editor responsible for ensuring that a specific task (such as the copyedit) is done by a more junior in-house editor or a freelancer; this role is often fulfilled by the project editor
- **Production editor**: an editor responsible for budget, schedules, and project specifications

One way to think about the editing process is to think of the distinct jobs, or tasks, that coincide roughly with the publication cycle sketched out in chapter 2. Another might be to think about people, each handing work off to the next in line; ideally, there would be one editor for each task, although that's not plausible in reality for a number of reasons. Practically, you might find it easiest to think about hats, or roles. Each stage of publication a manuscript moves through requires work from an editor fulfilling a specific task. It may be the same editor putting on and taking off a hat to do a particular piece of work, but each time she puts on a hat, she must fully inhabit that role.

the reader. Before we talk about that, however, we have to talk about workflow and manuscript preparation—apparently invisible work that occurs after the substantive edit and before the copyedit. Having a well-prepared manuscript makes subsequent processes smoother, and preparation is the responsibility of the project editor.

In this chapter more than any other, I need to clarify my use of the term *author*. As elsewhere, *author* refers to the person whose name appears on the full-title page of the book as the agent responsible for the book's existence. In some cases, there will be multiple authors. In the case of an anthology, a collection of letters or essays, or another edited volume, *author* refers to the volume editor, who is not the publisher's editor but is rather an authorial contributor to the manuscript (for instance, the person who chooses the letters to include or who writes the contextual introduction). In a small number of cases, *author* refers to a corporate body or other organizational entity, with no named individual responsible. When you're dealing with the physical details of the manuscript, it sometimes matters exactly *who*—or what—the author is.

Similarly, throughout this chapter I will refer to the primary editor handling the manuscript as the *project editor*. She may be the book's acquiring editor, or she may be someone taking over responsibility for guiding the book through its mechanical processes. In either case, the role of the project editor is coordination, supervision, evaluation, and communication; the editorial checklist in appendix A is an excellent resource for anyone in this position. This editor's role is to help realize the book in its final form.

The Elements of a Book

What makes a book a *book*, distinct from other forms of written communication?

Imagine you bought a package of index cards and wrote one fact on each of the three hundred cards in the pack. That task would certainly take a lot of thought, effort, and time; but you wouldn't likely call the resulting pile a book. Why not? How we explain why a pile of facts on pages is not a book gives us a vital clue to why much of the discussion around whether or not ebooks are "real" books is so misleading. It also gives us insight into the physical constructedness that makes a book a specific kind of text with specific functions. For example, a book's table of contents, index, chapter headings and subheads, illustrations and captions, and chapter previews and wrap-ups (in textbooks, for instance) are devices that help readers find a specific part of a book within its larger whole. These functional features help the manuscript transition into a book.

In chapter 5, we discussed substantive editing and how the book editor thinks about structure and presentation to make the book as effective as it can be. Readers are trained to read different kinds of texts in particular ways. For example, when we encounter a dictionary, we know that the words it defines will be presented in alphabetical order, so we flip to the part of the dictionary relevant to our search. This is not how a person usually reads a novel—but it does have something in common with how a person might read an anthology of poetry. Many textbooks have answers to in-chapter problems and quizzes in the back, so studying may involve a student flipping repeatedly between chapters and BACK MATTER. A textbook will be built for this kind of use because readers are primed to expect it. We might read a first-aid manual from front to back when taking a first-aid course, but in an emergency, we want to find precisely the information we need, quickly. Books can provide both random and sequential access, and over centuries, their physical presentation of text has evolved to make access comfortable and pleasant for various kinds of readers and various reading situations.

Most books are built from chapters, which may themselves be built from smaller units of content, such as recipes or anecdotes. Chapters may be organized into sections with a unifying theme, or they may be sequenced to provide a satisfying narrative arc. Some books are made up of essays or articles organized by an external logic—alphabetical by subject, alphabetical by contributor last name, or according to a knowledge arc the volume editor wants to build, for example. Sometimes the content of a book is so lengthy that it extends to multiple volumes (for reasons of both the reader's physical comfort and the limitations of print manufacturing), each of which contributes to the whole but must also be able to stand alone effectively. What we are discussing is the integral features of a book's structure and presentation, not as they relate to the topic of the manuscript but rather as sense-making devices for readers.

The publisher also has intentions for the book, and some of the sense-making devices applied to the book reflect the way the publisher imagines a book will be used (which may differ from how the author intended it to be used). For instance, the author may have written a guidebook to Alberta's ungulates (hoofed mammals) with the intention of communicating with a learned professional audience. When the publisher adds colour photographs, an easy-to-use identification key, and way-finding guides for each chapter, the book becomes a tool for a much wider audience, such as armchair naturalists, hikers, and hunters.

Before you begin to think about how to signal a book's use and value to readers, though, let's look at what's involved in manuscript processing. Manuscript processing involves preparing the manuscript to be worked on by other staff in the workflow and is the point at which the project editor reviews, creates, and assembles the paratextual elements that wrap around the author's manuscript to create a book as readers understand it.

Manuscript Processing

If you've never edited or prepared a book-length project before, the best resource I can recommend—other than the help of an experienced book editor—is *The Chicago Manual of Style*. From its title you might think *Chicago* is just another book of preferred spellings and mechanical decisions, and certainly that content is there—robustly so! But *Chicago* is more importantly a book about making books. It includes extensive discussion about thinking through textual problems in order to solve them best on behalf of readers. It also discusses, at length, publishing conventions and the reasons editors do the things we do; printing and the physical manufacturing of books; and working with other editors, writers, designers, and other staff involved in the publication of books and journals. For our purposes here, chapter 2 in the current (16th) edition discusses in detail how to edit specific parts of a manuscript, such as FRONT MATTER, back matter, and cross-references. Once you've edited a few book-length manuscripts, most of these processes will feel comfortable, but it never hurts to review this material, particularly if you're working on a type of book you haven't edited before.

As the project editor, you must clean up a manuscript to send it to the copyeditor. The copyeditor receives a fairly stripped-down manuscript. Inexperienced editors and authors don't always recognize that such a plain file is the best way to send the file to layout (particularly because today's word-processing software makes it so easy to style a manuscript extensively). The book's designer will have established appropriate formatting for the manuscript, which will be applied in the layout software. Layout software will overwrite most of the word processor's formatting (note that italics, bold, underline, and various diacritics can be compensated for), but won't eliminate small issues such as double spaces and extra hard returns. It's generally faster and cheaper for an editor to clean up a word-processing file than it is for the designer or layout technician to do so, but most designers will do a basic cleanup if they receive cluttery files. Designers often clean files as a simple search-and-replace function and may not be as conscientious as an editor would be, so there's a good chance for errors to be introduced into the text. Avoid having design staff do this sort of work to your files if at all possible. If you're working with freelance design staff, it's a good idea to discuss house standards and expectations *before* you prepare and send any manuscript materials.

The project editor is responsible for ensuring that every manuscript has been prepared for mechanical editing. This preparation may be more or less intensive. At some firms, the project editor sends the copyeditor a cleaned-up digital file, with copyediting tags or XML codes in place and with clear instructions about how to proceed. At other firms, the project editor sends the copyeditor a copy of the author's submitted file and expects the copyeditor to clean the file herself. Whatever the practice in your house, someone—presumably you—must be responsible for finding a copyeditor to do the edit, preparing the file (and any other materials required) for the copyeditor, and ensuring she has sufficient time to do the work necessary and returns the edited manuscript on schedule. (Note that, in this section, I am referring to the copyeditor as the next editor to work on the file. You may have a separate editor doing a stylistic edit prior to the copyedit. If that is your house process, please recognize that I understand stylistic editing as the first part of the overall copyediting stage, so for me, *copyeditor* encompasses *stylistic editor*.)

In some workflows, the copyeditor applies XML or similar markup by tagging every line in the manuscript. Tagging may also be done (by the project editor, an editorial assistant, or software) before the copyeditor receives the manuscript for editing. Be sure you give the copyeditor complete instructions for handling the tagged file, including how to adapt her word processor's settings so as not to overwrite the tagged file's defaults; otherwise, the editor may inadvertently undo the tagging or introduce formatting errors.

Here are a few more typical tasks for the project editor to do and issues to watch for:

- If the manuscript has been submitted as multiple files, assemble them into a single running file, or break them up appropriately (e.g., front matter, body, back matter). If required, separate figures and graphics (e.g., tables, charts) into individual files for specific treatment in copyediting and in layout.
- Regularize page margins, line spacing (normally to double spaced), and TYPEFACE. If the author has used a foreign-language typeface, be sure not to overwrite it with another typeface.
- Ensure the dictionary on the manuscript file is set to the correct default.
- Set the file to display formatting.
- Format or tag levels of subheads consistently.
- Convert underlined text to italic.
- Change any all-caps text to mixed case (or possibly small caps, for initialisms and acronyms).
- Remove multiple hard returns before a new paragraph, subhead, or section, and remove any column formatting and hard page breaks.

- Remove unnecessary tabs and double spaces after periods and within sentences.
- Ensure that bullet points and numbered lists are constructed manually and not with Word's auto-formatting tools.
- If applicable, collect footnotes and convert them to endnotes.
- Consult with design staff on elements of the text that require special handling, develop systems as necessary, and add callouts to the text reflecting any decisions made.
- Add callouts for images, tables, charts, and other graphics, and ensure the copyeditor is aware of house standards for treating images and captions.

A CALLOUT is an instruction, embedded in the digital file but not appearing in the final published work, that gives the layout technician direction about placement of images or other layout requirements. Here's a sample callout:

> *[Design: This section is the last piece of the front matter; it should be numbered with lower-case roman numerals; arabic numerals start on the first recto of chapter 1, below.]*

Callouts may also be used for communication between editor and author, if the word-processing software does not have a comment feature.

As you prepare the manuscript to hand over to the copyeditor, you should also assemble copies of the artwork (never originals), as well as captions for illustrative materials (if the captions are not written into the manuscript file itself) and any instructions for special treatment. Ensure that callouts are in place in the manuscript file for all artwork and graphics, or else ensure the copyeditor tags the manuscript accordingly. Callouts for art might look something like this:

> *[Design: Insert image 47 here.]*

When the manuscript has been copyedited and the project is moving to layout, you will send the designer or layout technician all original artwork, photographs, and illustrations (or high-resolution digital files thereof), as well as high-resolution versions of any tables, charts, graphs, maps, and other graphics; or you will provide clear directions for the designer to create some or all of these elements herself. Ensure that all artwork is referred to by a clear and logical numbering system (e.g., by chapter and order of appearance, so that the first photograph to appear in chapter 2 is image 2.01 and so on—specific practice will vary) and that the copyeditor has tagged all the art in the manuscript. Keep in mind that some artwork or graphics may have been added, eliminated, or altered during the editorial process. It's a good idea to double check that all elements are included in the package going to the designer and that all elements to be included are correctly numbered and tagged in the manuscript.

Permissions

By this stage in the process, all permissions should be in place. Permissions are normally cleared and paid for by the author, although they may be paid for by the publisher in some cases. Ideally, permissions are submitted with the finished manuscript, but sometimes the author is still waiting for permissions as the manuscript is moving into mechanical editing, because publishers sometimes take months to respond to permissions requests. As this is a contractual matter, the book's acquiring editor should ensure that the publisher is aware of any outstanding permissions. It is common for the publisher to ask the author to supply copies of the permissions he has cleared.

---

26 May 2016

Dear Permissions Department:

I seek permission to reproduce the following material from the book *Late Again? Procrastination, Creativity, and the Brain* by Charlotte Branwell (2014).

- chart on page 19: Hours of sleep relative to brain function
- passage "Scientists remain mystified ... the well-ordered life," pp. 127 to 129, approx. 470 words.

This material will be used in the forthcoming textbook *Individual Psychology for the Canadian Student* to be published by Kamloops University Press in Spring 2018. I request non-exclusive world rights in all languages for this and all future editions, including digital.

We will acknowledge your permission as follows:

> *Late Again? Procrastination, Creativity, and the Brain* by Charlotte Branwell copyright © 2014. Used by permission of Fantastic Publishing.

If there is any charge for the use of this material or if a different form of acknowledgement should be used, please contact me directly at CBush@goodmail. com. Thank you for your consideration.

Yours truly,

Catherine Bush, PhD

Figure 6.1 Sample permission letter

If you are preparing the manuscript and are not the acquiring editor, be sure to let her know about any permissions you are waiting to receive. Do not lose track of outstanding permissions. When you receive the copyedited manuscript or file back from the copyeditor, update any outstanding permissions if necessary. Be aware that at some firms, a manuscript cannot be sent for copyediting until *all* permissions are in place, because it is highly disruptive to production (read: expensive) if the publisher learns after copyediting—or, worse, during layout—that a permission has not been granted. Be aware, too, that the copyeditor may point out additional permissions that need to be cleared.

Version Control

A significant part of a project editor's work in a digital workflow is version control. *Chicago* refers to this as "retaining the version of record," phrasing that is not normally used with authors. Backups are emphatically necessary. Multiple versions are an imperative in editing, as in publishing generally, and every editor needs a protocol to ensure that work is done ONLY on the current version of the text. Find a system that works for you, and use it consistently. Never assume that other people are following your system or are as rigorous about backups as you are. Make the expectation of regular backups an explicit part of the workflow for everyone you work with directly.

Something many young editors do not realize is that even in the digital era, the edited manuscript is often sent to the author as a hard copy, not as a digital file, as a form of version control. This may seem odd and slow in an otherwise digital workflow, but the reason is straightforward: to prevent work from being undone or being done twice. When reviewing the copyedit, the author answers queries, accepts or rejects changes, and makes any last deletions or additions on a paper copy of the edit (keeping a copy for himself), then returns it with his signoff. The project editor needs tact and diplomacy when communicating with authors on this point. In the transmittal letter that accompanies the copyedit, give the author specific directions about what to do with the material that has been sent and when his changes and signoff are due.

If the author receives a digital file, you must be emphatic about file management; again, use the transmittal letter for this task. The author must not overwrite the transmitted file with her own version of the manuscript and must use the Track Changes and Comment functions to mark what has been accepted, rejected, and added. Otherwise, the copyeditor's efforts may be wasted (or will at least require extensive file-comparison work to recover). Unfortunately, some authors will overwrite the copyedited file and introduce new materials, and in the worst case, the copyeditor will have to edit the manuscript again. Always suggest that the author immediately save the copyedited file with a new file name so the transmitted file remains unchanged, in case the author needs to refer to it again later.

When the project editor has finished with manuscript preparation, the file will move into mechanical editing, which will include a review by the author. It will next go into layout, then be proofread, and an index may be compiled, if needed. Once the proofs are signed off, the book files will be submitted to a printer or prepared for live release as an ebook. Within a few weeks, the book will be officially published. Each of the foregoing processes takes days or weeks of time. Under normal circumstances, each involves multiple people alongside the editor. Missing any of these steps can be costly, or embarrassing, or both. Again, *Chicago* is instructive: "it is critically important to make all possible efforts to eliminate any errors or inconsistencies."

The Paratext

So far, this chapter has looked at how the project editor prepares the manuscript for mechanical editing. But project editors are also responsible for preparing the manuscript to be read as a book, by ensuring the manuscript contains the elements that allow the text to signal its genre and use immediately to readers. Many of the substantive decisions the editor and author made during the substantive edit will become features of the paratext, at least in a nonfiction manuscript. There are fewer signposts in fiction as a result of the way we read most fiction—that is, cover to cover. The project editor also adds textual components not created by the author and organizes the book's contents in conjunction with the substantive editor and the book designer.

In this section I discuss the title, the cover, and the body of the book from the perspective of what the editor and publisher add to the book's value for readers through the paratext.

The title

One critical element of the paratext is a book's title. Titles help readers meet books because they signal how the book is positioned in the market. They also help as mnemonic devices; the title, the subtitle, and the series title (if applicable), in conjunction with the book cover, enable readers to find the right book for a given purpose. Publishers try to ensure that both the title and the subtitle contain keywords to help readers discover the book through databases and search engines, even if the keywords make the title less graceful or catchy.

A manuscript always carries a working title, of course, but that's rarely its published title. (One of the suggested titles for *The Great Gatsby*, for example, was *Trimalchio in West Egg*—certainly not as pithy or appealing.) Titles are touchy things, frequently a point of fierce debate. Sometimes the author knows best, but not always. Sometimes the editor finds the title or subtitle during the editorial process, as the manuscript comes more fully into focus. Sometimes the sales and marketing staff offer suggestions, too, usually fairly early in the marketing conversations. The publisher may also have an opinion—and the publisher often wins.

In chapter 5, we discussed the idea that a book's title should clearly signal the boundaries of its interests. Look at these two examples: *Onward: How Starbucks Fought for Its Life Without Losing Its Soul* and *What If? Serious Scientific Answers to Absurd Hypothetical Questions.* First, notice that both titles also use antithesis cleverly. Second, observe how the titles bound their subject matter clearly while leaving space for a reader's curiosity. Subtitles are important for readers trying to find themselves as potential members of a book community. They are also crucial for book discovery, as so many readers find books by plugging keywords into databases and search engines. Today's meaty subtitles encompass key themes and probable search terms, such as *Play: How It Shapes the Brain, Opens the Imagination, and Invigorates the Soul*; *The Little Bookstore of Big Stone Gap: A Memoir of Friendship, Community, and the Uncommon Pleasure of a Good Book*; and *Daring Greatly: How the Courage to Be Vulnerable Transforms the Way We Live, Love, Parent, and Lead.*

Finding the right title for a book requires both art and science, drawing on both your intellect and your gut. Sometimes it's the music, sometimes it's the keywords, but when you've found exactly the right title, you know. Be careful not to fall in love with a title too quickly, though, because the author, publisher, and marketing director will all have their opinions, too. As you and the author refine the title for a book, consider both demographics (statistical information about readers) and psychographics (information about readers' motivations and loyalties): who is "the tribe" for a given book?

A CLOSE LOOK AT TITLE FORMULAS

Robin Quinn's short article "What's in a Name? Ten Plus Tried and True Formulas for Title Success" discusses formulas that help titles communicate content to their intended readers. Title formulas apply to nonfiction rather than to fiction. In fiction, the title needs to do literary work: illuminate character, signal themes, allude to another text, suggest the narrative arc—and, of course, attract readers' attention. In nonfiction, the title is a device that aids discovery. Underpinning every title must be a sense of utility or usefulness. The utility promise varies from book to book and from title to title, but it's important that a title signal the book's *usefulness*—that is, that it is the right book for a given purpose (even if that purpose is pure escapism).

Here I've used some of Quinn's formulas to demonstrate ways to develop an effective title. Note that many of the examples I've given adopt more than one strategy, and you can apply the formulas to either the main title or the subtitle.

Making a promise is a title formula that speaks directly to utility. The promise may be implied or explicit, but any book that promises to deliver a specific goal if the reader takes its advice is likely to be successful. *How to Never Look Fat Again*; *Cook. Nourish. Glow.*; and *Think and Grow Rich* are three titles that make clear promises, as do *The Business Book: Big Ideas Simply Explained* and *The Life-Changing Magic of Tidying Up*, somewhat more subtly.

Referring to sex, money, or personal fears is a traditional title formula. In advertising, sex, money, and fear are referred to as the prime motivators. Many book titles lean on these drivers directly, such as *Debt-Free Forever: Take Control of Your Money and Your Life*; *Fifty Shades of Pleasure: A Bedside Companion*; *The Carbon Bubble: What Happens to Us When It Bursts*; and *Don't Let Your Doctor Kill You*. The prime motivators can be applied in cute ways, too—consider the memoir *Sex in the Museum: My Unlikely Career at New York's Most Provocative Museum*—but be sure that your sly wink can't be missed and that cute doesn't become twee.

Sharing secrets is another strong formula. Who doesn't want the inside story, especially about anxiety-generating matters? As with promises, many of these appeals are direct, such as *The Secret Life of Money*; *The Surprising Secrets of Highly Happy Marriages*; *The Secret Language of Flowers*; and *The Big Book of Realistic Drawing Secrets*. Some are more fear- or conspiracy-oriented, such as *The Big Investment Lie: What Your Financial Advisor Doesn't Want You to Know*; *The Truth About Men: The Secret Side of the Opposite Sex*; and *All the Presidents' Bankers: The Hidden Alliances That Drive American Power*.

Presenting your content in superlative or absolute terms is a reliable formula that you've seen hundreds of times in titles like *The Year's Best Science Fiction* and *World's Best Cities*. Think beyond *best*, though: *Gut: The Inside Story of Our Body's Most Underrated Organ*; *Portraits of the World's Most Stylish Women*; and *The Most Important Thing*. *Top* and *greatest* are obvious synonyms for *best*, but don't forget about authoritative words such as *The Juicing* **Bible**; *The Intelligent Investor: The* **Definitive** *Book on Value Investing*;

Destinations of a Lifetime; *Canadian Living: The **Ultimate** Cookbook*; and *Wine Folly: The **Essential** Guide to Wine*. In certain contexts, underselling can also work, such as *The Little Book of Golf* and *O's Little Guide to Finding Your True Purpose*—but be sure that you're actually promising and delivering big.

Quantifying your content is another reliable formula. You've almost certainly encountered *The 7 Habits of Highly Effective People*, but might not have connected this title to all kinds of counting in current books: *The Confidence Factor: Seven Strategies of Successful People*; *The Future: Six Drivers of Global Change*; *100 Ways to Motivate Yourself*; and *101 Plus-Size Women's Clothing Tips*, for just a handful of examples. Large numbers can be striking—such as *1,001 Books You Must Read Before You Die* or *1000 Record Covers*—but simplifying problems to a manageable number of steps also has its appeal, as in *Prescription for Life: Three Simple Strategies to Live Younger Longer*. Unusual numbers are popular lately, such as *Brain Fuel: 199 Mind-Expanding Inquiries Into the Science of Everyday Life*; *Young House Love: 243 Ways to Paint, Craft, Update and Show Your Home Some Love*; and *The Novel Cure: From Abandonment to Zestlessness: 751 Books to Cure What Ails You*; as is the daily formula in *365 Golf Tips and Tricks from the Pros* and *Soup of the Day: 365 Recipes for Every Day of the Year*.

Emphasizing novelty is perhaps the most common formula. People want to know what is new and innovative so they are better prepared to deal with change and so they can remain current. Consider *Baby Bust: New Choices for Men and Women in Work and Family*; *Knockout Knits: New Tricks For Scarves, Hats, Jewellery, and Other Accessories*; and *Weight Watchers New Complete Cookbook*.

Using humour is another sure-fire formula, but remember that humour can be subjective. What you or the author finds funny must also be funny to the target audience. Consider the restrained humour of *Cooking with the Two Fat Ladies*; *Who Moved My Cheese?*; *Eats, Shoots and Leaves: The Zero Tolerance Approach to Punctuation*; and *Jump Up and Kiss Me: Spicy Vegetarian Cooking*.

Beyond basic formulas, many titles use figurative language and rhetorical schemes for appeal and memorability. Alliteration is especially common: *Lean In: Women, Work, and the Will to Lead*; *Year of Yes*; *The Defining Decade*; and *The Big Bad Book of Bill Murray* (along with any book titled *The Big Book of ...*). Parallelism is also common, often used in conjunction with climax, as in *Loveable Livable Home: How to Add Beauty, Get Organized, and Make Your House Work for You* and *Superbetter: A Revolutionary Approach to Getting Stronger, Happier, Braver and More Resilient*, for instance. Repetition is frequent, as in *Open Heart, Open Mind*; *My Fight/Your Fight*; and *Healthy Sleep Habits, Happy Child*; and so is rhyme, as in *Me and Earl and the Dying Girl* or *Silver Screen Fiend*. Antithesis can be effective, too, as in *Act Like a Lady, Think Like a Man*; *Rich Dad, Poor Dad*; and *Do Big Small Things*. Once you start looking for these features in titles, you'll discover them everywhere.

Startling or offbeat titles can work if they're clever. Many writers will recall Anne Lamott's quirkily titled memoir *Bird by Bird: Some Instructions on Writing and Life*. The unexpected image of *The Snowball: Warren Buffett and the Business of Life* also employs this formula, as does the apparently negative *Don't Waste Your Time in the Canadian Rockies: An Opinionated Hiking Guide* and the cheekily contrary *An Astronaut's Guide to Life on Earth*. The aggressive *Screw It, Let's Do It: Lessons in Life and Business* (by Virgin's Richard Branson) is arresting, as is the sharply contrasting *Furiously Happy: A Funny Book About Horrible Things*. But remember, no matter how clever and attention getting they are, titles must always be appropriate to both the content and the intended readership.

Of course, not every title adheres to a formula. Many books invite the potential reader to identify with a quality evoked in the title; for example, *Bold*; *The Rational Optimist*; *The Organized Mind*; *Reading Like a Writer*; and *What Happy Working Mothers Know* all adopt this tactic. Others invite the reader to join in a projected "us": *Stranger Than We Can Imagine: An Alternative History of the 20th Century* and *Who We Are: Reflections on My Life and Canada* are examples. Social trends also influence book titles.

LOOKING FOR COMMUNITY, TRENDS, AND ISSUES

In the following list of books published since 2010, what social issues, trends, and personal positions do you observe are staked out or appealed to? What do these appeals suggest to you about community and belonging? What else do you notice about this list of titles?

- *Nature's Beauty Secrets: Recipes for Beauty Treatments from the World's Best Spas*
- *Quiet: The Power of Introverts in a World That Can't Stop Talking*
- *Brown Eggs and Jam Jars: Family Recipes from the Kitchen of Simple Bits*
- *Big Magic: Creative Living Beyond Fear*
- *A Smart Girl's Guide to Knowing What to Say*
- *Everyday Super Food*
- *Unstoppable: Harnessing Science to Change the World*
- *We Are All Feminists*
- *Great Sex, Naturally: Every Woman's Guide to Enhancing Her Sexuality Through the Secrets of Natural Medicine*
- *Trim Healthy Mama Cookbook: Eat Up and Slim Down*

If you like, take this exercise further. Visit a bookstore, study books featured in the nonfiction section, and compile a list of ten to twenty titles that strike you for whatever reason. What themes do you observe in the keywords of these titles, if any?

Cover copy

The cover is primarily an instrument for selling the book, although its existence is also vital to the integrity of the book as a physical object. The cover speaks immediately to the book's market fit and positioning. Book covers tend to be commercial in their visual presentation and are affected by trends in the larger visual culture, such as webpages and advertising, and there are numerous options for making a book stand out on the shelf, such as covers using colour, foils, LAMINATES, varnish, die cuts, embossing, and other special effects. Even in sectors that are traditionally visually conservative, such as university press publishing, book covers are increasingly attractive; it's rare to see a one- or two-colour, words-only treatment today. Most importantly, Chip Kidd says, the cover has to work both when the reader has no clue what the book is about and when the reader is building an emotional relationship with the text. Developing the visual communication of the cover is the art department's responsibility, not the book editor's, although the editor may have input.

As a complement to the images and colours on the cover, the publisher adds cover copy, another form of paratext. Cover copy has to do many different kinds of work. The title and the cover copy together position the book in the market. Cover copy also has descriptive and functional roles.

The back-cover copy is the most important copy an editor writes—and ideally it *is* the editor, and not the marketing staff, doing the writing. When a potential reader picks up a book and reads the back cover (or the front-flap copy, in the case of a hardcover), a "buy" decision is either secured or lost. For that reason, the copy should be prepared by someone who knows the book well—and then *perhaps* tweaked by someone who understands marketing and consumer motivation.

Conventionally, the industry uses the terms JACKET to refer to the paper wrapper folded around the boards of a hardcover book and *cover* to refer to the COVER STOCK of a paperback book. For the sake of convenience, in this chapter and elsewhere I use *cover* as a catch-all term. Obviously, publishers have much more real estate on a jacket, which has front and back flaps as well as its front, back, and spine. Publishers use this extra space purposefully.

Typical components of a book cover include the following:

- the book's title and subtitle, and the author's full name
- an explanation of the book's content
- an author biography (Only a brief bio appears on some covers; in that case, a longer one, including an author photo—and a credit line for that photo—should appear inside the book itself.)
- BLURBS and advance quotations from credible sources and/or praise from credible reviewers (If appropriate, include reviews from previous books, too, either on the cover or on the first few pages of the front matter.)

- mentions of awards and honours (e.g., Canada Reads Finalist 2015, Governor General's Award, Giller Prize shortlist) in a COPY LINE or starburst
- other promotional tie-ins, if appropriate (e.g., reference to a film or a television series based on the novel) The tie-in may be textual or visual, if characters or scenes are immediately recognizable—think of the tie-in editions of Lawrence Hill's *The Book of Negroes* and Markus Zusak's *The Book Thief*, for example.
- technical data, including the price (Canadian and American on some editions), the ISBN, a UPC, and barcodes for the ISBN and UPC (Note that in certain sectors—such as textbook publishing and, increasingly, scholarly publishing—the price does not appear on the book itself.)
- a "Printed in Canada" notation if applicable (This point is important for cross-border distribution.)
- the publisher/imprint name, plus distribution information (if different), the publisher's website and, increasingly, Facebook page, Twitter handle or hashtag, or Pinterest boards
- credit lines for photography, cover illustration, and cover design, if not captured on the copyright page
- subject headings (The use of subject headings or store locations to categorize books is inconsistent today, mainly because physical bookstores rarely follow them and because online bookstores use METADATA; but they are still used by some publishers on some books.)

Depending on how large or small your firm is, cover copy may be prepared by an editor or by sales and marketing staff. Regardless of who develops the copy, it must be edited and proofread carefully and must adhere to the STYLE SHEET developed for the manuscript. Also, be sure the cover copy is cast in a tone similar to that of the book itself.

Certain kinds of copy conventionally appear on certain parts of the cover. For instance, the synopsis of a novel appears on the inside front flap or on the back cover. On guidebooks and cookbooks, sample text and images often appear on the back cover. It's not unusual for a strong blurb or review comment to appear on the front cover rather than on the back cover, with additional blurbs/reviews on the back; in fact, the entire back jacket of a hardcover may be given over to "praise": excerpts from positive high-profile reviews, endorsements, and enthusiastic blurbs. The main title, the author's name (often last name only), and the publisher's name or logo (correctly called a COLOPHON—see

WHAT IS AN ISBN?

An ISBN is an International Standard Book Number, a string of characters that identifies a book as a unique product in the marketplace. Today, the ISBN is a thirteen-character code; prior to 2007, it was a ten-character code. Current ISBNs are made up of a three-digit prefix element (978 or 979); a registration group element (one to five digits long), which identifies the country, geographical area, or language the book belongs to; a publisher or imprint identifier (up to seven digits long); an edition and format identifier (up to six digits long); and a single check character (which may be an X). Every edition of a book published requires its own ISBN. If, for example, a book is published in hardcover, in paperback, and in three ebook formats, there will be five ISBNs associated with that title. If a book is reprinted without an edition change, however, it retains its original ISBN. (An *edition change* means the content or format of the book has changed significantly from the previous edition; for instance, new material has been added, specific content has been updated to reflect new information, or the text has been issued in a new format. It is no longer the book it was. A *reprint* reproduces the existing edition in the same format with no significant textual changes.)

Books available for sale and distribution in the retail supply chain must carry an ISBN. In Canada, ISBNs are available from Library and Archives Canada (http://www.bac-lac.gc.ca).

page 145) appear on the spine reading from top to bottom. (French-language spines read bottom to top.)

Research has shown that blurbs really do sell books. According to *Publishers Weekly*, endorsements from recognized authors, business leaders, and celebrities positively influence consumers' decision to buy books. Blurbs appeal to the human desire to be part of a community. There are many potential problems with blurbs and blurbers, as with the overabundance of awards, but for the purpose of assembling your manuscript, be sure to solicit a range of writers and other commentators as potential blurbers. Think beyond the writers in your author's network and your region. If appropriate to the subject, reach out to community leaders, academics, high-profile bloggers, and writers with national and international profile.

Those of you interested in ebooks and other digital forms may have noticed that I've been concentrating on physical books in this section. Publishers producing ebooks recognize that ebooks lack spines and back covers, so buyers often receive much less information about an ebook than about a paper book, depending on the venue through which they buy their book. Metadata (data that describes and provides detail about other data—in this case, a digital book file) can be built into the ebook file, supplying the cover copy and other information about the text for those readers who want it. At this time, there is no consistent standard for what an ebook file may contain, and ebook retailers support or freely ignore publisher-supplied paratext. But these standards will come, and book editors (and sales and marketing staff) should adhere to them when they do.

Writing cover copy

Cover copy is some of the most consequential prose you will prepare as a book editor. The book summary, generally between 80 and 150 words in length, depending on space, balances informational text with sell copy. Cover copy must be promotional but not hyperbolic or self-congratulatory, and should reflect the tone of the book itself. The best cover copy describes the contents of the book in a way that is both accurate and appealing to the self-identifying book-buying audience we discussed in chapter 3. It speaks to the benefits readers will gain from the book and makes a call to action ("buy this and gain …"). On nonfiction books, the copy may itemize or enumerate the book's selling features, often in point form. All cover copy must tell the reader one thing, however: what's in it for the reader?

Cover copy is often refined from existing copy. The book editor has normally written catalogue copy and/or a paragraph describing the book for its presentation at the publisher's sales conference. This copy may have been drawn from a book description provided by the author, but should be further developed through commentary and feedback from the publisher, other editors, sales reps, and marketing staff, as well as the editor's own knowledge of the manuscript and the market.

Well-written cover copy usually requires many drafts—it is not something the book editor (or a marketing staffer) whips off in a few minutes. Space is limited, so every word counts. The cover copy is an instance where the editor must be at least as rigorous in editing herself (or another staffer) as she is in editing the author—and it's important to include other eyes in this process. Errors of any type in the cover copy are acutely embarrassing and will almost certainly affect the book's sales.

The Body of the Book

Having discussed the title and the cover components, we now turn to the inside of the book. I will review the components that make the body of a book recognizable and consistent, from front to back. Note that these components contribute to the structure and presentation of the book's content and, in many cases, make using the book easier for the reader.

Pagination

As a book editor, you must think about the details of a book's presentation. One of these details that is conventional but not particularly apparent (except to other editors) has to do with pagination. Take a look at a book of serious nonfiction, such as this book, a textbook, or a scholarly book. You'll likely see that the page numbers—usually called FOLIOS—in the front matter are different from those in the body of the book. Many pages in the front matter don't carry a folio, and those that do use lower-case roman numerals. The folios in the rest of the book are cast in arabic numerals, beginning on the first RECTO—or more fussily on the first VERSO, page 2—of the first numbered chapter. (The right-hand page of a book is referred to as a recto. The left-hand page of a book is referred to as a verso—think reverse or back side.)

Pages that are deliberately blank (such as the verso at the end of a chapter) do not carry a folio, and neither do part or section title pages; and the opening page of a new chapter may carry its folio in a different position than on subsequent pages, if the chapter opens on a recto. Similar practices apply to the inclusion or absence of RUNNING HEADS and FOOTERS. You may think such details are picky and inane, and perhaps they are. Yet it is these details that mark careful, conscientious professional publishing; they signal an awareness of tradition and craft, so ignore them at your peril. Of course, emerging ebook practices may eventually make these conventions of print books irrelevant or obsolete: only time will tell.

Front matter

When you open the cover of a book, you see a variety of paratext elements. Not all books will contain the same elements, but all books require some of them.

- half-title page
- full-title page
- copyright page
- dedication
- epigraph
- table of contents
- list of illustrations
- list of tables
- foreword
- preface
- acknowledgements
- introduction

Collectively, these materials are referred to as *front matter*. I have presented this list according to the conventional ordering of these elements. Depending on the genre of book and the firm's standards, you may see other materials here, too. Getting these matters in the right order with the right names is a mark of professional standards. Assembling the front matter is primarily the responsibility of the project editor, although, as you can see, some parts of the front matter are prepared by the author.

I have a few comments and observations to offer particular to the preparation of front matter materials.

- **Title pages**: A well-made printed book includes a half-title page. In a hardcover book, a blank sheet, called an ENDPAPER, appears before the half-title page. The endpaper is slightly heavier than and may be a different colour from the stock on which the body of the book is printed. The half-title page is integral to the physical manufacturing of the hardcover binding, and is present in paperbacks simply as a matter of convention. The half-title page usually includes just the main title of the book, without the subtitle. Sometimes the half-title page and its verso are used to carry paratextual information, such as a book description and/or praise for this book, and/or the author's previous work. The complete title of the book (main title and subtitle) appears on the full-title page, as does the author's full name and the publisher's imprint name, sometimes with the place of publication and the date. The title pages and their versos never carry folios.

- **Copyright**: The copyright page contains vital information and in a printed book normally appears on the verso of the full-title page; see below for additional comments on its content. The copyright page may be referred to in working conversation as *page iv* (pronounced *page eye-vee*) because it usually falls in manuscript order as page iv; the page itself does not carry a folio. In an increasing number of ebooks, the copyright page appears at the end of the book. Regardless of its pagination, it must be present somewhere in the text.

- **Table of contents**: Depending on how a reader is likely to use the book, the table of contents will be more or less developed. It is often plain and unadorned—simply a list of chapter numbers and titles. Some novels forgo a table of contents entirely if the chapters are only numbered and not titled. In serious nonfiction and textbooks, however, the table of contents may be sufficiently detailed to represent the skeleton and musculature of the book, making the architecture of the book obvious. The project editor must ensure that the list of sections, chapters, and subheads is correct, complete, and current: these names often change (or are added or eliminated) during substantive editing.

- **Foreword**: A foreword (note the correct spelling!) provides a context-setting overview of the book's content or its purpose for being, and is written by someone other than the author—for instance, a community leader, another author, or a celebrity. The purpose of the foreword is to introduce the book and to add an endorsement of its significance from a relevant authority. A foreword is *never* written by the author, always by a guest.

- **Preface**: A preface provides an overview of the book's content, context, and, sometimes, the process of its writing. The preface may include acknowledgements, or the acknowledgements may stand alone. A preface is *always* written by the author or the volume editor. In nonfiction, it may be called a prologue or an author's notice; note that this prologue is distinct from the manuscript prologue some authors use in fiction.

- **Acknowledgements**: Acknowledgements are increasingly developed and long in contemporary books, sometimes running to three pages or longer. The acknowledgements traditionally appear in the front matter in nonfiction and as back matter in fiction. Increasingly, publishers of trade nonfiction are including acknowledgements as back matter, however, perhaps influenced by the formatting of ebooks, which usually start with the author's text as soon after the cover page as possible.

- **Introduction**: An introduction provides a text's conceptual lead-in; it is normally written by the author and is a common feature of nonfiction work. In fiction, poetry, or other literary texts, an introduction sets a framework for the reader's understanding of what follows, and may provide an analytical or critical view of the text—in this case, the introduction is usually written by someone other than the author of the literary text, and the text itself may be annotated to complement the introduction. The introduction is often treated as part of the front matter in an academic book—in this case, its folios are numbered in small roman numerals. The introduction is generally treated as the first book chapter in trade nonfiction. You should have a standard house practice. If any materials are included in a book's front matter that are not included in my list above, they should appear after the introduction, if it is treated as front matter, or else after the acknowledgements, if the introduction is treated as chapter 1.

- **Abstracts and summaries:** In some books you will find an abstract or executive summary. This is more typical of business books than other forms of trade publishing, although abstracts may appear in some academic books as well. Abstracts and summaries may be prepared by the publisher's editor or by a freelancer who specializes in this kind of work.
- **Maps:** A common inclusion in the front matter is a map or multiple maps of relevant territory, in either fiction or nonfiction. Maps should appear after the acknowledgements/introduction in nonfiction, and before the author's text in fiction; maps may also be printed on a hardcover's endpapers.
- **Endpapers:** These aren't technically part of the front matter, or the back matter either, but they may need your attention. In certain books, the endpapers are printed, rather than blank, with content pertinent to the book's subject matter. In children's books, the endpapers often form part of the book's larger visual narrative and may differ from front to back. Obviously, any material to appear on the endpapers should be reviewed by the project editor; if it is textual material, it should be copyedited and proofread, and must conform to the style sheet for the overall book.

You may choose to deviate from conventions, and most deviations are fine if they are done purposefully. For instance, many publishers of guidebooks and collections of academic essays run the contributors' biographies in the front matter; others run them in the back matter. The dedication may be granted a page of its own; in many books, however, the dedication is squeezed onto the copyright page to save space and costs. Deviations such as printing the copyright page on a recto, however, look amateurish, may interfere with the reader, and should be scrupulously avoided.

The copyright page

So much important work happens on the copyright page that I need to dedicate further explanation to its contents. The copyright page—page iv—must contain some of the following elements, and may contain others, depending on your publishing situation:

- the publisher's imprint name and location (the publisher's insignia may appear here, too, but is not required)
- the copyright statement, and the statement *All rights reserved* (additional copy regarding rights, limitations, and reproduction may follow)

- an edition statement (e.g., first edition)
- a printing statement (printing location and print run/date; this may include information about the paper, particularly if the publisher has adopted Forest Stewardship Council [FSC] standards)
- the ISBN
- CIP data (or a statement that CIP has been requested; see below for more detail)
- staff credit lines (if credit is not cited elsewhere, such as on the cover)
- acknowledgements of grantors (and their logos, if required)
- permissions, if the number of permissions is small

Your firm may also include additional boilerplate text specific to your house or imprint.

The copyright statement is important: it is part of a publisher's contractual obligation to ensure that the copyright is clearly declared on the book. The copyright statement normally looks like this:

Copyright © Rights Holder 2016

or like this:

Copyright © 2016 by Author Fullname

Copyright is inherent in the creation of a document, so if for some catastrophic reason you were to omit the copyright statement, the book is legally still protected. It should be policy, however, to ensure that the book contains an explicit copyright statement.

If your firm belongs to Access Copyright, the Canadian rights collective agency, the copyright page will normally contain a boilerplate reference to Access Copyright as well the usual limitations of rights. Here's an example.

All rights reserved. The reproduction of any part of this publication by any means (electronic, mechanical, photographic, recording, or otherwise) without the prior consent of the publisher is an infringement of copyright. Excerpts from this book may be reproduced with the written permission of the publisher, under licence from Access Copyright, or under licence from another rights management agency.

As you likely perceive in this sample text, it's a good idea to include more language than just *All rights reserved.*

CIP statement

CIP stands for CATALOGUING IN PUBLICATION and refers to a data record that helps libraries catalogue and shelve new books appropriately. It's an important and valuable record, and its presence contributes to making a book look well planned and professional. In Canada, CIP is prepared by Library and Archives Canada and is easy to request. Go to the Library and Archives Canada website and find Cataloguing in Publication under the Services and Programs menu. (In the United States, Library of Congress CIP data is prepared by private agencies and the wait time may be months; this is the reason you will often see language like "A CIP record for this work has been applied for" on the copyright page of a book published in the United States.) Request CIP *at least a month* before your book is scheduled to be proofread.

Once your CIP record is returned, you must notify Library and Archives Canada if you make any changes to the title or the release date. Also, when you request CIP, you commit to sending two copies of your book to Library and Archives Canada as part of the legal deposit program. Through this program, your book—and all other books published in Canada—will be preserved as part of Canada's writing and publishing heritage. Be sure to send your two copies promptly upon publication of every title and every new edition.

Permissions redux

If the author has quoted lines from a contemporary poem, reproduced a table from an existing textbook, or otherwise incorporated materials protected by another party's copyright, the manuscript may require formal permission statements. Permission is particularly important with quotations of lyrics and with reproductions of photographs, artwork, and archival documents. Permission is not required for quoting from books in the context of education, review, and criticism, so many works of scholarship, some textbooks, and many books of serious nonfiction do not require permissions—but it depends on the content and its context. A smart project editor keeps an eye on quoted materials and knows which items fall under fair use, which items belong to the public domain, and which items require permissions. (Note that in the case of artwork, permissions may distinguish between copyright and use; be sure you're clear.)

If the manuscript includes a small number of permissions, these may be listed on the copyright page. If the list of permissions is long, a separate permissions page should be compiled and appended to the manuscript; this constitutes an extension of the copyright page and typically appears in the back matter, although it may appear in the front matter.

A brief line on the copyright page refers to the page(s) on which the permissions list appears. In the case of anthologies, the permissions statements often run at the bottom of the first page of each anthologized item.

It is author's responsibility to acquire the permissions and submit them to the publisher; it is the project editor's responsibility to ensure the permissions statements are included in the manuscript text and adhere to the requirements of the agencies giving permission. If there is any risk that a permission may have been overlooked, the copyright page may carry a disclaimer to the effect that "The publisher made every effort to identify and acknowledge copyrighted material included in this book. Any errors or omissions are unintentional and should be brought to our attention. We will be pleased to acknowledge any errors or omissions in future printings of this book." Here's one of the many points in mechanical editing where it's better to be overly cautious rather than careless.

The Author's Text

The bulk of a manuscript is made up of chapters, recipes, articles, essays, or similarly self-contained but linked portions, and may be divided into sections and parts. The content of the manuscript is not our concern here, but its presentation is.

If the manuscript is to be divided into sections or parts, you must think about how this division will be effected. Will you introduce a formal title page for each section, or can you signal divisions to readers visually (e.g., by changing the colour and text of the section heads)? Has the author provided text to introduce each part? How does the divided structure affect the length and the tone of the overall text? At times, it's valuable to ask the art department for suggestions about how to structure and identify divisions within the manuscript. Special treatments may affect your page count and therefore your budget.

It's also a good idea to talk with the art department about how photographic material will be incorporated into the book. Will photos be sprinkled throughout the text in the relevant parts, or concentrated in an eight- or sixteen-page section and printed on a heavier, glossier stock than the rest of the book? Do you need permissions for any of this material? If the materials are not already in digital form, who is responsible for digitization—both getting the work done and paying the bill? And who is responsible for taking care of original artwork while it's in care of the publisher?

The concept of *editorial design* is pertinent here. Editorial design refers to decisions made by the book editor and designer together in the interests of the readership and book use. In a guidebook or how-to book, for instance, a conversation about editorial design will ensure that the information most users want is most obvious on the page. Considerations for editorial design include examining the type area versus the image area on a page; selecting appropriate typefaces, type sizes, and line spacing for a particular readership; and using colour, headings, rules, and other decorative elements to drive the reader around the page in a particular way. Editorial design may also shape how chapters open and close, how illustrations will be integrated into the textual presentation, and how elements that are apparently disparate may be shaped to create continuity and flow for the reader.

Captions

One element of the author's text that may require particular attention is the captions (sometimes referred to as *cutlines*, although this is a newspaper term). Captions are the brief texts that appear alongside photographs, graphics, and other visual content. They are an afterthought for many writers, and as you process the manuscript, you may discover that the captions are incomplete, inattentively written, or missing altogether. It's good practice to include a caption (or at least a title) for every photograph, illustration, or other graphic.

Thus, as project editor, you may be writing or rewriting captions, or you may be examining them to prepare a model style for the copyeditor to apply. Here are a few points to consider:

- Think about punctuation and mechanics—in particular, whether the captions should be complete sentences, should start with a capital letter, and should end with a period. What mechanical style best suits the content and the overall tone of the book?

- How descriptive are the captions—purely factual, impressionistic, didactic? How closely do they tie into the running text? Do they simply complement the text, or do they require specific cross-referencing?

- Does a caption exist for every image and every graphic? If not, can you ask the author to write captions, or is that now your task? If a caption exists for every piece of artwork, are the captions comparable in their treatment and presentation, or are some noticeably shorter or longer?

- Some books contain only one kind of visual complement— photographs, for instance. Some books contain photographs, line art, tables, charts, and graphs. Different content may require different kinds of captions, so ensure your plans suit, or can accommodate, all captions.

Remember that mechanical consistency in captions, as in all other elements of the text, produces reader confidence in the text.

You may be preparing the manuscript for copyediting and layout, so callouts may accompany your captions, like this:

[insert IMAGE 46 about here City of Edmonton Archives EA-10-324]

[caption:] Edmonton's High Level Bridge under construction, ca. 1912; Rutherford House appears in the background. City of Edmonton Archives EA-10-324; used with permission

The information inside the square brackets won't appear in the book itself. It's just a cue for the designer or layout technician to insert the appropriate photo. This is not the stage to copyedit the captions. This is the stage for thinking about how best to integrate this element of the author's text into the larger apparatus of the book on behalf of readers. Consider the purpose of the captions and their relative length. Are they unified in their voice and presentation?

Back matter

Like the front matter, the back matter normally appears in a standard sequence, although some deviation is common. Again, not all books will contain all (or any) of these elements.

- afterword
- appendix
- notes
- glossary
- bibliography
- list of contributors
- index
- author biography

As with the front matter, some parts of the back matter are written by the author, while others are assembled by the project editor or other staff. Most of the back matter elements pertain to nonfiction more than to fiction.

Here are a few points to consider as you assemble or refine the back matter of a manuscript:

- **Afterword:** An afterword (also referred to as a *conclusion* or an *epilogue*) may be contributed by either the author or a guest writer. It runs as part of the body text, although it is technically back matter. Because an afterword ups a manuscript's page count, its inclusion may be a point of contention, so be sure it contributes to the strength of the manuscript as a whole.

- **Appendix**: Material that is ancillary to the text—relevant, but not necessarily of immediate interest to every reader—is often captured in an appendix (plural *appendixes*).

- **Notes**: Today, it is common for authors to gather their notes at the end of the manuscript, rather than running notes at the bottom of the relevant page as with traditional footnotes (that said, in a volume of articles or essays from various contributors, the notes are collected at the end of each article, not at the end of the book). Endnotes are particularly useful for authors of serious nonfiction who do not want to adopt scholarly citation practices (such as MLA or APA inline citations). Endnotes may be bibliographic, discursive, or both. The text used to set endnotes is typically smaller than the BODY TYPE, as few people read the notes from beginning to end and therefore ease of reading isn't a primary consideration.

- **Glossary**: In some nonfiction (and in a small number of works of fiction) it may be appropriate to include a glossary, which is like a miniature dictionary, but limited to terms that reflect the interests of the book. Words captured in the glossary are normally highlighted in the running text—using italics, boldface, or small capitals, for instance. In technical books, an illustrated glossary is useful. For instance, readers may understand the concept of a *petiole* or *midrib* better from a visual, rather than a verbal, explanation.

- **Bibliography**: The bibliography may also be referred to as the Works Cited, References, List of Sources, or Further Reading, depending on the genre of the book and readers' expectations. Not all books require a bibliography, but for those that do, the bibliography demands the same attention as the body text. It is the author's responsibility to ensure that the bibliography is accurate and appropriately formatted. Some novelists—particularly those who write historical and speculative fiction—now include lists of books relevant to their manuscript research or of potential interest to readers. In some trade nonfiction, appendixes and the bibliography may be combined into a Resources section.

- **Index**: According to the terms of most publishing contracts, it is the author's responsibility to produce the book's index, if it has one. Indexes (and for that matter abstracts) are a specialized form of editing and are often prepared by a professional indexer and paid for by the author. That said, in some areas of publishing, such as guidebooks and field guides, in-house staff may produce the index. An index cannot be prepared until the book has been laid out and PAGE PROOFS (sometimes called GALLEYS) have been generated. As the project editor, you may be responsible for specifying a maximum number of pages for the index (part of your costing), for ensuring that the compiled index is correct, and for transmitting the index to the designer or layout technician for layout. This work occurs very close to the point that the book is to be printed, so time tends to be short and deadlines are critical. As with endnotes, the type in an index tends to be quite small. Note that in some books, the index is an alternate version of the table of contents— for instance, an index of recipes by category or an index of poems by first lines.

- **About the author:** The author normally submits a short biography, generally with a photograph, either with the final manuscript or with the author questionnaire for the marketing department. This text may appear on the book jacket or inside the book as one of the final pages. In some cases, this text appears in both places. This paragraph, like all other ancillary matter, must be copyedited and proofread to conform to the style of the overall book. If the author has published with the house before, or if the book is one volume in a series, be sure the biography is correct and current—don't just assume it is. And be sure a credit is included for the author photo, since you can be pretty sure the author didn't take it herself (unless it's a selfie, of course—but even a selfie needs a credit).

THE COLOPHON

A part of the back matter that deserves a little more attention, the colophon is lovely detail that reminds readers of historical publishing and printing practices. In the age of manuscript books, copyists often left details about the work, or their experience of copying it, at the end of the handwritten text. In the early days of printing, the colophon referred specifically to the publisher's emblem, sometimes with other identifiers, in part because most early books were registered with the crown or another controlling agency.

Today, a colophon appears on the last or second-last page of some books, offering information about how the book was designed and manufactured, particularly when that information is pertinent to the book's subject matter. A colophon may also appear on the copyright page. Here is part of the colophon from a catalogue of an exhibition about Chinese opera on the Canadian prairies, for example:

The golden yellow used predominately in the design is the imperial colour of the Chinese emperor, reserved for his exclusive use. In Chinese culture, yellow is also considered the colour of the earth, which in an

> Alberta and University of Alberta context represents the wheat fields of
> the Canadian prairie. • Typeset in Quadraat Sans with titles in Boulevard,
> this catalogue was printed on Sterling Matte 100 lb. text by Friesens
> Corporation in Altona, Manitoba.

Colophons may also be instructive about typography, which many contemporary readers find interesting. For instance, here is part of the colophon from Patti Smith's memoir *Just Kids*, a work about art, creativity, and innovation:

> This book was set in Granjon, a type named in compliment to Robert
> Granjon, a type cutter and printer active in Antwerp, Lyons, Rome,
> and Paris from 1523 to 1590. Granjon, the boldest and most original
> designer of his time, was one of the first to practice the trade of
> typefounder apart from that of printer.
>   Linotype Granjon was designed by George W. Jones, who based his
> drawings on a face used by Claude Garamond (ca. 1480–1561) in his
> beautiful French books. Granjon more closely resembles Garamond's
> own type than do any of the various modern faces that bear his name.

As with so many practices that have been newly revived, however, colophons have a tendency to be flowery and ornate, and may sound something like effusive descriptions of wine. Long ago, I received a copy of this rather sardonic, anonymously composed colophon, which tells the tale:

> This book is set in 12-point Monotone Bimbo, with chapter headings in
> Basketball Overextended. Both faces were designed by the great Adolf
> Pflupfl and are characterized by noble, full-bodied proportions with
> complex, slightly fruity serifs. It was printed by upset lithophagy on 70 lb.
> Tropicana Ivory mislaid Cowabunga Slipshod Overcoat. The ink came
> out of a can.
>   This paper is 100% unrecycled. Whole forests were leveled, thousands
> of small furry animals left homeless, and vast virgin landscapes
> devastated, to make this book.

Colophon text is normally written by the designer and should be checked by the book editor or the copyeditor for both fact and clarity. As with all other paratext, the colophon must conform to the book's overall style sheet.

None of the writing the project editor contributes to a book, be it an abstract, acknowledgements, or captions, should be flashy or call attention to itself. It is present because it is important to the reader's experience of the book *as* a book. Yet because it is paratext, it is the publisher's responsibility. Do not expect authors to write or even think about most elements of paratext.

At the beginning of this chapter, I invited you to consider why a book is more than a pile of facts, more than an extended narrative. One of the things that makes a book a book is its specific structure and presentation.

If for some reason you as editor choose to defy the conventions of book structure, do so deliberately and thoughtfully, not out of ignorance or carelessness.

A well-structured book makes reading almost effortless. Readers approach text with a set of mostly unconscious conventions about how to use the book and its content. The book's structure determines how readers perceive its function. But of course, readers also use books in ways that we might not anticipate—to decorate their rooms, to make art, even to kill bugs!

Now that the manuscript has been reviewed and completed by the project editor, it is ready for further mechanical processes: copyediting, layout, and proofreading. Chapter 7 discusses copyediting and proofreading, and chapter 8 discusses some basic concepts of design, manufacturing, and production that all editors need to know.

7

Editing the Manuscript 2: Textual Editing

*"Editing is like giving mouth-to-mouth to a body
pulled from the water: out with the bad air, in with
the good. Hoping it coughs to life."—Andrew Pyper*

*"... editing itself is an excruciating act of self-discipline,
mind-reading, and stable-cleaning. If it seems like a
pleasure, something is probably wrong."—Arthur Plotnik*

We've discussed two of the most important aspects of book editing: acquisitions and the relationship with the author. We've talked about substantive editing and the structural elements that help transform a manuscript into a book. In this chapter, we turn our attention to TEXTUAL EDITING, considering, by turns, stylistic editing, copyediting, and proofreading.

Textual editing involves three levels of style. First, there are the standards of good prose: good grammar, punctuation, mechanics, and appropriate usage, to name the most basic elements. These standards also encompass *euphony*, the quality of being pleasing to the ear, through elements such as flow, rhythm, cadence, precision, and concision. These standards are dealt with primarily by the stylistic editor, secondarily by the copyeditor. Then there are the requirements of house style, dictated by a publication manual or disciplinary standards. (*The Chicago Manual of Style* is a given, but MLA, APA, or another style manual might also be applied.) This level of style encompasses mechanical consistency and textual accuracy, and is dealt with primarily by the copyeditor. Finally, there is the writer's own palette of choices and preferences—her idiom—expressing a voice that is unique to that author. Toronto-based editor Jennifer Glossop calls this "the sound of self," and maintaining this sound involves a fine balancing of the source text, your own editorial sensibility, and your knowledge of standards and conventions.

The purpose of the various forms of textual editing is to ensure that the writer's text conforms to the publisher's (house) standards. Interestingly, at many publishing firms, this kind of editing is increasingly done by freelance editors. In recognition of this fact, throughout this chapter, I position the working editor—the stylistic editor, copyeditor, or proofreader—as a freelancer from outside the firm.

The freelancing of this work puts a double burden on the book editor, whom I will refer to in this chapter as the assigning editor (recognizing that the assigning editor herself may be the stylistic editor, copyeditor, and proofreader, too). First, the assigning editor needs to maintain positive working relationships with the freelancers undertaking textual editing, ensuring they have the right tools and knowledge, are working to a sufficient standard, and are meeting their deadlines and estimates. Further, the assigning editor needs to maintain a positive working relationship with the author even if the editing work is being done by an out-of-house editor. She must keep the author informed about processes and deadlines, ensure the author is available to review edits and give a signoff, and also keep the author focused on the larger goals of the project—which might mean the editor is overseeing the writing of the next book while the current book makes its way through production.

Stylistic Editing

The Editors' Association of Canada explains the job of stylistic editing like this: "Clarifying meaning, eliminating jargon, smoothing language and other non-mechanical line-by-line editing." It deals with what in classical rhetoric is referred to as *elocutio*, or style of speech, encompassing the author's precision, clarity, appropriateness, and use of devices and ornamentation. The job of the stylistic editor, or line editor, is to produce a coherent, cohesive text that can be readily taken up by most readers, whether novices or experts. Good stylistic editing signals a willingness to communicate well and effectively.

Stylistic editing calls for a sensitivity to language that editor and writer Arthur Plotnik calls perception: "hearing what the author is trying to say while keeping an ear tuned to the sensibilities of the readers."

For me, choices that signal perceptiveness include text that reads well to the eye and on the lips, text that sounds pleasant to the ear, and text that is no longer than it needs to be. You'll notice here repeated references to the senses; we might distinguish between stylistic editing and copy-editing as the difference between editing for the ear and editing for the eye. Many editors will explain stylistic editing using terms like *voice, sound, rhythm,* and *music.* It is in this stage that the editor must particularly work to retain the author's "sound of self."

Stylistic editing generally requires some give and take. As Plotnik says, "The readers are served best when the editor has preserved the author's strengths and eliminated only the weaknesses in communication." Stand firm on your decisions where necessary, but be prepared to give elsewhere. Think of William Faulkner's advice to writers about killing their darlings—that is, that writers should be prepared to let go of their pet words, phrases, and writing devices. If the writer hasn't already done the dirty work, you are about to, and *perhaps* there are a few darlings you can spare. If you relax on elements of the text that are correct but not good, you'll have greater strength when you need to win a battle.

But at the same time, you must let the writer have her voice. Let unusual figures of speech, idiomatic usage, and stylistic tics stand unless they're plainly wrong. The work of the stylistic editor must be transparent: it's the writer who shines through the prose, not the editor. The editor mustn't drain the life from the text by forcing the author to adhere to some "objective" standard unless there's an overarching reason to do so. Assuming the prose is mechanically sound and basically comprehensible, you must let the writing speak for its writer. When you make a correction or a change, the writer retains the right to unmake it—that is, in the end, the writer has the right to be wrong. This is one of the most difficult lessons for editors to learn—and being closer to the production process than the author is, you may feel tempted to overrule her. Don't.

Sensibility redux: Editorial sensibility and stylistic editing

Any honest professional editor must acknowledge that stylistic editing—and for that matter even mechanical editing—involves a degree of subjectivity. Certainly editors generally agree about what's correct, some of us being more or less forceful about various stylistic hobgoblins than others, but every editor's sensibility influences how tightly or permissively she'll edit a text.

An editor's sensibility bears much in common with that of her editing peers and is always influenced by contextual considerations such as the author, the intended audience for the book, and general house practices. Even so, given the same text, three different editors would produce three different finished texts, and the differences might be striking.

Style manuals and professional standards provide a map, but ultimately it's the editor herself who moves through the terrain of the manuscript guided by her experience, sensibility, and instinct.

For instance, one editor may really dislike the use of *impact* as a verb and may change it to *affect* throughout the manuscript. Another editor might not be so sensitive to *impact* and therefore not make this change, but might be rigorous about removing split infinitives instead. One editor may have a relaxed sense of *they* used in contexts where a person's sex is indeterminate, whereas another editor may relentlessly recast such sentences to ensure *they* is never used this way. Are such decisions "right"? Only the readers can judge—and only in the context of the finished book.

The work of the line editor and copyeditor is to prepare the way for readers. As Leslie Sharpe and Irene Gunther observe, "A good editor remembers that he is a reader too. If a particular style or word usage bores or irritates him, it will probably do the same to the audience." But, Arthur Plotnik cautions, "Sometimes the author's voice is an integral part of a thought and must be preserved, even if it is loathsome to the editorial ear." I hope you don't find your authors' voices loathsome! But even if you do, keep Plotnik's advice in mind. Your editorial sensibility doesn't rule the project. A good book editor is able to work in many different idioms, with writers at various levels of their craft, with manuscripts the editor both loves and hates. We edit with both author and audience in mind.

EXAMINING YOUR SENSIBILITY
Think on your own or talk with a friend or colleague about your mutual formal or informal mechanical editing experiences. What did you concentrate on? Did you receive feedback after the job, and if so, about what? If you didn't receive feedback, what, if anything, were you concerned about? What makes mechanical editing easier? What makes it more difficult? What do you think you still need to learn?

What Is Copyediting?

At its most basic level, copyediting is mechanical editing. As the Editors' Association of Canada explains it, copyediting involves "Editing for grammar, spelling, punctuation and other mechanics of style" and "checking for consistency of mechanics and internal consistency of facts," among other points. It involves examining the manuscript as it stands, considering the work it's meant to do, and then making it the strongest possible tool to do that work. Copyediting involves much more than dotting i's and crossing t's, however. It's a sensitive act of caring for words and sentences—helping the reader and the writer meet in comprehension and trust.

Copyediting may be referred to as *line editing* (although, correctly used, that term in book editing refers to *stylistic editing*), or *text editing* (rather than *manuscript editing*, which is generally understood to refer to substantive editing). As I noted above, today copyediting increasingly fuses stylistic editing and mechanical editing, which once were distinct passes, into a single step in the editorial process. Because I've already discussed stylistic editing at a basic level in the previous section, in this section I'll discuss copyediting in much more detail, from time to time touching on both processes.

Careful copyediting removes ambiguity and produces credibility. Most readers can forgive a slip or two, but when a book contains a significant number of errors, readers notice and grow less willing to trust the author. Thorough copyediting should address the problems that interfere with reading and damage the reader's faith in the text.

Author and editor Arthur Plotnik calls the task of copyediting "functional compulsiveness." It is time-consuming, highly detailed work; it requires close attention to all areas of the manuscript. Whether we like to acknowledge it or not, there is a degree of subjectivity to mechanical editing, just as there is in substantive and stylistic editing. Most editors learn to copyedit by doing: by working with various kinds of text, by training with a more senior editor, and by trial and error with authors and audiences. Feedback is a big part of the learning process—and regrettably, sometimes that feedback means getting something wrong. For copyeditors, it's important to feel secure with what we know, but also to recognize what we don't know.

Copyediting Basics

Mechanical editing exists along five dimensions: *correctness, consistency, clarity, concision,* and *consideration.* Although correctness is often held up as the be-all and end-all of textual editing, a good copyeditor requires far more skills and sensitivity than rigid adherence to rules.

Manuscripts can be edited in a variety of ways. Some manuscripts need, or get, a "light" copyedit, ensuring that all words are spelled correctly, no words are missing, and the grammar and punctuation are sound, but not attending to issues of clarity or conciseness. (The "light" edit is a sour point today, in view of the "editors don't edit" debate.) Other manuscripts need a heavy edit, a copyedit so deep it verges on substantive editing. If you discover a manuscript requires work of this depth, contact the assigning editor; there may be a reason the manuscript exists in the state it does. Most manuscripts need a moderate edit, meaning that there are some typos, grammar errors, missing words, and other slips to catch, but the text does not require extensive rewriting or reorganization, and most of the text is clean and well composed. The editor is likely able to work through roughly six to eight pages in an hour of moderate editing. A heavier edit will obviously be slower; a light edit will be somewhat quicker. A thorough copyeditor can typically work through six to ten pages per hour, assuming 250 to 300 words per page. If you're getting through more than twelve pages in an hour, you may not be giving the text sufficient attention.

The copyeditor either takes her cue for the level of work to be done from the assigning editor or determines it based on a brisk read-through of the manuscript balanced against available time, the project budget, and the book's publication goals. And of course, the copyeditor's sensibility, or personal editorial style, overlays each level, meaning that one editor's "light" edit will likely not involve the same features as another editor's "light" edit.

When an editor talks about "clean" copy, she means that the text she has received contains few or no mechanical errors. It does not mean that she will not introduce other kinds of changes, however, such as the smoothing of phrases, the regularizing of various textual elements, and the elimination of redundancies and other minor infelicities. A copyeditor's best work is done invisibly, without drawing attention to itself, and the editor is most noticeable in her lapses. When copyediting has been done well, the author should feel the manuscript is precisely his own, polished to reflect exactly the light he wished to bring to his text.

Correctness

Correctness involves the mechanics of a document: grammar, syntax, punctuation, spelling, and conformity to a declared style (such as MLA or Canadian Press style). There are some common basic errors the copyeditor must be able to resolve: dangling or misplaced modifiers; unclear pronoun antecedents; faulty agreement between subject and verb; faulty parallelism; unintentional repetition; overuse of the author's "pet" words; inconsistent presentation of content such as dates, numbers, and abbreviations; and the careless introduction of jargon or specialized knowledge. (If you're uncertain about some of these concepts, consult appendix D for a quick refresher.)

For copyeditors, correctness may also encompass checking general-knowledge facts and observing concerns with names, dates, numbers, titles, quotations, descriptions, locations, and so on. (Specialized knowledge is the author's responsibility.) You may or may not have the authority to check these points. If you're the in-house editor, query the author.

If you're a freelance copyeditor, ask the assigning editor to confirm the level of detail she wants you to chase. Be especially cautious when working with unfamiliar content, unusual usage, and foreign words and phrases. In pursuit of correctness, your aim is not to prove how smart you are; rather, you want to act like a goaltender and save what could potentially be an embarrassing slip. The author is the expert, but you must be an informed reader.

It is the copyeditor's duty to be alert to anything odd or unusual in the text. Because copyeditors work at such a deep level of the text, they are the editors most likely to find irregularities in the presentation. Shifts in style or tone in a manuscript are not necessarily a problem, but they do require resolution. In the best case, such shifts may signal a long developmental period for the text; in the worst case, they may signal plagiarism. Shifts of argument or evidence, shifts in presentation, and unexpected omissions also deserve queries and extra editorial attention, and mean working deep in the text. If the text hasn't been through a substantive edit, the copyeditor may end up becoming a de facto substantive editor while also tackling stylistic and mechanical matters. In that case, completeness—matters of substance—ends up being bolted on to correctness. Has the author given readers all they need? What's missing? Is the argument logical? If there's a reference to a table or an image, does the table or image exist—is there at least a callout for it to exist? Asking and answering questions like this will slow down any copyeditor.

Consistency

Copyeditors create consistency by following and applying standard choices to text on points such as spelling, the treatment of numbers, heading styles (e.g., SENTENCE CASE or TITLE CASE), the use of punctuation, and other mechanical matters. Some projects come with mechanical and stylistic requirements already in place, such as a project dictionary and a project style manual. In other cases, you will have to select these elements based on your knowledge of both the manuscript's content and appropriate dictionaries, style manuals, and other resources. All editors should be more than passingly familiar with several style manuals and their application—and for book editors, knowing *The Chicago Manual of Style* well is essential. (If you don't know much about style manuals, appendix E contains a list of some of the most common options.)

In addition to following the style manual, copyeditors also build style sheets—running lists of the decisions they make—customized for each project they work on. Style sheets help editors and editorial teams bring consistency and congruence to the text; see the section starting page 162 for more detail.

Clarity

Clarity can be difficult to achieve because what is "clear" often depends on the audience and the purpose of the communication. Yet when prose is clear, the narrative or argument shines brilliantly. In his book *Style: Ten Lessons in Clarity and Grace*, rhetorician Joseph Williams observes that a reader knows, in a way that the writer herself can never know, what it feels like to read the writer's ideas. Writers usually know what they intend to mean, but only readers know what a passage actually means—that is, how it is received. A copyeditor has the same experience. For authors, the copyeditor's feedback on clarity is vital because it is likely to be echoed by future readers.

As the copyeditor, you are responsible for making the document as clear as possible. But when you are editing specialized content, you'll discover an ineffable quality of language: "as you try to write in a way people understand it moves away from accuracy, and as it moves very close to accuracy it becomes unintelligible," says Dr John Hoey, former editor of the *Canadian Medical Association Journal*. Clarity cannot be considered in isolation, but rather must be evaluated in concert with the author's intended audience and the text's purpose.

Concision

One of most important qualities of writing in our text-saturated world is concision. Think of all the reading you do each day. Have you ever felt alienated by a writer's vocabulary? Frustrated by a writer's acrobatic presentation? Annoyed by a writer's assumptions? Distracted by digressions before the author introduces a substantial idea? These responses underline why it is so important for authors to be concise.

Concision refers to the "short and sweet" of editing: the right number of words to express a thought. This is the principle evoked when we think of the editor slashing recklessly through prose, but remember that shorter is not always better. Concision refers not necessarily to the fewest number of words but to the *best* use of words.

There are many ways to effect concision at the level of word and phrase: using the active voice, deleting words that don't contribute to the sentence or the idea, deleting redundant expressions, replacing phrases with single words, and eliminating nominalizations. At the level of phrases and sentences, keep an eye out for metadiscourse, or throat-clearing; announcements of topic and argument ("Next I will discuss ...," "Now I will prove ..."); attributions to non-existent sources ("It has been said that ... "); and hedging and intensifying (*really*, *very*, *quite*, *almost*). Once you start to look for opportunities to distill prose, concision becomes easy.

Consideration

Consideration, and courtesy, is what both writer and editor owe to the reader. Who will be reading the book and under what conditions? What expectations or conventions surround the reading experience? Think about the books you encounter in your daily life. Some of them are written to be read front to back, as a continuous text; others are written as references, to be consulted as needed. Lengthy or gratuitously complex prose may be the feature that keeps a reader from sticking with or turning to a book as a trusted resource.

To edit with consideration and courtesy means bringing empathy to your editing. Remember both that someone is destined to read the words you're so carefully sculpting and that those words were composed by someone more or less invested in their success. Never let the author talk down to readers, but equally do not let the author assume that the reader has all the writer's knowledge. As an editor, your job is to help the writer become a better communicator. Anyone can fix mechanical errors, but only the writer knows the message she really meant to express; as the copyeditor, you want to become an ally in expressing that message.

Copyediting Process and Method

A copyedit is performed on text prior to layout. The copyeditor works through the text word by word, phrase by phrase, examining mechanical matters for correctness, consistency, clarity, concision, and consideration. Such close work normally requires two or three passes through the text.

As the editor starts the copyedit (or else immediately after concluding it), she runs searches on the digital file for global mechanical matters such as removing double spaces and extra hard returns; checking hyphens, en dashes, and em dashes; and eliminating paragraph indents and extra spaces after paragraphs. Some editors will also regularize certain spellings (such as *colour*, *labour*, and *neighbour*) and remove common tautologies (such as *period of time* or *personal opinion*). These sorts of global changes are normally made without tracking, often called *working silently*. All other changes on the digital file should be tracked unless the assigning editor or author has agreed otherwise.

Although virtually all copyeditors work with digital text, many still elect to do the copyedit on paper. In this case, the first pass may occur when the copyeditor performs a spell check and runs global searches. This pass will often reveal problems to anticipate in subsequent passes, such as mechanical inconsistencies, proper nouns that require attention, and stylistic quirks such as the frequent use of unintentional fragments or extra-long sentences. The second pass occurs as the editor slowly works through the manuscript on paper. The third pass occurs as she enters her marked-up changes into the digital file and reads through to confirm that changes are sensible and appropriate.

You may be surprised that book editors often still work on paper. Don't be: it's logical. Many editors recommend that we edit in the format readers will consume the text; in the case of books, that's ink on paper, for the majority of books. Editing on paper also mimics the flippable, manipulable nature of the physical book better than the screen does. Experienced editors consistently say they catch more errors on paper than they do on-screen. Some editors balk at the expense of printing out and shipping a book-length manuscript, or have environmental concerns about using so much paper. Build the cost of paper, toner, and shipping into your bids, use both sides of the printed sheet, and recycle all printouts when the edit is complete. Remember that you can scan your markup and create a PDF as a backup or to transmit to your client, if necessary.

If you're marking up on paper, remember that neatness counts in editing. You must be able to use and read conventional markup symbols, particularly if you won't be entering your own changes to the digital file. (If you're unfamiliar with markup symbols, see appendix C for examples of the common symbols and their use. *Every* editor should learn and use markup symbols: they are a shorthand that makes communication within our field easy and consistent.) The copyediting symbols are fairly standard, but each editor has a particular way of making them, like handwriting. In copyediting, markup symbols are made from the bottom of the line into the line. Directions (e.g., run in) are circled. Text to be inserted is not circled but is written neatly in the interline space above the insertion point (or in the margin or on the reverse side of the sheet, if the added text is long; attach an additional sheet if necessary). Don't obscure text when you delete it; there is no need to cross out and obliterate. You'll be glad you have tidy markup habits when you have to insert your own changes and when you're working with clients who are not editors.

Editing on-screen may be slower or faster than editing on paper. Copyediting on-screen tends to be quicker but tends to make proofreading take longer because the copyeditor may catch fewer errors. Editing on-screen enables quick global changes, but may obscure other areas of the manuscript that are inconsistent or uneven. It is *never* sufficient to run a spell check, a grammar check, and some standard global search-and-replace strings in lieu of a thorough copyedit; regrettably, this may be all the copyediting some manuscripts receive.

However it occurs, the copyedit should follow an agreed-upon protocol. The assigning editor should communicate her expectations, but you may need to establish rules with non-publishing clients. If you use Track Changes, be clear where changes were not tracked. If you edit on paper, someone—perhaps you, perhaps another editor or editorial assistant—will transfer your markup to the digital file. Mark up tidily and use ink or a dark pencil that will stand up to photocopying. It's also a good idea to keep a clean copy of the manuscript in case your markup gets complicated or messy. Apply good judgement to your markup: if the person who will be making the changes (assuming you're not doing it yourself) will not understand markup symbols, use marginal instructions extensively to communicate. Always try to check the marked-up changes against the edited file to ensure that everything that has been called for has been caught—and to ensure that you haven't missed anything.

Again, the editor should plan to go through the manuscript three times: once quickly and superficially, like triage, to get a sense of the text and its needs; a second time slowly and carefully, at the level of word and phrase; and a third time to check her own edits, to confirm that her changes are correct and clear, and to catch any lingering gremlins. Practically speaking, today it's unlikely that the editor can go through a text more than twice; but if nothing else, she should ensure that the edits she's called for have been entered correctly and work as she planned.

The Editors' Association of Canada observes that some factors make copyediting easier, some more difficult. If you're working on a badly formatted manuscript, particularly one with many auto-applied styles, the work may be slow. (This is one reason a project editor should prepare the manuscript file for the copyeditor in advance.) Editing text that contains a large number of tables, figures, or cross-references will also be slow, as may be editing highly technical or unfamiliar content. Working with a first-time author often requires extra effort, as can working with a writer whose first language is not English, if you're trying to regularize phrasing and idiom for your audience. Of course, in both cases, let the manuscript itself be your guide: there is no reason to assume a non-native English speaker or a first-time author will produce a manuscript that needs extra attention. I've worked with first-time authors whose manuscripts have been conscientiously prepared and exquisitely polished, and with non-native English speakers whose grammar and style were impeccable; equally I've worked with experienced, native-English-speaking authors whose manuscripts were incomplete and sloppily prepared (but only a very small number of these, thankfully).

Working on a manuscript written in a distinctive but unconventional style will also slow you down until you work out the internal logic of the text. Finally, editing text written by multiple authors, or a manuscript that covers multiple subjects, will require extra effort to unify the treatment, voice, and presentation. One factor that particularly complicates copyediting is working with unclear or incomplete direction. Regrettably, this is not an uncommon experience for freelance editors: sometimes the assigning editor fails to provide sufficient direction about the depth of the edit expected, the style to follow, or the scope of the freelancer's authority to make changes. The hesitation and uncertainty generated by an ambiguous assignment wastes time, money, and good will on both sides. For the sake of good relationships, it's important for freelancers to ask questions until they feel confident about the assigning editor's expectations, and equally it's important for assigning editors to provide freelancers clear, complete, and unambiguous directions. Obviously, having clear project guidelines and agreement on the level and kind of work to be done makes both the textual editing and the process better overall. It's particularly important for freelancers to understand that our opinion of the work to be done must be tempered by the assigning editor's opinion of the work to be done; when freelancer and assigning editor don't see eye to eye, the freelancer needs to be judicious and smart.

It's easy to do a disservice to writers—and readers—by being either too timid or too aggressive. "Push the red pen firmly" is advice you'll hear in many editing seminars; it means be confident, but not abrasive, about your choices. Copyeditors are paid for their expertise, so they must bring that expertise to the task. Throughout the process, the copyeditor must know when to speak to the author, when to consult another professional, and when to trust herself. An editor strives for excellence, but must balance excellence against time and resources—which is to say, the editor must know when to stop. Some texts will only ever be correct, never good, and that's acceptable.

Something many novice editors—and even experienced authors—do not recognize is that some errors may remain in the text at the end of the copyedit. The copyeditor may have missed one slip while in pursuit of another, or may have introduced an error in the process of making changes. That's why the process of textual editing isn't finished yet. The next step is for the text to be formatted, followed by thorough and rigorous proofreading.

Queries in Copyediting

In the context of copyediting, *queries* refer to questions the editor directs to the writer, just as in substantive editing. The principle behind queries to the author is *tact*: address your queries clearly, concisely, and respectfully. I shouldn't need to mention this point, but NEVER embarrass an author with a query. Do not try to show off how much you know or how well you can argue; query only to let the author know about a relevant concern with the text. As a good guideline, ask yourself what the reader might wonder about. If the reader might wonder, you should wonder. Query the author for clarification.

When you query, either provide a clear direction (e.g., *rewrite, add, check, resolve*) or offer a solution the author can accept (e.g., "Try rephrasing like this ... "). Always have a sense of which queries must be addressed and which are less critical—that is, that won't hurt the quality of the book if the author elects not to act on them. You want to retain as many opportunities as possible to say yes to the author, places where you're willing and able to be flexible. That way, you have more strength when you must say no to something—and sometimes you must say no.

In chapter 5, I talked about the so-called shit sandwich. The same idea applies to good query technique. If your criticism is major (or might be understood to be major), praise some aspect of the text before you criticize it. Call for changes only in the interests of the project, not to reflect your tastes or needs. Phrase your queries carefully; use softening words and offer suggestions and options (such as *may, might, perhaps, in my view, sometimes, seems, please, OK*), but don't simply fall back on *I think* or *I feel* if you can't clearly justify your suggestion. When it's possible, offer an alternative, especially if you're suggesting a major change.

If you're the assigning editor, you have a relationship with the author to fall back on; the author will likely trust you and take the best from your questions. Freelance copyeditors rarely have such trusting relationships with authors. Regardless, it never hurts to be both firm and kind when you have the option. Arthur Plotnik is instructive on this point: "An author's greatest fear is to appear, as a result of revision, less than brilliant. The good editor convinces authors that *without* revision their genius will be obscured."

Writing and Rewriting

Something many writers don't recognize, but should, is that copyeditors need to be more-than-competent writers (although not necessarily flashy or stylish writers). Copyeditors, particularly those working in-house, may be called on to produce all kinds of incidental copy, such as abstracts and summaries, acknowledgements, authors' biographies, descriptive copy, and image captions. A degree of recasting and rephrasing—and in some cases, rewriting—also falls within a copyeditor's purview. Some of this writing is ordinary, such as solving awkward agreement issues, shifting from unnecessary passive constructions to active voice, and transitioning from one paragraph to the next. Some of it is more extensive, though, and may put the copyeditor on slippery ground with authors.

Some editing jobs involve considerably more rewriting than others. For instance, an editor working at a small regional press with a program strong in natural history and gardening might find herself composing sentences from the point form information provided by subject-matter experts because the experts can't be bothered with "all the grammar" or "don't have time" to do the actual writing. Editors working with writers who do not write as a primary job, or who have largely lost their sense of style after years of opaque institutional writing, may need to coach these authors to find and trust their authorial voices. Other authors, though brilliant thinkers, cannot find the simplest, clearest way to express themselves. For these authors, corralling the content is as much as they can do. In such cases, the stylistic editor or copyeditor may become the de facto "writer" on the project.

Editor and instructor Ruth Wilson advises that if a copyediting job seems to require an unusual amount of rewriting, alert the assigning editor. Rewriting, particularly if it involves reorganizing structure or rethinking presentation, may quickly trespass on substantive editing. If that's not what the assigning editor requested, you must confirm that the editor understands the issue, agrees with your solution, and is willing to adjust the schedule—and presumably the budget—to accommodate the work.

Once you have the assigning editor's approval, you have two possible work paths. You can identify the material that requires rewriting, determine how best it could be reworked, and then send it back to the author. In many kinds of book editing, this is the preferred course. If you take this route, be prepared that you may need to invest considerable time coaching the author to produce what you want—and you may meet considerable resistance. After all, if the author could do the work easily, you probably wouldn't be calling for a rewrite in the first place. Your other option may be to undertake the rewriting yourself, based on the materials provided. (If you charge a higher rate for writing than for editing, confirm that the assigning editor knows that and will pay your invoice.) If you undertake the writing yourself, you face a few potential risks. First, you may go too far with your revision before you contact the client. Work on a small portion of the text and then have the editor or author review it. If author or editor has suggestions or concerns, pay close attention to the feedback and figure out how to accommodate it. Many writers would rather do their own rewrites than have the editor do them. Don't assume the author is happy to let you rewrite; check explicitly.

Another risk is that you'll squeeze the life out of the author's project, the author's words. The best part of writing is style; no one enjoys reading text with the colour and consistency of paste. Even if you dislike it, you must maintain the author's voice and style as best you can, particularly the quirks and flashes that signal personality. A writer's style is transmitted even in minute choices, so try to retain these unique glimmers through the editing process whenever you can. When you solicit feedback from the editor or author, ask specifically about voice and style.

Finally, it's easy to misunderstand the value or purpose of a project. You might be agonizing over the author's awkward prose or abstract, artful language and miss the fact that the author's text is only the supporting tissue in a book that is largely factual, visual, or ephemeral. Before you dive into rewriting, ensure the effort is appropriate to the goal. And of course, when you must create new copy for whatever reason, work through your own sentences at least as critically as you did the author's original writing.

Style Sheets: An Editor's Control Systems

A style sheet is a project-specific list of decisions the copyeditor makes as she works through a manuscript. Its purpose is to capture every mechanical decision you make for consistency, such as the presence or absence of the series comma, how dashes are treated, how numbers are handled, and how dates are formatted. It also captures author spellings that you change to conform to the project dictionary. The style sheet includes any unusual spelling or usage choices, once you have determined they are deliberate and consistent, as well as your decisions whenever the text is inconsistent. You should also record proper names, especially if they have unusual features, and any compounds or acronyms specific to the project. In general, note the manuscript page number on which the first instance of the name, compound, or acronym occurs.

It's important to know what to record on a style sheet if you haven't used one before. Start by writing down the project dictionary and project style manual. These documents are part of the overall stylistic presentation of the manuscript and form the foundation of the style sheet. Even if the author has followed a discipline-based style manual, such as Canadian Press or MLA style, house style or publication styling may create exceptions or issues. Rather than check these deviations every time, add them to the style sheet.

The style sheet is meant to be a tool that makes your work easier and more efficient. If the project dictionary or style manual dictates a point you may have trouble remembering, note it on the style sheet rather than looking it up repeatedly. Also note your definitive decision when the style guide permits a choice and the text is inconsistent, as well as for any non-standard decision you make to support the aims of a particular manuscript.

There are several ways to create a style sheet. Alphabet boxes are a common format. In this kind of style sheet, one or two sides of a piece of a paper are broken into boxes, each box identified by a range of letters or other descriptor. Stylistic and mechanical decisions are recorded in the box under the appropriate headings; see Figure 7.1 for an example.

AB	CD
EF	GHI
JK	LM
NO	PQR
ST	UV
WX	YZ
PUNCTUATION, MECHANICS	OTHER

Figure 7.1 Alphabet boxes are a common format for style sheets.

STYLE SHEET: STUDENT REFUGEES AND SCHOOLING
—spelling follows *Canadian Oxford Dictionary*, mechanical style follows APA, publication styling follows CMS

Terms, Spelling, Usage

anti-colonial theory

art-making

audiotape (N or V)

backyard (closed)

behaviour

biracial (no hyphen)

capacity building

caregiver, caregiving

centre

child care (hyphenated as prenominal adjective)

co-operate, co-operative

coordinator

counselling, counsellor

data: treated as singular rather than plural

e-learning

email

ethno-cultural

Eurocentric

first-hand

focus, focuses, focusing

frontline (adj)

geopolitical

health care (open in most adjectival compounds)

high-rise (N)

homeland

instill

interracial

judgement (note e)

labelled, labelling

labourer

lifelines

lifespan

map-maker, map-making

migrant-worker families

modelled, modelling

mortarboard (closed)

multicultural (no hyphen)

Multicultural Act (caps, roman)

multi-dimensional

multi-ethnic (hyphen)

multi-faceted

multilingual (no hyphen)

multiliteracy, multiliteracies (no hyphen)

multiracial (no hyphen)

multivocal (no hyphen)

non-medical

non-verbal

okay

ongoing

participant-observer

person-centred care

place-identity

policy-maker

post-secondary

post-traumatic stress disorder (note lc)

practice (N), practise (V and verbals)

preclinical

pre-departure orientations

pre-existing

preschool

prescreening

preventive (NOT preventative)

prioritize

program, programs

pro-social

psychosocial

RCMP (no points)

Figure 7.2 Sample style sheet using a running-file format (page 1 of 2)

school-readiness (adj; open when nom
    phrase)
schoolyard
self-care
settlement workers (lc)
socio-cultural
socio-cultural–historical (note hyphen,
    en dash)
socio-economic
socio-political
speech-language pathologist
storyline
storyteller, storytelling
T-shirt (uc)
tape-record (V)
time frame (open)
toward (not towards)
transnational
travelling, travelled
underemployed, underemployment
underuse, underused
US (but prefer United States)
videotape, videotaping
well-being
Western (in reference to the US, Canada,
    western Europe)
workshop (all forms)
X-ray

Mechanics

series comma in
em dashes set close
ellipses set off for treatment in design: ...
no period after chapter number in ToC
lc after colon
all headings are in title case,
    distinguished by format
captions: "Title of Work"; credit to ...
    (no end punctuation); if caption is
    discursive, end punctuation may
    appear
grades: spelled out, lc
no periods in academic and professional
    designations (per CMS), e.g., PhD,
    MD
no hyphen in -ly compounds (e.g.,
    culturally sensitive)

Proper Names

Adrienne Chui (Crown Prosecutor)
American Medical Student Association
Nichole Condé (note h in Nichole)
Foothills Medical Centre
Herman Gray
Andrea-Jane Latourneau (Red Cross PR)
Su Cheung De
UNHCR (AKA the Office of the United
    Nations High Commissioner for
    Refugees, the UN Refugee Agency)
Lucas van Leyden (lc on van)
—in contributors' bios, contributors
are usually referred to by **first name** on
second and subsequent reference, if not
by pronoun or as "Dr."

Figure 7.2 Sample style sheet using a running-file format (page 2 of 2)

Another format involves index cards. Index cards are less common today than they once were, but can be handy for manuscripts that contain numerous proper names, especially if any of the names are unusual. A stylistic or mechanical decision is recorded on each card, usually with a manuscript page number for the first instance of the decision. The cards are kept in logical order and may later be used to compile the index.

The most common way to create a style sheet today is to maintain a running file, a word-processing file that is open alongside the manuscript document file. Items are added to the running file as the editor makes stylistic and mechanical decisions. The example style sheet in Figure 7.2. shows what a finished running-file style sheet might look like.

FOCUS ON STYLE

Look carefully at the items listed on the style sheet in Figure 7.2. Did the style sheet make sense to you? Which items that the editor listed seem obvious to you? Which items surprise you? Do you think working with a style sheet would help or hinder you? If you've worked with a style sheet before, what was your experience?

Find something you have written in the last year (such as an essay, a long email or a series of messages, or a report for work). Treat this text as your source manuscript. Based on the choices you made in the source manuscript, create a personal style sheet. It's fine if you were consistent in the manuscript itself; think about how you might have styled words or mechanics differently. Your style sheet should contain at least fifteen items, including notes on forms to avoid, if necessary. When you have compiled your style sheet, do some reflection. What do you notice about your own style?

Transmittal Letters

As I explained in chapter 6, a transmittal letter summarizes the process of the edit. A transmittal letter sent at the conclusion of the copyedit should highlight any decision making that was generally applied (e.g., "I changed any lingering past-tense references to present tense") and point out any areas that caused difficulty or that need further attention. Importantly, it does not review every change and every mark. You have been hired as a copyeditor to do specific work and are assumed to be an expert in it, so don't cast doubt on the work you've been hired to do. If you've tracked changes on the manuscript, the assigning editor or client can follow the specifics of the edit anyway.

If the copyedit has generated queries, you might list them in the transmittal letter, if there aren't too many, or you can summarize the kinds of queries the author should anticipate. If you've used the Comments tool to insert queries in the manuscript itself or written them directly on the printed manuscript, the author will be able to address them individually. If you need the author to take further action on the manuscript, make your expectations clear in the letter (e.g., "Please return the rewritten paragraphs before the end of November").

Some freelance copyeditors like to offer further comments or observations on the project, such as pointing out a strong copy line for the book cover, suggesting a likely blurber, or offering a solution for a potential layout problem. If you think these comments will be welcome and useful, and you have a receptive assigning editor, go ahead and make them. But do not invest *extra* (i.e., billable) time in coming up with such suggestions unless you've been asked to do so specifically.

As with queries, build your transmittal letter by offering praise before criticism. If you have genuine concerns, particularly legal concerns, express them; but if the project, the style, or the presentation simply isn't to your taste, keep that to yourself. A transmittal letter should be friendly, enthusiastic, and approachable—it's as much about your soft skills as your technical skills. Always invite questions or feedback, and offer your sincere thanks for the opportunity (if you're a freelancer) or your encouragement to the author (if you're an in-house staffer).

In Figure 7.3 you see a sample transmittal letter from a freelance editor. This letter is addressed to the author but was copied to the assigning editor and the book designer so everyone involved in the process can follow the events of the edit. In this case, the freelancer is well known to the firm, so the letter is fairly casual; it could easily be more formal. Note that the editor has gone beyond the work of a typical copyedit and made two structural changes to the manuscript. From her prior work, the freelancer has established that the assigning editor trusts her judgement and will support her suggestions. It would not be prudent to take such a leap the first time a freelancer works with a client.

Once the author has reviewed the copyedit, addressed any queries, and made any last changes, the manuscript is effectively final. At this point, the book editor or project editor may require a formal signoff from the author; at some firms, the submission of the final file may stand in lieu of a written signoff. The digital text can now be sent to the art department for layout.

In chapter 8, we will discuss some of the processes editors need to understand about design, layout, and production. But for our purposes in this chapter, the next stage in mechanical editing occurs when there are pages to proofread. Once again, I have positioned the proofreader as a freelancer from outside the firm, being overseen by an assigning editor.

Copyedit of your manuscript   _ ☑ ✕

To   Shazia Rham   **Bcc**

Cc   Ella Phont, Ty Tschip

Subject Copyedit of your manuscript

Dear Shazia,

Shazia, hello! I want to let you know how much I've enjoyed copyediting your manuscript. I can't wait to see it with the images in place. It's going to be spectacular!

This letter is a quick overview of my editorial process. I used Track Changes most of the time, although I turned it off when making mechanical changes like turning hyphens into en dashes, removing double spaces, etc. I've also attached a style sheet that should show you much of my process. When I deviated from a spelling you had used, for instance, I made a note on the style sheet. The style sheet also reminds me about consistent choices you made that were outside my resources (e.g., the pinyin spellings).

I've made two significant changes, both having to do with the physical presentation of the text: a re-ordering of the front matter and a shifting of notes.

I followed *The Chicago Manual of Style* directions for ordering the front matter. This choice does make the list of works exhibited appear a little more prominent than it might otherwise (you'll also note that I took the italics off these works; I can restore them if you wish), but I think Ella Phont's layout should make the list less prominent again. Please let me know what you think. I hope there are no other concerns with the front matter.

I hope the switch of the footnotes to endnotes is not a concern, although I recognize that it is a more significant change. I consulted with Ella about this decision before I made it, and would have consulted with you too except that our time is getting so tight and I didn't know your travel schedule. What informed the decision Ella and I came to was that the footnotes were of varying lengths—some quite long—and were both discursive and bibliographic. Ella feels the design will look better on the page with the notes collected at the end, and I feel readers who need the notes will be better served by their collection in a single place. To emphasize that there are endnotes, I have added a pointer in the table of contents. Again, please let me know what you think. More importantly, if this is a major concern, let me know right away so I can fix the text over the weekend and re-submit it to Ella, so we don't lose time in layout.

Thank you for forwarding the comments from Björn Anderrson. I have made his proofreading catches where he identified something that was obviously wrong. Where I felt a change Björn suggested made the text clearer, I have made the change and am grateful for his help. Where I felt a change Björn suggested was a matter of authorial voice, though, I have not made the change. I would ask you to take a close look at these spots (there aren't many) to ensure you agree with my sense of your authorial voice.

Do you want to add Björn to the acknowledgements? I have not done so on your behalf; perhaps Björn could be acknowledged on the copyright page, if you are comfortable with that. I have added credit lines for myself and for Ella Phont there. Is there anyone else who should receive a credit line, or be added to the acknowledgements?

That's pretty much it. Again, I've enjoyed working on this project and am looking forward to seeing the proofs—and a finished book not too long from now. Please don't hesitate to let me know if you have any questions about my work on the text. Thanks and best wishes!

Ann Editor
AFM Editing Services

Figure 7.3 Sample transmittal letter

What Is Proofreading?

Proofreading refers to a close read-through to confirm that the text of a book will appear as intended. Proofreading is not the kind of reading we do every day; rather, it involves examining words letter by letter, then assembling those words into units of meaning. While you may encounter proofreading errors in your everyday reading, the process of proofreading is different. This work requires that you be slow, calm, and methodical.

Proofreaders, like indexers, are specialized editors, and not every editor is a good proofreader. Proofreading requires a specific mindset. The proofreader reads one word at a time, one line at a time. In book production, the proofreader reads for several levels of concern: spelling, punctuation, grammar, sense, and production matters. The proofreader's job is to correct misspellings, correct any faulty grammar and mechanics, ensure consistency, note or correct deviations from visual specifications, and catch any other glaring errors. Unless the proofreader has been given explicit permission to work deeper, she queries anything else. The proofreader is not the author and is not the copyeditor; she is a backup for both.

Proofreading happens late in the production process. The pages you are working on are composed, or laid out; the next stage, after the proofreading changes are made, is printing. Thus changes at this stage are disruptive and generally costly. Proofreading is not the stage at which to second-guess the work of an earlier editor—for instance, the copyeditor. You may not like what the earlier editor has done or has left standing, but, assuming the point is not an outright error, you cannot overrule it. If you have real doubts about a point, ask the assigning editor. Never assume that an editing decision was careless or thoughtless.

Proofreaders must know and respect three boundaries: authority, time, and style. Authority is serious: the assigning editor grants only so much authority to the proofreader. Remember, earlier editors have a longer view of the project and know why certain decisions have been made, and also why certain steps cannot be taken. It's the proofreader's job to bring the text *as it stands* as close to perfect as possible, not to fix the text to her own tastes or remake the text to her own preferences.

Time and respect for its limitations are critical in proofreading. If you agree to a due date or deadline, you cannot miss it. Even if the assigning editor wants to give the proofreader more time, other pressures, such as a looming press date, can turn a late submission into a big problem. It's also important to recognize that time is usually related to money: if you spend more time on the job than was budgeted, you're likely also invoicing more for the job than was budgeted. At this stage in book production, the proofreader can do only so much.

Finally, house style, the project dictionary, and the copyeditor's style sheet are central to the process. The proofreader's role is to apply conformity to decisions that have already been made and to ensure the correctness of the various aspects of the text. The style may not be one you like, but as proofreader, your job is to apply it correctly and consistently.

What these boundaries mean in a practical sense is that the proofreader must negotiate among competing interests: time available versus the rigour of the work, or time versus consistency, or rigour versus type of text. For example, a publisher will be more concerned with errors in a textbook than with errors in a marketing mailer, although in an ideal world there would be no errors in either document. In book publishing, our deadlines are usually much more relaxed than those in magazines or newspapers, so negotiations among competing interests shouldn't produce conflict very often. If you find yourself wondering which compromises to make, talk to the assigning editor or your publisher. As a guideline, consider that the best proofreaders find every error within their authority and don't waste time or money with unnecessary queries.

> **PROOFREADING IN THE WORLD AT LARGE**
> Find three examples of proofreading errors from writing published
> in print or online (from a major website, not a personal site or a blog)
> within the last twelve months. Analyze each error—what is the problem?
> Provide a correction. Then suggest some strategies to help proofreaders
> catch similar kinds of mistakes in the future, such as a simple memory
> trick, or propose a way to anticipate this kind of mistake.

Soft proofing

Historically, proofreaders checked proofs on printed pages, but SOFT PROOFING is becoming popular. Soft proofing refers to reviewing and marking up PDFs rather than printed pages; there are obviously some cost savings associated with soft proofing, particularly with respect to shipping manuscripts across a distance. Some editors are well accustomed to soft proofing, but for book-length projects, I strongly recommend proofreading on paper. Remember that the proof will be going to back to a designer or layout technician, so be sure to mark up cleanly, clearly, and consistently.

Proofreading as Process

Proofreading is extremely detail-oriented work; expect to consult resources and to keep a style sheet (in addition to the style sheet you should have received with the project). One of the areas where novice proofreaders go wrong is in assuming they have all the resources they need in their heads. The sidebar Tools for Proofreading provides a list of tools and resources you should have available when you're proofreading.

Yet, contrarily, while proofreading is detailed work, it is also in a sense superficial work. While you must expect to find errors, you should assume that most of the text is final. You are not re-editing the text.

TOOLS FOR PROOFREADING

You might not need all of these tools for every manuscript, but it's good to have them on hand.

- good light and a quiet space
- an eye guide (a straight edge: a ruler or an index card works well)
- bright ink pens: red, light green, pink, purple, light blue (never mark up in pencil, and avoid black and dark-blue inks)
- correction fluid
- the project dictionary (if possible, own several; use the dictionary assigned for the project)
- the project style guide (if no manual has been assigned, choose an appropriate guide but refer to it only to resolve inconsistencies; keep a running style sheet)
- language resources (grammar books, punctuation manuals, usage guides, etc.)
- an atlas, an almanac, a desk encyclopedia, and other specific references pertinent to the text
- a current calendar
- a PICA ruler (for measuring line lengths and character heights)
- a calculator
- a scratch pad (for testing corrections before you commit them to the proof pages)

The proofreader must work at an appropriate level for the situation. Proofreading isn't copyediting. If you're working at the level of phrases and sentences, you're working too deep—you're not proofreading. And obviously, proofreading does not involve rewriting or restructuring, except in rare circumstances. If you're making major changes at this stage, you will need to proofread again later.

The reality at small firms, of course, is not so straightforward. In a small publishing house, it is entirely possible that the proofreader was the copyeditor, and time pressures may mean that the editor rushed or compromised at an earlier stage. Enough time must have passed for the proofreader to have forgotten the text if she hopes to do a good job of finding lingering errors, and she needs enough time to do a thorough job on the proofread if she had to skimp on earlier steps. If you're in this situation, give the author extra time to proofread, compare your catches and the author's catches carefully, and pay particular attention to the weak spots listed in the sidebar Typical Weak Areas for Extra Attention.

One of the reasons authors may not be the best proofreaders of their own work is purely psychological. For our own sense of self, we expect not to see errors; we tend to read past errors and see instead what we expect to read. The same psychology applies to the editor who copyedited the text. An objective proofreader who is expecting to find mistakes is crucial to rooting out lingering errors. In high-stakes situations, where accuracy is paramount, a book may need two proofreaders (in addition to the author); three is even better if time and resources permit.

TYPICAL WEAK AREAS FOR EXTRA ATTENTION

Certain elements of a book tend to require extra attention. These areas should be proofread at least twice, even three times. An extra set of eyes is valuable for this work. Remember to work calmly, slowly, and methodically.

- Pay particular attention to proper names and to strings of small words.
- Check titles and subtitles, heads and subheads.
- Compare the chapter title to the running heads or footers, chapter by chapter, section by section.
- Be alert to any text that incorporates numerals, including the front matter (e.g., phone numbers, addresses, edition numbers).
- Look at the first few paragraphs after a head or subhead; the last few paragraphs before a chapter or section break; and the front matter (particularly the paratext).
- Watch out for pages containing a small amount of text, and be cautious at any place the type changes.
- Be aware that production processes can delete or duplicate text— watch for abrupt, nonsensical shifts in the text.
- Read the title on the cover character by character, word by word: it's easy to perceive words on the cover as graphic content rather than as words.
- Scrutinize all late corrections; never assume *standing copy* is correct as supplied. (Standing copy refers to text that has been repurposed from another situation, such as the boilerplate text from a copyright page or a previously published list of your firm's top sellers.)

Never assume that the body is the most important part of the book for proofreading. Front and back matters need rigorous attention, too.

I cannot overemphasize the need for slow, calm attention to the page. Proofreading is slow work: you must examine every character and element, and your care and attention must persist. Depending on the size of the page and the complexity of the composition, expect to be able to proofread eight to twelve pages per hour. You may be able to work faster if you're planning multiple passes for certain materials. You cannot get bored halfway through the job—although frankly, that sometimes happens. There is a well-worn belief in publishing that at about page forty in a book, you'll start to notice an increase in the number of errors, presumably because the editor's focus diminishes at roughly this point. Take heed and beware!

Proofreading method

As a basic method, plan three major "sweeps" through the text, working at a different level each time.

1. **The scan:** On this sweep, you evaluate the level of work likely needed and the type of copy involved. Identify any obvious problems or concerns, and note any areas that will require special attention.
2. **The particular read:** On this sweep, you read carefully, letter by letter, for spelling, punctuation, grammar, usage, meaning, accuracy, and visual presentation. Make repeated passes through the text as required, focusing on different elements each time. For example, read all the chapter opening pages one after another to compare their formatting, or read all the running heads in a single pass to ensure they are all correct and consistently formatted.
3. **The review:** On this sweep, you adopt a scattershot or snapshot method. Let your eyes roam around the pages randomly. Sometimes an error will pop out at a glance, even though you haven't seen it before. This seems to be how proofreading misses reveal themselves *after* the book is printed!

On most books, multiple passes will be necessary. Multiple passes are not a waste of your time. On each pass, you concentrate on a specific element, such as the running heads, the footers, the captions, the cross-references to back matters, and so on. Don't assume you can give equal attention to every element when you look at the whole page at once. It's a smart idea to proofread similar materials together for the sake of consistency, such as proofreading all the footers side by side, one after the other. Then read the whole document through continuously for correctness and coherence.

The style sheet is a control mechanism for ensuring that an editor applies consistent choices to a manuscript. When you receive a manuscript to proofread, the assigning editor should provide a copy of the project style sheet. If for some reason you don't receive a style sheet, follow the directions on pages 162–166 to create one as you go. As you work, add any new style points to the existing style sheet.

Traditionally, the proofreader reads the galleys (the "live" copy) against a marked-up copy of the manuscript (the "dead," or reference, copy). Today, we use that system when we check that the proofreading changes called for have indeed been made to the text. In book editing, most proofreading is done without a reference copy. The proofreader simply reads the text as it appears on the page proofs, which are visually more or less as the finished book will appear.

I encourage you to proofread on paper. This suggestion may sound anachronistic in this age of omnipresent screens, but it's a bad idea to proofread on-screen, even when you're rushing—especially when you're rushing. It's easy to miss an error on-screen because of the way the human eye deals with emitted light (versus reflected light from paper). Yes, digital tools are helpful, and yes, they make editing easier in many respects. But not when we proofread: good proofreading happens on paper.

The final step is crucial. The proofreader, or a more senior editor, must check that the changes the proofreader has called for have been made, and that no new errors have been introduced in the process. Check and check again. Only then is the proofreading complete.

Proofreading symbols

The concept behind using proofreading symbols is brevity. You don't have time to write out complex instructions, so the symbols function as shorthand, taking the place of long descriptions.

A proofreader's marks are similar to a copyeditor's marks, but the symbols are used differently. When we proofread, we double mark—that is, we place a caret or dele (deletion mark) in the text, and we mark the correction or change in the margin next to the line concerned. *The Chicago Manual of Style* advises using either margin, adopting the margin closest to the error; other authorities recommend using only one margin, normally the right-hand margin. Double marking reduces the chance that your marks will be missed by the person entering the changes. If a line requires two or more corrections, the corrections should be separated by vertical lines.

Importantly, text insertions are not written between the lines as they are in copyediting. At this stage of production, the type is set, so

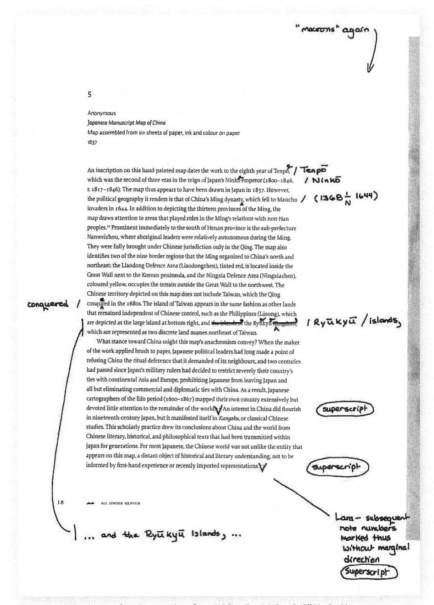

Figure 7.4 Sample proofreading markup from Walter Davis's book *All Under Heaven*

there normally isn't room to write words clearly, and the possibility of a change being missed or misread in the line is high. If for some reason a major correction is required, the affected passage should be crossed out and rewritten clearly in the margin (if space permits; above or below the text block if not) or on a separate, attached sheet. In general, make the smallest number of marks possible: simplicity aids clarity. Indicate your intentions clearly without wasting time or being redundant.

Use standard markup symbols when you proofread, even on short tasks such as flyers and brochures. (If you don't know the standard symbols, see appendix C.) You may also need to explain the symbols to some clients or co-workers. Think about your situation as proofreader. Are you working with an experienced editor at a well-known publishing house? Chances are she'll know how to read markup symbols, and so will the other editors and the layout technician. If you're working with a self-published author or with an organization whose normal business is not book publishing, then mark up accordingly. The key is to ensure that the client/typesetter/editor will understand your intentions. Whatever method you use, be consistent. And remember, neatness counts!

I started this section by mentioning that you should be attentive to spelling, punctuation, grammar, sense, and production matters. Let's consider each of these areas in a little more detail.

Spelling

There are several points about spelling to consider. Most importantly, don't guess. If you're not positive a word is correctly spelled, check the project dictionary. Be sure to consider alternative spellings in context (e.g., Canadian versus American spellings—these are trickier, and more encompassing, than merely adding a *u* to a handful of words). Consistency is also important. Proofreaders quickly grow attuned to words with variant spellings and alert for inconsistent treatments. Remember, however, that there are limits to consistency; for instance, you don't change spellings in quoted materials to conform to your style sheet.

Be aware that many words that are legitimate but uncommonly used look similar to other, commonly used words, such as *numinous* (versus *luminous*) or *intestate* (versus *interstate*). Proofreaders sometimes assume that the common word is the intended one and change the uncommon word, especially if both words are the same part of speech. By doing so, of course, they alter the writer's original meaning and may introduce an error into the text. As a guideline, be sensitive to diction. Pay attention to the author's overall language use, and if you're not sure about a point in diction, query the editor or the author. (There is an apocryphal story about *New Yorker* editor Harold Ross and the final lines of T.S. Eliot's poem "The Hollow Men," which ends, "This is the way the world ends / Not with a bang but a whimper." Ross was allegedly so concerned a proofreader might "helpfully" correct *whimper* to *whisper* that he went to the printing plant and checked the type on the press.)

Editors should use digital tools whenever we can, so proofreaders should assume that a manuscript has been run through a spell checker and basic spellings are under control. Still, recognize the limitations of the technology. Never assume a spell checker has caught all the errors. Also, be aware that the operator may not have used the spell checker correctly. Sometimes people accept a correction prompt without confirming that the word offered is appropriate. A common example of such a correction is the word *defiant* standing in place of *definite*, which is often misspelled as *definate*. Global search-and-replace changes require special care. I recently read about a book that contained the word "particitrousers." Presumably, through a flawed search-and-replace operation, the "pants" in *participants* had been overwritten. This is an egregious example, and a proofreader should have caught it; but be aware that digital shortcuts make such examples—and errors—all too easy to produce.

Be especially careful with names. There are several variant spellings of most names, and an error involving a name is not just a spelling mistake but an error of fact. When possible, get source copy that verifies the spelling of individuals' names; don't simply trust the writer to get it right (e.g., Pierre Burton vs. Pierre Berton).

Here are a few more tips on proofreading for spelling:

- Watch for silent letters and unusual spelling patterns (such as clusters of consonants).
- Read long words syllable by syllable.
- When a text introduces foreign-language words, check both the spelling and the mechanical treatment (e.g., italics, diacritics).
- Certain suffixes tend to be frequently misspelled, such -able/-ible. If you're in doubt, check.
- Some spelling "errors" are the result of mishearing or confusing one word with another, such as *faze* (versus *phase*) or *parity* (versus *parody*).

The key takeaways for becoming adept at proofreading for spelling: get used to consulting dictionaries and other reference texts, don't assume, and don't guess.

Punctuation

Writers punctuate according to convention as well as for clarity of expression. Sometimes the writer or editor may use punctuation to aid reading. When you proofread, consider how punctuation is used throughout the document. Consistency is important, but it never trumps clarity.

Several punctuation errors are typical. Watch for missing terminal punctuation, such as absent periods and questions lacking question marks. Also, be sure colons have been removed from the ends of heads and subheads. They are grammatically unnecessary and look typographically sloppy. Another point to watch for is trouble with quotation marks. Are they single when they should be double? Have they been positioned correctly with other punctuation? Have they been used in pairs? Extend this scrutiny to other forms of paired punctuation, such as parentheses and brackets.

Internal punctuation marks require judicious attention. Don't introduce or strike punctuation because you hear the sentence differently in your mind's ear. Know and apply the conventions—and recognize when they've been violated. Comma errors are particularly common, including missing parenthetical commas and the variable use of the serial comma. Watch out for misused semicolons, but be sensitive to the artistic application of semicolons in some kinds of literary publishing. Strike out colons used between verbs and objects or between prepositions and objects in series or lists (e.g., *this example should include:* ... or *please give to:* ...; in both instances, the colon after the verb is wrong).

Punctuation advice attributed to the Oxford University Press observes, "If you take hyphens seriously, you will surely go mad." Most editors care about hyphens, but not all editors agree about their use. (For instance, you'll note that I'm fond of hyphens and let them stand where some of my colleagues would strike them.) If you think you see errors with hyphens, review a good number of proof pages before you start adding or striking them; pay attention to how author and copyeditor have applied hyphens in prenominal adjective phrases, in noun phrases modifying nouns and predicate adjective phrases, and in place of en and em dashes. Many copyeditors run a global check for hyphens, en dashes, and em dashes as part of their basic file preparation. If they don't, sometimes the layout technician does. You can ask the assigning editor whether this step has been taken. If not, keep a sharp eye on these distinctions. It's easy to distinguish between the hyphen and the em dash, but an en dash can fool even an experienced editor.

But there's more to hyphens then their in-line use. Hyphens are also used to indicate the break in a word at the end of a line. There is, or at least should be, a method to word division. You'll need to turn to a dictionary for assistance. The preferred British word-division method is based on etymology. The preferred American word-division method is based on pronunciation. Don't let the design software's algorithm decide for you: check. In fine typography, at least three letters should be retained on the line with the hyphen. Proper names should not be broken across a line (or a page) unless it's absolutely unavoidable. If three or more consecutive lines end with hyphens, they're called *stacked hyphens* and are considered a mark of poor typography. To correct stacked hyphens, write a callout to the layout technician.

One further area to watch closely is punctuation applied repeatedly, such as in bulleted lists, in dialogue, in captions, in DISPLAY TYPE (in cover copy, for example), and in image captions. If you read similar materials side by side (e.g., look at all the image captions in a single pass, then at all the bulleted lists), inconsistencies are much easier to notice.

Grammar

Most grammar errors should have been caught during the copyedit, but some may be lingering. Sometimes they are artifacts of the editing process—for instance, an agreement error created when a subject is changed from plural to singular and the verb is not changed accordingly. Sometimes they're tricky points in grammar that both author and editor missed. Regardless of why they remain, grammar errors need your thoughtful attention.

There are several issues to consider. First, there are the basics of correctness: that verbs agree with their subjects, pronouns agree with their antecedents, pronouns take the correct case, adjectives and adverbs are correctly used and positioned, and so on. Next, there is context. "Poor" grammar may be used as a stylistic device. You should be reading sensitively enough to know whether this is the case; watch for patterns or other textual cues. The assigning editor will likely have mentioned if dialect or other non-standard issues need your attention.

Level of formality is a further consideration. Again, minor points such as contractions, split infinitives, the loose use of *you/your*, and poorly placed modifiers (e.g., *only*) should have been dealt with during the copyedit. At this stage, call for a change only if communication is actually impaired by informality or if it's strikingly different from the rest of the text. Think about the audience, too: their reading level, sophistication, expectations, and comfort with language change. Adherence to many grammar "rules" exists on a spectrum, and what is appropriate for one audience may not be so for another. Remember too that grammar is not usage; keep these two aspects of language distinct.

Typical grammar errors include comma splices and run-together sentences (two independent clauses joined by a comma or with no punctuation at all). These errors can usually be solved with a semicolon, but be sure that choice is right for the audience. Inserting a period at the end of the first sentence and capitalizing the second sentence may be a better solution, or you might be able to insert a coordinating conjunction. Agreement is also usually straightforward. Singular subjects take singular verbs, and plural subjects take plural verbs; likewise, singular pronouns should have singular antecedents, and plural pronouns should have plural antecedents. Be alert for problems with hypercorrection (such as the ever-popular *between you and I*) or errant cases that emerge because the pronoun position in the sentence is unclear.

A degree of subjectivity and thought is needed when you encounter sentence fragments. In general, don't correct stylistic fragments, only uncontrolled fragments. Misplaced or dangling modifiers can be a problem at this stage. Unless they truly impede communication or are laugh-out-loud obvious, you may need to leave them. If the fix is easy, mark the change; if the fix involves rewriting the entire sentence, evaluate the situation carefully. You may also run into trouble with the use of *they* (treated as a gender-neutral singular pronoun), especially in governmental and educational documents. You may want to ask the author or assigning editor in advance how to handle this, but be alert to patterns: if it happens repeatedly, it may be an intentional choice.

Sense

The proofreader's job is to check that what will be published is in fact what is meant—that is, that the text communicates sensibly. For that reason, you must confirm that the text makes sense both as a whole and in its parts. Proofreading for sense is challenging because your brain must move rapidly between the micro and the macro. For this reason, two different proofreaders should be used, one to read for mechanical matters and one to read for sense alone.

As you proofread for sense, think about words carefully. Are the words that appear the correct words, or were other words intended? Consider whether a word is correctly used in context. Should it be the noun form or the adjective form? Are the words in the correct order? Have any words been omitted or repeated? Little words are often a problem; similar-sounding or similar-looking words may have been substituted. Very familiar words are often overlooked simply because they *are* so familiar: we take for granted that they are correct.

When materials are organized according to a pattern, ensure the pattern is followed. For instance, check alphabetical order and numerical order, and ensure that if five points are called out, five explanations follow. In addition to words, pay attention to names, dates, phone numbers, addresses, prices, and totals. Use a dictionary, a calendar, a map, or other resources to help you solve a problem, but keep in mind that the book has already been copyedited and you're not responsible for fact checking. With fiction in particular, adherence to strict facts may not be necessary or even desirable. If some point of fact seems jarringly wrong and cannot be readily fixed, query the assigning editor (or the writer, if necessary). You'll discover that many sense problems cannot be solved by the proofreader and must be queried.

Production matters

Your job as a proofreader will normally include production proof-reading, in addition to textual proofreading. Production proofreading involves checking the correctness and consistency of the visual elements of the layout. Page proofs, or galleys, are typeset and appear in near-final form. As proofreader, you ensure the pages look good as well as read correctly.

The major focus of production proofreading has to do with type specifications. Examine the type size; note any inconsistencies or deviations. Watch margins and ensure justification is consistent. Most books are published fully JUSTIFIED—that is, with even left- and right-hand margins—but some books have a rag-right margin. Ensure that page ends are even, that paragraphs are indented where they should be (paragraphs immediately after a subhead are normally not indented), and that appropriate styling has been applied to various levels of subheads, as well as to running heads and footers.

Then, start looking at the typography. Look for items such as hyphens that break across columns or pages, hyphens on already hyphenated words (such as *ethno-cultural*), paragraphs that end with the second half of a hyphenated word, and paragraphs that end with short single words. Be sure to mark any words that are obviously incorrectly hyphenated

Justified margin

Lorem ipsum dolor sit amet, consectetur adipiscing elit. Sed at ante. Mauris eleifend, quam a vulputate dictum, massa quamdap ibus leo, eget vulputate orci purus ut lorem. In fringilla mi in ligula. Pellentesque aliqua quam vel dolor. Nunc adipiscing. Sed quam odio, tempus ac, aliquam varius ac, tellus. Vestibulum ut nulla aliquam risus rutrum interdum. Pellentesque lorem. Curabitur sit amet erat quis risus feugiat viverra. Pellentesque augue justo, sagittis et, lacinia at, vene natis non, arcu. Nunc nec libero. In cursus dictum risus. Etiam tristique nisl a nulla. Ut a orci. Curabitur dolor nunc, egestas at, accum san at, malesuada magna ut nulla aliquam.

Rag-right margin

Lorem ipsum dolor sit amet, consectetur adipiscing elit. Sed at ante. Mauris eleifend, quam a vulputate dictum, massa quam dapibus leo, eget vulputate orci purus ut lorem. In fringilla mi in ligula. Pellentesque aliquam quam vel dolor. Nunc adipiscing. Sed quam odio, tempus ac, aliquam molestie, varius ac, tellus. Vestibulum ut nulla aliquam risus rutrum interdum. Pellentesque lorem. Curabitur sit amet erat quis risus feugiat viverra. Pellentesque augue justo, sagittis et, lacinia at, venenatis non, arcu. Nunc nec libero. In cursus dictum risus. Curabitur dolor nunc, egestas at, accumsan at, malesuada nec, magna.

Figure 7.5 Justified versus rag-right margins. Justified type feels formal and orderly—appropriate to most books—while rag margins feel informal, even friendly.

Uneven page ends

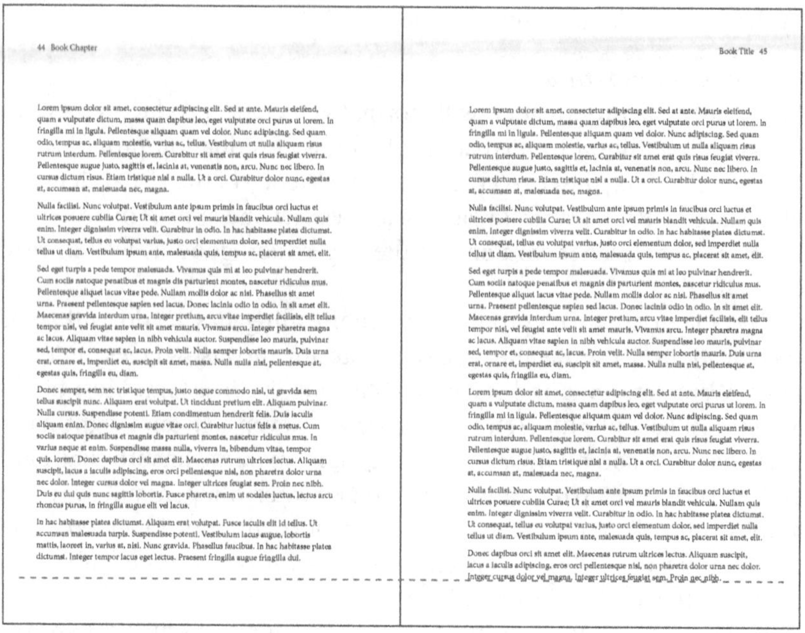

Even page ends

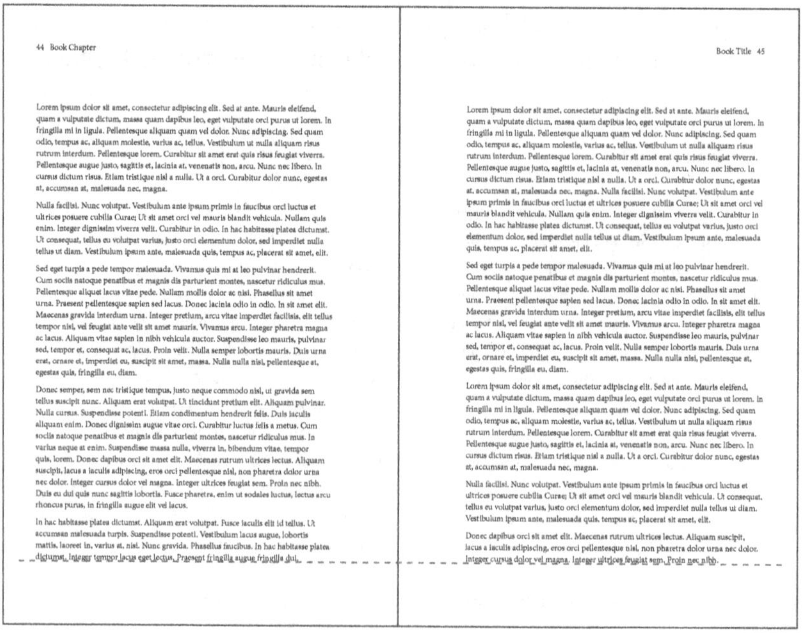

Figure 7.6 Uneven versus even page ends. The even page presentation feels more graceful and complete.

Figure 7.7 The overall distribution of the page is sometimes referred to as its colour; it should be evenly "grey," in that you don't want to see rivers of white flowing through the type or odd shapes forming in the right-hand margin.

(for instance *gre-/enwashing*, which I saw in a book I was reading recently). You may also flag WIDOWS and ORPHANS (single lines that are separated from the rest of a paragraph by a column break or page turn). Widows and orphans should be resolved by wrapping the single line back or forward to the preceding or following page or column. In justified text, watch for loose lines; on rag-right type, watch for evenness and consistency.

Images require your attention as proofreader just as much as the text does. Examine every image. Beyond matching the image with its in-text description, check its placement and quality. Also ensure captions and any credit lines required are present, accurate, and correctly formatted. The same advice applies to tables and graphs: check their titling, cross-referencing, scale values (if appropriate), and overall correctness.

In any place where text characters are used graphically—such as on the front and back covers and the half- and full-title pages—proofread the text carefully. Text used as a graphic may have been rekeyed by the designer or layout technician, may not have been reviewed by an earlier editor, and may be a comparatively new element in the layout. This is a weak link in the production sequence, so never assume text-based graphics are correct as presented.

Finally, watch out for folios, or page numbers. No folio should appear on a page that is otherwise blank, and the folio treatment on the opening page of a chapter is often different from the folio treatment on other pages. Watch the pagination of the front matter in particular—there should be few folios, and those that do appear should be run in lowercase roman numerals.

Many layout technicians will comb through their layouts shortly before production to finesse the typography. At this point they look for many of the same kinds of issues the proofreader looks for, such as loose

Unkerned

Wave

Track

2010

Kerned

Wave

Track

2010

Figure 7.8 Unkerned and kerned text. Note the readability of the kerned text—and how readability may break down.

lines and bad breaks. Some will also run checks for KERNING pairs (e.g., Aw, Av, We, and Ya) and LIGATURES (e.g., ff, fi, fl, and ffl). Ideally, the designer runs these checks prior to generating galleys for the indexer (in the case of nonfiction), author, and proofreader, but not always. The risk with adjusting the type after proofreading and layout is that words or lines may flow to new pages—a small problem, but one that is important to avoid once the book has been indexed.

Ligatures

The first fjord flowed stiffly around the land.

No ligatures

The first fjord flowed stiffly around the land.

Figure 7.9 Note that text set with ligatures is more graceful and "clean" looking than the text set without them.

Even small changes may cause text to overflow the space originally assigned to it. If the layout technician is unable to accommodate the overflow by adjusting word spacing and kerning, the proofreader may fit the copy to the space by eliminating a few characters or words in the surrounding text. Such alterations are called COPY-FITTING.

Thanks to digital typesetting, copy-fitting is less of an issue than it once was. Whenever late changes are introduced to a book, however, copy-fitting may be necessary, particularly if the book has already been indexed. If you're asked to make something new fit an existing page, check the changes you've already called for on that page. Can you alter them to make them more compact? Look for short lines at the ends of paragraphs: you may be able to cut a word or two earlier in the paragraph and wrap up the text. Look for modifiers that could be eliminated, nominalizations that could be rephrased, and passive voice that could shift harmlessly to active. Failing a textual solution, examine the graphic elements that could be altered, reduced, or cut to accommodate space needs.

Copy-fitting at the proofreading stage is unusual and generally disruptive to the production schedule. Never adjust copy this way unless you are asked to do so or a serious change makes it necessary.

Queries in proofreading

Queries are questions about the text that the editor cannot answer on her own. In proofreading, queries are normally addressed to either an editor—most likely the assigning editor or project editor—or a layout technician (the person responsible for the visual formatting). At this stage, queries should be brief and clear; the respondent should be able to answer "yes," "no," or "doesn't matter" in most cases. Here are some sample proofreading queries:

- Myrna's grandmother's full birth name is given here. Should it be included in the index?
- Author has alternated between first name and last name throughout this chapter. Should this be unified with a quick search and replace? I would recommend last name only, as in other chapters.
- Eye colour in chapter 2 was blue. Strike descriptor here as it is not essential to the action, or ask author to confirm?

One important thing: never query aspects of the text that it is your job to know or evaluate, such as spelling, grammar, level of heading, and so on. Asking about these points, rather than making an outright correction, undercuts your professionalism. If you really can't figure out the problem, it's likely pretty serious. So here's another dictum: know what you know; query what you don't know—that is, what a reader would query.

Different proofreaders handle queries in different ways. At this stage, if all has gone well with earlier stages, you shouldn't expect to generate many queries. Keep a running list on a piece of paper or a digital file, and hand the list to the client/editor with the rest of the project. You normally mark the text with a question mark or the letters QU in the margin of the manuscript, circled. Number your queries on the manuscript to make referring back to your running list easier.

A FEW MORE PROOFREADING TIPS

- Use an eye guide—a ruler, an index card, or some other straight edge that covers most of the text and forces you to focus on a small portion at a time. It's easy to let your eye wander and lose your place in the line. The eye guide keeps you on task.

- Look for matching pairs: train yourself to put a pointer (a pencil point, your finger) on the text when quotation marks open, and then confirm that they close. Ditto when a parenthesis opens, and so on.

- Errors tend to cluster. If you find an error, expect to find another nearby.

- Watch out for transpositions of letters *(form/from)*, keyboard keys *(previous/precious)*, and words *(at a/a at)*.

- If you're interrupted in the process, mark your place and then resume the process a few lines above where you broke off to get back in the groove and to catch anything you might have missed when your attention was beginning to be distracted.

The proofreader is responsible for checking every part of every page and ensuring it communicates correctly and effectively. If you want to be an effective proofreader, slow down! Proofreading is not a race, and a book is not well served by frantic proofreading. Working slowly but efficiently is one of the hardest lessons to learn about proofreading. Take it from the experience of editors who have gone before you: you cannot proofread well on the run.

WHERE ARE YOU NOW?

After thinking about editing relationships and responsibilities over the last three chapters, think about where you see yourself now as a possible book editor. What do you think you'll be good at, what still concerns you, what do you still need to learn?

If you're a working editor, this might be a good time to ask professional peers and colleagues about their perception of your strengths and their experiences (if any) working with books and authors. Remember, editing is a mentored profession, so it's important to ask other editors about what they believe and value.

Wrapping Up Mechanics In-House

Although for the purposes of the discussion above, I assumed that the proofreader is a freelancer, not an in-house staffer, the same processes apply if you are proofreading a manuscript you or an in-house colleague edited. The in-house editor, however, is also responsible for guiding the author through the process of reviewing proofs. Your role with the author continues to involve managing expectations, particularly with respect to schedules and changes.

In most publishing contracts, the author has the right and the obligation to review proof pages prior to publication. Most book editors need an author signoff at this stage, confirming that the author reviewed the proofs and raised no significant concerns (or that any concerns were addressed). Once the book goes to the printer, of course, there is effectively no turning back, so you may need to emphasize the seriousness of this signoff to the author. Also, because time is vital at this stage, you need to set a short and firm deadline for turning around the proofs. Here is where any goodwill you have earned in your relationship becomes important.

The book editor or project editor sends the proofs to the author with a brief transmittal letter, setting out how the author should mark up any changes or concerns and when the proofs must be returned. Warn authors explicitly about the costs and potential risks of late changes. Many authors who have grown up with word processing do not understand that changes in a book that has gone through layout are significantly more complex than changes in a word-processed document. If authors disregard this advice and insist on late changes, you may have big problems—compounded if the book has an index—and may face significant additional production costs as well as an increased risk of errors. In the worst possible case, the book will need to be proofread again. Some presses charge late changes back to the author, deducting their cost from the author's first royalty payment. Rather than start down this road, however, you're better off to ensure the author understands the production sequence from the beginning and respects both the process and your authority over it.

Once you have the author's proofreading changes, you either supply them to the proofreader or amalgamate the proofreader's changes with the author's changes. The compiled marked-up pages are sent to the layout technician for correction, and new pages should be generated for you to review. Be sure to confirm that all proofreading changes have been made correctly and no new errors have been introduced. (I'm not kidding. Check, and then check again.) If a change has been made to a sentence, read the whole sentence when you proofread it—this method will help you find agreement problems you've introduced with other edits. When you are certain that the pages are as close to perfect as they can be, give the design department your okay to send the book files to production. In just a few weeks, you'll be holding a new book in your hands. Or you'll be opening a freshly coded ebook on your ereader—but this isn't quite as romantic as the gleam of a newly printed cover and the tang of fresh ink!

In this chapter, I've raised issues of design and layout repeatedly, and in the day-to-day operations of most publishing houses, mechanical editing and design/layout are inseparably linked. For that reason, chapter 8 provides a fairly comprehensive overview of tasks, processes, and concepts involved in the design and manufacturing of books.

8

Book Design and Manufacture

"In an ideal world, one could judge a book by its
cover—or by its type and binding and paper. In an ideal
world, surely the makers and vendors of things, such
as physical books, would obey the inner promptings of
the spirit."—Warren Chappell and Robert Bringhurst

This chapter provides a brief overview of the processes of book design and manufacturing from the perspective of a book editor: the basics of what the editor needs to know. It won't prepare you to work as a designer—design is a specialized field that requires extended study—but it is intended to prepare you to work intelligently alongside designers, layout technicians, and the art department at large, as well as to ask informed questions of print sales reps and press operators. Learning about design, production, and manufacturing offers the book editor excellent opportunities to understand more about the publishing industry and how it is changing.

The art department represents something of a black box for many editors. We send files to the art department, and a few weeks later we get proof pages in exchange. It's a mistake not to understand, or even be interested, in how the art department works, however. As with so much else in editing and publishing, there are standards and conventions associated with book design and layout, yet every book poses a distinct bundle of problems to be solved. While the book editor solves some of these problems, the designer and layout technician solve others. The book editor must understand the issues design and production face because ultimately their problems become her problems. This chapter is intended to provide a vocabulary and a background to help book editors work with designers and others toward potential solutions.

With that aim in mind, this chapter is divided into three related parts. The first part considers the art and technology of design. The second discusses the practical elements of manufacturing books of various kinds. The third identifies a business role that some book editors undertake and that in other cases is its own area of specialization: production. While all these areas fall under the banner of design and manufacturing, they encompass a wide swath of skills and experience. At points my discussion is necessarily general and may not align with your prior experience, or with what you'll experience in the workplace. In some firms, book editors are routinely involved with design and production decisions, while at others design, editorial, and production are highly segregated. Still, just as editorial decisions inform design decisions, production constraints and possibilities inform editing and design. Beyond their textual existence, books are eminently *functional* objects. It is in their physical realization, whether as printed books or as ebooks, that they fully meet their purpose.

BRAIN PUZZLER
True or false: A single sheet of paper folded once produces four pages. Not sure? Try it yourself!

PART ONE: THE ART AND TECHNOLOGY OF DESIGN

Design

Design refers to how visual communication is structured. Most book design has an explicitly commercial purpose—it is an applied art. Successful book design requires a designer to interpret and balance how best to address the needs of the text, the publisher, and the audience.

All design is a problem-solving process, planning and shaping the form of a specific kind of communication product. Book design aims to produce attractive relationships on the page between the type, the page shape, and the images while optimizing readability and maximizing communication of the message. A well-designed book suggests to readers how to take in the content presented to them—or to put it another way, good book design yields a book someone *wants* to read.

BASIC DESIGN TERMS AND DEFINITIONS

I believe you need vocabulary to be able to communicate effectively with the people you work with; hence the numerous terms and concepts explained throughout this book. Here are some basic design- and type-related terms and definitions every book editor should know.

- **Font**: all the characters of a particular size and style of type, named for the box, or font case, in which moveable type was stored (see Figure 8.1)

- **Typeface**: the complete set of a specific design (or FONT) of characters, encompassing all heights, weights, and styles; although in the computer age this term is often used interchangeably with *font*, typeface is the wider term, while font is the narrower term

- **Point**: a unit used for measuring the height of type and for line spacing; a POINT is 1/72 of an inch (i.e., there are 72 points in an inch); designers still use points as a base measurement in page composition, rather than inches or millimetres, because type is measured in points

- **Pica**: a unit used for measuring vertical and horizontal space, such as the length of a line; a pica is 12 points, or 1/6 of an inch (i.e., there are 6 picas in an inch)

- **Tracking**: the consistent relationship of space between one letter and the next within a word, and from one word to another, without regard to a letter's form or shape (which is the role of kerning)

Figure 8.1 A font case

Figure 8.2 Using software such as Photoshop, an editor can check the size of images to see whether they have enough resolution for print. This image, at 300 pixels per inch, would only be 1.6 inches wide. Making the image wider will reduce the resolution.

- **Kerning**: the adjustment of space between one letter and another to produce a complementary visual relationship, as in letters that change width from top to bottom—e.g., W, Y, V, A—adjacent to other letters that also do so

- **Ligatures**: two or more letters represented through a single character in a font for greater readability, e.g., fl, ffl, fi; although they make type more legible, ligatures are an artifact of moveable type that hearkens back to calligraphy and are thus a little "fussy"; some designers consider them an affectation and therefore do not use them

- **Old-style figures**: numerals that move off the baseline and read visually more like text than lining figures do; although old-style figures are appropriate in some applications, they are not well suited to scientific and technical publishing

- **Lorem ipsum** (also known as GREEKING or *dummy text*): meaningless text, placed for position only, to represent the way the finished text will look in the layout; it includes long and short words to provide a sense of line length, word spacing, hyphenation, and line rhythm; using meaningless text keeps designers and editors from being distracted by the working text when they evaluate a design mock-up

- **Rag margin**: an uneven, or unjustified, margin on a column of type, reflecting unadjusted line ends; usually rag-left, sometimes rag-right

- **Trim size**: the dimension of the finished, bound book

- **Bleed**: an image or screened area that reaches beyond the trimmed edge of the sheet; when content is intended to print to the edge of a trimmed page, bleeds are necessary to compensate for the potential movement of the paper in the press; a document that contains BLEEDS may cost slightly more to print, depending on the finished TRIM SIZE and the original sheet size, because it might use more paper

- **Dummy book:** a bound block of unprinted pages produced in the specified paper stock to allow a designer or client to preview how the finished book will appear; most printers or paper suppliers will produce a dummy at no cost for clients

- **Vector graphics:** mathematically drawn graphics that can be manipulated almost infinitely; an image that can be scaled from very small to very large

- **Raster graphics:** pixel-based graphics, meaning the image is composed of pieces of data within a frame; such images are necessarily constrained by their resolution, or the amount of data they contain (see Figure 8.2). Digital photographs are an example of pixel images. When using pixel images, you must have an appropriate resolution for the size of the image. Regrettably, many authors and new editors mistakenly assume that if an image is digital, or if it looks good onscreen, it can be used in any application at any size, which is simply untrue for conventional printing.

Vector graphic   **Raster graphic**

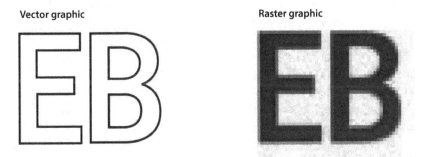

Figure 8.3 Vector versus raster graphics. The lines and curves in a vector graphic, such as that on the left, are built mathematically and thus are infinitely scalable. A raster image, such as that on the right, is built from dots and its resolution is limited, meaning its reproducible size is constrained.

The mechanical nature of the book affects the reader's experience, and this materiality is captured in many of the terms above. Book conventions have evolved over centuries and exist for the sake of function, based on how readers hold, use, and interact with books of various kinds. This point underscores why it's important for editors to be especially careful when working with non-book designers. What might be done in another visual communication context, such as an annual report or a brochure, may not be at all appropriate for a book.

If editors could ask only one thing of designers before they undertake a design, it would be that designers read the manuscript—not just a few pages, and not just a flip-through. Book editors want designers to read the text front to back and understand its tone, characters or key figures, symbolism, plot points or architecture, imagery, and purpose. Not all designers do so, but this effort makes subsequent editorial and marketing work much easier. In exchange, many designers would ask that editors have a greater understanding of design. Two books I recommend for editors are Robin Williams's *The Non-Designer's Design Book: Design and Typographic Principles for the Visual Novice* (4th ed. 2014) and Ellen Lupton's *Thinking with Type: A Critical Guide for Designers, Writers, Editors, and Students* (2nd ed. 2010). If both sides make an effort, authors and readers are sure to benefit.

Design is not layout

Design is not layout, although often the same person is responsible for both tasks. Design and layout are both problem-solving activities, but each role addresses a different set of problems. *Layout* is the process of arranging text and/or images into complete pages in a printed product. It is sometimes referred to as *text formatting* or *page formatting*, although these terms are less common in book publishing and more common in newspapers and magazines. The designer determines the page size, the number of pages to be printed, the type of paper to be printed on, colours and inks, the kind of press the job will be printed on, how the book will be bound, and other finishing considerations, as well as the typeface to be used; the type size, LEADING, and margins; the position and weights of various textual elements (e.g., subheads, rules, captions, images); and how colour will be incorporated. The layout technician (or the designer acting in this role) enacts the designer's decisions on individual pages and balances the designer's ideal vision against the realities of the author's text. For this reason, designer and book editor (or production editor, as I will explain below) must discuss the budget and the design specifications before layout begins.

Principles of design

There are five basic principles to design: balance, proportion, sequence, emphasis, and unity. (Designers will find that statement rather reductive, I know; of course there is much more to design than that, but the complexity of the discipline is a topic for another book.) The challenge for the designer involves knowing which of these five principles to draw on most in any given project, as different projects call for greater emphasis on one principle than the others. Most book design tends to emphasize unity, but not absolutely. Designers have to be versatile. The solution to a beautiful volume of poetry is very different from the solution to a four-colour guide intended for beginning gardeners.

Many experienced designers have a signature style, and it's frankly easy for book designers, like any other professionals, to grow complacent. Sometimes a designer needs to be encouraged—or challenged—to come up with a better idea rather than reach for what is familiar, what she knows will work. Similarly, designers can get hooked on a concept and be reluctant to scrap it, even when it's wrong for the book. It's valuable to learn the patterns of the designers you work with most often and how a given designer responds to feedback, so you can communicate effectively to achieve the goals of the project. As with book editing, book design is not supposed to be about egos, but sometimes it is. Back matter in particular often requires extra thought, and the book editor may be able to offer insight, particularly if she has done the book costing. The pages available for back matter may be limited, so the designer's solutions may need discussion.

Layout technicians are responsible for the integration of illustrative material but generally not for producing it. Do not expect a book designer or technician to be an illustrator, a photographer, or a painter. If she is one, you may be able to use those talents to accomplish additional work, but producing photography, illustration, and original artwork is not the normal province of design and layout. Rather, designers integrate and prepare graphics and art that others have created for reproduction.

Most designers work with styles, and to a lesser degree, templates, not just in their designs but also in layouts. They use paragraph styles, colour palettes (swatches), object styles, and other shortcuts to save time and ensure uniform treatment of similar materials, in much the way editors use style sheets. If you flip through a book and observe how many distinct typographical treatments you encounter even within a small number of pages, you'll easily understand why styles and templates lend the layout technician control and consistency in realizing the designer's intentions.

As with book editing, there are numerous conventions specific to book design, and designers who produce webpages, annual reports, and posters as the majority of their work may not have a good sense of what to do with gutters, bottom margins, copyright pages, and other book-specific matters without clear and specific guidance—that is, they may miss the balance between the page and the book, the part and the whole. That said, the onus is on the book editor to be clear and precise. Designers aren't editors and don't necessarily think like editors or share the vocabulary of editors. Never assume the art department or a freelance designer will somehow "get" your imagined use of a text or its intended market. Be prepared to discuss your sense of the audience and its needs clearly and specifically.

Editorial design

When visual presentation is part of the book's purpose or use, book designer and book editor may work together in a process called *editorial design*. In this kind of collaboration, the designer's visual communication decisions are integral to ensuring that the author's message reaches its audience in the most appropriate or efficient way. Design, like writing, can be a kind of invention, even a kind of exposition; in editorial design, the designer, rather than the editor, takes the lead. From their experience in working with visual, rather than verbal, communication, designers bring a different but complementary set of tools to the work. A designer can support and extend the editor's intentions for a project, but only if she understands those intentions fully. A solid trust relationship is clearly important for this work. Just as editors may pride themselves on their textual expertise, designers bring visual expertise to the relationship. Communicate what the reader needs and trust the designer to discover a solution, using the tools available within the project's scope.

Typography

The job of typography is to support the communication of content as text in an attractive manner. Type and its placement should visually communicate an idea complementary to the written meaning of the text.

More than 20,000 typefaces are available, with many new faces released every year, and it's sometimes difficult for new book editors to know what questions to ask or comments to offer about type. There's a reason most book faces look similar, though, and it's not because designers are lazy or unwillingly to experiment. Rather, relatively few typefaces are legible for the sustained reading that most books require; most typefaces are better suited to display. If you want to learn about the history and significance of typography, I strongly encourage you to read Robert Bringhurst's smart and lovely book *The Elements of Typographical Style* (4th ed. 2013). Bringhurst says, "type exists to honour content" and "well-chosen words deserve well-chosen letters." It is the role of the designer to select the type, but the role of the book editor to confirm that the selection suits the tone and purpose of the book.

Let me tell you a story about my own experiences with this point. I was the editor on a book of poetry—very sophisticated but also fairly ribald poetry. When I received the first set of proof pages from the designer, I was taken aback. These playful, sexy poems had been typeset using a font called Mrs Eaves, an elegant Baskerville-like face—tonally completely wrong for the poems. Fortunately, after a long discussion, the designer agreed to reset the type, this time in a modern, less ornate face. While the original type was beautiful, it was not the right design decision in context.

Type basics

Most typefaces can be classified in one of two ways. Some are SERIF types, meaning that the letterform possesses small hooks or extensions—serifs—reflecting the movement of a hand lifting a chisel or a pen nib. Some are SANS SERIF types, meaning that the letterform lacks serifs. (See Figure 8.4 for examples.) Serif types are easy on the eyes and well suited to sustained text, such as a book's body text. Sans serif types may not be as easy for the eyes and the brain to discern and therefore are better suited to display purposes, such as chapter heads, subheads, and running heads/footers. However, these conventions emerged from centuries of print culture. Online reading and digital texts are slowly changing these practices, making the type more "present" (in the sense that readers are more aware of type than they used to be since they can do things like choose and change fonts) and the reading experience less "invisible" and effortless. This is one quality that upsets some people who dislike ebooks (even while they might enjoy the ability to adjust the type *size* for their comfort), but it is also a learned, internalized response. Sans serif types are now becoming more prevalent in digital materials. Perhaps in the future the distinction between serif and sans serif types will matter less.

Figure 8.4 Serif and sans serif type. Note the strong serifs on the M, in particular.

Type may also be characterized by its *weight*, referring to the thickness of the strokes that make up individual letters. The weight of a type is expressed in naming conventions such as *ultra-light, light, regular, bold, extra-bold*, and so on (see Figure 8.5).

Helvetica Neue Ultralight	**Helvetica Neue Medium**	Minion Pro Regular
Helvetica Neue Thin	**Helvetica Neue Bold**	Minion Pro Medium
Helvetica Neue Light	**Helvetica Neue Heavy**	**Minion Pro Semibold**
Helvetica Neue Regular	**Helvetica Neue Black**	**Minion Pro Bold**

Figure 8.5 Examples of type weights

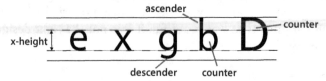

Figure 8.6 Letterforms

Imagine letters printed on ruled paper. The x-height refers to the basic height of a letter's body, minus ascenders or descenders, such as a lower-case *m, o,* or *s.* The ascender refers to the part of the letterform that extends toward the top of the rule—as on a *t* or an *f.* The descender refers to the part of the letterform that hangs below the rule, as on a *g* or a *q.* The counter is the space contained within some letterforms, such as inside an *O* or a *D,* or a *p* or a *q* (see Figure 8.6). Type is measured in points from the bottom of the descender to the top of the ascender. For most type, the larger the x-height is relative to the type size, the easier the type will be to read—but keep in mind that good type design relies on balance. Medium-weight typefaces are considered most readable for sustained passages. Appropriate size depends on the content, but for most books for adults, 9 to 12 points is best, and for children's books, 12 to 16 points is best.

The school represents a crucial institution of social

Figure 8.7 The line above the type represents the coastline. It can be difficult to find errors in print when we read by scanning because we "cruise" the coastline; instead, proofreaders learn to read letter by letter.

The pattern the letterforms make above or below the x-height is called the COASTLINE. Most people learn to read by scanning the upper coastline, but proofreaders must break this style of reading and read each character distinctly. Body, or reading, types have comfortable letterforms and balanced weight; they are used at sizes smaller than 24 points. When a reading type is used for display, however, it usually appears in a heavier weight as well as a larger point size. Display type—typically seen on covers, captions, and marketing materials—is normally used at sizes larger than 18 points.

Letters don't normally appear in isolation, of course. They form words, phrases, sentences, lines, and paragraphs, and the presentation of these units affects the reader's experience of the book. Traditionally, line lengths were measured in picas. With the migration to layout software, however, it is now more common to measure line lengths in characters

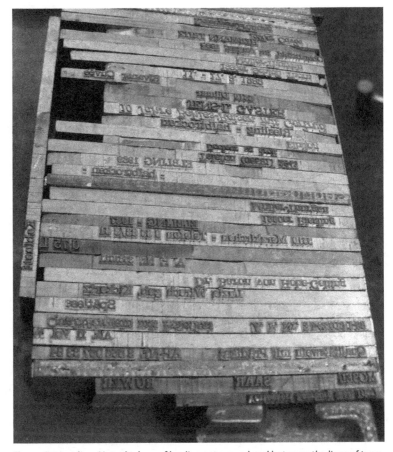

Figure 8.8 Leading. Note the bars of leading set around and between the lines of type.

(or in centimetres or inches). Line lengths shorter than forty characters or longer than seventy-five characters are difficult to read and are not appropriate for sustained texts. Long lines exhaust our eyes, while short lines disrupt how we perceive the structure of the sentence, and may cause readers to miss content; therefore, the designer must plan a comfortable line length that suits the overall dimensions of the page and the selected typeface.

The space between one line of type and the next is called *leading* (which rhymes with *heading*), or line spacing. The term refers to the strips of lead inserted between lines of type in the days of moveable type. Leading for a serif type is usually roughly 120 percent larger than the text face size, but there are exceptions; leading for a sans serif type is generally slightly greater. Like line length, leading requires consideration because too much leading damages the pattern of the coastline,

Figure 8.9 A typeset page. This is a complete page of handset type, plus an image, locked in a chase and ready for printing.

while too little leading exaggerates the pattern and slows down reading. Too little leading also creates a very grey page (also referred to as dark colour) and may encourage the eye to miss a line when scanning back from the right margin.

Different types have different tones and rhythms. Certain types are appropriate for certain settings, while others are not—as communication scholars William Ryan and Theodore E. Conover suggest, "Think of type as the clothes that words wear." A well-composed page feels, visually, rhythmically appealing. But readability is the key to typography in books. Designers and editors may approach readability from different perspectives. Sometimes designers focus on producing pages that are visually appealing but not necessarily readable; it's the editor's role to protect the interests of the reader and readability. When conflict arises, it's important to remember the purpose for the words and type is to communicate with an audience. What does the audience need?

According to Marshall Lee, readability may be evaluated by the following factors: the typeface or typefaces the designer has chosen; the size of these types; the length of the line; the overall page pattern (which refers to the margin, the gutter, and elements that break up the running text); the contrast between the ink colour of the type and the paper it will be printed on (more contrast means greater readability);

the relationship between the running text and other typographical elements, such as subheads; and the suitability of the type to the content. Regrettably, these factors are where most of the problems occur with self-published books and books created by non-book designers. Few books can get away with challenging readability, even when readers are highly motivated to consume the content.

An ideal page displays *good colour* for its readership. This means the page demonstrates a balanced distribution of the "black" of the type against the "white" of the paper to produce an even "grey." Many books— novels, serious nonfiction, professional and academic books—should be grey in this sense. Other books, of course, should have a lighter colour, created by breaking up the type with images, using larger leading, and adopting wider margins. For instance, in a book for young readers or readers struggling with literacy, larger type with wider leading is appropriate (to make reading easier) and produces a lighter, or less grey, page.

Book basics

Look at Figure 8.10, which presents the physical parts of a book. There's a lot of detail here that is important to editors. The hard cover of a hard-cover book may be referred to as the *case*; you may also hear it referred to as *boards*. The boards are made from very stiff cardboard (historically, thin sheets of wood) covered with decorative cloth (hence the term CLOTH BINDING), printed paper, or leather. The *spine* connects the boards and provides additional sturdiness to the cover as well as protection for the block. The removable paper wrapper around the case is referred to as the *jacket* (more properly, the *dust jacket*). The pages that make up the reading text of the book may be referred to as the *book*

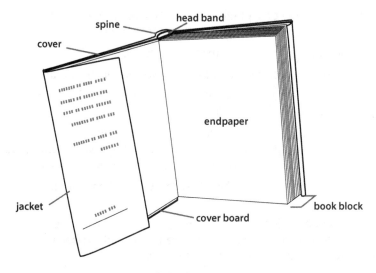

Figure 8.10 Parts of a book

THE VISUAL SIDE OF HYPHENATION

In chapter 7, I quoted an editing truism: "If you take hyphens seriously, you will surely go mad." Hyphenation was once painstakingly done at the typesetter's table. Today, it is generated automatically by computer software. A balance between these approaches, however, generally yields the best production outcomes. Here's a smattering of points about hyphenation and lineation that editors need to consider when they evaluate design and layout.

Lorem ipsum dolor sit amet, consectetur adipiscing elit. Sed at ante. Mauris eleifend, quamvulputate dictum, massa quam dapibus leo, eget vulputate orci purus ut lorem. In fringilla min ligula aliquam. Pellentesque aliquam quam vel dolor. Nunc adipiscing. Sed quam odio, tempus ac, ali lacina quam molestie, varius ac, tellus. Vestibulum ut nulla aliquam risus rutrum interdum. Pellentesque lorem. Curabitur sit amet erat quis risus feugiat viverra. Pellentesque augue justo, sagittis et, lacinia at, venenatis non, arcu. Nunc nec libero. In cursus dictum risus.

Etiam tristique nisl a nulla. Ut a orci. Curabitur nunc, egestas at, accumsan at, malesuada Edmonton nec, tempus ac. Nulla facilisi. Nunc volutpat. Vestibulum ante ipsum primis in Jodie Hamilston orci luctus et ultrices posuere cubilia Curae; ut sit amet orci vel mauris blandit vehicula.

Fantastic Publishing Author Questionnaire

Headers Are Nullam quis enim. Integer dignissim viverra velit. Curabitur in odio. In hac habitasse platea dictumst. Ut consequat, tellus eu volutpat varius, justo orci elementum dolor, sed imperdiet nulla teut diam. Vestibulum ipsum ante, malesuada quis, tempus ac, placerat sit amet, elit imperdiet.

Sed eget turpis a pede tempor malesuada. Vivamus quis mi at leo pulvinar hendrerit mollis about tempus ac, placerat sit amet. Pellentesque aliquet lacus vitae pede. Nullam mollis dolor ac about tellus eu volutpat varius. Praesent pellentesque sapien sed lacus.

Figure 8.11 Examples of problem hyphenation. See if you can spot the problems listed below.

- A large number of hyphens on the right margin suggests the line length is wrong for the content. It also looks messy.
- Avoid hyphens on three or more consecutive lines.
- Avoid breaking proper names across two lines unless it is unavoidable.
- Never break a word unnaturally in a chapter head, subhead, or caption: find another solution.
- Never leave the stub-end of a hyphenated or a single short word alone on a line. Instead, ask the layout technician to adjust the letter spacing in the line so that the stub wraps up or another word wraps down.
- When possible, avoid starting two consecutive lines with the same word.

These details may feel fussy, but they contribute to greater readability. As good practice, designers will overrule the default hyphenation settings on layout software—these controls are adjustable.

block. The *endpapers* are added to attach the block to the case. Head bands, tail bands, and ribbons may be both decorative and functional.

Next look at Figure 8.12, which presents the elements of a *spread* (i.e., an open book displaying two pages, sometimes called an *opening* in academic discourse). Remember the single folded sheet in the puzzler at the beginning of this chapter? The single folded sheet represents the basis of book making; the verso facing the recto creates a spread.

The main reading text, or print block, may be referred to as the live-matter area. The white space surrounding this area is generally referred to as the *margin.* The *face margin* (or outer margin) refers to the margin on the outside edge of the page; the *gutter* (or inside margin) refers to the margin on the inside edge of the page (right margin on the verso, left margin on the recto). When you work with book designs, you must think not of the single sheet but of the spread, the pages functioning in pairs. It's important that text and images not be lost in the gutter, and depending on how the book is bound, the size of the gutter may increase slightly with the page count.

The margin at the top of the page is called the *head margin*; at the bottom of the page, the *foot margin.* The foot margin is often slightly larger than the head margin to accommodate a reader's fingers grasping the book from its bottom edge. Type that runs consistently between the reading text and the head margin is called a *header* or *running head* (plural *running heads*). Type that runs consistently between the reading text and the foot margin is called a *footer* or *running foot* (plural *running feet*). Sometimes people will use *folio* to refer to both the page number and the running foot; note that the folio might appear in either the head margin or the foot margin.

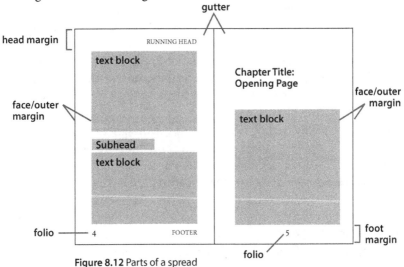

Figure 8.12 Parts of a spread

THE ALCUIN SOCIETY

The Alcuin Society is a Canadian organization dedicated to the tradition of fine printing, tasteful design, and the book arts in general. The society's name refers to Alcuin of York, Charlemagne's court scholar, who in the late eighth century was responsible for developing Caroline minuscules, or what we recognize today as lower-case letters. Prior to that time, European letters were written only as capitals.

One of the society's best-recognized programs is the Alcuin awards—properly called the Alcuin Society Awards for Excellence in Book Design—which annually recognizes outstanding design accomplishment in a variety of categories. Winning an Alcuin award is a mark of professional accomplishment.

The Digital Workflow and Ebook Production

Today, virtually all new books are born digital—that is, they move through a digital workflow from word-processor file to layout file to printer's IMPOSITION. For instance, most editorially complex files are tagged or coded during copyediting. The tags are included so the designer knows how to treat various text blocks, and may be coordinated with layout software styles so that when the text is imported, it flows in seamlessly. Ebooks are the realization of an entirely digital publishing process, and XML is the system underpinning it.

XML (eXtensible Markup Language) is a system for tagging the parts of a running text according to the content, such as title, heading level 1, heading level 2, caption, note, and so on. XML is the format of choice for text that will be used in a variety of applications (print, ebook, online). The XML file describes which text elements are found in the text but does not apply typographical treatment—that is, the file contains no data about typography, which makes XML a very versatile format. Once an XML file is imported, the technician determines how each text element will be treated. The technician's determination for variable display depending on context forms the basis of various ebook formats and digitally adaptable formats.

In a digital workflow using XML coding, the designer may be responsible only for developing a visual template and a palette of appropriate formats for the various elements of the XML code. A technician (often overseas) is responsible for actually formatting the layout, although the designer may be consulted during the proofreading stage to ensure the design has been correctly implemented. Book designer Carol Dragich Bishop comments, "Working with an XML file allows me to focus only on the appearance of the book, rather than applying styles. This saves time and allows for a more creative focus. However, it creates some limitations based on simple things like font names. For example, *Italic* works great, but *Regular Italic, Semibold Italic,* and *Bold Italic* are problematic for a character style."

XML format lends itself particularly well to projects that feature repeated structures, such as textbooks and reference books. Display treatments and limitations suit the specific application (e.g., seamless reflow at different text sizes on one ereader versus another) and also support generalized functions such as internal and external links.

Controls for design and layout of ebooks are still evolving and are not as consistent or as straightforward as for print, but EPUB3, an XML-based format, has been advanced as a potential global standard. For most ebooks, EPUB is the format in which the consumer receives the book file. Digital rights management (drm) software, referring to a digital lock—may then be applied by the publisher, or more often the retailer, once the file exists in EPUB format. In ebooks, all content is XHTML (eXtensible Hypertext Markup Language, which is a part of the larger XML markup language family and acts as an extension of HTML). Cascading style sheets (CSS) describe how the book is displayed, and metadata such as bibliographical information, the table of contents, copyright, and more may be bundled with the file.

The larger questions behind the search for an ebook standard engage the book as both physical and textual object. Is the book the physical container—the dead tree product—that society has valued for centuries, or is a book content, ideas, more abstract than material? When people repudiate ebooks, they may be cleaving to the traditional container, a specific kind of reading experience they feel an ebook cannot emulate. As tablets and ereaders grow more sophisticated, however, such arguments grow more specious (although I confess to being frustrated when I have to restart my ereader, or when it runs out of batteries—experiences I have never had with printed books). Book design is integral to our experience of the book as this abstract object—something more than just words on a page, regardless of how we take up these words.

PART TWO: PRACTICAL CONSIDERATIONS IN MANUFACTURING

Specifications

In determining a book's design and visual presentation, the designer can make almost infinite choices in terms of typography, colour, integration of artwork and graphics, line lengths and column widths, page size, paper colour, and so on. These choices are realized in finite ways, however, bound by the cost of manufacturing the physical object. It may be up to the art department to develop the specifications for a book project, or it may be the responsibility of the book's editor. Either way, it's important for book editors to know something about physical specifications and manufacturing.

Paper

In printing estimates, paper makes up the largest cost, so it's important for editors to know a fair bit about paper. Designers often have relationships with paper sales reps, so ask your art department or some freelance designers who their paper reps are and get in touch. You may be able to take a tour of the warehouse and get paper samples and support materials so you can learn more about paper specifications, costs, and applications.

One basic consideration involves the weight of the paper. In Canada and the United States, paper weight is measured in pounds per ream (500 sheets) of the basis sheet—but note that the size of the basis sheet is not consistent for all papers. A basis sheet for text weight, for instance, is 25 by 38 inches, while a basis sheet for cover stock is 20 by 26 inches. Offshore paper is measured in grams per square metre (gsm, referred to as *grammage*). In general, heavier paper is more expensive and lighter paper is cheaper. Heavier paper may produce greater readability, but your decision depends on how your book will be read and other reader needs.

A reader's experience of paper is influenced by three other factors: a paper's surface, its colour, and its opacity. The surface of a paper may be coated or uncoated; COATED papers have a fine, smooth finish created by a thin layer of clay applied to the paper fibres during manufacturing and may be matte or glossy. (Matte paper has a duller finish than glossy has.) Uncoated papers are rough and more porous. The smoothness or roughness of the surface affects a paper's contact with the printing surface (the press blanket, as described below) and therefore the paper's ability to take up ink. Printing ink absorbs (*dries back*) into the fibres of uncoated papers, producing slightly duller, less precise type and images. Ink sits more fully on the surface of coated papers, producing sharper, brighter type and images. Depending on the number of images in a book, the saturation of colour in those images, and the balance of images and type, different weights and finishes of paper may be called for. Paper can carry only so much ink, and different papers have different tolerances. Uncoated paper is generally cheaper than coated paper of the same weight, all other factors being equal.

Colour refers to the colour of the stock itself, although by far the majority of book papers are nominally white. *Whiteness* describes how evenly a sheet reflects all colours in the visible spectrum; whiteness can be manipulated to produce a warmer or cooler white. Some papers complement the presentation of colour images; some papers are better suited to carrying type; some papers are well balanced for both type and images.

Opacity describes how much light penetrates the paper, or how well the paper absorbs and spreads light. Paper with high opacity is less translucent—that is, it lets little light pass through—and paper with low opacity is more translucent—it lets light pass through easily. The opacity issue for book editors and designers is SHOW-THROUGH: the degree to which the image or type from the reverse side of the printed sheet shows through on the reading side. Oil in printing inks affects opacity, making a printed sheet less opaque than an unprinted sheet, so you cannot always trust a dummy for evaluating show-through. In books that contain a large number of images, show-through can be a significant problem affecting readability—this is why high-quality art books tend to be printed on heavier, coated paper. But such papers are expensive and heavy—they add to the unit cost of manufacturing and make books more expensive to ship. So while opacity is important, it must be balanced with other elements of the design and the budget.

A key feature to understand about printing ink is that it's translucent, not opaque. It works because paper reflects light back to the reader through the eye. *Brightness* refers to how much light a paper's surface reflects and produces contrast between the paper and the ink. If a sheet lacks brightness, it will absorb too much light and little light will reflect back through the ink. Either too much contrast or too little may impair reading; for the paper in books, unlike other kinds of printed material, brightness is a critical factor. Paper that is too bright makes sustained reading uncomfortable.

One particular quality of paper affects printing and binding: grain. *Grain* refers to the direction in which most, but not all, fibres lie in a sheet. Paper is much stiffer across the grain than along the grain, so it's easier for paper to bend along its grain direction. It is also easier to tear paper along its grain rather than against its grain. Running sheets through the press against the grain may lead to registration problems in colour printing. (REGISTRATION refers to the accuracy of printing with multiple inks.) Similarly, the grain should run parallel to the binding, creating a smoother fold, making the pages easier to turn, and allowing the paper to swell across the grain in humid conditions. If the binding runs across the grain, humidity changes may cause the book to buckle and the binding to break as the paper swells or shrinks.

THREE BOOKS IN THREE PLACES
Choose three different books from your own collection or from a local library. Pick books of different sizes and lengths, with different bindings, and printed with different amounts of colour.

Try reading each of the three books (just a few pages—you needn't read each book through) in three different locations in your home or workplace—for instance, at your kitchen table, in your bedroom, in front of the television, in the bathroom, at your desk. For the sake of experimentation, visit your locations at different times of day, at different points in your schedule.

After you read a few pages from each book, make notes about the experience of your reading in that location. How do your eyes feel? Did reading give you energy or take it away? Do you recall what you read? How did the illustrations (if there were any) strike you? How do you feel about the book? Anything else you notice, positive or negative? Take notes at each location. You may want to compare and contrast your reading experiences as you move from place to place.

Page counts and imposition

A book can be long or short, but the number of pages that may be successfully bound is constrained by binding technologies. The number of pages in a book is its page count, which starts from the first sheet in the book, regardless of the book's page numbering. Most books are printed in *signatures* (although there are exceptions, as I'll explain in a moment), which control the page count. A SIGNATURE is made from a folded press sheet, and therefore its length is mathematically determined in multiples of four, eight, sixteen, or thirty-two, depending on the size of the sheet and the number of folds. The number of signatures in a book affects its unit cost—the more signatures, the more paper and therefore the more expensive the unit cost. The book editor must understand how to correctly identify a book's overall page count to be able to cost it appropriately.

Imposition refers to how pages are set up on a printing PLATE to take best advantage of the size of a printing sheet and the folding and binding processes. Most presses produce signatures in multiples of eight or sixteen, sometimes thirty-two or even sixty-four (although that's uncommon). If you examine the length of several books, counting all sheets in the block, you'll likely notice common breaks in multiples of sixteen and thirty-two, which reflect the most economical use of the press: 128 pages (32 times 4), 160 pages (32 times 5), 192 pages (32 times 6), 224 pages (32 times 7), 256 pages (32 times 8), 288 pages (32 times 9), and 320 pages (32 times 10).

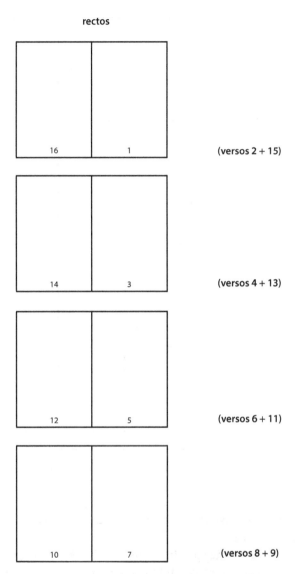

Figure 8.13 Imposition for 16 pages, saddle stitch

Depending on your bindery options, you may be able to bind in a signature of eight pages, rather than sixteen (see Figures 8.13 and 8.14); and in some cases you may be able to bind in a four-page signature. If you're using a SADDLE-STITCHED binding, as for some paperback picture books, you bind in fours, but never in twos. The cost of a book depends primarily on how much paper it uses, but also reflects the amount of work the printer has to do. If the press's standard signature is thirty-two pages, creating a 152-page book versus a 160-page book may not save

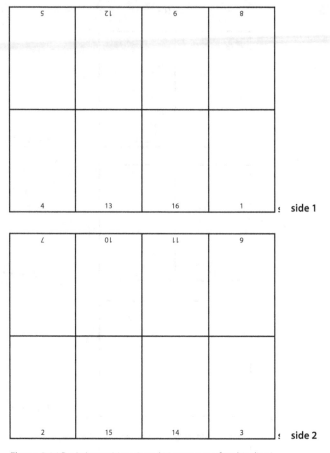

Figure 8.14 Basic imposition, 8 up (16 pages, perfect binding)

you money because the printer has to do extra work to accommodate the short signature.

When you set the specifications for a book, you determine its length in printed pages, then assign that length to the different functional areas of the book itself: the front matter, the body, the back matter. If you don't use every page you spec, you'll end with blank pages somewhere (often at the end of the book). Blanks are not necessarily a problem if it's only a page or two, but it's a waste if it's five or six. They are less common today because of layout software; if necessary, the type may be adjusted and even repoured to make more efficient use of paper. Still, blank pages can be easy to overlook, especially in a workflow where printed proofs are limited or absent, and you may discover the issue only when it's too costly to correct.

Standard book sizes

Books are made with fairly standard trim sizes to take best advantage of standard-sized press sheets. Here's a list of typical trim sizes in inches (still the standard in Canada and the United States):

$5^1/_2 \times 8^1/_2$
6×9
7×10
$7^1/_2 \times 9^1/_4$
8×10
$8^1/_2 \times 11$
9×12

Book dimensions always read width by height, so a 6×9 book is 6 inches wide by 9 inches tall. Books can be trimmed to other sizes, of course, but you must consider the economics and mechanics of using paper in non-standard ways because non-standard book sizes generally result in wasted paper, which is the biggest factor in your printing cost. A print rep and a dummy book may be useful to your costing.

Prepress: Proofs

As a book editor, you must know how to look at proof pages and detect what is wrong visually. When proofreading, you are responsible for both textual and visual corrections. In particular, watch digital images. Their resolution must be sufficient for effective printing. For example, a 72-ppi image that looks great on a laptop screen will look terrible when printed; 300-ppi images are standard for printed books.

However, a book editor may also be responsible for checking prepress proofs, which are created after proofreading is complete and the book file has been submitted to the printer. The printer preflights the file—that is, runs it through a number of prepress checks, such as ensuring all necessary fonts have been supplied and all the images are saved in the appropriate format. The printer then generates proofs, which show roughly how the book will look when it's printed. This is your last chance to make changes.

Depending on the kind of book being printed, you will receive one or more sets of proofs. Cover proofs are usually separate from the body proofs because covers are printed on different stock and often on different equipment. Common printer's proofs include the following:

- **Plotters:** Plotters are low- or medium-resolution colour proofs, often printed on uncoated paper. They are generated from the preflighted files and are folded into signatures. Plotters allow you to review image position and basic quality, but the colour may not be true to either the original or the press. Plotters are not produced for one-colour, type-heavy books.

- **Digital blues**: Digital blues, or digital bluelines, hearken back to the concept of traditional bluelines, which were made from film exposed on light-sensitive paper (like an old-fashioned blueprint). Digital blues are digital proofs, printed black on blue paper or black on white paper, from preflighted files. Printed on a large-format laser printer or digital copier, digital blues have about the same resolution as an office printer (300 to 600 dpi, or dots per inch) and may be presented in signatures, according to the press's imposition plan. They are generated for books being printed in black ink only; they tend to make poor-quality black-and-white images look even worse. Digital blues are best used for one-colour books with few or no images.

- **Composite proofs**: Composite, or composed, proofs are high-resolution colour proofs; depending on the system your printer uses, these proofs may have a proprietary name. Composite proofs are generated from preflighted files and are presented in signatures. If they are ink-jet proofs, their resolution may be as high as 2880 dpi; if they are dye-sublimated proofs (also called *thermal transfer proofs*), their resolution may be as high as 2540 dpi. The colour likely won't match the colour on the plotters—the composite proofs are closer to what's in the layout file than the plotters are. Some composite proof systems can accommodate Pantone colours if required. Composite proofs are best used for books that feature full-colour images. Because the various systems used to create colour proofs and the actual printing process are different, your ability to examine colour proofs and predict what will happen on press will improve as you gain experience—it's as much an art as a science.

The printer's proofs are sometimes referred to as CONTRACT PROOFS. Your signoff on the proof forms a contract with the printer: you agree to accept the print job based on the quality and correctness demonstrated on the proof. You are normally expected to turn the proof around within one or two working days.

At this stage, you make critical changes only, as the cost for changes is relatively high and a delay puts your press appointment at risk. These proofs are not normally shown to the author, who has signed off on the proof pages days or weeks earlier.

Printing Basics

Today, the majority of commercial printing is done using OFFSET LITHO-GRAPHY. The printing plate is the key to offset printing. Lithography uses plates (originally stones, but today, thin sheets of aluminum) divided chemically into printing and non-printing areas. Ink is chemically formulated to be greasy. Non-printing areas of the plate repel ink and attract water; printing areas repel water and attract ink. A plate is created for each colour to be printed; in most commercial printing, there is a plate for each of the four process inks, with the possible addition of one or two more to carry a SPOT COLOUR or varnish; see the discussion of colour, below. In the printing press, the ink image—type, illustration, or other matter—is offset, or transferred, from the plate onto a device called a *blanket*; the blanket then offsets, or transfers, the ink image onto the paper sheet. Because this process is so ubiquitous today, throughout this book, unless I specify otherwise, I have assumed you are printing books and other materials using offset lithography.

Offset printing is a right-reading format, also known as indirect printing. The image on the plate looks like the image that will be printed. (It is wrong-reading—a mirror image—when it is transferred onto the blanket.) If you've ever used Silly Putty to lift and copy a picture, you understand how a press blanket works. Silly Putty is pressed onto an inky surface, picks up some of the ink, and then is pressed onto a new surface, where it leaves a copy of the image. The blanket functions the same way. The plate is inked, the blanket is pressed upon it, and the inked image is transferred from the blanket to the printing sheet.

Two kinds of book printing are common today: *sheet-fed* and *web* printing. Both are forms of offset lithography. The distinction between the formats lies in how the paper moves through the press. In a SHEET-FED PRESS, the printing paper is cut into standard-sized sheets that move through the press one at a time. In a WEB PRESS, the printing paper is pulled continuously through the press from a very large roll (called a web) and is cut into sheets after being printed. Whether you choose to print on a sheet-fed press or a web press usually depends on your quantities. Sheet-fed printing is best for producing quantities from several hundred to about forty or fifty thousand copies, and the overall quality is very high. Web press printing is best for quantities from tens of thousands to hundreds of thousands. The quality is very good but not necessarily as consistent as sheet-fed printing is, and the paper choices are somewhat more limited. That said, the quality of current web presses is more than sufficient for all but the most exacting colour work, such as high-end art books.

Figure 8.15 A sheet-fed press. Note the towers: one ink is applied in each tower.

Figure 8.16 A web press

Books employ one of two general processes: one-colour printing or FOUR-COLOUR PRINTING. On a one-colour press, any number of colours may be printed (the limiting factor is the ability of the paper to withstand the ink), but each colour is applied to the sheet by a separate plate on a separate pass through the press. The default is black, of course, but you can print with any ink colour, and a second or third spot colour could be used in concert with the black ink—in a red-letter edition of a religious text, for example. The Pantone Matching System (PMS),

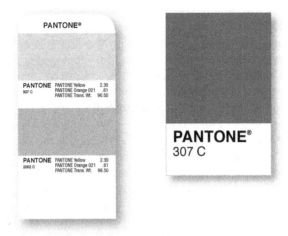

Figure 8.17 A Pantone swatch

among others, offers inks in a large range of colours, any of which could be used instead of, or in addition to, black. Pantone is a system similar to paint swatches at a hardware store. Each colour has a specific formulation, and a designer chooses a colour for a particular application. Your art department or any freelance designers you know will likely have a PMS formula guide. If you haven't seen one, ask to examine it. Printing with black plus spot colours does not produce what we recognize as full-colour printing, however.

Full-colour printing—more commonly referred to as four-colour printing—involves four or more inks, each applied by a separate plate. The four standard inks are called the PROCESS COLOURS: cyan, magenta, yellow, and black; additional spot colours or varnishes may also be applied. Four-colour printing is sometimes referred to as CMYK, the initials of the four process inks. (The *K* in CMYK refers to black, which is called *key* in printer jargon.) A full range of colour can be achieved using only cyan, magenta, and yellow; black is used to add sharpness to detail and to reduce the density of the other inks.

In CMYK printing, the four inks are applied in tiny dots overlapping and adjacent to one another by using four different patterns, called screens. SCREENING converts the full range of colour we see in the world around us into dots that can be printed. Screening is also applied to continuous-tone black-and-white images, a process once called creating a HALFTONE.

Colour images used in offset printing are normally saved as CMYK. You'll often encounter colour images saved as RGB, which stands for red,

LETTERPRESS PRINTING

Letterpress printing, which is how printing was done historically, is not offset but direct. Pages are made up from individual pieces of metal type, set by hand, plus images and ornaments. The areas to be printed are inked, and paper is pressed directly onto the inked area. Letterpress and other direct printing methods (such as rubber stamping) are wrong-reading: the inked area appears as a mirror image to the way it will appear on the sheet. Letterpress printing gives type a tactile quality, too, as the paper is slightly embossed when it is pressed on the type. Letterpress printing is uncommon today, but a few publishers—such as Gaspereau Press in Nova Scotia—use it. It brings an elegant, formal aesthetic to the printed word.

Letterpress printing has been largely displaced by offset presses, but the artisanal movement (think Etsy, Make It! and crafters fairs) has raised its popularity again. Depending on where you're based, you may not be able to find a letterpress printer easily. However, if you're producing a special or limited-edition text, have substantial lead time, and want to manufacture something memorable and valuable, letterpress printing might be an option—at least for part of the project (for instance, the cover). Choose letterpress if the following points apply to your book.

- You want to evoke history, tradition, or continuity.
- You want to evoke a handmade aesthetic or want to emphasize the physical product of the book.
- You are willing to accept a small degree of imperfection and variation in the finished books.
- You need a relatively small number of copies (a few dozen to a few hundred).
- Cost is not your biggest constraint.

Making books into beautiful, one-of-a-kind objects can be a savvy strategy for independent publishers looking to appeal to readers. Be sure to use it with the right text and the right audience.

green, and blue, the colour system used by computer monitors. RGB images are fine for on-screen display, but may fail a printer's preflight tests and will not print correctly. In one-colour printing, all images should be saved as grayscale (sometimes still called a halftone). Ideally, your author will submit images in the required format, but you may need to verify that images are correctly formatted (although you should not format the images yourself unless you know what you're doing). This is another task that requires communication. Printers' technologies and standards change regularly; your print rep can provide current expectations for file delivery.

Xerography: Print on demand

XEROGRAPHY refers to printing done with dry ink, or toner, fused to paper using heat. There is no wet-ink transfer as in offset or letterpress printing. Xerography may be high-speed digital photocopying or laser printing, depending on the printer's system. The Espresso Book Machine is a xerographic system intended, as its name implies, specifically for printing books. Other digital printing systems are intended for a wider range of applications, such as flyers, brochures, and posters; books are only a small part of their output. The key to xerography is that it's an on-demand system, perfect for printing limited quantities (from a single copy to a few hundred copies) affordably.

The resolution of xerography, while not quite as good as that of offset printing, is improving as the technology advances, and is appropriate for many on-demand applications such as small-circulation books, dummies, and ADVANCE READING COPIES (ARCS). (ARCs are copies of edited but uncorrected manuscripts that are formatted simply and printed inexpensively and on demand.) Current digital printers can boast resolution as high as 600 dpi in both black-and-white and colour. Paper selection is often a limitation, however. Your print rep should be able to give you current specifications and options.

Print-on-demand (POD) technology has enabled many publishers to take advantage of just-in-time inventory management, producing only as many copies of a book as they need. Files exported from layout software may require some preparation for appropriate assembly, as the imposition of a POD book is based on double-sided single pages, not folded signatures. This construction may lead to concerns about the book's shelf sturdiness and durability, especially if you're selling books into the library system, where the rigours of circulation require certain standards.

Binding

Binding refers to the way in which the printed sheets are joined into a single piece. The book block must also be attached to the cover in some way. There are various forms of binding available for most printing, but the two most common book bindings are PERFECT BINDING and SEWN BINDING. You may also encounter saddle-stitched books as well as other kinds of binding and fastening.

Saddle-stitched binding

Relatively few books are saddle stitched, but enough are that you need to understand what saddle stitching is. In a saddle-stitched book, the printed sheets and the cover are stapled together along a vertical fold

Figure 8.18 A saddle-stitched book

that forms the spine of the book (see Figure 8.18). Saddle stitching is effective on short books, such as children's picture books, that do not run beyond sixty-four or ninety-six pages (depending on the thickness of the paper stock). Be aware, however, that some granting programs have a minimum page count—usually forty-eight pages—for a text to be recognized as a book (except in the case of books obviously intended for children). Short, saddle-stitched books, such as chapbooks, may be disqualified from grant funding and awards consideration.

Perfect binding

Perfect binding produces the flat, square spine we see on all but the slimmest paperback books. The printed sheets are folded into signatures. The signatures are then assembled into correct book order. The folds that will form the spine are ground or sawed to create a rough surface, glue is applied to the surface, and the cover is wrapped around the signatures (see Figure 8.19). The book body is then trimmed. The finished book has a tight square spine.

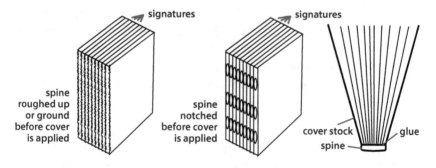

Figure 8.19 On a perfect-bound book, the gathered signatures are lightly ground by machine, giving the spine a rough, uneven surface to which glue will later be applied.

Sewn binding

Sewn bindings are more common on hardcover books but are sometimes found on paperbacks as well. The process for making a sewn binding is similar to that for a perfect binding. The printed sheets are folded into signatures and are sewn through their centres (much like saddle stitching, but with cloth thread). The sewn signatures are then stacked in correct book order, and long threads are shot through the stacks. Endpapers are attached to the stack, and the block is attached to its cover (see Figure 8.20).

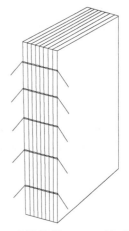

Figure 8.20 Making a sewn binding

Case binding

On a paperback book, the cover is printed on cover stock, stiff paper that protects the block and helps to keep the book pages upright when the book is shelved. The cover of a hardcover book is more complicated to manufacture. Hardcover bindings may be called CASE BINDINGS. The hardcover case, which may be made from paper, cloth, or leather wrapped around paper boards, is manufactured apart from the book block and then attached to it using spine cloth and the endpapers. There are many choices to make when you specify the case; your printer or bindery rep will walk you through your options as you build specifications for an estimate (see Figure 8.27). Case-bound books have a much higher unit cost than paperback books because of the additional manufacturing.

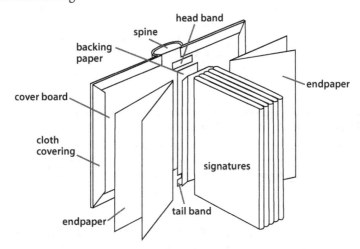

Figure 8.21 Details of a case binding

Other bindings

Some books are bound using spiral binding, Cerlox binding, Wiro binding, or similar open bindings. These systems are used on books that must open flat and that are intended for intermittent reference rather than continuous reading, such as handbooks and recipe books (see Figure 8.22). Although you might think these bindings are inexpensive, they can actually be surprisingly costly. They also make finding books difficult, if the book isn't shelved face out, and they lend only limited support to the pages, so the book may collapse on itself when shelved unless the cover stock is stiff and heavy. Specify these bindings only when it's appropriate for the book project.

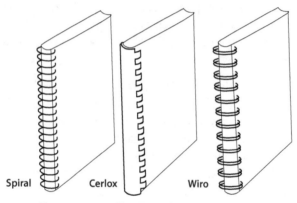

Figure 8.22 Examples of other bindings

EXPLORING BINDINGS

Using the resources of your home library or a local public library, find an example of a saddle-stitched book, a perfect-bound book, a case-bound book, and a book with a spiral or Wiro binding. Spend some time with each book and observe how the paper selection and the binding affect your experience of the book. What does each book's physical presentation communicate to you about its content or its tone? Do you agree with the publisher's manufacturing choices? Why or why not?

SUSTAINABLE MANUFACTURING

Most publishers want to be environmentally and socially sensitive, but we are in the business of making products that consume resources, and we want those products both to be affordable and to make a profit.

If your firm wants to lighten its effects on the globe, here are a few points you may want to consider:

- **Paper:** When you're seeking printing estimates, ask about recycled papers. If a paper is recycled, what proportion is post-consumer recycled? Is the paper manufactured without chlorine and chlorine derivatives? If you're interested in using papers made from non-tree fibres, how do the cost and quality compare? How is the fibre sourced? Can the waste be taken back through domestic recycling? Be aware that recycled and non-tree papers tend to cost more than other papers. Ask the printer how its plant manages recyclables. If environmental standards certification is available, does the printer have it? Remember to consider paper use throughout your operation, not just for printing books. Could your firm reduce its consumption of paper by adopting greener behaviours?

- **Ink:** Today, many printers have access to vegetable-based inks, which avoid using petroleum-based carriers. You may also want to ask the printer about how the shop disposes of waste ink and handles other chemicals. Printing in four colours uses more ink and may require more press time than printing in one colour. Not every book needs full-colour printing, so think carefully before you specify.

- **Cover finishes:** Many books have coatings applied to their covers to make them wear resistant and give them visual appeal. Varnishes, UV coatings, and aqueous coatings are on-press options. Laminates are options at the bindery. Each has its own environmental consequences and benefits. Ask which choices are best for your needs.

- **Binding:** All bindings have drawbacks. Permanence is usually the most important factor in book making, so consider glued or sewn bindings, which will make stronger, more durable books. If you choose an open binding, be sure it's sufficiently strong to stand up to the book's shipping and display. Think about the environmental consequences of producing unnecessary waste when books become unsellable due to damage.

- **Volume:** The number of pages in the book, as well as the number of books being manufactured, may be a consideration. At a minimum, adopt standard book sizes, which use printing sheets most efficiently. Consider page counts carefully, and work with designers to use paper and ink thoughtfully. Print only the number of books your firm needs so you aren't storing large quantities in inventory and potentially pulping or destroying large numbers in a few years.

- **Sourcing and shipping:** Book printing is often done far from your local centre. Is a local printer better suited to your needs, or does a remote printer have ways to offset its clients' environmental impact? Sourcing can also be a trap for some organizations—for instance, those trying to avoid using virgin fibres but also seeking to use local materials may not be able to find the materials they need or may not be able to afford paper that is both post-consumer recycled and locally made. Don't assume; ask specific questions.

The same ideas apply project by project, of course. If you're publishing a book about environmental or sustainability issues, you'll need to ensure the book's manufacturing is as green as possible.

An excellent resource for learning about sustainability issues is the Forest Stewardship Council (ca.fsc.org). FSC seeks to respect environmental, social, labour, and economic standards. At a minimum, you can specify FSC-certified papers when you print, but you may discover there's much more you can do.

Keep in mind that sustainable practices extend beyond green purchasing. Your sales rep should be able to answer your basic questions, but you may need to do additional research about a firm's ownership and politics. If environmental concerns are important to your firm, ask your suppliers about their own practices, such as recycling, shipping, and green sourcing; many printers are involved in tree planting, low-emissions programs, carbon-offset purchasing, and other environmentally responsive activities. If you order offshore printing, be aware that industrial practices and labour standards are major issues in some countries. Refraining from printing is sometimes seen to be the most environmentally sensitive choice, but do consider the implications of digital waste from laptops and smartphones, issues regarding access due to poverty, and ethical concerns associated with conflict resources. How does your own firm measure up on these scales?

As with any other decisions regarding production specifications, choose a service provider who normally works with the types of materials you're considering, and use the right medium for the job. If sustainability is important for your organization, you may need to commit to regular professional development and training to keep up with changing technology, because this area is advancing rapidly. If you want to make sustainable decisions, it's up to you to learn where each supplier shines.

PART THREE: PRODUCTION

Production Editing

Marshall Lee defines book production as "the execution of the design, i.e., purchasing materials and services, scheduling and routing the work, coordinating the manufacture of the book with distribution requirements, and maintaining records." Someone must be responsible for this execution, and in many firms, responsibility falls to a production editor or production manager (who, at some firms, might be the book's editor).

The production editor acts as a go-between, bridging editorial and the art department. This editor is typically responsible for schedules, costing, and budgets. She may be responsible for hiring freelance staff, or for overseeing their contracts if others hire them. She may be responsible for getting estimates, bids, and quotations from various suppliers. She is typically responsible for ensuring that all the people and processes involved in the publication of a book come in on schedule, and that the book arrives in the publisher's warehouse and in stores when it is promised. She may also be the staffer responsible for managing PRESS CHECKS (often in collaboration with the art direction, if the firm has one), and her signoff may have financial authority as well as responsibility.

Production editing engages two kinds of thinking at once. First, it refers to a set of ever-expanding knowledge about specific techniques, processes, tools, and products. Second, it refers to a problem-solving orientation toward a set of tasks. Production editors speak of learning to think forward and backward simultaneously, and this is a crucial aspect of their posture. Production editors must be strongly linear thinkers; even more so than book editors and designers, they anticipate and solve problems. Different books will require different solutions and different suppliers, so the production editor must be flexible in her thinking and versatile with her suggestions. A production editor spends her days collaborating with others who have deep and specialized knowledge; her knowledge and skills complement theirs. The production editor must know what other people's jobs are—that is, what they are doing, what they are responsible for, and when they will deliver—yet she does not need to know how to do their jobs herself. As such, this editor cannot simply trust that others are providing what she needs; her role is to be clear, specific, somewhat mistrusting, organized, and ever prepared for contingencies.

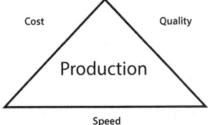

Figure 8.23 The production triangle

The production editor's work is always performed with an eye to the three points of the production triangle: cost, quality, and speed. The production editor can rarely have all three factors in her favour, so the job in production is generally to maintain a favourable balance (with cost usually being the most important to the publisher, who is the firm's ultimate boss). Production editors learn to think backward because every stage of production is constrained as much by the step that preceded it as by the step that follows it, and the production triangle is affected by these constraints. As such, the production editor must anticipate what later steps will require and plan earlier work to suit those requirements. For instance, let's imagine you're responsible for a cookbook. If the cookbook will be bound with a plastic spiral binding, you need to know the book's final page count early enough to order the correct size of spiral binding, and you need to know the correct offset for this binding method so the designer specifies an appropriate gutter. If the recipe pages will be printed in two colours with glossy four-colour pages of food photography inserted every so often, you need to know the imposition plan early enough to oversee the layout of the recipes so that a colour page doesn't fall at an unfortunate break. (For example, you don't want to give up a page of your colour section to an all-text page with no images: the colour pages can be inserted only between one signature and the next.) One of the critical teachings of production is that the later in the process you discover an issue, the higher the cost of fixing it.

A production editor's most important skills are communication, organization, the ability to manage others' expectations, flexibility, and firmness. She must communicate with people in the workflow to ensure they are staying on time and are prepared to deliver on their due dates. She must maintain a schedule and keep the schedule up to date to be able to report to others; similarly, she may have to maintain a budget and keep it current for the sake of reporting to others. The production editor cannot compromise her schedule to try to meet an impossible deadline unless she has abundant resources to throw at the project—and such resources are frankly rare in book publishing. She must equally not compromise her budget to try to accommodate late changes in goals or outcomes without clear direction from a senior editor or the publisher. To do otherwise is to set herself up for failure.

Production editors learn early to schedule deadlines well ahead of when they really need the materials and to build in flex time. It's always a strength in a relationship to be able to give someone a day or two of "extra" time. If the production schedule has been set too tightly, without some flex, the first missed deadline can scuttle the whole project, like a line of falling dominos.

Supporting the art department

As the book editor prepares a manuscript for mechanical processes, she needs to think about artwork: photographs and graphics. How does the art department want these materials supplied? When does the designer need them—how far in advance of receiving the copyedited text file? Who is responsible for naming/numbering files, keeping custody, and returning any original materials to the author once the book has been published? These details don't emerge magically: someone—probably the book editor or the production editor—must make decisions and communicate expectations and responsibilities.

A specific point the book editor must know is how the layout technician wants to receive the copyedited file. This file is normally transmitted when the text is signed off and needs only proofreading after layout. (Some layout software does have provision for an editor to make editorial changes to the file while it is in layout, but in general this feature makes the layout technician's job more complicated.) How does the art department want to receive the word-processed file—as one long file? As a number of distinct, sequential files? How should the text be prepared—are bold and italics okay? Will other character styling (such as diacritical marks) persist once the file is imported into the layout software, or will it be lost? It's possible the designer's templates will overwrite file formatting unless the file is thoughtfully imported. Will the typeface (or faces) the designer has chosen support certain symbols or languages? If not, time may be wasted when the type has to be changed to accommodate the needs of the manuscript.

In short, the book editor or project editor must try to anticipate both the needs of the manuscript and the needs of the designer or layout technician. As with so many other aspects of life and work, communication is the key.

Press check

From time to time, you may be asked to attend a press check. At a press check, a member of the publisher's staff goes to the printing plant to review samples of printed sheets (called MAKE-READY). You look at the colour and the reproduction quality of any critical images. (Press checks are not normally done for one- and two-colour jobs.) Your print rep is usually with you and will guide you through the press check, at least the first time. Press checks are more usually attended by design staff, but as an editor, you'll learn a lot about production and manufacturing by attending one if you can.

When you examine the sample press sheets, you are looking for colour density and correctness. At this stage of production, it is normally too late to make any other kinds of changes. First, look at the printed sheets themselves. Pay attention to bands of solid colour, especially blue, green, yellow, and red (e.g., look at the green of grass, the blue of sky or water). You should have a signed-off high-resolution proof to compare to. Are the colours too strong, too weak, or just right? Then look at the colour bar (also known as a colour strip or control strip—it is printed outside the trim area, on one edge of the sheet). The colour bar contains technical information about dot size, ink saturation, and registration; the press operator will explain these details to you if there is a concern.

Next, listen to the press operator. What is the operator concerned about? What is the operator asking you to comment on? Operators know their equipment; they know what they can adjust—relative CMYK values and ink density, for example—and what they cannot. Listen to the print rep, too. Print reps want their clients to get the best job possible, and the reps usually know printing—and printing problems—well. What is the rep concerned about? What does she suggest the operator do?

Your task is to make a decision about priorities. What elements on the page matter most? This is your last opportunity to affect the printed page, so think through the consequences of your decisions carefully. The press check is not a moment to act on impulse, and not a time to pretend you know more than you do.

Some typical problems include dot gain (some is inevitable), misregistration (some is likely), ghosting (which occurs when there is a large volume of ink on one part of the plate and a small volume of ink on other parts of the plate—it's difficult to balance the ink flow for both needs), hickeys (which are caused by an imperfection or defect on the printing plate or the blanket), and picking (which occurs when ink pulls fibres or coating from the surface of the paper, leaving spots on the printed surface). Listen before you speak; your job is to evaluate the situation and ask for a solution if necessary, not to find fault or to direct the solution. When you are satisfied with the quality and correctness of the colour, you (or the designer) sign off on a make-ready sheet. The press operator will use this sheet as the basis for the settings on subsequent plates—you will not normally be asked to check more than one setup. Your signoff indicates that the publisher will accept the print job on the finished books. You may also be allowed to take some make-ready sheets (called FLAT SHEETS) with you.

Book Costing and Book Budgets

In chapter 3, I mentioned that a book editor will often prepare a rough costing of a book (the P&L statement) in order to determine how much of an advance to offer an author. The editor may also prepare a revised P&L statement after the book's first year in print to evaluate the project's profitability. Now let's look at what goes into book costing, the intermediate step in which a book's costs are first estimated, then confirmed as the work is done.

Figures 8.24, 8.25, and 8.26 present simplified costing sheets, just to give you a sense of what to consider when you cost a book. (Note there are some differences in the models used in each scenario.) Costing

sheets are usually prepared on spreadsheets with formulas bu
as information changes, you update the figures and recalculate
It's important to keep costing sheets current so that the decisions you
make reflect a realistic budget.

Title: A Light-Hearted Novel

Author: Sunny Day

Edition: paperback

ISBN: 978-1-89630-123-4

Proposed publication date: September 2016

Proposed price: $18.95

Unit cost: $4.32

Ratio of PP&B: 4.39

PRODUCTION STAFF

Editor: Lowly Editor
Designer: Hunt Peck
Layout: Hunt Peck
Printer: Houghton Boston

PRODUCTION SPECIFICATIONS

Overall page count: 160 pages
Trim size: 6 × 9
Interior pages: B&W
Cover: 4C 1 side
Binding: perfect

SALES INCOME

First printing: 1,000 copies
Forecast sales, first year: 800 copies
Sales at 47% discount: 700 copies
or $7,030.45
Sales at 20% discount: 0 copies
Sales at 60% discount: 100 copies
or $758.00
Gratis: 100 copies
(includes author copies)
Forecast sales income: $5,893.45
Forecast rights income: $0
Forecast grant income: $8,000
Forecast gross income: $5,893.45

IN-HOUSE COSTS

Rights and permissions: $0
Artwork: $350
Editorial: $1,000
Design and layout: $2,200
Print, paper, and binding: $4,320
Advance: $500
Additional royalties earned: $1,016
Total in-house costs: $9,386

SALES AND MARKETING COSTS

Sales commission:
$471.48 (8% of net sales)
Distribution and fulfillment:
$707.21 (12% of net sales)
Marketing:
$294.67 (5% of net sales)
Total sales and marketing costs:
$1,473.36

Gross costs: $10,859.36
Forecast net income: $3,034.09
(without grant, -$4,965.91)

Figure 8.24 Sample book budget 1: Small press literary novel

Title: A Colourful Field Guide

Author: May Flowers

Edition: paperback

ISBN: 978-0-55109-799-0

Proposed publication date: September 2016

Proposed price: $19.95

Unit cost: $3.98

Ratio of PP&B: 5.01

PRODUCTION STAFF

Editor: Vallia Green

Designer: Claire Eaux

Layout: Claire Eaux

Printer: McCallum

PRODUCTION SPECIFICATIONS

Overall page count: 288 pages

Trim size: 5 × 8

Interior pages: Full colour throughout

Cover: 4C 1 side

Binding: layflat

SALES INCOME

First printing: 5,000 copies

Forecast sales, first year: 4,500 copies

Sales at 47% discount: 4,000 copies or
$42,494

Sales at 20% discount: 0 copies

Sales at 60% discount: 500 copies or
$3,990

Gratis: 100 copies
(includes author copies)

Forecast sales income: $44,289

Forecast rights income: $0

Forecast grant income: $0 (not grant
eligible)

Forecast gross income: $44,289

IN-HOUSE COSTS

Rights and permissions: $0

Artwork: $1,000

Editorial: $3,300

Design and layout: $4,600

Print, paper, and binding: $19,899

Advance: $1,000

Additional royalties earned: $7,977.50

Total in-house costs: $37,776.50

SALES AND MARKETING COSTS

Sales commission:
$3,543.12 (8% of net sales)

Distribution and fulfillment:
$5,314.68 (12% of net sales)

Marketing:
$885.78 (2% of net sales)

Total sales and marketing costs:
$9,743.58

Gross costs: $47,520.08

Forecast net income: ($3,231.08)

Figure 8.25 Sample book budget 2: Regional press trade book

Title: Thorough-Going Criticism

Author: T.H.E. Mann

Binding: paperback

ISBN: 978-0-88863-283-X

Proposed publication date: September 2016

Proposed price: $39.95

Unit cost: $6.15

Ratio of PP&B: 6.5

PRODUCTION STAFF

Editor: Ann Editor

Designer: Ella Phont

Layout: Ella Phont

Printer: Hignell

PRODUCTION SPECIFICATIONS

Overall page count: 256 pages

Trim size: 6 × 9

Interior pages: B&W

Cover: 4C 1 side

Binding: perfect

SALES INCOME

First printing: 800 copies

Forecast sales, first year: 500 copies

Sales at 47% discount: 150 copies
or $3,176.03

Sales at 20% discount: 300 copies
or $9,588.00

Sales at 60% discount: 50 copies
or $799.00

Gratis: 100 copies
(includes author copies)

Forecast sales income: $9,568.03

Forecast rights income: $0

Forecast grant income: $2,000

Forecast gross income: $11,568.03

IN-HOUSE COSTS

Rights and permissions: $250

Artwork: $450

Editorial: $3,300

Design and layout: $3,500

Print, paper, and binding: $4,920

Advance: $0

Additional royalties earned: $1,997.50

Total in-house costs: $14,417.50

SALES AND MARKETING COSTS

Sales commission:
$765.44 (8% of net sales)

Distribution and fulfillment:
$1,248.16 (12% of net sales)

Marketing:
$478.40 (5% of net sales)

Total sales and marketing costs:
$2,392.01

Gross costs: $16,809.51

Forecast net income: ($5,241.48)

Figure 8.26 Sample book budget 3: University press scholarly nonfiction

Let's walk through a model costing sheet using these figures. Keep in mind that you will prepare a fresh costing sheet for each binding and format you plan to publish—one for the hardcover, one for the trade paperback, one for the ebook. Note also that the ISBN for each edition will be different, too.

Remember, the proposed price of the book—its cover price— is ideally between five and six times the unit cost to manufacture the book (expressed as a ratio, it's 5–6:1). The unit cost is the overall cost of PRINT, PAPER, AND BINDING (PP&B) divided by the number of copies to be printed. In the differential between the unit cost and the cover price, you should be able to cover all the other costs associated with publishing the book. If you feel the market can bear it, use price breaks like $19.95, $24.95, $29.95, and $34.95. Prices in whole dollars (e.g., $36, $40) tend to be reserved for hardcovers, gift books, and high-end cookbooks. Your sales force will likely tell you if your proposed price is too high or too low.

Based on the proposed cover price, you can forecast your sales income. Remember that the publisher rarely receives the full cover price of a book; the model I've used here presents some typical discounts, but of course you'll plug in the numbers that suit your publishing situation. Don't forget gratis copies—the AUTHOR COPIES and any finished copies to be sent to reviewers or as desk or examination copies—because these represent a cost to the publisher. For textbook publishers and some academic publishers, dozens or even hundreds of copies will be sent out to instructors who might assign the book to their classes and need to see a copy before making the decision to adopt the text (although publishers are increasingly using ebooks for this purpose). Your forecast gross income is the total of forecast sales income, grant income, and rights income.

Now let's look at in-house costs. Rights and permissions refer to charges your firm pays on behalf of the book. In many cases, rights and permissions are paid for by the author or are charged back against the author's royalties, so the figure here might be very low or even zero. Artwork costs refer to any charges associated with the creation of original artwork, such as commissioning a map for the book's endpapers or hiring an illustrator to draw herb plants and edible flowers to accompany the recipes in a cookbook.

Editorial costs include charges for the substantive edit, copyediting, and proofreading. If the firm is paying for indexing or an abstract, this is charged to editorial as well (although it might be charged back to the author, depending on the book contract). Whether you include editorial and design and layout costs is an important question. At some firms, these figures are included in a costing sheet only if the work will be done by freelance staff. In this case, you will need a current quotation from the freelancers in question. At other firms, all costs must be captured in the costing sheet, including in-house staffers' time. In this case, charge costs based on the number of weeks a staffer will need to complete a task. Each workweek is worth one-fiftieth of a staffer's annual salary.

PP&B refers to the overall cost of manufacturing the book and shipping it to the publisher's warehouse. You'll need a range of estimates from printers who are best equipped to produce the kind of book you're costing. Some printers offer full service, including in-house bindery. Some printers specialize in colour but will bid high on one-colour bids; similarly, some printers are best suited to one-colour jobs and will be unable to bid competitively for four-colour work. To request appropriate estimates, you need to talk to sales reps and learn what equipment each printer has. Be sure to provide the printer complete specifications when you request a bid.

Finally, note that the advance (or at least the portion paid to date) is a sunk cost. You can rarely get it back if the book ends up becoming a ghost (i.e., being announced but never published).

You'll notice that sales commission is a fixed percentage of sales income, as is distribution and FULFILLMENT, and so is not a cost you can adjust. Marketing costs are discretionary and may have some flex, but typically run five to ten percent of sales income. This is a place where a firm may feel it can save significantly, but remember that while digital marketing looks "free" superficially, it involves substantial work. If you include in-house staff's salary cost in editorial and design and layout, you may have to include marketing staffers' salary costs in this line, too. Be careful about squeezing marketing too hard. Every book needs some market attention. You can always spend more on marketing, depending how hard you want to push a book, but always remember that costs are a reality while forecasts are a fantasy. Bills tend to come due much earlier than your sales income is remitted.

Common costing problems

Book editors run into a few typical issues when they prepare costing sheets. One involves guessing badly, or too early in the process, how long the finished manuscript is likely to be. Paper is the biggest cost item in printing, and even eight additional pages tacks on a significant cost over the run of a few thousand books. A related error is failing to consider a manuscript's special requirements, which may add to the cost of everything from editing to layout to manufacturing. Even a small number of permissions can add several hundred dollars to the overall cost of a project. You must think clearly and completely about a project's full requirements when doing your initial costing.

Date: January 29, 2016

Client: Magic Publishing House
12345 67 Avenue
Edmonton, AB

Project: **Design, layout, and production management**

Grade 4 social studies textbook

4cp throughout, 8×10 inches, 256 pages (incl. front and
back matters), 1–2 images per page, first in a series

Design of interior pages	**$3,200**

including choosing palette, illustration style, creating system of topic pages
and icons for easy navigation; master file to include templates and styles

Production of interior pages	**$2,500**
Production management	**$6,000**

includes consultation with editors, cartographer, illustrators, photographers;
sizing, labelling, and preparing photographs for printing, based on
1–2 photos per page; preparing other artwork for printing

Cover design and production	**$1,200**
Total estimate	**$12,900**

The above project will be completed and provided in InDesign CC 2015. Client to
provide all artwork and text. The above quote includes four sets of major changes
and two sets of minor changes, as well as up to 20 hours of consultation with other
suppliers. Additional consultation time will be billed at a rate of $80/hour. Production
time beyond what is quoted will be billed at $55/hour.

Invoices will be issued as stages are completed (i.e., upon interior design approval,
images requiring scanning, cover design approval, final files sent out to service
provider).

This quote does not include GST or courier fees.

Thank you for the opportunity to quote on this project. If you have any questions or
concerns, please call. I look forward to working with you.

Art Ist
Winning Covers Graphic Design
art@winningcovers.com

Figure 8.27 Sample design estimate

Another typical error arises from using out-of-date estimates for freelancers' work or from deliberately underestimating freelance expenses to bring the cost of the project down. See Figure 8.27 for a sample design estimate—note that this estimate encompasses more costs than typical projects require. Underestimating freelance costs is frankly a common short-term strategy, but it's fraught in the long term. Similarly, harried editors will sometimes use old printers' estimates rather than get a current quotation or a quotation specific to the project in question, yielding cost estimates that can be misleading. Be sure to provide detailed specifications and ask for a range of quantities (e.g., 1,000, 3,000, and 5,000 copies).

Some errors arise from problems during the process. You must add unbudgeted costs into the costing sheet as you go, such as having to redo an edit or cover design or producing multiple sets of proof pages because of the author's late changes. Have some stretch in your budget to accommodate these exigencies, or at least ensure that you adjust your cover price to cover the extra costs. Although we like to imagine that every book will go smoothly—and many do—it's generally a better idea to build in a margin for error. You can always be happily surprised when the book out-earns its budget.

At the beginning of this chapter, I wrote that books express their purpose fully only when they are realized physically. This seemingly simple statement has been picked at over the last decade as questions of the form versus the content of a book have become central to contemporary book culture. Today, we ask in all seriousness if a book is only a book when it is consumed on paper, suggesting that digital books—ebooks—are somehow not really books. But how? How is the content of a book segregated from its container, and what are the consequences when it is? These questions are not merely aesthetic, either. Recent studies have suggested that reading comprehension and retention are reduced when readers read on a digital device rather than on paper, a finding that plays on our human fear of loss or exclusion—our fear of missing out—at the same time that it disparages the emerging technology of digital reading. Book design and manufacture—whether on paper, as audio, or as ebook—underpin these larger social conversations, and we'll return to some of these themes at the conclusion of this book.

This chapter has underscored the importance of knowledge and communication in the relationship between editorial and design. In chapter 9, we look at yet another important relationship: that between editorial and marketing.

9

Sales and Marketing

"... what writers finally want more than good editing and smart marketing and ten-city tours and two-book contracts and appreciation (make that worship) and lucrative movie deals and hoity prizes are readers. Loyal, avid readers."—Betsy Lerner

This chapter introduces sales and marketing from the perspective of a book editor: the basics of what the editor needs to know. Once again, it is not intended to prepare you to work in sales and marketing; as with design, marketing is an area of specialization in itself. What this chapter will do is explain some marketing and PUBLICITY activities to you; discuss those aspects of sales and marketing that are expected of most editors; and relate these processes to the larger arc of publication. Editors are involved with sales and marketing staff throughout a book's lifespan. However, at most firms, the editor has specific work to do prior to publication, around the publication date, and following the book's release. Although the description of these processes here may suggest that each book gets exclusive attention, at most firms the attention of the sales and marketing staff is no more exclusive to a book or an author than the book editor's attention is to a single manuscript. Staff may be working on several titles, sometimes dozens, at one time.

Let's start by defining our terms. *Sales* refers to the work of moving books from the publisher to the retail chain and involves sales representatives who visit bookstores and booksellers. The sales area also includes warehousing and distribution. *Marketing* refers to the work of bringing a book to the attention of potential buyers, using a variety of tactics, including PROMOTION and publicity. Unlike sales messages, which give direct encouragement to buy or consume a product or service, marketing messages are indirect and suggestive. *Promotion* refers to activities that the publisher pays for to raise awareness about a book or books, such as buying ads in industry publications or producing book-related swag. *Publicity* refers to opportunities for other media to direct awareness to the book, such as an author appearing on a noon-hour newscast or the book's appearance on a bestsellers list. While these terms are sometimes used loosely, they do involve distinct processes. All the activities planned for the promotion and publicity of a book are articulated in the book's MARKETING PLAN, a document prepared soon after the manuscript is acquired (or maybe even before).

Another key term in marketing discussions is *positioning*, and this is where editors have some insight. Positioning means using a variety of marketing tactics to identify a book to its audience and to the sales force. As you assessed the manuscript and developed the book substantively during your editorial work, you were inherently positioning it. The cover and paratext similarly position the book, and various decisions made by the sales and marketing team will further refine the book's positioning.

Go to a bookstore and study the fiction section—not just the romance novels or the science fiction, although these books will make my point nicely. Look at the covers of trade novels. Chances are that from the image, the type, the trim size, the relative positions of the title and the author's name, and even the blurbers, you have a good sense of the novel's kind of storytelling and the quality of the prose even before you turn to the back cover. Nonfiction tends to be more variable, but

YOUR PICKS

If you've been in a bookstore recently, you've likely seen a shelf or a wall of staff picks, books recommended by the people who work in that store. Put yourself in the shoes of a bookstore staffer. Which five books—current or classic—would you recommend to others? If you like, take your list to a bookstore and see how your tastes compare with those of local booksellers.

To extend this exercise, write about each of the books you've selected and share your writing with others (for instance on Facebook or on your blog). Provide a short plot description (no spoilers, please!) or an overview of the content, and explain in a few sentences what you like about the book and why you would recommend it to others. Be specific and detailed: does the book have a gripping story, lush prose, fascinating characters, amazing plot twists, admirable research, unexpected insights, or other admirable qualities?

increasingly the covers in serious nonfiction hail their potential readers similarly. Consciously or unconsciously, readers recognize the signals a book's positioning sends them.

The Author's Key Role

When the manuscript leaves editorial care and enters the realm of sales and marketing, the author may feel left behind. In most cases, publishing firms promote books, not authors, although certainly there are exceptions. As with editing, a big part of the marketing job involves managing expectations. Another important part of the job is to involve the author. Most authors want their books to be successful and are receptive to marketing staff who can help them promote their books and find publicity opportunities.

Regrettably, without marketing, a book may fail. In a world in which thousands of books are published every month, an author who refuses to promote herself and her book actively is a liability to the book's success, yet some authors resist doing promotional work. They feel shy and uncomfortable when they give readings and don't want to appear on radio or television. They don't like having a professional audience on Facebook, resist tweeting on Twitter, and resent carving up their writing time to maintain a blog or to contribute to your firm's blog. And some authors have full-time, non-writing jobs and simply cannot be as involved in marketing as a full-time author might. If an author is reluctant to do promotional work, the editor may need to lean on her relationship with the author. The publicity clause in most contracts requires that the author make some effort at publicity; ideally you won't have to push this point, but you might. Do what you can to encourage your author to get involved in promotion, and communicate early to allow the author to anticipate scheduling conflicts and competing demands for her time and attention. Also, encourage sales and marketing to come up with promotional strategies that can work for individual authors. Not everyone is comfortable doing an interview on radio or television, but guest blog posts or a Twitter account might be perfect. In some circumstances, the marketing strategy will evolve with the goal of simply keeping the book from disappearing into obscurity because of unfortunate timing (imagine the fate of books published in the United States in September 2001) or a topic that just doesn't click.

Marketing Conversations

Many conversations will occur between an author and the marketing staff. The book editor may have no more than passing familiarity with the marketing plans for the book, but if the relationship between editor and author is secure, the book editor will likely hear from the author regularly as marketing gears up. Early in the editing process, however, there are a few marketing-related conversations editors should be prepared to have with their authors.

One of these conversations has to do with the title, as you read in chapter 6. If the sales and marketing staff, or the book reps, have concerns about a book's title, pay attention and get ready to discuss the title with the author. As I mentioned before, authors tend to be fiercely protective of the title they've chosen, particularly on fiction and poetry, but the author's title is not always the best pick. The publisher tends to win the argument, creating the potential for a resentful author. As the book's champion and the publisher's ambassador, the book editor can help reach a middle ground and keep the relationship positive and productive.

Another conversation topic, which I will discuss further in a few pages, is reviews. Ask the author where she imagines seeing her book reviewed, who she dreams of being reviewed by. Your sales and marketing team will likely have extensive lists of potential review outlets, but only the author knows which outlets she reads and admires. Be careful to manage expectations here. Reviews can be solicited, but they are never guaranteed. You want to know where your author wishes to be reviewed, but be sure she understands you are not promising to make it happen, because you cannot. Start discussing where to send advance reading copies and REVIEW COPIES early, and have the conversation again shortly before the book's publication date to ensure you and your author still have the same goals and expectations.

A further marketing-related conversation you may need to have has to do with the cover. If your author doesn't like the cover, you have a problem. Even if your art director loves it, and sales and marketing staff adore it, if the author won't show the book face out to others and won't hold the book proudly at events, you're losing tremendous marketing power. As with discussions about the title, the author may not win the battle over the cover, but an unhappy author generally makes for an unhappy publisher, so this conversation, though often uncomfortable and sometimes unsatisfying, is important.

A closely related conversation may need to occur around branding. If you've acquired a series, your firm's art director may try to signal sequence and continuity among the volumes with a consistent visual identity or brand. Similarly, if the book fits into a specific interest for your firm or if the house wants to promote the idea of a particular kind of reading experience, the book may look and feel "branded," even if it's not formally so. Not all authors are keen to be branded, though, even when a series or imprint is highly successful. This is another potentially uncomfortable conversation, and putting it off won't make it easier. If necessary, remind your author about the book contract, which usually says that the publisher has the final say on marketing-related decisions. If visual identity is a stopper, it's important to know early enough in the marketing process to adjust the plan—or jettison the plan entirely. Editor and author must also talk if either side has concerns about how the book is positioned. For instance, I worked with a first-time author on remaking her master's project into a novel. After publication, she confessed that she didn't really like her book's cover, which she felt positioned the novel as young adult and not literary comedy. Regrettably, the author did only limited self-promotion, and the novel failed to receive the attention it should have had.

The author questionnaire

Most marketing conversations begin after the author completes an author questionnaire. It is normally sent to the author within a few weeks of the manuscript's being formally accepted. The author knows the book better than anyone else (except perhaps the book's editor) and may have excellent insight into how best to promote it. The questionnaire also allows marketing staff to get an early look at the author's expectations for the book. The sample author questionnaire in Figure 9.1 is typical, although most publishers have their own form with its own idiosyncrasies.

Marketing Meets the Sales Channels

A few years ago, market analyst Craig Riggs described the supply chain in Canada and the United States aptly and succinctly: "Big likes to play with big." The increasing reach of Amazon, the merger of Penguin with Random House, and other changes in the industry have only amplified Riggs's observation. Sales and marketing are challenging for any publisher, but in the context of Big Publishing and Big Retailing (terms I'll return to later), sales and marketing for small independents are particularly difficult. A book's editor has an important role to play.

Remember the sales channels? Let's plug some specific details into that general discussion. When sales and marketing staff refer to "the chain" in Canada, they mean Chapters/Indigo (which also owns Coles bookstores and sells both through physical outlets and online). Chapters/Indigo is the major buyer for most Canadian publishers. Many Canadian cities also have independent bookstores, but even the independents tend to buy more from the major publishers than from small publishers (because the books from large publishers tend to get substantial marketing and are in demand by average consumers). Walmart and

Fantastic Publishing Author Questionnaire

We are thrilled to be publishing your book! The following questionnaire is designed to help us work with you to promote your book to the biggest audience possible, including media, reviewers, bloggers, and, of course, readers. Your help is essential to your book's success!

Information requested on this form will also be used to request a Cataloguing-in-Publication record from the National Library of Canada and may be shared with Revenue Canada.

Please provide as much detail as you can in your responses. If you wish, you may also send a brief version of your résumé or CV when you return this questionnaire.

YOUR CONTACT INFORMATION

FULL NAME _____

YOUR NAME AS IT WILL APPEAR ON YOUR BOOK _____

DATE OF BIRTH _____

CITIZENSHIP   CANADIAN   LANDED IMMIGRANT   OTHER

SOCIAL INSURANCE NUMBER _____

GST NUMBER (IF APPLICABLE) _____

HOME ADDRESS _____

MAILING ADDRESS (IF DIFFERENT FROM HOME ADDRESS) _____

WORK ADDRESS _____

MOBILE TELEPHONE _____ DAYTIME TELEPHONE _____

EVENING TELEPHONE _____

NUMBER WHERE WE CAN LEAVE URGENT MESSAGES, OTHER THAN ABOVE _____

FAX NUMBER _____

PRIMARY EMAIL ADDRESS _____

ALTERNATE EMAIL ADDRESS(ES) _____

WEBSITE/BLOG URL _____

FACEBOOK_____ TWITTER _____

LINKEDIN _____ _____

OTHER SOCIAL MEDIA (PLEASE LIST)_____ _____

Do we have your permission to provide your telephone number
to media if they wish to contact you about your book?   Yes   No

Figure 9.1 Sample author questionnaire (page 1 of 4)

GETTING TO KNOW YOU

Please provide a brief biographical statement (approx. 25 to 30 words) and a longer, developed biography (approx. 100 to 150 words). Don't be shy! Include information about where you were born and raised, where you have studied, where you have lived for work, your profession and training, your hobbies and interests, any awards or honours you have received, and any interesting anecdotes about your book.

What is your current job title?

_____

Are you a member of any professional, academic, or writers' associations? If so, list them.

_____

_____

_____

_____

List your previously published books. If this is your first book, list any journals or periodicals you have been published in.

_____

_____

_____

_____

ALL ABOUT YOUR BOOK

Explain your book in 25 to 30 words—the elevator pitch.

_____

_____

_____

_____

Explain your book in 80 to 100 words. We may use this description for our catalogue, website, etc.

_____

_____

_____

_____

_____

_____

_____

_____

_____

Figure 9.1 Sample author questionnaire (page 2 of 4)

What do you feel are the most important features of your book?

_____

_____

_____

_____

If someone were searching for your book online, what keywords do you think would lead them to it?

_____

_____

_____

Who is the ideal reader for your book?

_____

_____

What is the primary market for your book?

_____

Does your book have a secondary market? If so, what is it?

_____

What three places would you like to see your book reviewed in?

_____

_____

What three people would you like to provide an advance comment ("blurb") about your book? If possible, please provide complete information for these people, particularly email addresses.

_____

_____

_____

What existing books are similar to yours in topic or presentation?

_____

_____

_____

Are there any publications (including small magazines, local papers, and journals) that should review your book? If so, list.

_____

_____

_____

Figure 9.1 Sample author questionnaire (page 3 of 4)

Would organizations or associations you belong to announce your book in their newsletter or other communication? If so, list.

_____

_____

_____

Are there any awards for which your book might be eligible? If so, list. (No need to mention the GGs or the Giller Prize.)

_____

_____

_____

Are you aware of any organizations that might purchase a large quantity of your book? If so, list.

_____

_____

_____

Do you have a local bookstore? Do you shop there (i.e., are you known there)?

_____

_____

_____

Please provide a list of contacts (names and email addresses) we can send information about your book and promotional opportunities.

_____

_____

_____

What are your marketing and promotion ideas for your book? Please list.

_____

_____

_____

_____

Are you willing to travel for promotional events?   Yes   No

Please send your completed form to marketing@FantasticPub.ca within two weeks. If you have further ideas or discover marketing opportunities at any time, please let us know.

Thank you for your time and information. We look forward to working with you!

Figure 9.1 Sample author questionnaire (page 4 of 4)

Costco are the major non-traditional book outlets. Despite the resurgence of bricks-and-mortar retailing since 2012, Amazon continues to dominate bookselling—particularly ebook sales—and is noticeably shaping the terms of trade. In Canada, Chapters/Indigo, Costco, and Amazon tend to be most publishers' biggest accounts. The smaller the publisher, however, the less likely this is so.

Beyond the concentration of retailing, we must also be aware of the concentration of sales. As Chris Anderson observed in *The Long Tail*, a small number of books will sell extraordinarily well—hundreds of thousands or even millions of copies—but most books will sell only a few copies through each retailer. Craig Riggs found that the top five hundred titles accounted for roughly a quarter of all book sales in Canada, and the Big Five publishers account for by far the majority of sales (more than 65%). This situation is particularly precarious when we realize that the supply (i.e., the number of titles available for purchase) is far outpacing demand (the number of people buying and reading books), not to mention library use, digital piracy, and the still-healthy trade in used print books.

Many small- and medium-sized publishers depend on direct sales to consumers, either on the publisher's website, through book groups, or at events, and recently some major publishers have returned to direct sales through their websites, too. Special sales are another area of increasing importance to smaller publishers' incomes. I raise these points because as Big continues to get Bigger, smaller publishers feel the squeeze. Smaller publishers need to be ever nimbler and more adaptable to survive. Sometimes this means exploiting markets and tactics abandoned by larger publishers, and sometimes it means adopting large publishers' tools at a scale that's right for smaller operations.

The best marketing tool you have is the manuscript itself. As the book's editor, you did research to evaluate the book's market prior to acquiring it. Share this information with the sales and marketing department, but also share your personal enthusiasm. Why are you excited to be publishing this book? If you get the sales and marketing staff excited about the book, they can communicate that excitement to retailers and consumers. As Pat Walsh says, "Publishing is a business largely based on enthusiasm and validation." If you can transfer your enthusiasm for the manuscript to others, they will do their best to validate it through sales, awards, and other forms of success.

The Marketing Plan

Throughout this book, I have noted that at least some authors struggle with the tension between art and commerce. For most authors, your publishing firm's strength in marketing, sales, and publicity matters. Expectations certainly vary, but no author sets out to fail in the market-place. Authors want to know that your firm can sell their books well, and their faith may need to be won early. When a book is being chased by several publishers, it's the marketing plan that may ultimately impress the author (and the agent).

A marketing plan is exactly what it sounds like: a document that outlines the sales and marketing team's plans for a given book. It is normally prepared by the marketing manager with information drawn from the author (from the author questionnaire, an in-person meeting, or both) and the book's editor. Although marketing plans tend to have common features, a plan should be customized for each book in the season. As a planning document, it is subject to change as the manuscript moves through editing and production.

For marketing plans to be well executed, the author must be energetically involved in both the planning and the activities. Much of the pre-publication activity will involve generating "buzz" or market anticipation. The marketing plan may use the author's own resources, such as her blog, her Twitter account, and her Facebook page, as well as other pertinent social media (e.g., LinkedIn, Pinterest, Instagram). It will also use the publisher's traditional tools, such as the catalogue, lists of reviewers, and media relations. The plan will also take advantage of specialized tools, such as book trailers, Goodreads giveaways, and emerging social media. Cathie Crooks, Sales/Marketing Manager for University of Alberta Press, says, "Given the thousands of books published every few months, promoters and their authors go to great lengths to help readers discover their books. No one activity is sufficient, and publishers and authors need to work together cohesively to maximize their efforts."

Here is a list of typical elements of a marketing plan. As we get deeper into this chapter, I will explain some of these elements—and others—in detail, particularly where book editors should be involved:

- book launch
- author tour
- online presence
- social media
- advertising
- point-of-sales materials

For more information about a marketing plan, see the sample marketing planner in appendix B. One of the most difficult parts of marketing books is that each book is in effect a new product and needs a unique campaign. Your experience as the editor of previous books and your current knowledge of the book industry at large will help the marketing department tailor a plan appropriate to both book and author. But keep in mind that coming up with the marketing plan and doing the work of sales and marketing is primarily the business of that department, not yours (unless, of course, you *are* the marketing director as well as the book's editor).

Building Anticipation Prior to the Publication Date

Today, a book may have as little as sixty days to prove itself on the shelf. As Monique Sherrett of Boxcar Marketing observes, publishers need to start book promotion early—as early as the book is signed, in some cases—and to keep promoting the book (and the author) as long as possible—ideally beyond the book's first season. In this section I'll survey several documents and processes marketing and editorial staff may use to build anticipation of an upcoming book.

At a minimum, the title-information sheet and cover copy should be prepared by the book's editor, who should know the manuscript better than anyone except the author; ideally, that editor should also review any other copy generated on behalf of the book. All sales and marketing copy must be copyedited and proofread, and many publishing firms have a house style sheet to support conformity and consistency of textual presentation.

Catalogue copy

Catalogues are a tool publishers use to present books to potential buyers—at the consumer level, but also to booksellers, wholesalers, and library buyers. They are often printed, but increasingly you'll find publishers' catalogues online in PDF form or published on hosting sites such as Issuu, too. Catalogues are important yet subtle tools; the way a book is presented in the catalogue is part of its overall positioning. A book that gets a two-page spread in a catalogue signals to book reps and retail buyers that the publisher intends to spend a great deal of time and effort on the title, unlike a book that appears on a quarter of a catalogue page alongside three other titles.

Cover copy is often based on catalogue copy, so it's important to write an appropriate, effective description for every book. Remember that catalogue copy is also sell copy, so it shouldn't be dry or uninteresting. Ideally, catalogue copy should be written by editorial staff, not by marketing staff.

The title-information sheet

A TITLE-INFORMATION SHEET (TI) is a statement of a book's key features, prepared by the book's editor for presentation to sales and marketing staff, to the sales reps, and to reviewers in advance of the book's publication date. The sheet may look fairly straightforward but is based on substantial research. You should be able to back up any claims you make on your TI sheet. Your sales force is made up of knowledgeable people who will call you out on faulty or misleading information, so don't try to bluff them.

The sample TI in Figure 9.2 is typical, although your firm might ask for more or less detail. *Competing titles* refers to books from the publisher's own list and from other publishers' lists. Competing books appear in the same category and may affect the potential sales of the new book. Similarly, *related titles*—which include titles that are not in direct competition but may have relevance because of their audience, content, or style—may appear on the publisher's own list or may be published by a competitor. Accurate lists of competing and related titles may be helpful for a publisher's cross-promotional plans and may be used for comparisons when sales reps describe a book to retailers.

The sales handle

A sales handle, which appears on the TI sheet and elsewhere, is a phrase or sentence that communicates the essence of the book, signals its vital qualities, and/or makes a comparison to a well-known book. An excellent example of a sales handle is this, for the book *How to Build a Girl* by Caitlin Moran (2014): "Imagine *The Bell Jar* written by Rizzo from *Grease*." Or Gregory Maguire's description of his book *Egg and Spoon* (2014): "*The Prince and the Pauper*, except with girls, meets *Frozen*, except everything is melting instead of freezing."

A sales handle is sales oriented and commercially appealing. It should be crisp and memorable and ideally possesses a hook for its intended audience. Most importantly, a sales handle is *not* a statement of theme. A sales handle sells books!

The sales conference

A *sales conference* is a meeting, usually lasting several days, at which book publishing sales representatives hear from the publishers they represent. The sales reps may work for a single publisher (usually with a large number of imprints or client publishers) or for a number of publishers at once; their job is to sell their publishers' books to retailers who sell books. Sales conferences are usually held twice a year (coinciding with the sales seasons, fall and spring), and it's common for book editors to attend sales conferences to present their lists of books for the upcoming season.

WWW.FANTASTICPUB.CA

Book title: _____

Author: _____

Author hometown: _____

Publication date: _____

Format and trim size: _____

Print run (specify format if necessary):_____

Retail price (specify format if necessary): _____

Sales handle: _____

Additional sales points:

- _____

- _____

- _____

Catalogue description:_____

_____

_____

Market (may specify primary, secondary): _____

Author bio: _____

_____

_____

_____

Previous work(s) by the same author:_____

_____

_____

Competing titles (outside of house/imprint): _____

_____

_____

_____

_____

Related titles (inside of house/imprint, for purpose of co-promoting): _____

_____

_____

_____

_____

Figure 9.2 Sample title-information sheet

Going to the sales conference gives you an opportunity to learn about your firm's sales channels and to get feedback about your past books from bookstores across your sales region. Therefore, your goal at the sales conference, in addition to introducing your upcoming titles, should be to develop open and regular communication with your sales force.

Book reps tend to be advocates for the editors, publishers, and authors they represent, and your success is their success. They are, in a sense, the "human face" of the publisher, since most booksellers will never meet the staff of most publishing houses. Your best strategy is to think in terms of fit, just as you did when you acquired the book: figure out the distinction that suits your book's position and communicate this idea to the sales reps.

Most sales reps have substantial background in books and marketing. From this experience, they try to balance the interests of the publisher—that is, selling books—with the interests of the consumer—that is, finding the right book for a given purpose. It is not in either the reps' or the publisher's interest to oversell a title. If the bookseller can't move the copies, they will be returned to the publisher's warehouse, battered and possibly unsellable. So when you talk to the reps, be enthusiastic but not hyperbolic; keep your expectations reasonable. Honest communication will ensure your titles are well represented in stores and may encourage the continuing sales of your backlist titles, too. Independent booksellers have a real advantage in meetings with book reps. They know their clientele and will usually order appropriately if they've been given correct information. Chain retailers, despite having access to mountains of data, do not behave quite the same way. Chain retailers may order hundreds of copies of a title, then return them, sometimes in unopened boxes, just a few months later, causing disruption for both publisher and author.

To do its best work, your sales force needs basic, reliable information from you about every title you introduce.

- Who is the market for this title?
- What is the competition for this title?
- What are the promotional plans for this title (advertising, regional touring, Goodreads giveaways, etc.)?
- What promotional support materials may be available (posters, bookmarks, bag stuffers, etc.)?

The reps need the book's presentation in the catalogue to be clear and accurate because, as we'll discuss in a few paragraphs, the catalogue is an important sales tool. They also want you to think about the support materials you provide. A table of contents is welcome for nonfiction; a chapter sample is welcome for fiction. Reps want to see advance reading copies of LEAD TITLES, but don't expect the reps to read them unless a book truly has legs. Although they may love books and reading, reps don't have time to read most of the books they sell.

The reps also expect you to be well prepared for your presentation. You will have a very short time—perhaps only fifteen or twenty minutes—and this is not the place to wing it. Go to the sales conference with a strong, concise pitch for each book. More importantly, use your role as the book's editor to give the reps insider information that exceeds the catalogue presentation. For instance, if you have anecdotal information about the author's background or about how the book was acquired, now's the time to share it. The reps might be able to use this information to intrigue retailers and overcome their resistance to ordering.

At the sales conference and during the selling season, expect to hear feedback from the reps. You'll likely get questions at your presentation, which will suggest how the reps themselves perceive the book and its positioning. The cover tends to be particularly important. Reps may also offer suggestions about the title, the price, the release date, and promotional plans. Once they're out in their territories, the reps may communicate with you (or more likely with your marketing manager) if they encounter particular problems with a title, such as the price, the content, the timing, or support.

Your obligation to the reps extends beyond the sales conference. The reps need to know if your production schedule slips and a book will be delayed. They also need updates on books with very low inventory, books being reprinted, books going out of print, books changing price or format, and books with new rights sales. Although you have direct contact with your book reps only once or twice a year, they are working for your firm every day and need your consistent and engaged support.

The tip sheet

A tip sheet is another sales and marketing document; its purpose is to support your sales force. Editors and marketing staff provide tip sheets alongside catalogues and TI sheets to ensure book reps have the information they need to understand a particular book and to sell it correctly—appropriately—to booksellers and other sales channels. The information provided on a tip sheet is in point form; the reps will glean additional information from your sales conference presentation and supporting materials. For most projects, it should be no more than a single page long.

Online presence

There are two components to a book's online presence. First, the author must have a web presence. If the author has a website, it should link to the publisher's website (and vice versa) and should feature the current book prominently. The author's website should function as a hub where all the author's online activities come together, including her blog (see below). Be sure that it's possible to follow the author on Facebook, Twitter, Instagram, Pinterest, or other social media through a direct link—you don't want to lose a potential follower because she has to go to a social media platform and search for your author rather than just clicking through. And obviously, as a book editor, you are expected to follow your authors on Twitter and retweet their book-related content, become Facebook friends, and so on. You should also be active on social media so you can amplify the work your authors and your marketing team are doing, and create your own fanfare when books you are responsible for are published.

The book itself must also have an online presence so potential readers and buyers can find it easily. This means listing the book with the major online retailers (Chapters/Indigo and Amazon) and ensuring that the book's metadata is maintained. Most of these activities are beyond the scope of this chapter and fall squarely into the realm of sales and marketing staff, but the section on BookNet Canada below explains some of the reasons why a book's online presence is so critical today. Another tactic is to list the book on Goodreads and LibraryThing once advance reading copies are available, to create more opportunities for discovery and to generate anticipation.

Blogging

In addition to or as part of their websites and social media presence, many writers maintain a blog (a web journal) on which they write about their writing, their personal interests, or other topics that might interest other people. John Scalzi's blog *Whatever*, for example, is a popular site on which the author discusses his own work, his personal life and interests, and other authors. In this way, the author becomes approachable, almost like a friend, and readers can quickly become fans simply by getting to know the author as a human being. YA author John Green, with the help of his brother Hank Green, has taken blogging a step further and created a blog-like YouTube channel called *VlogBrothers*, where fans can learn about the Greens, John's writing, and numerous other topics of personal and social interest.

Blogging software is freely available and setup is simple. Blogging is a commitment, however: a blog needs to updated regularly, at least two or three times a week, if not daily, and there are literally millions of abandoned blogs cluttering up the web. In addition to posting on his own blog, your author might contribute guest posts on your press blog and on other book-related blogs.

Book trailers

Book trailers are increasingly popular tools released prior to a book's release. Even self-publishing authors are creating them. Unlike a movie trailer, a book trailer does not provide the narrative arc of the story. Rather, it introduces the book to the reader, often with the author speaking directly to the topic or the process of writing. There are normally no actors in a book trailer, just words, images, music, and the author.

As a book editor, your perspective is valuable to ensuring that the trailer maintains the tone of the book itself. Also, be sure to respect other creators' rights when you introduce images and audio to the trailer—use Creative Commons materials and give appropriate credit, or ensure you have explicit permission from the rights holder to use the material.

CRITIQUE BOOK TRAILERS

If you've never seen a book trailer, you may be surprised by how different a book trailer is from a movie trailer. Shelf Awareness (www.shelf-awareness.com), a book-industry newsletter, regularly highlights new book trailers. Go to the Shelf Awareness site and explore past issues of the newsletter. View several book trailers using links from Shelf Awareness. What do the trailers do well? What could they improve? Do you want to read any of these books, having viewed the trailers? Which ones?

Reviews and reviewing

Conventional book reviewing has contracted in the last decade or two for a number of reasons, the most significant of these being changes in newspaper and magazine publishing, where most formal book reviewing was done. (For what it's worth, the loss of reviewing—or at least of thoughtful, serious reviewing—has been considered an issue for decades.) In the place of books pages and noteworthy book reviewers, we have book sites on social media (Goodreads, LibraryThing), numerous thoughtful book blogs, and customer-generated reviews on online retailing sites such as Amazon. While these sites certainly support a book's sales and an author's success, well-placed reviews may still be important to a book's success. Scholarly books need to be reviewed in important academic journals, for instance, just as fiction needs to be reviewed in major newspapers, textbooks need reviews from instructors who use and like them, and poetry needs to be reviewed in relevant journals and small magazines. A book that isn't reviewed is a lonely creature indeed.

Authors need reviews as much as books do. Reviews—even if they are lukewarm or downright negative—tell authors that their books have found readers, have been acknowledged by their peers, have a place in the community. While many authors refuse to read their reviews, they still need to know they exist. An author may be excited about her ranking on Amazon, but she probably cares more about whether her peers have noticed her book's arrival.

Novice publishing staff are often surprised to learn that the publisher doesn't determine which books will be reviewed. Never imagine that a book wasn't reviewed in the *Globe and Mail* or the *New York Times* because the publicist failed to think of these outlets. Publishers do not—and should not—control reviews, positive or negative. It's a coup to get a starred review in *Publishers Weekly* or the *Globe and Mail* specifically because the publisher does not tell a newspaper or magazine what, when, or how to review. A book is sent out as an offer, and marketing staff hope the offer is accepted. Because there are fewer spaces and more books to choose from than there once were, competition is fierce. The best a book editor can do is hope for positive attention and encourage the author to stay focused on her next project.

Ask for reviews well in advance when you can. Some outlets require three or four months' lead time, or longer, to have reviews completed by your book's publication date. You will, of course, continue to try to get reviews after the book's publication date, too. Sales/Marketing Manager Cathie Crooks says, "Apart from providing great metadata for a book, the area I work at most diligently is getting review coverage, as this aids in both discoverability and credibility."

Advance reading copies

Advance reading copies may be supplied to book reps, librarians, book bloggers (including BookTubers—book lovers who post reviews and other book-related content on YouTube), and other reviewers. ARCs may also be given to booksellers in stores where HAND-SELLING—sales made directly from a bookseller's recommendations—is important, such as the bookstore in an author's hometown or in a city's leading independent bookstore. These books are made to be disposable. The type is reproduced at office-printer resolution (300 to 600 dpi), so they're not suitable for books with colour images or even with a significant number of black-and-white images, and they are bound with glue, so ARCs tend not to last long. Most importantly, ARCs are uncorrected proofs, so reviewers should not quote from them because the text is still subject to change and correction.

ARCs allow you to provide copies of a book to blurbers and reviewers months in advance of the publication date so you can get the blurb or the

Avi D. Reader
9711 Anywhere Boulevard
Nanaimo, BC V9S 4N4

July 3, 2016

Dear Avi,

Thank you for requesting *All These Green and Perfect Places* by Emile Dickens from the
January LibraryThing Early Readers program. Congratulations! You have been selected
to receive the enclosed review copy on behalf of Fantastic Publishing.

When you post your review on LibraryThing, please also take a moment to send us
the link or email a copy to us (marketing@FantasticPub.ca). We would love to hear
what you think about this book, as well as any other Fantastic titles. Be sure to include
your name and the title of the book you've reviewed. We send LibraryThing reviewers'
comments to our authors, who love to hear how readers have responded to their work.

Enjoy the book with our best wishes!

Yours truly,

Marion Sales
Marketing and Promotions
marion@FantasticPub.ca

Figure 9.3 Sample letter to reviewer

excerpt from an advance review you're hoping to put on your cover. As
you might imagine, having to produce ARCs puts pressure on the book's
editor to move the manuscript through editorial processing rapidly.

Digital ARCs are becoming popular, particularly with self-publishing
authors and very small publishers. Digital ARCs, like other ebooks,
greatly reduce the costs of manufacturing and shipping, so they're valuable for presses with tight budgets. But for readers who want to experience the physical book, eARCs are not a substitute. And digital ARCs do
not relieve the pressure of speed on the book's editor.

Publishers are also using ARCs as giveaways to ordinary readers
on social media as a mechanism for building buzz. Goodreads and
LibraryThing are the major outlets for such giveaways, but an author
could easily host a contest on his Facebook page or blog to give away
ARCs, the only costs being that of the ARC itself and shipping it to the
winner.

Publication Date and After

DISCOVERABILITY—a title's success at being found by its ideal readers—
is any book's greatest challenge today. Monique Sherrett asserts that
"The key to book discoverability is not SEO [search engine optimiza-
tion]." Rather, publishers need to mix traditional promotional activities,
such as reviews and media appearances, with social sharing to generate word of mouth on social media and references to the book and its
author. Digital tools help to keep the promotional window open longer,
but they work best as part of a larger promotional spectrum.

News releases and media kits

A NEWS RELEASE (sometimes wrongly called a press release) is normally
prepared and circulated two or three weeks prior to a book's publication date. The point of a news release is not to announce that a book is
about to be published, because books are published every day and no
one in media cares. The job of the news release is to promote opportunities for media to cover your book away from the book page—as a
segment on breakfast television, for instance, or in a dedicated seasonal
shopping guide.

With the loss of review pages and book sections, publicists have
increasingly pushed to gain attention for books elsewhere in newspapers and magazines. This approach is not new, but it is much more
important today than in the past. Getting the book "off the book page"
means seeking publicity through a feature article about city history that
refers to your book, from the food writer doing a round-up of important cookbooks, in an op-ed column by your author, or on the sports
page as a human-interest story. For example, *Edmonton Journal* political
affairs reporter Graham Thomson wrote a column about the fortunes of
Alberta's premiers in which he dedicated several paragraphs to discussing Kevin Taft's then newly published book *Follow the Money: Where Is
Alberta's Wealth Going?* (2012)—a great example of getting a book off
the book page and into a key section of the newspaper. The cookbook
Alice Eats (2013) was featured in an article with colour images on the
front page of the food section of a major daily, with an excerpt of recipes
on the second page. In either case, the publisher could hardly buy better
exposure. A great news release can create such opportunities.

News releases are intended to communicate with journalists and
therefore should adopt a journalistic format and style. Keep your words,
sentences, and paragraphs short; stack the information using the inverted
pyramid structure; provide contact information and be available to
respond if you're contacted; and offer opportunities for journalists to
find their own angle on the subject.

December 1, 2016

FOR IMMEDIATE RELEASE

DON'T WAIT TO EAT YOUR VEGETABLES

Regina, Saskatchewan—Did you know that many common garden vegetables are also aphrodisiacs? As you choose the vegetables to complement your holiday meals in the coming weeks, you just might want to ponder their value beyond great flavour and good nutrition.

In his latest book, gardening guru Jerry Haricot reveals how phytochemicals found in ordinary garden foods can improve people's sex lives. He explains why carrots are good for more than just your night vision, how snap peas can put the snap back in your relationship, why every woman of a certain age should grow broccoli, and more.

Building from more than 20 years of research in greenhouses, gardens, and farms, *The Phytochemical Connection: How Fruits and Vegetables Can Change Your Life* lets readers in on the chemical secrets that make vegetables and fruits so stimulating. With his trademark wit, Haricot explains how scent, taste, texture, colour, and freshness add to the erogenous appeal of vegetables and fruits. He also includes a variety of recipes tailored to improving readers' charisma, physique, and stamina.

The Phytochemical Connection invites you to look at vegetables in a new way—a sexy way. Holiday dinners may never be the same!

-- 30 --

For more information, to obtain a review copy of the book, or to arrange an interview with Jerry Haricot, please contact:

Luce Talker
Fantastic Publishing
101 Midtown Exchange
Regina, SK S4R 1Z0

Tel: **306.555.1234** | Email: **publicity@FantasticPub.ca**

www.FantasticPub.ca

Figure 9.4 Sample news release

WRITE A NEWS RELEASE
Write a sample news release for a book that is already in print. (Make up the details as required.) What is the news angle for a local media outlet? For a regional outlet? Be sure to announce something more than just the publication of the book itself.

A MEDIA KIT is a package of materials to support a book's publication; it forms part of your basic media-relations strategy. Back in the 1990s, media kits went over the top. Book publicists sent journalists and editors fresh-baked muffins to support cookbooks, baskets of flowers to promote gardening books—anything to set a book apart and grab the journalist's or editor's attention. Since then, publicity budgets have fallen, and today's media kits are leaner, stripped-down information packages. Ideally, the media kit for any book should be available on demand through the publisher's website and will include the news release; a developed author bio; a high-resolution author photo; facts about the author, the book, and if available its reception (including any awards it wins); and a media advisory, which includes information about the author's availability (such as tour dates and scheduled interview and photo opportunities). The kit may also include an excerpt from the book, an author interview or Q&A, a sample feature story, and other materials to make reporting easy.

The purpose of the news release and the media kit is to pitch the unique features of the book. Can you tie the book to a current news issue? Can your author speak authoritatively to matters involving high-profile themes, personalities, or organizations? Can your author give an interview highlighting what's quirky, nostalgic, values-rich, or otherwise engaging about his book for a wide public? These are the qualities to bring out in your media communication.

It's generally easier to get the attention of local media than of regional or national editors. However, pitching to national outlets is worth the effort. Getting a book on CBC's *The Next Chapter* with Shelagh Rogers or having an author featured on *Writers and Company* with Eleanor Wachtel (or on NPR's *Fresh Air* with Terry Gross in the United States) usually results in a marked sales bump. Of course, it's easier to gain this attention when the book has accomplished something notable, such as winning a national award or becoming a surprise bestseller.

Advertising

The common belief in publishing is that advertising doesn't sell books, yet book ads show up in certain settings because readers do look at and act on ads. Books are rarely advertised on television or radio because the cost is so high relative to margins, but books are regularly advertised in magazines and sometimes in newspapers. Advertising may be directed to the trade (booksellers and librarians) or to consumers (the general public).

Most book advertising is about positioning the book for its audience. It also engages recency—that is, the ad complements positive reviews, publicity, and word-of-mouth promotion a book is already receiving, and thus reminds potential readers about a title already in their awareness. If advertising is part of the marketing plan, watch costs carefully and support ads with other promotional activity. Advertising by itself is not enough.

BOOK-RELATED PERIODICALS IN CANADA

The following periodicals are excellent places to advertise to both the general public and the book trade. These publications review books and feature excerpts.

- *BC Bookworld* (www.bcbookworld.com)
- *Prairie Books Now* (ambp.ca/pbn)
- *Montreal Review of Books* (mtlreviewofbooks.ca)
- *Atlantic Books Today* (atlanticbookstoday.ca)
- *Quill and Quire* (www.quillandquire.com)

Another book-friendly publication is *Geist* (www.geist.com), which positions itself as a magazine of ideas and culture and features new writing and reviews. You'll see quite a few book ads on its pages. *The Walrus* (thewalrus.ca), which emphasizes cultural issues and high-quality writing, also regularly includes book ads. Finally, *Alberta Views* (albertaviews. ab.ca) features regular advertising inserts dedicated to Alberta books and publishers, as well as ample, thoughtful reviews. Advertising in these venues is reasonable and within many independent publishers' budgets.

Book launch

If you ask anyone who's been in publishing for more than a few years, you'll hear that book launches are expensive, they're a lot of work, and they don't sell books. Regrettably, in many cases, that's true. But some authors will insist on a launch, on or shortly after the book's publication date. How can you make the best use of your resources?

Many small publishers are now holding joint launches, either launching several books from the same season at one event or involving several publishers at a single event. For small publishers, working in partnership with other presses can help all the partners reach more people and minimize costs. Whenever possible, let other organizations do your events for you—that is, tie your book to other organizations' activities, which may mean that your author has a book "event" rather than a launch. For instance, a book about the early history of Edmonton might be launched as part of the opening weekend at Fort Edmonton, a living-history site. Such an event would be fairly demanding to organize, but would expose the book to thousands of people, some of whom might buy the book at the event and others who will talk about it to their friends and family after the fact.

There is, however, a lot of competition out there for readers' attention, and authors rarely remember a reading for three people positively (especially when two of them were the publicist and the book editor). If you must have a book launch, invite four or five times as many people as you expect will attend. Some publishers find that using an event-planning website, such as Eventbrite, helps manage expectations and avoid a badly disappointed author. With launches and any other scheduled events, *be sure the books will be available* on the date of the event—don't schedule an event hoping another department can speed up its processes to make your deadline. I've attended book launches without the books present, and they are incredibly uncomfortable.

Author tour

Book tours amplify the costs and logistics problems of a book launch over great distances. In Canada, relatively few authors tour, and when they do, it is often in conjunction with other events, such as the fall literary festivals circuit. In these cases, it's best to retain a publicist in remote cities to manage your author on tour, rather than leaving the author to manage on her own or trying to run activities from a distance. (Your budget likely won't stretch to allowing someone in-house to accompany the author on the tour.)

Some of the best author tours are author directed, such as Lisa Guenther's tour in support of her novel *Friendly Fire* (2015). Lisa toured with musician Carmen Loncar across Saskatchewan and Alberta, providing music and literature in a high-energy package. Lisa reflects:

> I was hoping to connect with readers through the tour and, of course, sell books. I also hoped that by teaming up with Carmen, we would together pull in slightly bigger, more diverse audiences than we would have individually. I think the tour accomplished all those things. Attendance was good. ... It was really lovely to meet people interested in our work, and for this reason alone it was worth it. Sales were also good. My book reached number two on the bestseller lists in Edmonton and Saskatoon, for a week. I'm sure this was because of events in McNally Robinson and Audrey's [bookstore]. Carmen's sales were also good—she had to order more CDs part way through the tour. We had several stops in rural communities, along with the major cities. The cities were great, but I really want to emphasize that rural communities can be great places for readings.

But, Lisa cautions,

> *It was a tremendous amount of work. It's harder than you might*
> *think finding the right venue in each town, especially if you're*
> *doing it remotely. It took several months of planning to pull it off.*
> *... Our friends and family suggested venues in their communities,*
> *promoted the shows, came to the show (often bringing their own*
> *friends), gave us a place to stay, and often fed us. I think they*
> *were key to the tour's success. ... Despite the work, I certainly*
> *think it's worthwhile for authors, especially when they're*
> *launching books. It was an interesting, worthwhile experience,*
> *and I intend to do another when my next book is published.*

Whether you direct the tour or the author does, you must provide tour support. Be sure the author and the bookstores have sufficient copies of the book for the events, and be prepared to drop-ship more inventory (i.e., ship it directly from your office or warehouse without going through your distributor) if the book develops legs during the tour. Be available to coach the author if his media experience is limited, and look for additional promotional opportunities along the author's route. Many schools, colleges, and university classes would appreciate a visit from a creative writer, particularly if the cost is low and the host has advance notice to promote the event. In some cases, you may even have access to grant funding to support an author tour—but almost never as much funding as you really need.

Book readings and signings

Once the book is launched—with or without a formal event—an author's follow-up visits to bookstores offer value to the bookseller and customers. Readings and signings, by a single author or as a group event, can be a low-cost way to bring interested readers to bookstores and to keep the promotional window for a book open—as well as to build excitement about future books.

Rick Lauber, author of *Caregiver's Guide for Canadians* (2nd ed. 2014) and *The Successful Caregiver's Guide* (2015), reflects on his experiences:

> *I have found that bookstore signings can be an enjoyable and*
> *effective way to promote your own work. These events can be*
> *quite easy to arrange. I have simply called bookstores, politely*
> *introduced myself to bookstore managers as a local author, and*
> *asked to be slotted in on the store's "visiting author" calendar.*
> *Try to coordinate your scheduled signings with a busier shopping*
> *day (e.g., Saturday). Personally, I like scheduling signings from*
> *noon to four to reach the peak number of customers. Remember*

that the holidays can be popular times for other authors looking to reach customers ... therefore, you can be proactive and start asking for holiday signings several months in advance.

Bookstores welcome visiting authors as they help to increase business (I haven't been turned down once yet with my own signing requests). If the bookstore carries your title, sufficient book stock can be ordered in for your signing. If you are a self-published author, expect to work on consignment (where you will supply your own book inventory—known in the business as "car/trunk stock"—and the bookstore and you both get a percentage of your sales). Either way you choose, signings make for excellent opportunities for customers to meet authors and for authors to market their book(s).

Author-led signings can keep a book visible for months, even years, helping it find new readers and extending its sales.

Point of sales materials

POINT OF SALES (POS) materials, also known as MARKETING COLLATERAL, are non-book materials used to promote a title. Bookmarks, posters, and buttons are common, inexpensive giveaways, and DUMP BINS and SHELF TALKERS may be part of a larger POS strategy. POS materials are especially valuable with children's books and can be distributed prior to publication to generate anticipation. Most of these materials cost relatively little to create (for instance, bookmarks can be produced on the same stock as the book cover and printed at the same time), but readers tend to value them highly. As an example, I have collected dozens of bookmarks over the years and keep them tucked carefully inside the books they came with. Your English teacher may have had posters from the Penguin Classics series hanging in his classroom, and people who have attended book fairs may use the crested carrier bags they've received for years. As with every strategy, of course, be sure the giveaway material suits the promotion.

Social media

As I noted above, promotional work on social media should start early and continue well after a book's publication date. For book editors, social media can raise potential issues. Authors must be aware of and respect copyright, libel, and privacy laws; be sure you or the marketing manager has had clear conversations about your expectations for the author's professional profile on social media.

The following list suggests some basic social media resources to consider. New media continue to emerge regularly, and you must evaluate which social media tools offer the best fit for the book, the author, and the audience.

- **Facebook**: Best suited to adult readers, Facebook allows authors and books to connect with readers, much like a book group. Authors can distinguish between their professional and personal pages.

- **Twitter**: An excellent tool for promoting books, authors, and book culture. The tight character count suits sales handles especially well. This example from House of Anansi demonstrates how to use a sales handle on Twitter: "#JaneAusten meets #GoneGirl in @missjanetellis's debut novel 'The Butcher's Hook.'" The ability to include pictures allows you to promote book covers and interior pages as well as your authors and book events. Be sure to retweet your authors' self-promotions.

- **Tumblr**: An excellent resource to support a book, Tumblr can be used like a scrapbook for readers who want to learn more about the world of a given book. Authors can post images and link to content relevant to a book's topic or context. Tumblr pages can be static or dynamic, depending on what suits the project—be sure the page links to book-purchasing options, the author's other social media, and the book's catalogue page on the publisher's website.

- **Pinterest**: Similar to Tumblr, but particularly suited to certain kinds of publishing, such as cookery, crafting, home and garden, and lifestyle. Many publishers post book covers, author images, and book-related links on Pinterest.

- **Instagram**: Publishers post photos of book covers, authors, book events, and book-related materials (such as cover reveals, crested coffee mugs, and "shelfies"), as well as other aspects of book culture. This platform particularly suits photography of subject matter that also plays well on Pinterest: food photography, house and garden images, lifestyle photography, natural history, and so on.

- **YouTube**: If your organization regularly generates video, it may be worthwhile to develop a YouTube channel on which you can post book trailers, interviews with authors, and other video content. YouTube is an excellent tool if your authors' content is something that can be easily demonstrated, such as gardening, cooking, painting, or other technique-based pursuits.

Author Rick Lauber, whom I introduced earlier, observes,

> *While I began by blogging (even before my first book was published), I now prefer Facebook, Twitter, and LinkedIn for both reach and response. I tend to avoid shamelessly plugging my books on all of these platforms, expecting people will quickly tire of being bombarded with sales pitches. Make the majority of your posts fun and informative and people will not mind you slipping in the occasional sales message. ... For best results, post regularly on social media at different times of the day (readers will not always visit your pages routinely).*

An author's best success with social media comes from his intrinsic motivation. If an author is willing to integrate the work into his daily routines, social media can keep a book's promotional window open indefinitely—and offer added value to readers who engage with the author directly.

Mailing lists

We live in an age of permission-based marketing. This means consumers seek out and welcome communication from specific producers, such as publishers. Books tend to be high-trust objects, so publishers may be able to reach out to readers directly in a way that other manufacturers cannot—almost like friends. The notion of permission-based marketing is particularly important in social media, where people look to friends and social influencers to tell them where to focus attention. Monique Sherrett explains that people buy what their friends and the people they admire have for a very simple reason: "ads tell us what's available; our friends tell us what's desirable."

By building mailing lists, marketing staff create opportunities for ongoing, permission-based communication that emulates the friending and following models on social media. In newsletters and updates, marketing staff communicate as members of the book community: *we're readers, too*. They invite readers to interact with authors and with staff themselves, not just as book-industry insiders but as people who love to read.

Hand-selling is a term both editors and marketing staff should know. The bookseller's ability to provide a personal recommendation for a book by talking and listening to the customer, and knowing the store's inventory and sales patterns intimately, is one of the features most valued at independent bookstores. This is the quality most permission-based marketing tries to emulate.

The key to permission-based marketing is that it's opt-in only. When consumers are ready to move on, they must be able to stop your communication easily. In Canada, recent federal anti-spam legislation (commonly referred to as CASL) threatens fearsome penalties for non-compliant companies.

Direct mail

Direct mail may sound hopelessly old-fashioned, but for some buyers, it's still the right tool. In many cases, direct mail is now email, targeted to opt-in audiences (such as sending professors announcements about newly published textbooks or sending scholars announcements of new works in their field). But direct mail may also be lettermail for the right book, particularly if the intended audience is older or more conservative.

Libraries, festivals, and talking about books and reading

During the early and mid-twentieth century, libraries were an important and reliable sales channel for most publishers. Since the 1990s, that relationship has changed, but libraries remain an important way to promote books, authors, reading, and book culture. Even if the local library won't buy more than a few copies of a book, it may still offer a low-cost venue for hosting readings and signings, with a built-in audience of committed readers. Many libraries are now embracing an activist role in the community, pushing reading for social change and social justice. They may be some of the best allies publishers and authors could wish for.

Another outgrowth of our social conversations about reading and book culture is the popularity of author festivals. The International Festival of Authors hosted at Toronto's Harbourfront Centre is perhaps the best recognized of these, but there are writers' festivals and reading series in every province in Canada, as well as in Yukon and Northwest Territories. For some books—particularly literary fiction, creative nonfiction, popular but serious nonfiction, and poetry—festivals offer excellent promotional opportunities. If your author has published previously, you may be able to get her invited to a festival at which she can read from and sign her current book. An appearance at a festival tends to generate its own publicity, which can benefit not only the current book but also the author's earlier work. Festivals help books come to the attention of a wider community, build authors' reputations, and may contribute to books' and authors' success with awards and prizes.

For books with strong pop-culture connections, look into science fiction and fantasy expos, anime and cosplay conventions, comic and pop-culture fairs, and similar events. Most major cities host at least one or two such events each year. Attendance can be expensive, and these events are a fit for only some books and some authors, but don't discount "fans and cons" when you have the right book.

One more way many authors are finding success is by promoting their books to book groups, one at a time. Authors willing to attend a book group meeting—in person or electronically—form strong relationship bonds with readers and foster long-term reader loyalty, potentially translating into opportunities for backlist sales and anticipation for the author's future books. Of course, not every book suits book groups—these groups are often, though certainly not exclusively, meetings of middle-class suburban women—and the publisher may need to sink some money into developing a book group apparatus, such as questions about the book, additional information about the book and its context, and additional information about the author. All of this material may appear online. Book groups remind us that, in its history, reading was a social act; importantly, book groups and the conversations about authors, writing, and reading they generate are renewing and strengthening book culture.

Discoverability: The Book's Biggest Issue

To be read, to be purchased, to be valued, a book must first be found. The process of finding a book, from a marketing perspective, is referred to as *discovery*. Discoverability has emerged as the number-one issue books in the early twenty-first century face. There are so many books available from so many outlets in so many formats that it is increasingly challenging for a single reader to find a single book. Add to this academic research that demonstrates that humans tend to demonstrate bias toward the kinds of media we already consume and to resist new forms and new perspectives. Yet discovery—particularly the discovery of local authors and books from the place that is ours—is vital to sustaining book culture.

One practical outcome of discoverability is that responsibility for promoting books has shifted from the retailer to the publisher. There is comparatively little hand-selling of books today, even at independent booksellers. In the late twentieth century, a city's independent bookstores were leaders in book culture: they set the agenda for readers by presenting books and authors that suited the tastes of the store owners, who were also readers. Since the 1990s, however, the scene has changed dramatically. Today, independent bookstores are few, and big-box retailers compete with Amazon online to offer the largest selection possible—hundreds of thousands of books within a single store, and only a few of them promoted specifically (on sales tables and end caps, positions paid for by publishers). For that reason, publishers must retake responsibility for identifying the right book for every kind of reader.

In a bookstore, a potential reader looks at the front of the book, then at the back of the book (for blurbs, awards, endorsements), and then maybe inside before making a decision to buy. In the online environment, the front cover and the option to preview the interior of the book must do similar work. One aspect of the potential reader's evaluation lies in determining who else is buying in—who has reviewed the book positively or provided an endorsement. Therefore, it's important to communicate buy-in from the front cover and throughout your promotional package (particularly in whatever metadata your firm uploads to online retailers). Who else endorses this book? Has a brand-name author provided a strong blurb? Has an earlier edition of this title won awards? Has this author won previous awards? People value the sense of a reading community, knowing that a book they have selected speaks to their own motives and values. Online buyers also want low prices, easy purchasing options, and a wide selection of titles—but that's a somewhat different matter.

A question sometimes posed to the marketing department is whether a book can be over-praised or over-promoted. Can a book feature too many blurbs, win too many awards? Does recognition by peers really sell more books? Most publicists would say no, there's probably no such thing as too much publicity, too much good press, mainly because there are so many books and comparatively few opportunities to promote them. Yes, some readers are turned off by an Oprah O emblazoned on the cover of a book, and some readers resist reading Giller Prize and Governor General's Award winners, but these readers are uncommon, and they are not the readers you're trying to reach. Those readers have clearly heard of your book and are making a deliberate choice at this time not to select it, although that doesn't mean they will never do so. Research has shown that awards and other high-profile recognition do lead to increased book sales—for instance, in the "Oscar effect" that occurs when a book is adapted to film and subsequently is nominated for or wins an Academy Award. However, marketing staff must work carefully with editors and the art department to ensure that the book's positioning is upheld when blurbs, award notices, and other endorsements are added to a book's paratext. There's nothing designers dislike more than a book cover marred with award starbursts, even though they help to sell books.

POSITIONING A BOOK PROJECT
Now that you understand editorial assessment and positioning, it's time to synthesize that knowledge by trying to position the following books for marketing.

- *No More Downward-Faced Dog: Using Yoga to Control Depression,* by Ellia Hopchin
- *Monkeywrenches: Memoirs of an Industrial Education Teacher,* by Michael J.R. Effringham
- *Food Without a Face: Easy Recipes for New Vegans,* by Liliah Enraab
- *Shaking Hands: My Brushes with Fame and Random Conversations with Important and Emerging Authors,* by Lilly Stargazer
- *Ride Along and Write Along: A Guide to Writing an Impeccable Police Procedural,* by Ryan Garrison
- *The Letters of Sanford Mowbrey, Rupertsland Trapper,* by Gabriel Peters
- *Bloodless: The New Tradition of Canadian Diamonds,* by James Dimas

Here's a rough-and-ready assessment strategy to use for the purpose of this activity.

1. Is this project really a book, or would it be better treated as a magazine article or other form? (Questions to consider: How long is the text—does the concept support a book? What does it look like physically—hardcover, paperback, ebook only? What's on the cover? How does the running content appear? What's in the front matter and back matter, if anything? What visuals support the text, if any?)
2. Who is the audience? (Questions to consider: How big is this audience? Does it see itself as an audience? How will you reach/ motivate this audience?)
3. Position this book. (Questions to consider: Is it frontlist, midlist, or backlist? Who should provide a blurb? What features will you highlight on the cover copy? What price will this market bear? What events would support the publication date?)

List your positioning ideas for each title and annotate how you would signal this positioning.

Throughout this book I have referred to the tension between commerce and creation—between books (and authors) and the market (readers and buyers). This tension seems to be heightened in the last few years, perhaps due to the public's greater awareness of writing and publishing, particularly in media reporting of the exigencies of Big Publishing and the rise of self-publishing. Today, marketing success intersects with editing importantly—and at times controversially—in the realm of reception: how the book's sales figures affect subsequent acquisition processes and publishers' relationships with authors. Book editors must therefore understand how sales data is captured and used. In Canada, this means understanding the role of BookNet Canada.

BookNet Canada

BookNet Canada (BNC) is the Canadian publishing industry's supply-chain agency. BNC works between publishers and retailers to make bookselling easier. BNC is responsible for a number of programs, which I'll talk about in a little detail, but most significantly, BNC tracks sales data, which has led to controversy among authors and agents. As a book editor, you may not be interested in ONIX and BISAC CODES, which are part of everyday life for marketing staff; yet these factors are changing the way books are promoted, discovered by readers, and acquired, so they are vital new information for book editors.

The publishing supply chain today is much more complex than it once was. BNC, alongside international agencies, has been involved in developing global supply-chain standards to help publishers streamline and regularize their books' metadata, as well as other sales data. Data standards allow any publisher to work with any retailer, which may be one way for small publishers to confront the "big likes to play with big" problem. However, authors and agents have real doubts whether sales data and metadata are working to authors' advantage.

BNC is part of various international organizations responsible for the shift to ISBN 13 (from the earlier ten-digit ISBN), which identifies a book uniquely in the market; I'll return to the significance of the ISBN in a few paragraphs. You may also encounter other identifiers, such as EAN, UPC, and ISTC, as you work with books.

- EAN stands for European Article Number, which is a barcode that identifies a book and its price.
- UPC stands for Universal Product Code, which is another barcode that identifies a book and its price. (The EAN is normally on a book's cover or jacket; a UPC may appear beside the EAN or inside the cover on certain books.)
- ISTC stands for International Standard Text Code, a code that allows different formats of the same book to be linked, despite having differing ISBNs.
- ISNI stands for International Standard Name Identifier, a code for identifying and distinguishing authors, which is particularly important for academic and research-intensive books.

These codes and others are important to standards and processes within a global supply chain, and to the movement of data from publishers to retailers, wholesalers, and libraries. Again, BNC is responsible for a range of programs and sales tools, but here I will concentrate on two that should be of interest to book editors as well as to sales and marketing staff: BISAC codes and ONIX.

BISAC, Thema, and ONIX

BISAC (Book Industry Standards and Communications) codes communicate information about subjects, merchandising, and regional themes (e.g., book geography, author location) through nine-digit alpha-numeric codes. BISAC codes provide a way to tag books to make them more discoverable. The codes form part of a title's metadata and allow retailers to shelve the book (physically or virtually) appropriately. With BISAC codes, consumers can find books that suit their needs, interests, and age group using online retailers' databases. In late 2015, for instance, a huge announcement in the BISAC world was the addition of several hundred new codes dedicated to identifying fiction and nonfiction for young adults.

Thema is a relatively new bibliographic standard. Thema is an international standard designed to reduce confusion among the various national cataloguing schemes used around the world. BISAC is still the standard used in North America, but current best practice is to include Thema in metadata as well.

For this book, the BISAC and Thema subject codes are as follows:

> *Main BISAC subject code, heading: LAN022000, LANGUAGE ARTS & DISCIPLINES/Editing & Proofreading*
> *Secondary: LAN027000, LANGUAGE ARTS & DISCIPLINES/Publishing*
> *BISAC region code, heading: 4.0.2.0.0.0.0, Canada*

> *Main Thema subject code, heading: CBW, Writing & editing guides*
> *Secondary: KNTP, Publishing industry, book trade, the press & journalism*
> *Thema geographical qualifier code, heading: 1KBC, Canada*

ONIX (ONline Information eXchange) is the metadata standard for providing information about a given title to the retail community. ONIX refers to a standard set of XML-based rules that are used to transmit book data and that have been customized for the publishing industry. ONIX describes products, not works, so each edition of a book a publisher issues will have a distinct ONIX record. If you submit your books to any online retailers, such as Amazon, you do so using ONIX. Every product record must pass a schema validation (a program that verifies the metadata is well formed) to be considered an acceptable ONIX file.

A file that fails validation must be fixed before it can be released to the supply chain. For this reason, sales and marketing staff invest significant time in developing ONIX data, which is proving to be vital to book marketing in the online world.

```
<Title>
  <TitlePrefix>The</TitlePrefix>
  <TitleWithoutPrefix>Complete Canadian Book Editor</Title-
WithoutPrefix>
</Title>

<Contributor>
  <ContributorRole>A01</ContributorRole>
  <NamesBeforeKey>Leslie</NamesBeforeKey>
  <KeyNames>Vermeer</KeyNames>
  <LettersAfterNames>PhD</LettersAfterNames>
  <CountryCode>CA</CountryCode>
</Contributor>

<NumberOfPages>400</NumberOfPages>

<Publisher>
  <PublishingRole>01</PublishingRole>
  <PublisherName>Brush Education</PublisherName>
  <Website>
  <WebsiteLink>www.brusheducation.ca</WebsiteLink>
  </Website>
</Publisher>

<CityOfPublication>Edmonton</CityOfPublication>
<CountryOfPublication>CA</CountryOfPublication>
<PublishingStatus>02</PublishingStatus>
<PublicationDate>20160831</PublicationDate>
<CopyrightYear>2016</CopyrightYear>
<YearFirstPublished>2016</YearFirstPublished>

<SalesRights>
  <SalesRightsType>01</SalesRightsType>
  <RightsTerritory>WORLD</RightsTerritory>
</SalesRights>
```

Figure 9.5 Selections from the five-page ONIX record for this book

ONIX data allows a publisher to identify the nationality of a book's contributors, regardless of the book's content. Some online destinations want this information to develop their own promotions. ONIX data can also include regional codes, which may identify a topic relevant to a region regardless of whether the author is Canadian. ONIX data also includes audience information, which allows a publisher to identify the intended readership for the product—for instance, to specify an age range or grade range for a title. Libraries often want this information, and some retailers will use this information to assign in-store locations.

The big draw for sales and marketing people, however, is ONIX records' capacity to include various kinds of descriptive text, such as excerpts, reviews, and a book's table of contents. This kind of content can help with discoverability, especially for nonfiction. Listing the awards a book has won can also help readers find books and can assist retailers with building local promotions. As a book continues to be reviewed and recognized, the descriptive text can be expanded. This is certainly one way to extend a book's shelf life and to make it easier to find after its first season. Ideally, robust metadata from BISAC codes and ONIX records will yield more sales—or at least greater sales potential. More metadata should also mean fewer problems for retailers and for readers searching for books; metadata is generated on the premise that there is no such thing as too much information.

The ONIX program is tied to 49th Shelf, an online book-discovery website that features Canadian content. Although 49th Shelf is not a sales site, it can direct viewers to bookselling sites. It is supported by the Association of Canadian Publishers and various other agencies (including Amazon) to increase the discoverability of Canadian-authored and Canadian-published books. It is also intended to host and support an online community for readers.

The SalesData program

I mentioned above that BNC tracks sales data. BNC's SalesData program, as its name implies, collects sales data (using ISBNs) from various traditional and non-traditional retailers. By paying a fee, publishers have access to the tracked data. Here's how BNC explains the program:

> SalesData collects weekly point-of-sales data from over
> 2,000 retail outlets across Canada, covering an estimated 85%
> of the Canadian trade print book market. It's much more than
> a sales tracking tool: Use it to investigate market trends, identify
> sales opportunities, plan print runs and book orders, and more.

Data generated by SalesData may be used to compile bestseller lists and reports on seasonal and title-by-title sales. It's the reporting feature that is causing authors and agents unhappiness.

Records of bestselling books have been collected for more than a century. If you're interested in the history of bestsellers, former Simon and Schuster editor Michael Korda published a book called *Making the List* (2001), in which he surveys bestseller lists reaching back to the late nineteenth century. From those records we know that bestsellers lists have always suffered from bias. They were collected from the major bookstores in major cities and didn't necessarily reflect local trends (a problem regional publishers continue to feel even today). They were collected from bookstores that advertised extensively in media and were based on booksellers' subjective experience rather than the objective fact of which books were actually selling. This last point is the big one. SalesData captures ISBN-based transactions in real time to report sales figures with a remarkable degree of accuracy that often affirms booksellers' subjective sense of sales. For instance, prior to the arrival of SalesData, Canadian booksellers recognized that Robert Munsch's book *Love You Forever* was a consistent bestseller. Anecdotally, it was the top-selling book in Canada year after year. With SalesData, booksellers and publishers have discovered exactly how well *Love You Forever* sells, and how it stacks up against other top-selling books every year—and yes, it continues to sell year after year, although it is not necessarily the top-selling book in Canada. SalesData allows publishers to track their sales daily, and while that information might be used to support publishers' inventory and the supply chain, what it has enabled publishers to identify is money-making and money-losing authors and projects, in almost real time.

Scholars and others have long known that there is a gap between the canon of great books (if such a thing exists at all) and the bestseller list. In fact, many of the most studied and most revered books of the twentieth century were sleepers: they did not appear on the bestseller lists at the time of their original publication. Similarly, most of the books that hit the top of the bestseller lists have long been forgotten.

Where SalesData is changing the nature of book editing is with the process of acquisitions. When authors with previous publishing history present a new manuscript to a publisher, the acquiring editor will likely look up the sales data on the previous book or books. Authors, editors, and agents who work with major publishing houses have been reporting for several years that if an author's sales history isn't strong, the publisher will likely reject the new manuscript, or the advance offered will be modest. And there is nowhere for authors to hide from this process: a publisher who buys SalesData can look at other publishers' data as well as his own firm's data. It's a database, after all. Publishers pay for access and increasingly use it to make acquisitions decisions.

The process of rejecting authors' new work on the basis of their sales histories is particularly acute for the so-called midlist authors—who have often been the source of important, serious books despite what is being said about the midlist now—as well as for literary experimentalists and emerging authors. If the sales on an author's first book aren't strong, that author may have a much harder time getting a second book contract, even with a small, independent publisher.

The implications of using sales history to inform acquisitions decisions are controversial, if not downright negative. Historically speaking, small independent publishers and regional presses acted like farm teams for the major publishers and the Big Five. A system of mentorship and development existed, allowing writers to be sheltered from the economic demands of multinational publishing. The use of sales history has led to midlist authors having multi-book contracts cancelled and to writers adjusting manuscripts to be what they or their editors imagine is more saleable. At the same time, this aggressively economic decision making has driven many authors away from conventional publishing and toward self-publishing. Authors are justified to wonder if the book as a commodity has become more important than the book as an element of culture when so many contemporary publishing decisions seem to depend on selling, targets, numbers, and income. Yet if books don't sell, publishers cannot afford to produce more books—publishing *is* a business, even for the smallest independent publishers.

Again, you may think SalesData, ONIX, and BISAC and Thema codes are concerns for the marketing manager, not for a book editor, but in that you would be wrong. You may not deal with these matters every day as a book editor, but they matter to your authors and the publishing industry as a whole, so you have an obligation to pay attention. The circular relationship between authors, acquisitions editors, and sales and marketing success is an important theme—one of several we'll take up in chapter 10 as we survey issues on the horizon for book editors.

10

On the Horizon:
The Future for Book Editors

"In fact, new technologies will save
book culture."—Sherman Young

In chapter 2, I referred to publishing as taking place within a fragile ecosystem. It is indeed fragile, but it's also surprisingly resilient. Despite numerous body blows in the last two decades (such as the financial turmoil of the early 2000s, the loss of numerous independent bookstores, and the sale or closure of several major publishers), book publishing in Canada remains world class, and not merely because of the presence of the Big Five publishers. The tremendous success of André Alexis's *Fifteen Dogs*, published by Coach House Books in 2015, which won the Giller Prize and the Writers' Trust Fiction Prize, among numerous other honours, is only one example of Canada's strong and creative independent publishing community. And Coach House's success may be all the more remarkable in view of the fierce competition independent books and authors face from Big Publishing.

Many of the issues we are currently confronting in book editing, and in publishing in general, have to do with scale and expectations. Today, it is easier than ever before to get published, if you are willing to embrace the tools of self-publishing and ebooks; it is simultaneously harder than ever before to be read. Never before have human beings produced so much information, so many books. Never before has the challenge of discoverability—finding *le livre juste* for a specific reader at a specific moment—been greater. How does a reader find the right book in an environment where literally hundreds of books are published every day?

Book publishing today faces one big question: what might encourage more reading—and more book buying? Book editors should be central to that question. Book editing is a job that emerged at the end of the medieval ages with the invention of moveable type (although people had been working as copyeditors and proofreaders in the monasteries for centuries before that). In the fifteenth century, editors were in effect writers, compiling and commenting on the received knowledge of the time. Over centuries, writers who themselves created original works of art, scholarship, and entertainment emerged, and the divide between writers and editors developed. Book editing matured as a profession in the early twentieth century alongside rising levels of literacy, increasing divergence in the publishing business, greater narrowing in education and professions, and a larger industrial movement toward specialization and expertise. As a profession, book editing depends on the existence of book culture. As a future book editor, then, something for you to consider is the future of books. And therefore this chapter, unlike the preceding hands-on, practice-oriented chapters, offers a more theoretical, philosophical approach to a number of issues on the horizon for book editors, and for writing and publishing in general.

The Ebook Revolution

The issue that is likely to continue to challenge the publishing industry as a whole is the debate over paper versus digital books. Recent figures suggest that ebooks are no longer cannibalizing print sales and that the market division between print books and ebooks is stabilizing. Yet questions about ebook pricing, rights and distribution, and the value of ebooks versus print books remain.

Whether we recognize it or not, the price of printed books is low, particularly in Canada; and for most titles, if an ebook edition exists, the ebook price is even lower. As both academic and industry research have shown, the price of digital books has been driven to an artificial low to encourage readers to buy ereaders and try ebooks, which are potentially much more profitable than the manufacturing, warehousing, and shipping of paper books. However, according to the Writers' Union of Canada and to the Authors' Licensing and Collecting Society (in the United Kingdom), writers are earning less today than they have for decades, and are doing more work to earn it; the Writers' Union of Canada characterizes the situation as "a cultural emergency for Canadians." Many factors are in play in this finding, but the income authors derive from the sales of their books—and ebook sales in particular—is certainly part of the problem. The very low price of ebooks, divided first between retailer and publisher, and then between publisher and author, means that authors receive only a tiny sum for the sale of their work in digital form; that sum is even tinier when books are licensed to libraries, which, facing their own budgetary restrictions, are increasingly subscribing to ebook repositories to reduce the overall cost of their collections. Self-publishing has amplified the income problem for many authors. But the economics of publishing affect the incomes of everyone in the supply chain, including editors. If authors are hurting, book editors should be concerned.

Another issue is our society's changing sense of ownership. When readers buy digital books, unlike printed books, they do not own anything physical. Rather, they have purchased a licence, which is a limited right that may be granted, and that equally may be revoked. Such licences are often protected by digital rights management (DRM) software. Importantly, it's not always publishers who apply DRM to ebooks; in fact, some publishers sell their ebooks from their own websites without DRM. Rather, DRM is being applied by book retailers, suggesting a significant shift in concerns about piracy and rights protection from the companies that create ebooks to the companies that distribute them. We might ask, however, whose rights are really being protected. Certainly not readers' rights. DRM restricts readers' legal uses of the books they "purchase" (most consumers don't recognize that, according to the terms of service, they do not own their ebooks outright) and may tie readers to proprietary purchasing systems, such as Amazon's Kindle ereader. Here is what Amazon's content licence states:

> *Upon your download of Kindle Content and payment of any applicable fees (including applicable taxes), the Content Provider grants you a non-exclusive right to view, use, and display such Kindle Content an unlimited number of times,* solely on the Kindle or a Reading Application *or as otherwise permitted as part of the Service, solely on the number of Kindles or Supported Devices specified in the Kindle Store, and solely for your personal, non-commercial use.* Kindle Content is licensed, not sold, to you by the Content Provider. (emphasis added)

Editors need to be aware of the terms of the licences their authors' ebooks will be sold under, if only to be able to explain these licences to authors. Be aware, however, that agreements between publishers and ebook retailers are proprietary, so as a book editor, you may be able to speak to a particular agreement only in general terms. Digital books also challenge authors' rights on the matter of editions that never go out of print and therefore never revert back to the author. What are the implications for authors if nothing ever goes out of print?

Some publishers are turning to ebook publishing for environmental reasons, and there is no way to ignore the fact that traditional print publishing affects the environment. It's not just the paper, but storage, shipping, and the chemicals used in printing that raise concerns. Of course, ereaders, tablets, smartphones, and other digital tools have their own ecological consequences, which we have not resolved to date, and the servers where ebooks and digital retailers are hosted consume power and resources, too. As I noted in chapter 8, printers are increasingly aware of and trying to mitigate their environmental consequences. For publishers looking to have a smaller ecological footprint, digital publishing may be part of the solution, but it is certainly not all of it.

As ebooks and ereaders have evolved as technologies, publishers and others have tried to speculate on what makes digital reading attractive. One of the frequent answers is convenience, the ability to hold dozens of books in a device that weighs less than two hundred grams. Another answer refers to the potential for richer media (rather than the relatively "poor" media experience of the book) in what is called an *enhanced ebook*, which may include animation, videos, music and other sound effects, games, and social interactivity. Editors need to think about this issue carefully: should an ebook be text and image only, or should it be enhanced? Which books should be enhanced, and why? The answers depend on what consumers want and expect from electronic text. Well-formatted, easy-to-read text satisfies most readers most of the time. Some writers may want to enhance the experience by having multiple entry points, divergent narrative paths, and variable endings, but obviously these strategies don't suit every author, nor every book. Editors must also consider that adding enhancements to ebooks may drive the cost up: the content must come from somewhere, and licensing can be expensive. Certainly the author cannot be expected to produce all of it himself. A related matter is the suggestion that authors should be producers, not just writers—on top of authors' increasing responsibility for promoting their books through social media and other web tools. And if we step back from the matter, we might wonder whether the impulse to produce enhanced ebooks implicitly asks what a book is meant to do. Is it really the job of a book to compete with other forms of media?

Right now, ebooks handle long-form fiction and nonfiction well. They are somewhat less effective with heavily illustrated books and with books that have complex formatting requirements, such as field guides and some textbooks. This limitation exists primarily because of format issues and the diversity of devices on which readers are reading. To reach the next stage of success with ebooks, we need fully reflowable digital text with anchors for images and other ancillaries that can be presented on a variety of devices at a variety of dimensions. Currently, the iBook software is leading in this quest. Ironically, however, reflowable formats behave something like scrolls—long rolls of text that are easily adapted to different devices—and thus turn the history of the codex book back on itself. Perhaps Marshall McLuhan is right that all technologies eventually reverse upon themselves and their users.

Scholar Sherman Young proposed the concept of the heavenly library, in which readers might find an on-demand digital edition of every book ever published (not too far off the concept behind the Google Books project, really). Book editors should be able to see the strengths and the weaknesses of such an idea. Should the heavenly library be our goal? If it existed, how would we control access to it—if at all? How would such a resource benefit consumers, publishers, and authors? And if books are always cheap or even free, how will the authors (and editors and publishers) of the future survive?

The existence of print-on-demand technologies such as the Espresso machine (which publishers and editors such as Jason Epstein have been championing for more than a decade) and their potential to create books almost instantly have shown that even when we have the technology, we don't necessarily have the will to use it. Digital publishing generates many new questions in addition to the questions it advances from traditional publishing, questions such as the right balance of writers to readers, our obligation to objects intended to be ephemeral, and our desire to explore new models of compensation and financial support for those who create.

In a global supply chain, moving large numbers of heavy, returnable objects across long distances for very small margins makes little sense. Ebooks certainly reduce some of the costs and some of the environmental consequences of publishing, but they cannot entirely replace printed books, for any number of reasons. Perhaps we need to stop thinking about book publishing as an *either/or* strategy and start thinking about it from a *both/and* perspective—that is, that some books will continue to need to be produced in paper and some books are more effectively consumed electronically on well-made readers, depending on the book, its audience, its author, and its purpose.

Self-Publishing

One response to the changing landscape of publishing, and various threats to books and their authors, has been authors taking their power back by self-publishing. Two very successful Canadian examples are David Chilton's *The Wealthy Barber* (1989) and *The Wealthy Barber Returns* (2011) and Janet and Greta Podleski's Looneyspoons series

(1996 to 2012). Digital tools have enabled at least some authors to opt confidently out of waiting to be published by a major publisher (although they may turn to conventional publishers for assistance with distribution and international rights sales).

No one can reasonably deny that self-publishing has become an acknowledged, if inconsistently respected, part of the publishing industry. Among publishers and some writers, self-publishing is still seen as threatening but often also as laughable. Despite a small number of writers who have been successful—particularly those using self-publishing as a way to extend their brand, such as Chilton and the Podleskis—much self-publishing is still perceived as amateurish. There is definitely a hierarchy in self-publishing, and conventional publishers have been quick to cooperate with the most successful self-publishers. E.L. James's Fifty Shades series, for example, was initially self-published, but its success mushroomed when it was published by Vintage Books, a Penguin Random House imprint, which also published James's 2015 follow-up Grey. Self-publishing "vanguardista" Amanda Hocking has commented that although she has been successful as a self-publisher, she wrote many novels before she found that success and certainly does not endorse self-publishing as a route to fame or riches.

The bigger question in self-publishing may be capacity—the question about finding more readers and buyers. I cannot deny that traditional publishing is frustrating for many would-be authors, but I am unsure self-publishing is any more empowering if the author cannot find an audience. As one of my colleagues in publishing observes, it's easy to make a book; the trick is to sell it. One reason people in conventional publishing evaluate self-publishing so poorly is their sense that the lack of gatekeeping produces an unmanageable oversupply of books (print and digital), so many of them languish in obscurity. Who is reading self-published books? How are these books discovered? Is writing self-published books any more sustainable as employment than writing for conventional publication? How do we correct the balance between writers and readers—or should we?

Self-publishing does pose an opportunity for freelance book editors. As self-publishing becomes an increasingly common part of the industry, more authors will presumably be looking for editors to assist them with the functions in-house book editors have traditionally fulfilled. One way to make a self-published book stand out is with high quality, which professional editors and designers can bring to self-publishing authors. But quality alone is not sufficient to address the issue of discoverability.

Big Publishing

In our larger social discourse, people often refer to abstractions such as Big Oil and Big Pharma. Multinational publishing—which I have characterized in this book as Big Publishing—perhaps deserves similar scrutiny. Some of the world's top ten publishers are names you likely know: Pearson, Thomson Reuters, Penguin Random House, Hachette, and McGraw-Hill Education, each of which earned billions of dollars in revenue in 2015. How can a press with a regional focus that produces ten to twenty books a year—which describes a lot of Canada's independent publishers—compete? Can it? Should it?

Maybe I'm posing the wrong questions. Maybe the small press isn't supposed to compete. Maybe the resistance—or outright hostility—many emerging and midlist authors feel toward major publishing is telling us something important about book culture. According to Sherman Young,

> Book culture is what distinguishes the book. ... Book culture is
> centred on continuing the great human conversation through
> a process of writing, reading, editing and ultimately publishing
> ideas. ... book culture is not about books themselves; it is about
> the process of interacting with books. Of writing them, publishing
> them and reading them.

Based on what I've discussed in the preceding chapters about the processes of editing and marketing books, it seems that Big Publishing should be at the centre of book culture. Yet it is Big Publishing that self-publishing authors and many so-called midlist authors are rejecting. Is scale the problem? Perhaps the giants of publishing are the issue, and smaller, independent publishing—hearkening back to the so-called Golden Age of early twentieth-century publishing—is the solution.

There is arguably a qualitative difference between Big Five publishing and the rest of the industry—it's not just a matter of scale. I'll be blunt: Big Publishing is greedy. Not because the people at these firms are any less concerned about literature, quality, talent, or authenticity than staffers at independent publishers are, but because Big Publishing is accountable to shareholders. Big Publishing has a corporate obligation to return a profit quarter after quarter, year after year.

On the other side of the relationship are consumers. Today's book buyers expect to be able to buy books anywhere, at any time, and they expect books to be cheap. Big Publishing (and Big Retail, to stretch the metonymy just a little further) has been selling just-in-time buying experiences for more than a decade. One of the underanticipated consequences of permission-based marketing and the immediacy of the online economy is that people want to read what they want to read when they want to read it, and many independent publishers are not well set up to respond to an on-demand economy. Is so much instant availability to text harming literature itself? I would say no, it's not, but it may be changing the way people value books and reading. Whether this is a positive or a negative change is a matter of debate—and a place where upcoming book editors may have an important stake.

Chris Anderson has argued in *The Long Tail* that publishers (and other producers) need to rethink their business model. Rather than relying on the massive success of the small number of million-selling books, publishers need to extract more sales over a longer period from all the books on their lists. Marketing consultant Monique Sherrett's idea of keeping a book's promotional window open longer perfectly complements this idea. This is certainly the model that many small independent publishers recognize, and it is closely akin to the traditional model of bookselling, too—and it is exactly the opposite direction from where Big Publishing and Big Retail are heading. But another writer, Gabriel Zaid, points out that the abundance of books enjoyed in the Western, overdeveloped world is not a problem that underdeveloped economies experience. In emerging economies, local books tend to be expensive relative to other needs, and the market is often overtaken by translations of Western titles, leaving only a small space for local authors to publish and compete. The West rarely publishes books from the writers of the emerging economies, although it routinely publishes Western writers into these nations—yet another iteration of the problem social theorists call *technology transfer*. In these places, Big Publishing is squelching local writing and publishing, local book culture. Perhaps Sherman Young's heavenly library could address this disparity—or perhaps it would only amplify it.

Postliteracy

Of course, the ongoing success of publishing in any market, in any economy, depends on the continuing relevance of books and reading, which I have referred to elsewhere in this book as book culture. The first half of the twentieth century was an era of innovative publishing in the West. Whether or not it was truly a golden age, this period saw the establishment of the global book publishers we know today. It saw Allen Lane establish Penguin Books and publish the first paperback books to balance literary quality against affordability, thereby changing many people's relationship to book ownership and reading. It saw the tremendous expansion of publishing for children, a movement away from the tradition of books aimed at character development and toward a celebration of childhood as a unique moment in the human lifespan. But the profusion of early twentieth-century publishing also produced a highly fractured book culture, in which reading and the love of books acquired a moral tone. We see this today in our panic over illiteracy (particularly in association with poverty) and aliteracy. *Aliteracy* refers to a choice that people who have the technical skills to read and write make to opt out of reading and literate culture. Aliteracy and the power of the image, or image culture (think television, advertising, and the rise of digital photography and photo manipulation), are producing human behaviours that scholars refer to broadly as *postliteracy*.

For more than a century, books have been used for purposes other than reading. Books have become part of the expression of our individual tastes and preferences. Some books are produced in expensive, artistic editions intended primarily for display. Some people collect books as furnishings and organize their bookshelves artfully. In early 2014, Kara Bloomgarden-Smoke published an article claiming that

> *physical books have become a prop. Vintage books are repurposed to make lamps, clocks, night tables, iPod docks and key holders. Book covers adorn shirts, bags and high-end wallpaper designed to look like the covers of vintage Penguin Classics ("reproduced by kind permission of Penguin"). Books are everywhere, that is, except in tote bags and purses where Kindles now reside in their place.*

Yet if we look back to the early twentieth century, scholar Janice Radway tells us that

> *people bought the fine book sets ... not simply because they wanted to read them but also because they wished to display them as prized possessions. ... the book itself became a symbol of all that [people] had acquired through their education ... the book as an abstract concept was further invested with symbolic significance by a generation of Americans desperately in need of markers to signal their accession to middle-class comfort and their command of middle-class refinement, achieved increasingly not by the accident of birth but by the rigorous process of institutional education and apprenticeship.*

We might like to imagine we've come a long way since the 1920s, and obviously in many ways we have; but our lives continue to be structured by a cultural form that is irrelevant to many people.

One of the consequences of the arrival of paperbacks has been a change in the way readers value the physical object of the book. While fine editions were, and are, still published, increasingly the quality of the edition matters less for many readers than the quality of the text it contains—that is, that an editor had worked with the writer to produce a specific and desirable kind of reading experience. This separation between the text and its presentation arises again with ebooks, displacing the physical object of the paper book and enabling its uptake in popular culture for other purposes.

Who we are as people is displayed in our artifacts, and it is this display that marketing people tap into when they use our friends and the people we admire to influence our purchasing decisions. We are, in a capitalist sense, "working" when we organize and present our books in our homes because we are showing others how to live by demonstrating how to consume. What's really going on is that we are asserting our place in our social world through a battle on the field of cultural consumption. For publishers in particular, and for our society in general, books and literacy are no longer at the centre of culture, if they ever were. But as we are all shaped by books and print, whether we choose to read or not, books, book ownership, and reading habits encourage us to make judgements about other people. When we associate reading with life outcomes (for instance, the finding that people who have higher socioeconomic status tend to have more advanced reading abilities) or with social goods (such as findings that reading makes people more intelligent, more compassionate, more empathetic, and more socially conscientious), we take a moral position on literacy, and postliteracy, that may neglect the larger social structures that produce these outcomes, such as policies that benefit the wealthy and harm the poor or political ideas that are taken for granted rather than scrutinized. Instead, our popular culture is laced with arguments about the morality of using books as decorative objects, claims about the moral value of reading, assertions in favour of book snobbishness, and judgements about other people's reading tastes—matters that distract us from the reality of poverty, racism, and the digital divide, among other issues. As upholders of beliefs about taste, editors are implicated in these arguments. When we look at ourselves, who are we? Who are our peers? Where have we come from, and what kind of world do we reflect?

One thing the abundance of books in the world should teach us, amplified by the speed and reach of digitization, is to focus on the relationships that emerge from the experience of reading (the content, if you will) rather than the objects from which texts are consumed (the containers). That is, books are more experiential than just their physical presentation *or* their intellectual/aesthetic content. As Robert Bringhurst says in his book *The Surface of Meaning* (2009), "we know that, to be real, a book must be more than a physical object. What makes the tangible form of a book rewarding is that it stands for an intangible reality alive in the heart and mind." Whether we recognize it or not, books and other print and print-derived forms shape us importantly as individuals, whether we choose to read these forms or not.

It's not really much of a stretch for book editors to connect their work in publishing to larger questions of economic policy and political dynamics. As we think about how the distribution of information in our world affects various outcomes, including education and opportunity, status and wealth, and public security, we need to ask difficult questions, such as these suggested by political economy scholar Peter Wilkin: "Do all citizens gain from these developments? Do they all gain equally? Does this inequality matter? Who is excluded from these benefits, and why?" To this list I would add, How does inequality affect how we do our jobs as editors?

HOW BOOKS REPRESENT US TO OTHERS

Earlier in this book I asked you to think about books as commodities—as interchangeable objects with exchange value—rather than as vehicles for ideas, instruments of culture, or physical manifestations of our larger social concerns. This view of books is changing. Marketing experts now see commercial books not merely as products but also as aspects of lifestyle. The book is a projection of our ideals, a representation of the self we want others to acknowledge us to be. From this point of view, books don't have readers or audiences; they have *communities*. Social reading sites such as Goodreads and LibraryThing (and to a lesser degree portals such as All Lit Up and 49th Shelf, two sites dedicated to discovering, buying, reading, and enjoying Canadian literature) reflect this emerging understanding of books as lifestyle markers.

Today, we buy books because they help us express, to ourselves and to others, who we are and who we want to become. This idea may seem farfetched, but it isn't. Janice Radway identifies a similar purpose for books in the 1920s and 1930s as the professional–managerial class grew stratified: they displayed their books to show off their wealth, their level of education, their currency within their professions and social groups, and their impeccable taste. If we look at the substantial rise in books about cookery, recreation, fitness, grooming, diet, health, and well-being today, we can see that we've come a long way from Julia Child's *Mastering the Art of French Cooking* (1961) and *The Complete Scarsdale Medical Diet* (1978). Both were top-selling books in their day, but they were also much more practical and much less aspirational than many of today's top-selling cookbooks and lifestyle titles.

Diversity in Publishing

If you read memoirs and biographies of editors and publishers, one feature of those books might strike you: they're written from a sharply limited perspective, primarily male and almost exclusively white. Regrettably, even as Western societies become ever more diverse, publishing in the West remains a strongly white, upper-middle-class profession. Far more women work in publishing today than fifty years ago, but they tend to have much in common with the gentlemen of publishing in the early and mid-twentieth century.

In the last few years, concerns about diversity in publishing—as in many other communications and technology businesses—have again come to the fore. (The last time these matters were discussed was in the late 1970s and early 1980s.) In 2014, a public conversation began in the United States and Canada regarding diversity in children's and YA books, thanks in part to a pair of articles: "The Apartheid of Children's Literature" by Christopher Myers and "Where Are the People of Color in Children's Books?" by Walter Dean Myers. It was taken further by the work of Lee and Low Books, which conducted surveys in 2014 and 2015 regarding diversity in the United States publishing industry. Jason Low reports that "the number of diverse books each year over the past twenty years has been stuck in neutral, never exceeding, on average, 10 percent." The discussion turned quickly to questions of diversity among acquiring editors, who are felt to be drawn to character representations and topics that reflect their own backgrounds; Lee and Low's 2015 findings were clear: eighty-two percent of editorial staff were white, eighty-four percent were female, and eighty-six percent identified as heterosexual. A similar discussion emerged in the United Kingdom in 2015 in the realm of publishing for adults, and members of Canada's publishing industry have started questioning its composition. So far, though, the discussion hasn't moved very far toward real change, and that is a problem.

When we turn our gaze inward, many people in publishing recognize that the people they work with come from similar backgrounds. Diversity concerns are not only about race. While most book editors are women, there are fewer women publishers, publishing vice-presidents, and senior marketing directors, and the profession is made up almost entirely of men and women from white, middle-class homes. Almost everyone working in publishing is able-bodied, too. Importantly, the lack of diversity reaches across firms, from publishers and publicists through acquisitions practices (editors selecting white writers with similar levels of education and socio-economic status), and across the industry, encompassing reviewers, booksellers, and librarians. Whose books are published? What kinds of characters and topics are discussed in these books? What audiences are these books marketed to? How do the authors of tomorrow perceive themselves represented in the texts of today?

Think about the books you read. What do you notice about representation and diversity? Do you regularly read books featuring characters or key figures whose gender, race, class, or ethnicity differs from your own? Do you notice how books intended for "ethnic" audiences are marketed? Do you observe and question who is winning awards, who is announcing handsome deals in industry publications? Questions about diversity, or its absence, in books and the book industry should help us recognize how "taste" is constructed in mainstream publishing as well as the urgent need to change the status quo.

Looking Ahead

As I suggested at the beginning of this book, it's an inspiring time to be working with books and authors. Book editors now appear in the media regularly, and book culture—and owning and reading books—grows ever more appealing. Book editing is certainly a labour of love, but it can also be a viable form of employment.

The discussion in this chapter may make you wonder whether there is any hope for conventional book publishing and how much need there may be for in-house and freelance book editors in the future. The relationship between book editing and marketing is undeniably growing closer. You will probably find it difficult to get a job in contemporary book publishing without a sound sense of book marketing and its related issues. And because of changing employment structures, related to the changing economics of the industry as a whole, you may find it difficult to gain an in-house position; your career path may involve freelancing or editorial consulting instead. From what we can see now, freelance editors will continue to be responsible for copyediting, and increasingly for substantive editing. In-house editors in large firms will do less textual editing themselves as their responsibility for financial matters grows. On the current landscape, a book that sells well is more valuable than a book that is well edited.

But the dominance—and the economic precariousness—of the Big Five publishers could indicate the potential for a resurgence of independent publishing. Independent publishers, with their smaller scale, lower marketing expenses, and reduced overheads, may be better positioned to withstand a book that fails, a downturn in the economy, or even a surprise bestseller (yes, being suddenly successful can be harmful). Much of the data experts draw from to analyze sales and marketing effectiveness comes from the Big Five and other major national and international publishers. We know much less about the successes of smaller regional and specialized publishers, except anecdotally; yet small publishers continue to make and sell books, continue to develop and support authors, continue to foster bookstores and book culture. Small publishers can be more creative and may be faster to adapt to changing circumstances than large publishers. The inward, buy-local turn happening in many communities may represent another opportunity for small, independent publishers and their books.

Regardless of who they publish with, authors need insightful, well-trained editors to work on their manuscripts with them at various points. Bringing economic concerns into the mix is increasingly necessary in commercial publishing, making the editor's (and the author's) job more complicated, but it need not harm the underpinning relationship between editor and author. Especially by using print on demand and digital publishing tools, independent publishers and their authors can experiment, play, and innovate with limited exposure to risk. What's vital to success at this scale, however, is an adjustment in everyone's expectations—including authors'. Not every book will, or should, sell a million copies, or even a hundred thousand copies—in fact, very few do. But sales income is certainly not the only value that matters in books.

As technology continues to develop, particularly in the area of mobile computing, and as wireless communication continues to expand, perhaps Sherman Young's heavenly library concept is becoming more feasible for authors and publishers alike. We need only step away from the *either/or* expectations we've built and embrace the *both/and* of publishing's various strengths. When the industry is less dependent on massive bestsellers to drive sales and reader interest, and can instead allow books and authors time to find their audience and voice, then surely readers— and writers—will only benefit. Social media and other digital tools will presumably be part of this effort. What I'm really advocating, however, is the concept of *enough*—publishing on a sustainable scale.

This chapter has posed a number of questions, and I hope reading these questions has generated even more questions for you personally. Book editing is a profession of intellectual labour, and questions—even about that which is taken for granted in our industry—are some of our most basic tools. The answers you bring to these questions—as an editor, as a writer, as a reader—will shape how book publishing operates in the decades to come.

Conclusion: The Process Begins Again

Over the course of this book, I've walked you through the basic tasks of being a book editor, from acquiring a manuscript and offering a book contract to manufacturing a printed book and getting that book into the retail supply chain. But unless your work as a book editor is unusually focused and tidy, in real life these processes are all happening more or less simultaneously. While one book is in layout, another is arriving with the author's substantive changes in place, while another has just been published and its author is being celebrated, and yet another has been proposed and is awaiting evaluation. The real life of a book editor can be chaotic.

I also observed that writing is an iterative process: a writer writes, and readers read and respond, encouraging the writer to write again or the readers themselves to write in their turn. This constant renewal of texts is one of the most exciting aspects to a career in book publishing. As former book editor Betsy Lerner says, "The best part of being an editor is the promise of making those discoveries again and again."

Editors and iteration

If you've worked through the chapters in this book in sequence, you can imagine the hypothetical book we've been following from acquisition through production through marketing now swimming independently in the world. Mechanisms of the market—both the retail marketplace and the marketplace of ideas—are in motion, a process referred to as *reception*. There are formal aspects to reception, such as the book's being reviewed and winning awards, as well as informal aspects, such as the way ordinary readers talk about and value the book—and even, at a more mundane, albeit very important, level, how well the book sells and how many copies are still in inventory. A book's reception affects not only the book and its author but also the publishing context into which the book is released. A massively successful book, such as Stephenie Meyer's novel *Twilight*, may create numerous opportunities for its author and also may spawn successors, imitators, and opportunities for other authors. A more quietly successful book can be just as important in its own way, although it may need several seasons or even years for its influence to be felt. This is one reason why many book editors—and authors—resent the churn of today's retail environment.

Frontlist-heavy retailers can allow a book only a few weeks to find its audience before it may be swept aside to make space for new competitors. Many books simply do not have the chance to be found by their intended readers in this brief window. Fortunately, digital tools allow marketing and editorial staff to keep a book visible even after its moment in the spotlight. Book blogs, virtual book groups, and book-centric websites allow readers to discover books and authors they might otherwise have missed. And word of mouth—one reader's recommendation to another—continues to be one of the most important aspects of a book's long-term success. For many books, what matters is not finding numerous readers, but finding the *right* readers.

Authors have different motives for publishing. Some need to share a story that's smouldering within them. Some want to stake a position, to advocate for change. Some have practical goals, like securing tenure or being invited to join the lecture circuit; others want something intangible, like admission to a community or recognition in a field. And some seek fame and fortune, despite that these are elusive qualities for so many books and so many authors.

Importantly, your goals for a project and your author's goal may diverge, especially as the book becomes "real" at publication. That is not wrong or in any way unusual. After all, it's the author's name on the front of the book; the book's success or failure is exceptionally personal. Regardless of your mutual or divergent goals, reception is the realization of a highly abstract process. Some authors may never know the true reception of their work: it may be years, even decades, before a book finally finds its cultural niche. Other books were created to be ephemeral and leave few traces even in the lives of their authors. Although reception is the ultimate judgement of a project, it is a granular process that emerges from the responses and actions of individual readers, sometimes widely dispersed in location and time. Whether your author is jubilant, or panicky, or ambivalent after publication, all you can do is go forward. What's the next project?

Book editors are professional readers whose jobs depend on our belief that we know what other readers will like—what they will enjoy as story, what they will find valuable as information. When we assess manuscripts, we're looking for something that adds meaning or value to readers' lives. In a message to employees in 2014, Penguin Random House CEO Markus Dohle wrote,

> *Everyone at Penguin Random House, no matter where you work or what you do, shares the same motivation: We want to change the world—one book at a time. Our collective belief in the power that a book can have is what inspires us to keep on sparking conversations, challenging the status quo, surprising readers, and creating must-reads—in short, nourishing a passion for reading.*

In the same vein, Betsy Lerner writes, "The greatest compliment any writer can hear from a reader are the words *Your book changed my life.*" When a teacher wrote to J.K. Rowling to say that he used her books with students from impoverished backgrounds to encourage them to read and write, Rowling tweeted back to him, "There is nothing— NOTHING—better to hear than that, so thank you and please send my love to your class!" Perhaps not every book can be profoundly life-altering, yet the potential for a spark between book and reader always exists, sometimes in ways neither author nor editor may anticipate. It is the promise of this spark that turns an editor into a project's champion, and that we try, in collaboration with colleagues, to reveal through the process of publication.

Sometimes we get it wrong, of course, for any of several different reasons. That's part of a book editor's career, too, and not an entirely negative part. Editing is as much an iterative process as writing is. With every manuscript you edit, you become a better book editor. The decisions you make in one setting are informed by decisions you made in other settings, and will in their turn inform future decisions—sometimes as direct and basic as *Never do* that *again*. You discover new ways to solve problems in prose, new aspects of your own and others' editorial sensibility, new tastes and new preferences. You learn about new ways of presenting text, new manufacturing processes, new ways of making a book. You find new ways to reach readers. But you always return to the basic task of reading a manuscript and the feeling that you know how to edit it best.

The books that don't succeed often teach book editors more than those that do. They reveal what we didn't anticipate about an author, a manuscript, or a market, or what we didn't acknowledge about our resources and our abilities; good book editors reflect on these moments and grow from them, rather than feel defeated by them. As awful as reading reviews may be for authors, it may be valuable for book editors. Reading reviews, for instance, can tell you what other readers see in a book that you might not have perceived or that you decided to overlook. And I would argue that a book that isn't successful is never a failure. Publishing is a business of taking economic risks on voices and ideas; but the risks in publishing are smaller than those in many other businesses, and the rewards are greater than a P&L statement can itemize. Whenever we take a chance on a manuscript, book editors add a strand to the web of human creativity. Like teachers, we can never know where or when its influence may be realized.

Readers are not passive in this transaction—nor, for that matter, are authors. Today, more so than ever before, if readers can't find what they like, when they want it, from traditional publishing, there's a burgeoning wealth of self-publishing, author-directed publishing, and micro-publishing that may suit their needs, and many readers are motivated to find it. Readers' problems are not problems of selection or choice; they are problems of accessibility, quality, and discoverability. Increasingly we are understanding that readers' problems are book editors' problems,

problems of our industry's scale, expectations, and profusion. The perceived dysfunction of corporate commercial publishing and the growing access to self-publishing have made book editors into highly visible targets for authors' discontent, and in some cases readers have taken up the notion that editors are adversaries, not allies. Editors should never pit themselves against readers or authors: we have too much in common. But as the fable of the blind men and the elephant reminds us, what we know to be true depends on where we look.

I emphasized in chapter 1 how important it is for book editors to be book readers, a theme that runs throughout *this* book. It's not enough for us to make books for others. We must also consciously commit to reading and talking about books as part of the reception cycle. That means engaging in the social conversations that build our book culture, whether online, in book groups, in classrooms, or even in the conversational question, "What are you reading?" If one major problem our industry faces is that of encouraging people to read, book editors must be leaders in solving the problem—and we are some of the people best equipped to do so.

Learning is another iteration

A second theme that runs through this book is the need for book editors to commit seriously to ongoing education. Whether that education comes through the pursuit of formal coursework and advanced degrees or through a regular program of professional development and self-directed study, the days when a book editor stayed with a single firm for her entire career are long gone. You are likely to change positions and firms many times before you leave the industry, and your commitment to further learning of various kinds is essential.

Today, it is breadth of experience, not depth, that makes a book editor attractive to the next potential employer or client. The more you know about the whole of the publishing process, the more valuable you are and the more likely you are to advance in the profession, should you choose to do so. For in-house editors, this advice means that you need to understand the business side of publishing, particularly the economics of sales and marketing. For freelance editors, career advancement may involve extending your reach and reputation through your network of influence, so that you work consistently on projects at which you can excel and so that you can depend on a secure roster of clients. Say yes to opportunities to learn more, to take professional development, to attend workshops and seminars. You never know who you might meet there, or how what you learn could benefit you in the future.

GETTING STARTED IN BOOK PUBLISHING

If you're not currently working as a book editor—or as an editor at all—you may be wondering how to get started in book publishing. In-house jobs aren't common, but they do exist, so keep your eyes open and let friends and family know you're looking. Most book editors get their start as freelancers, however, so here are some tips for finding work as a freelance editor.

- **Talk to people:** Let people know you're looking for freelance editorial work. You'll be surprised how many people know someone who's looking for someone to do some proofreading or copyediting. At the same time, start a website to let people know you're ready to work.

- **Learn to do by doing:** I don't advocate working for free to gain "exposure," but do be open to taking small jobs, maybe even a few volunteer gigs. You'll quickly build experience and develop a healthy portfolio. Community papers and local non-profits are just some of the organizations that need sharp editorial eyes, and you never know who you might meet on the job.

- **Build your skills:** If you don't already have formal training as an editor, get some. Universities and colleges in most major cities offer credit and non-credit courses in editing and publishing, either through a journalism or communications program or through a faculty of extension. The Editors' Association of Canada also offers training, some of it local, some of it online, as well as self-teaching resources. If you're really serious, explore the publishing program at Simon Fraser University or the Creative Book Publishing program at Humber College.

- **Network:** Find the other editors in your community and get to know them socially. If you demonstrate that you're smart and skilled, one might offer you subcontract editing work or give you a lead on a potential client. And you'll get to know some of the most wonderful people you'll ever meet, people who share your love of words, books, and correctness.

- **Find the book community:** If you want to work as a book editor, remember that where there are books, there are authors looking for editors. Attend book launches and author festivals, and become a regular at your local bookstore. Join a writing group. Contact your provincial book publishing association and find out who its members are.

- **Do your homework:** Be sure to find out about taxes and accounting, as well as the need to have business insurance and a local business licence. Talk to writers and editors in your region about freelance rates so you neither overbid nor undercut the profession. Research your technological and software needs, and get the right tools as soon as you can afford them.

- **Persevere**: It's not easy to get started as a freelance editor. Most freelancers I know eased into the role, holding a full-time or part-time job while slowly accepting more clients and projects. Sometimes there isn't much work; sometimes there's more than you can handle. If book editing is really what you want to do, you'll find a way to do it.

More immediately, I encourage you to actively support your profession and the industry. The key characteristics that sociologist John B. Thompson says distinguish independent publishing from Big Five publishing are community and cooperation; independent presses must be interdependent and collaborative, while the multinationals may be aloof. Perhaps that's so on a business level, but it should never be so at a personal level. Whether you work for a Big Five imprint or the tiniest of start-ups, your career will flourish when you get involved with the publishing community at large. Attend author readings and book events, not just those for your own firm or clients, but for other publishers as well. Your province likely has a book publishing association. Can you attend its events? Can you join the board? Perhaps you can find opportunities to teach relevant skills or hone your leadership abilities in industry-relevant organizations such as the Editors' Association of Canada or the International Association of Business Communicators. Consider volunteering with causes that support books, reading, and publishing. Literacy learners could benefit from a book editor's skill and knowledge, as could schools looking to micropublish and organizations looking to create commemorative books. Public libraries are vital community resources that need volunteers for all kinds of work. Working with any organization that invigorates reading and book culture gives you an opportunity to learn and to grow—and perhaps to lead and to teach others in your turn. It's great for your résumé, and it's fundamental to the renewal of our community and culture.

If there is one last message I want to leave with you, it is this: above all, enjoy the work. Whether you work in-house or freelance, full time or on contract, being a book editor means being one of the world's readers. It is work that is rewarding in so many ways—because of the people, because of the creativity of the work, and because of the books. Now, go make some beautiful books.

PUBLISHING HUMOUR

I often give the following to students as a handout at the end of my four-month credit course on book editing. If you've worked your way through this book, you should get the jokes.

Q: How many copyeditors does it take to screw in a light bulb?
A: I can't tell whether you mean "change a light bulb" or "have sex in a light bulb." Can we reword the question to remove ambiguity?

Q: How many book editors does it take to change a light bulb?
A: Only one. But first she has to rewire the entire building.

Q: How many art directors does it take to change a light bulb?
A: Does it *have* to be a light bulb?

Q: How many project editors does it take to change a light bulb?
A: You were supposed to have changed that light bulb last week!

Q: How many copyeditors does it take to change a light bulb?
A: The last time this question was asked, it involved project editors. Is the difference intentional? Should one or the other instance be changed? It seems inconsistent.

Q: How many production editors does it take to change a light bulb?
A: Who made this change? I didn't call for a change here.

Q: How many marketing directors does it take to change a light bulb?
A: It isn't too late to make this neon instead, is it?

Q: How many proofreaders does it take to change a light bulb?
A: Proofreaders aren't supposed to change light bulbs. They should just query them.

Q: How many authors does it take to change a light bulb?
A: But why do we have to *change* it?

Q: How many publishers does it take to change a light bulb?
A: Three. One to screw it in, and two to hold down the author.

Q: How many booksellers does it take to change a light bulb?
A: Only one, and she'd be glad to do it, too, except no one shipped any.

11

Exercises

Practise Making Proofreading Marks

Following the markup prompts, make the corrections needed in the following sentences. If necessary, refer to appendix C for a list of markup symbols.

Make lower case	Dear MR. Smith
Close up	They can not have been given the codes!
Insert a character	He works in the goverment procurement office now.
Set in boldface	You must act immediately!
Transpose	They endlessly must fantasize about holding absolute power.
Set roman	The term resumes in two *weeks*.
Mark superscript	The theorem is represented thus: a2 + b2 = c2.
Insert a word	Parvesh is working to afford a in Europe.
Set in small caps	Brian Mulroney was responsible for the FTA.
Delete and close up	Did you know that your tail-bone is exquisitely sensitive?
Spell out	His grandson is 4 months old now.
Capitalize	I live in Victoria, British columbia.
Delete a character	I need cofffee to get me started in the morning.
Set in italics	D.H. Lawrence wrote the novel The Rainbow.
Let the change stand	I find proofreading really exciting.

Key to Practise Making Proofreading Marks

Make lower case	Dear MR. Smith (lc)
Close up	They can not have been given the /c codes!
Insert a character	He works in the goverment /n/ procurement office now.
Set in boldface	You must act immediately! (bf)
Transpose	They endlessly must fantasize (tr) about holding absolute power.
Set roman	The term resumes in two weeks. (rom)
Mark superscript	The theorem is represented thus: a2 + b2 = c2. (super)
Insert a word	Parvesh is working to afford a in Europe. /vacation/
Set in small caps	Brian Mulroney was responsible for the FTA. (sc)
Delete and close up	Did you know that your tail/bone is exquisitely sensitive?
Spell out	His grandson is ④ months old now. (sp)
Capitalize	I live in Victoria, British columbia. (uc)
Delete a character	I need cofffee to get me started in the morning.
Set in italics	D.H. Lawrence wrote the novel The Rainbow. (ital)
Let the change stand	I find proofreading really exciting. (stet)

Proofreading Exercise 1: Emphasis on Spelling

Proofread the following sentences using correct markup symbols. Correct only spelling; query any other issues.

1. Yolanda was suprised by my vociferous tone.

2. Petunia is loathe to interrogate the issue of meritocracy.

3. My son was dissappointed that he received only socks for Christmas.

4. World scientists despair over the impending enviromental catastrophe signalled by global climate change.

5. Staff working in this facility must be innoculated against rubella, diphtheria, meningitis, and anthrax.

6. In the new millenium, our party promised to ameliorate the publically funded health-care system.

7. This genus represents a unique catagory: insectivorous plants.

8. Would you pass me a marshmellow, please?

9. For a novice to speak this way is sacreligious.

10. As a doctoral candidate, I was privleged to work with Professor Drager.

11. Before you begin painting, ensure you have a healthy dollop of ochre on your pallet.

12. Our office manager is a sensible and discrete woman.

13. This plant is most commonly identified by
    its pendant blooms and luxuriant foliage.

14. The Oregon Boundry Dispute in the 1940s led
    to a crisis in British—American relations.

15. The would-be restauranteur produced an
    opulent dinner, but his application was
    rejected.

16. The anthropologist watched with wrapt
    attention while the shaman performed the
    rain-calling ritual.

17. The colonel noted that locals often take
    advantage of conflict to misappropriate
    materiel.

18. The clampdown on democratic expression that
    proceeded the events of Tiananmen Square
    in 1989 suggested how the state might deal
    with a mass protest.

19. These charges relate to vandalism committed
    in the Santa Altos Cemetary.

20. The fauna of this estuary includes urchins,
    leaches, molluscs, and crustaceans.

Key to Proofreading Exercise 1: Emphasis on Spelling

Ensure you've used correct proofreading marks to identify the errors you've caught. You'll notice that running a spelling check would catch some of these errors, but not all of them.

This exercise intentionally mixes common and unusual diction. Proofreaders can be distracted by difficult words and may unintentionally overlook errors in basic language. In my explanations, I've also mentioned a few other points about these sentences.

1. Yolanda was *surprised* by my vociferous tone.

2. Petunia is *loath* to interrogate the issue of meritocracy.

   The distinction between the adjective *loath* and the verb *loathe* confuses even experienced writers and editors—so much so that I've known colleagues to check a dictionary to confirm it. Watch this one.

3. My son was *disappointed* that he received nothing but socks and underwear for Christmas.

   English spelling is loaded with doubled consonants. *Disappoint* is just one example of many words commonly misspelled because of confusion over doubled and single consonants.

4. World scientists despair over the impending *environmental* catastrophe signalled by global climate change.

   Be aware that there are numerous differences in Canadian and American spelling; the doubled final consonant in *signalled* is a common one.

5. Staff working in this facility must be *inoculated* against rubella, diphtheria, meningitis, and anthrax.

6. In the new *millennium,* our party promised to ameliorate the *publicly* funded health-care system.

Unsurprisingly, in 1999, *millennium* was one of the world's most mis-spelled words. Watch out for *-ally* versus *-ly* endings—this one is a common slip.

7. This genus represents a unique *category*: insectivorous plants.

8. Would you pass me a *marshmallow*, please?

9. For a novice to speak this way is *sacrilegious*.

10. As a doctoral candidate, I was *privileged* to work with Professor Drager.

    Privilege often shows up on lists of commonly misspelled words: there are so many places to go wrong with it!

11. Before you begin painting, ensure you have a healthy dollop of ochre on your *palette*.

    Watch out for homophones! This one's great, with three possible mis-cues: *palate/pallet/palette.*

12. Our office manager is a sensible and *discreet* woman.

13. This plant is most commonly identified by its *pendent* blooms and luxuriant foliage.

    Watch out for differences between adjectival and nominal forms.

14. The Oregon *Boundary* Dispute in the *1840s* led to a crisis in British–American relations.

    Be especially careful to read each word in a proper name: it's easy to assume that a name is spelled correctly, and many misspellings slip through this way. Note also the fact error, but recognize that fact errors are not a proofreader's basic responsibility.

15. The would-be *restaurateur* produced an opulent dinner, but his application was rejected.

> *Restaurateur* is controversial; some editors would accept the spelling in the exercise, but most dictionaries prefer the spelling provided here, which shows the word's derivation.

16. The anthropologist watched with *rapt* attention while the shaman performed the rain-calling ritual.

17. The colonel noted that locals often take advantage of conflict to misappropriate *matériel*.

> This spelling refers to a particular usage, suggested by the subject *The colonel*. It's easy for a zealous copyeditor or proofreader to guess and call for the wrong correction. Don't assume; check.

18. The clampdown on democratic expression that *preceded* the events of Tiananmen Square in 1989 suggested how the state might deal with a mass protest.

> This misspelling derives from another common confusion: *precede/ proceed*.

19. These charges relate to vandalism committed in the Santa Altos *Cemetery*.

20. The fauna of this estuary includes urchins, *leeches*, molluscs, and crustaceans.

> Again, watch out for homophones like *leech/leach*, particularly in contexts that may lead you to be less than diligent. Also, be aware of the differences in Canadian and American spelling: in the United States, *mollusk* is the preferred spelling.

Proofreading Exercise 2: Emphasis on Punctuation and Mechanics

Proofread the following sentences using correct markup symbols. Correct only punctuation and mechanics; query any other issues. Actors in these sentences must not perform any illegal, illogical, or immoral acts.

1. Thats the ugliest shirt Ive ever seen its right out of 1969

2. Why he left baffled us

3. Id like to go said Tom but unfortunately I have to work

4. Hes not only a great teacher hes also my best friend

5. The panel included three women Mary Contrary a doctor Jennifer Jones a lawyer and Missy Elliott a producer

6. Childrens books on the other hand dont sell

7. Didi Blitzen she was my graduate supervisor at Cambridge won the award last week

8. You should bring your own clubs there are no rentals

9. Charlie Brown Linus said dont you think Lucy has become rather obnoxious over time

10. The colonel stopped at the café to eat the private and the sergeant fixed the tire

11. If you want to succeed in life you need one thing perseverance

12. Bran a natural grain product is an important source of vitamin K

13. Finally he realized what was wrong the cars
    headlights werent working

14. Income tax favours the poor sales tax
    favours the rich

15. The problem Mr Jones said is you never tell
    the truth

16. While you watch the tiger eat its dinner Im
    going to check out the zoos new display of
    raptors

17. The goalie wasnt very good he made the team
    anyway

18. There are three choices for dinner tonight
    ham and eggs fish and chips or pigs feet on
    toast

19. As long as that horrible tie lasts Mother
    and I are afraid it will last forever Dad
    will wear it

20. Time is money therefore our time is limited

21. Its late but its necessary that we see the
    situation to its conclusion

22. Her hobbies include gardening reading
    books taking hikes and walks and cooking
    elaborate meals

23. What isnt wrong in this sentence

24. As we approached we heard music blaring
    from James backyard

25. When youre cooking Jim please dont touch
    your nose or mouth

Key to Proofreading Exercise 2: Emphasis on Punctuation and Mechanics

Here's how I would correct these sentences; other options are possible. Note that a grammar check would catch some of the problems, but not all of them.

1. That's the ugliest shirt I've ever seen!
   It's right out of 1969.

2. Why he left baffled us.

   No other punctuation is needed here. Avoid inserting a single comma between the subject and the verb.

3. "I'd like to go," said Tom, "but
   unfortunately I have to work."

   Here I have followed Canadian conventions for punctuating speech. Be aware that, following British conventions, quotation marks should be single, not double, and minor punctuation appears outside, rather than inside, the quotation marks.

4. He's not only a great teacher; he's also my
   best friend.

   This structure is often allowed to stand with just a comma, but the comma creates a comma splice. *Not only* is not a conjunction on its own; it needs *but* or *but also* to form the correlative. If you omit the *but*, use a semicolon or create two sentences.

5. The panel included three women: Mary
   Contrary, a doctor; Jennifer Jones, a
   lawyer; and Missy Elliott, a producer.

   Note the convention of using a semicolon to separate items in a complex list.

6. Children's books, on the other hand, don't
   sell.

7. Didi Blitzen—she was my graduate supervisor
   at Cambridge—won the award last week.

8. You should bring your own clubs; there are no rentals.

> A full colon is also acceptable here. It will emphasize the *why/because* relationship between the two clauses.

9. "Charlie Brown," Linus said, "don't you think Lucy has become rather obnoxious over time?"

10. The colonel stopped at the café to eat; the private and the sergeant fixed the tire.

11. If you want to succeed in life, you need one thing: perseverance.

> Some writers, particularly those with a background in journalism, will want to omit the comma after *life*. It's certainly not wrong to do so, but many style guides recommend the comma after an introductory subordinate clause. Similarly, some writers will want to use a dash to connect perseverance to the sentence as an appositive, but a colon creates a stronger pause and focus.

12. Bran, a natural grain product, is an important source of vitamin K.

13. Finally he realized what was wrong: the car's headlights weren't working.

> Here the colon is a better choice than the semicolon because of the relationship between the clauses.

14. Income tax favours the poor; sales tax favours the rich.

15. "The problem," Mr. Jones said, "is you never tell the truth."

16. While you watch the tiger eat its dinner, I'm going to check out the zoo's new display of raptors.

17. The goalie wasn't very good. He made the
    team anyway.

    You could, of course, use a semicolon instead of forming two sentences
    here.

18. There are three choices for dinner tonight:
    ham and eggs, fish and chips, or pigs' feet
    on toast.

19. As long as that horrible tie lasts—Mother
    and I are afraid it will last forever—Dad
    will wear it.

20. Time is money; therefore, our time is
    limited.

21. It's late, but it's necessary that we see
    the situation to its conclusion.

    Watch its/it's confusions: they're extremely common.

22. Her hobbies include gardening, reading
    books, taking hikes and walks, and cooking
    elaborate meals.

    Even if your style sheet requires that you omit the series comma, it's
    useful here for clarity. Also, don't put a colon immediately after a transi-
    tive verb such as *include*.

23. What isn't wrong in this sentence?

24. As we approached, we heard music blaring
    from James's backyard.

    Some people will omit the addition of the *s* after the apostrophe.
    Consult your style guide. The rules in *The Chicago Manual of Style* are
    particularly detailed and useful.

25. When you're cooking, Jim, please don't
    touch your nose or mouth.

Proofreading Exercise 3: Emphasis on Grammar

Proofread the following sentences using correct markup symbols. Correct only grammar and punctuation errors; query any other issues.

1. Renovations should add something to the value of the house, otherwise resale value will diminish.

2. Even if you wear the same suit over and over again, the cost of shirts and ties are always a lot cheaper than the suit.

3. One in four children have an undiagnosed vision problem.

4. It is important that all participants receive a meal including volunteers, directors, and special guests.

5. The designers of each of these German-made cars takes a unique approach to their craft.

6. Surrounded by over-packaged and over-produced pop, it's easy to forget just how nice a simple acoustic guitar can be.

7. A typical restaurant meal accompanied by a selection of hot sauces, only a few of which could match our sauce for heat.

8. The clerk told me before I left my order would be sent to my home.

9. Your responsibility isn't to her, though, or even to him, it's to yourself.

10. A list of two hundred suspects was compiled by the FBI, who were to be detained for questioning.

11. Home-improvement trends fluctuate, and the consensus among industry leaders is to not lose sleep over resale value.

12. One meat cutter says the cost of thighs and drumsticks have already increased by seventy cents a kilogram.

13. Painting in an office with bad lighting.

14. Once in the icy north Atlantic, there is little chance of survival.

15. Jeremiah will bring me another blanket, then he will turn off the lamp.

16. Born in Kansas and raised on her grandparents' cattle ranch, her poetry is infused with the details of rural life.

17. The list of nominees for Britain's Booker Prize have been announced.

18. From the beginning of Jimmy's desperate bid to become President of the United States in 1974.

19. A self-professed redneck and die-hard westerner, his life experiences provide an interesting perspective on the singing voice.

20. Each of the developmental stages are related to a specific genetic trait.

Key to Proofreading Exercise 3: Emphasis on Grammar

Here's how I would correct these sentences; other options are possible. Note that a grammar check would catch some of the problems, but not all of them.

1. Renovations should add something to the value of the house; otherwise, resale value will diminish.

2. Even if you wear the same suit over and over again, the cost of shirts and ties is always a lot cheaper than the suit.

3. One in four children has an undiagnosed vision problem.

4. It is important that all participants, including volunteers, directors, and special guests, receive a meal.

5. The designers of each of these German-made cars take a unique approach to their craft.

6. Surrounded by over-packaged and over-produced pop, listeners easily forget just how nice a simple acoustic guitar can be.

   Note how often the passive voice produces dangling modifiers.

7. We ordered a typical restaurant meal accompanied by a selection of hot sauces, only a few of which could match our sauce for heat.

8. Before I left, the clerk told me my order would be sent to my home.

   This type of error may be called a squinting, or ambiguous, modifier. Another possible solution is this: *The clerk told me my order would be sent to my home before I left.*

9. Your responsibility isn't to her, though, or even to him; it's to yourself.

10. A list of two hundred suspects, who were to be detained for questioning, was compiled by the FBI.

11. Home-improvement trends fluctuate, and the consensus among industry leaders is not to lose sleep over resale value.

> Most editors do not consider split infinitives to be an error, particularly at this stage of production, but this simple change may be appropriate for anyone editing for highly formal or linguistically conservative audiences.

12. One meat cutter says the cost of thighs and drumsticks has already increased by seventy cents a kilogram.

> You might query the treatment of the number in this example—many style guides would recommend numerals rather than the word *seventy*.

13. Painting in an office with bad lighting is a bad idea.

> This solution interprets the fragment as the subject of a sentence. Alternatively, you might have interpreted the fragment like this: *We hung the painting in an office with bad lighting.* You'd need more context to know which solution to use.

14. Once a sailor falls into the icy north Atlantic, there is little chance of survival.

> This solution adds an actor to the sentence, eliminating the dangling modifier and adding clarity.

15. Jeremiah will bring me another blanket. Then he will turn off the lamp.

16. Born in Kansas and raised on her grandparents' cattle ranch, she infused her poetry with the details of rural life.

17. The list of nominees for Britain's Booker Prize has been announced.

18. From the beginning of Jimmy's desperate bid to become president of the United States in 1974, he felt his success was unlikely.

   Note that some writers assume that if a fragment is long, it can stand as a sentence. This is the case only when a fragment makes sense in its context, which this one did not.

19. He was a self-professed redneck and die-hard westerner, and his life experiences provide an interesting perspective on the singing voice.

20. Each of the developmental stages is related to a specific genetic trait.

Proofreading Exercise 4: Synthesis

Proofread this excerpt from a high school-level biology textbook. Remember your limitations, and mark up or query accordingly.

The Endocrine System

A woman's body is controlled by a system of glands referred to collectively as the ENDOCRINE SYSTEM. The glands release specialized chemicals, called HORMONES, into the bloodstream. Numerous body processes are initiated by hormones, such as METABOLISM and body temperature regulation, growth, MENSTRUATION, sexual activity, contractions during LABOUR, LACTATION, and the woman's response to and STRESS. The effects hormones produce may be rapid or delayed, short term or long-lasting.

It is through hormones that a women "experiences" her emotions. Stimuli activate the central core of the brain (loosely known as the LIMBIC SYSTEM), which sends signals to the CEREBRAL CORTEXT and other brain areas. Emotions are "registered" by the HYPOTHALAMUS and the PITUITARY GLAND—sometimes referred to as the master glands—and appropriate hormones are released. A woman experiences emotion through distinct hormonal responses, each of which triggers a bodily reaction. For instance, fear causes the ADRENAL GLANDS to release CATECHOLAMINES. Catecholamines in turn instigate the body's FIGHT-OR-FLIGHT REPONSE.

Hormonal Production

Hormones may have either a short-term effect, such as in the variable amounts of INSULIN the pancreas releases in response to blood glucose level or a long-term effect, such as in the extended activity of ANDROGENS on a woman's sexual development during PUBERTY.

The hypothalamus and the pituitary gland regulate and monitor the endocrine system through feedback. This controlling function is the reason we call them the master glands.

The hypothalamus receives most message traffic between the brain and the body. As such, the hypothalamus "knows" about all the sensations a woman experiences, such as the pain she feels when the cuts her finger or the pleasure she fells at hearing a loved one's voice. The HYPOTHALAMUS also experiences thing that do not come to a woman's consciousness, such as levels of various hormones and nutrients in her body.

The pituitary gland, which sits just below the hypothalamus, helps to balance the responses of the endocrine glands. When the pituitary receives an electrical or hormonal messages from the hypothalamus, it releases hormones of its own (called trophic hormones) into the bloodstream. The blood carries the trophic hormones to target cells, including the other endocrine glands. Two particular hormones the hypothalamus produces—OXYTOCIN and antidiurectic hormone, or ADH—are stored in the posterior lobe of the pituitary gland to be released into the blood stream as needed. They pass to the pituitary over nerve fibres.

How Hormones Work

An intricate feedback system between individual glands, the hypothalamus, and the pituitary gland maintains the balance of hormone production in a woman's body. The master glands "recognize" the amount of various hormones in the bloodstream and whether a gland is over- or underproducing. The master glands regulate the hormonal production in individual glands by adjusting the release of other hormones.

The system is highly accurate despite tat hormones in the blood pass thoughout a woman's body. However, each hormone transmits only a certain chemical message, like a key. The chemical message can fit only into the correct receptor in particular target cells—like a lock. Some hormones, such as the steroid hormones, demonstrate exquisite precision. Oxytocin, for example, acts on the UTERUS during labour and on the MILK DUCTS of the breast in response to the LETDOWN REFLEX during lactation. In contrast, the protein hormones fit receptors in many target cells and may cause a more generalized response from the body. Hormones may amplify or inhabit the pace at which target cells perform their usual functions. They may usually activate or deactivate certain GENES within the nucleus of the cell to initiate particular functions.

Key to Proofreading Exercise 4: Synthesis

The Endocrine System

A woman's body is controlled by a system of glands referred to collectively as the ENDOCRINE SYSTEM. The glands release specialized chemicals, called HORMONES, into the bloodstream. Numerous body processes are initiated by hormones, such as METABOLISM and body temperature regulation, growth, MENSTRUATION, sexual activity, contractions during LABOUR, LACTATION, and the woman's response to ~~and~~ STRESS. The effects hormones produce may be rapid or /ﾉ/ delayed, short term or long-lasting. /=/

It is through hormones that a woman "experiences" her /a/ emotions. Stimuli activate the central core of the brain (loosely known as the LIMBIC SYSTEM), which sends signals to the CEREBRAL CORTEX and other brain areas. Emotions /ﾉ/ are "registered" by the HYPOTHALAMUS and the PITUITARY GLAND—sometimes referred to as the master glands—and appropriate hormones are released. A woman experiences emotion through distinct hormonal responses, each of which triggers a bodily reaction. For instance, fear causes the ADRENAL GLANDS to release CATECHOLAMINES. Catecholamines in turn instigate the body's FIGHT-OR-FLIGHT REPONSE. /s/

Hormonal Production

Hormones may have either a short-term effect, such as in the variable amounts of INSULIN the pancreas releases in response to blood glucose level or a long-term effect, such as /,/ in the extended activity of ANDROGENS on a woman's sexual development during PUBERTY.

The hypothalamus and the pituitary gland regulate and monitor the endocrine system through feedback. This controlling function is the reason we call them the master glands.

The hypothalamus receives most message traffic between the brain and the body. As such, the hypothalamus "knows" about all the sensations a woman experiences, such as the pain she feels when she cuts her finger or the pleasure she /s/

fells at hearing a loved one's voice. The HYPOTHALAMUS also /e/
experiences thing that do not come to a woman's conscious- /s/
ness, such as levels of various hormones and nutrients in
her body.

The pituitary gland, which sits just below the hypothalamus, helps to balance the responses of the endocrine glands.
When the pituitary receives an electrical or hormonal message from the hypothalamus, it releases hormones of its own /ℐ/
(called trophic hormones) into the bloodstream. The blood
carries the trophic hormones to target cells, including the
other endocrine glands. Two particular hormones the hypothalamus produces—OXYTOCIN and antidiuretic hormone, /C
or ADH—are stored in the posterior lobe of the pituitary
gland to be released into the blood stream as needed. They
pass to the pituitary over nerve fibres.

How Hormones Work

An intricate feedback system between individual glands, the
hypothalamus, and the pituitary gland maintains the balance of hormone production in a woman's body. The master
glands "recognize" the amount of various hormones in the
bloodstream and whether a gland is over- or underproducing. The master glands regulate the hormonal production in
individual glands by adjusting the release of other hormones.

The system is highly accurate despite tat hormones in the /h/
blood pass thoughout a woman's body. However, each hor- /r/
mone transmits only a certain chemical message, like a key.
The chemical message can fit only into the correct receptor
in particular target cells—like a lock. Some hormones, such
as the steroid hormones, demonstrate exquisite precision.
Oxytocin, for example, acts on the UTERUS during labour /C
and on the MILK DUCTS of the breast in response to the LET-
DOWN REFLEX during lactation. In contrast, the protein
hormones fit receptors in many target cells and may cause
a more generalized response from the body. Hormones may
amplify or inhibit the pace at which target cells perform /i/
their usual functions. They may usually activate or deactivate /ℐ/
certain GENES within the nucleus of the cell to initiate particular functions.

Copyediting Exercise 1: Nancy Cunard and the Hours Press

The following passage is an excerpt from a popular history that surveys the work of women writers and publishers in the early twentieth century. Copyedit it as you see fit, using correct markup symbols.

Nancy Cunard and the Hours Press

Even today heiress, author, and socialite,

Nancy Cunard, is probably better known for her

personal life than her creative work. Readers

in the early 21st century receive her as more

of a legend than anything else, a reception

enhanced by the numerous visual images of

Nancy that survive alongside the reminiscences

of her many friends, lovers and admirers. As

a poet of some note, an occasional literary

critic, an avid collector of African jewellery

and artifacts, and an early champion of black

rights, Nancy Cunard comes to us wearing many

guises. But perhaps the most problematic is

Nancy's role as publisher as founder and owner

of The Hours Press.

Nancy Cunard was born in 1896, one of the

youngest of the so called Modernists. Her

paternal grandfather, Samuel Cunard, had
founded the Cunard lines, and while the
family no longer profited from the company by
the end of the nineteenth century, Nancy's
father was sufficiently well-off to provide
a mansion for Nancy's childhood residence.
Nancy's mother Maud Alice Burke, later Lady
Emerald Cunard, actually owned the serious
wealth of the family; her fortune being
derived from her American father's industry.
Nancy's childhood was typically of English
rural upper-class, and from her earliest
days she would retain a love of finely-made,
beautiful things. This appreciation would
later inform Nancy's press-work.

Nancy's late teens and early twenties were
turbulent. She was enormously popular with
both women and men although her apparently
scathing personality might have put some
people off. She is always remembered, in
countless memoirs, as extremely attractive

and slim with especially memorable eyes.
She had numerous sexual liaisons, such that
she quickly developed a wild reputation.
Michael Arlen would eventually portray Nancy
as Iris March, the out of control heroine of
his novel The Green Hat. Her sexuality was
an important aspect of her personality and
greatly affected her working relationships,
although her memoir of the Press, These Were
the Hours, defied this assessment with its
detached, highly-professional reminiscing.

From a very young age Nancy was actively
engaged in literature, first as a voracious
reader, then as a developing poet and
eventually as a published writer. Ironically
it was her mother's connections and influence
made getting published much easier for Nancy
then it was for most writers. Parallax,
originally published for Nancy by the
Woolfs' Hogarth press in 1925, is generally
considered Nancy's best creative work and its

publication is presumably the reason Nancy developed an interest in book publishing, which led her to purchase a press and learn as much as possible about the process of printing. The Woolfs are famous for their potentially discouraging remark "Your hands will always be dirty", at which Nancy simply laughs. Cunard was certainly aware of the numerous small presses then fourishing in England, France and elsewhere in Europe. She lists the atmosphere into which she launched her venture, noting such operations as Ovid Press, Black Sun Press, Black Manikin, and Seizin Press (about which she remarked, "their books were nicely designed"). It was in 1928 that Nancy estalished the Hours Press in Reanville, France with something of a fellow-feeling.

---

525 words
Time required for you to work through your first pass: _____

Key to Copyediting Exercise 1: Nancy Cunard and the Hours Press

Here's what I would mark up for this text. Your markup should be similar, at least as far as outright errors go. Remember that there is a degree of subjectivity to copyediting, so I may have marked some changes that you did not, and vice versa.

Nancy Cunard and the Hours Press

Even today heiress, author, and socialite

Nancy Cunard is probably better known for her

personal life than for her creative work. Readers

in the early ~~21st~~ twenty-first century receive her as more

of a legend than anything else, a reception

enhanced by the numerous visual images of

Nancy that survive alongside the reminiscences

of her many friends, lovers, and admirers. As

a poet of some note, an occasional literary

critic, an avid collector of African jewellery

and artifacts, and an early champion of black

rights, Nancy Cunard comes to us wearing many

guises. But perhaps the most problematic is

~~Nancy's~~ her role as publisher, as founder and owner

of the Hours Press.

Nancy Cunard was born in 1896, one of the

youngest of the so-called Modernists. Her

paternal grandfather, Samuel Cunard, had founded the Cunard lines; while the family no longer profited from the company by the end of the nineteenth century, Nancy's father was sufficiently well-off to provide a mansion for Nancy's childhood residence. Nancy's mother, Maud Alice Burke) (later Lady Emerald Cunard) actually held the serious wealth of the family; her fortune having derived from her American father's industry. Nancy's childhood was typical of the English rural upper-class, and from her earliest days she retained a love of finely-made, beautiful things. This appreciation would later inform Nancy's press-work.

Nancy's late teens and early twenties were turbulent. She was enormously popular with both women and men, although her allegedly scathing personality might have put some people off. She is remembered in countless memoirs as extremely attractive and slim, with especially ~~memorable~~ striking eyes. *Q: OK change? So close to memoir*

~~She~~ Nancy had numerous sexual liaisons, ~~such that~~ and

~~she~~ quickly developed a wild reputation.

Michael Arlen would eventually portray ~~Nancy~~ her

as Iris March, the out of control heroine of *Q: should be Iris Storm?*

his novel <u>The Green Hat</u>. ~~Her~~ Nancy's sexuality was

an important aspect of her personality and

greatly affected her working relationships,

although her memoir of the Press, <u>These Were</u>
                                          Hours

the Hours, defied this assessment with its

detached, highly professional reminiscing.

From a very young age, Nancy was actively

engaged in literature, first as a voracious

reader, then as a developing poet, and

eventually as a published writer. Ironically,

~~it was~~ her mother's connections and influence

made getting published much easier for Nancy

then it was for most writers. <u>Parallax</u>,

originally published for Nancy by the

Woolfs' Hogarth press in 1925, is generally

considered Nancy's best creative work and its

publication is presumably the reason Nancy

developed an interest in book publishing,

which led her to ~~purchase~~ buy a press and learn

as much as possible about the process of

printing. The Woolfs are famous for their

potentially discouraging remark "Your hands

will always be dirty(,)" at which Nancy simply

laughed. ~~Cunard~~ Nancy was certainly aware of the

numerous small presses then flourishing in

England, France, and elsewhere in Europe. In her memoir, she

~~lists~~ describes the atmosphere into which she launched

her venture, noting such operations as Ovid

Press, Black Sun Press, Black Manikin, and

Seizin Press (about which she remarked,

"their books were nicely designed"). It was

in 1928 that Nancy establised the Hours Press

in Reanville, France, with something of a

fellow-feeling.

---

525 words
Time required for you to work through your first pass: _____

Copyediting Exercise 2: Families and School Outcomes

The following passage is an excerpt from an intermediate-level sociology textbook. Copyedit it as you see fit, using correct markup symbols. You may want to make a style sheet to keep track of your decisions.

Families and School Outcomes

Research from scholars in the field of education foundations has consistently shown a link between schooling outcomes and "parenting styles". Children tend to achieve superior schooling outcomes if their parents display a more "authoritative" parenting style as opposed to an "authoritarian" or "permissive" style. The way an authoritative style is characterized is by responsiveness and warmth and a careful monitoring of children's behaviour, whereas authoritarian parents tend to be over-demanding, less flexible, and lacking responsiveness and warmth. Permissive parents tend to be overly indulgent as parents, and set few limits on children's behaviors. In this chapter examines whether the relationship between children's outcomes and SES is mediated by differences in parenting styles. Our

analysis goes beyond previous research in this

field by examining in the specific, distinct

ways that different dimensions of socioeconomic

status are related to parenting styles and

schooling outcomes.

Behavioural, emotional or psychological

disturbances are displayed by a significant

proportion of Canadian children, which are

sufficiently serious to warrant concern

for their current functioning and future

developmental health. In order to guide

policy and practise intended to address

these problems, it is important that a

better understanding of the sources of these

developmental disturbances be developed by

teachers, principals and educational policy

makers. We have drawn from data describing the

sample of 3 and 4 year olds (preschoolers) and

12 and 13 year-olds (students in grade seven

at the time of survey) to investigate the role

of parenting especially as it relates to the
effects of SES on behavioral disorders during
childhood. [...]

A cliche of Canadians' modern life is
"spending quality time" with one's children.
Do some children succeed, despite social and
economic difficulties, mainly because their
parents are more engaged in their lives. Is
there really such a thing as "quality" time,
or is it simply a question of the amount of
hours that parents are engaged in play or
school activities or non-work with their
children? Our conclusions at the end of this
chapter addresses questions concerning parental
involvement as a mediating factor between
socio-economic status and child outcomes and
takes on some of the thorny issues involved in
balancing work and family life. [...]

These findings are likely going to be of
particular interest to mothers and father as
well as the policy community, as they confront

some of our perceptions about the way in which children's outcomes are influenced by family income and social class. It is a comfortable lie our society perpetuates that schools are social elevators and social equalizers, when in fact our data show that SES is in fact fixed and stable over generations and schooling in isolation has little or no influence on children's lifetime SES outcomes.

---

450 words
Time required for you to work through your first pass: _____

Key to Copyediting Exercise 2: Families and School Outcomes

Here's what I would mark up for this text. Your markup should be similar, at least as far as outright errors go. If you prepared a style sheet, be sure to capture mechanical decisions such as the treatment of the series comma and the use of Canadian spellings.

Families and School Outcomes

Research from scholars in the field of education foundations has consistently shown a link between schooling outcomes and parenting styles. Children tend to achieve ~~superior~~ better schooling outcomes ~~if~~ when their parents display a more authoritative parenting style, as opposed to an authoritarian or a permissive style. ~~The way~~ An authoritative style is characterized ~~is~~ by responsiveness, and warmth and a careful monitoring of children's behaviour, whereas authoritarian parents tend to be ~~over~~ demanding, less in flexible, ~~and~~ ~~lacking responsiveness,~~ unresponsive and ~~warmth~~ cold. Permissive parents tend to be overly indulgent ~~as parents~~ and set few limits on children's behaviors. ~~In~~ this chapter examines whether the relationship between children's outcomes and ~~SES~~ socioeconomic status is mediated

Q: glossary re parenting styles?

by differences in parenting styles. Thus, Our

analysis goes beyond previous research in this

field by examining in the specifier distinct

ways that different dimensions of socioeconomic SES

status are related to parenting styles and

schooling outcomes.

Behavioural, emotional or psychological

disturbances are displayed by a significant

proportion of Canadian children, which are display

sufficiently serious enough to warrant concern

for their current functioning and future

developmental health. In order to guide

policy and practice intended to address

these problems, it is important that need a

better understanding of the sources of these

developmental disturbances be developed by

teachers, principals and educational policy

makers. We have drawn from data describing the a

sample of 3 and 4 year olds (preschoolers) and

12 and 13 year-olds (students in grade seven

at the time of the survey) to investigate the role how

of parenting ~~especially as it~~ relates to the
effects of SES on behavioural disorders ~~during~~
childhood. [...]

has become

The idea of spending "quality time" with one's children a cliché of Canadian ~~modern~~ life ~~is~~

Do some children succeed, despite social and
economic difficulties, mainly because their
parents are more engaged in their lives? Is
there really such a thing as "quality" time,
or is ~~it simply~~ the issue a question of the ~~amount~~ number of
hours that parents are engaged in play or
~~school~~ activities or non-work with their
children? Our conclusions at the end of this
chapter address questions ~~concerning~~ about parental
involvement as a mediating factor between
SES ~~socio-economic status~~ and child outcomes; and
takes on some of the thorny issues involved in
balancing work and family life. [...]

These findings are likely ~~going~~ to be of
particular interest to ~~mothers and fathers~~ parents as
well as to the policy community, as ~~they~~ our data confront

some ~~of our~~ common perceptions about ~~the way in which~~ how

children's outcomes are influenced by family

income and social class. ~~It is~~ (a comfortable

lie) our society perpetuates that schools are

social elevators and social equalizers, ~~when~~ in

fact, our data show that SES is ~~in fact fixed~~

~~and~~ stable over generations, and schooling

in isolation has little or no influence on

children's lifetime ~~SES~~ outcomes.

---

450 words

Time required for you to work through your first pass: _____

Copyediting Exercise 3: Literacy Learners

The following passage is a stand-alone article from a school newsletter.
Copyedit it as you see fit, using correct markup symbols. If you feel you
need to work at a substantive level, express your suggestions as queries.

Announcing Literacy Learners!

Little Red School is proud to offer it's

students the Literacy Learners! Program. Ms

Goldman is heading the program and is very

pleased with the progress of our students.

Literacy Learners! is an early intervention

program designed to assist the lowest achieving

children in first grade who are having

difficulty learning to read and write. Children

meet individually with a specially-trained

teacher for 30 minute each day for an average

of 12-20 weeks. The goal is for the children

to develop effective reading and writing

strategies. During the short-term intervention,

these children make faster than average

progress so that they catch up with their peers

and continue to work on their own within an

average group setting in the regular classroom.

Literacy Learners!™ has one clear goal: "to dramatically reduce the number of learners who have extreme difficulty with literacy learning and the cost of these learners to educational systems.

Literacy Learners! is an investment in the professional skills of teachers.

Every Literacy Learners site systematically collects data on every child for a central national evaluation center. In Canada, that center is in Toronto at the Canadian Institute of Literacy Learners!™.

Literacy Learners!™ has two positive outcomes:

1. The child no longer requires extra help, and service is "discontinued."

2. A recommendation is made early in the childrens' schooling. If a child did not achieve success in the Literacy Learners! program, they will be sent for additional assessment and programming. (Only 1—2% of children are referred for additional help.)

Well-planned implementation determines the

success of the Literacy Learners! Program.

   Literacy Learners! is a not-for profit

program that involves collaboration among

schools, districts and universities.

Contact Mrs. Goldmen for more information.

---

280 words
Time required for you to work through your first pass: _____

Key to Copyediting Exercise 3: Literacy Learners

Here's what I would mark up for this text. Your markup should be similar, at least as far as outright errors go. You likely noted that several of the paragraphs should be combined, and some might be reordered.

Announcing Literacy Learners!

Little Red School is proud to offer its students the Literacy Learners! Program. Ms. Goldman is heading the program and is very pleased with the progress of our students.

[margin note: Q: confirm teacher name + spelling]

Literacy Learners! is an early intervention program designed to assist ~~the lowest-achieving~~ children in first grade who are having difficulty learning to read and write. Children meet individually with a specially trained teacher for 30 minutes each day for ~~an average of~~ 12 to 20 weeks. The goal is for the children to develop effective reading and writing strategies. During the short-term intervention, these children make faster than average progress so that they catch up with their peers and can continue to work on their own ~~within an average group setting~~ in the regular classroom.

Literacy Learners! ~ has one clear goal: ↗to ~dramatically~ reduce the number of learners ~who~ **struggling** ~have extreme difficulty~ with literacy/ ~learning~ ~and the cost of these learners to educational~ ~systems.~

— insert at Ⓐ

~Literacy Learners! is an investment in the~ ~professional skills of teachers.~

— insert Ⓑ

Every Literacy Learners! site systematically collects data on every child, **assisted** for a ~central~ national evaluation cent(er). In Canada, that cent(er) is in Toronto at the Canadian Institute of Literacy Learners! ~:~

└ move this ¶ to below

Literacy Learners! ~ **may have** ~has~ two positive outcomes:

1. The child no longer requires extra help, and service is ↗discontinued.

2. **That** ~A~ recommendation is made early in the child ~ren~ **'s** schooling. **before bigger problems develop** If a child ~did~ **does** not **succeed** ~achieve success~ in the ~Literacy Learners!~ program, ~they~ **she or he** will be sent for additional assessment and programming. ↗Only (1–2%) of children are referred for additional help.↗

insert Ⓐ here
←

Well-planned implementation determines the

success of the Literacy Learners! Program.

— insert at B (circled)

Literacy Learners! is a not-for profit [^=]

program that involves collaboration among

schools, districts and universities.

Contact Mrs. Goldmen for more information.

Q: as above — confirm name + spelling

280 words
Time required for you to work through your first pass: _____

Q: Note that I've reordered the discussion points and deleted some information that's not relevant to the parent audience. OK with you?

Appendixes

APPENDIX A

An Editorial Checklist

The following checklist is built on a model that a colleague shared with me when I was getting started in book editing. I have updated it, adding and removing steps as processes and job expectations have changed. Note that the timelines here exist as ideals; your own situation may vary.

1. At contract signing or within six months of MS due date
   - ☐ send Author Questionnaire to author
   - ☐ when Author Questionnaire is returned, send to Marketing

2. One month before MS due
   - ☐ contact author to confirm that MS will be on time

3. MS submitted
   - ☐ read MS for acceptability; confirm acceptance
   - ☐ (if necessary) contact Accounting to release advance
   - ☐ confirm receipt of any original artwork/photographs/graphics
   - ☐ check length against contract; estimate typeset length; send details to Marketing
   - ☐ start edit or assign; confirm deadline and editorial budget
   - ☐ based on sub edit deadline, schedule copyeditor
   - ☐ assign designer
   - ☐ designer to develop cover concepts, interior concepts
   - ☐ prepare for sales conference presentation
   - ☐ write catalogue copy

4. Substantive edit complete
   - ☐ send MS to author re any queries; first signoff
   - ☐ (if freelanced) submit editor's invoice to Accounting
   - ☐ confirm all permissions are now in place
   - ☐ confirm any additional images are now in place
   - ☐ confirm cover treatment with designer; send cover treatment to author

5. Manuscript returned
   - ☐ prepare MS for copyedit (checklist, details)
   - ☐ send MS to copyeditor with checklist, deadline, budget
   - ☐ (if required) send for legal read

6. During copyedit
- ☐ request CIP
- ☐ prepare front matter as required
- ☐ confirm interior treatment with designer; confirm specs
- ☐ based on design specs, request print bids; confirm printer
- ☐ (if required) size art/images based on design specs and send for scanning

7. Copyedited manuscript returned
- ☐ review edit; address queries
- ☐ send MS to author; second signoff
- ☐ send copyeditor's invoice to Accounting
- ☐ schedule page layout; confirm deadline, budget
- ☐ (if required) based on layout deadline, schedule indexer
- ☐ write jacket copy; send to designer with other materials for final cover
- ☐ write any remaining incidental copy; add to file
- ☐ prepare ARCs, eARCs; alert Marketing re advance reviewers
- ☐ send MS to potential blurbers

8. Page layout
- ☐ send text file (plus images if necessary) to designer for layout
- ☐ based on layout deadline, schedule proofreader
- ☐ confirm final cover; signoff
- ☐ schedule print date; alert Marketing of expected delivery date

9. Page proofs received
- ☐ copy of proofs to author with instructions (copy to agent if required)
- ☐ copy of proofs to proofreader with copyeditor's style sheet; confirm deadline, budget
- ☐ (if required) copy of proofs to indexer
- ☐ review prelims re CIP, permissions, credits, etc.

10. Page proofs returned

☐ confirm receipt of author's changes; final signoff

☐ consolidate changes; transmit to designer for corrections

☐ (if required) check index file for accuracy; send index file to design for layout

☐ check revised page proofs as necessary; signoff

☐ send proofreader's invoice to Accounting (ditto indexer's)

11. Final signoff

☐ transmit PDFs to printer

☐ confirm printer's shipping date with warehouse, Marketing

☐ send designer's invoice to Accounting

12. Plotters/Digital blues received

☐ review proofs; signoff

13. Books received

☐ notify author; ship author copies (copy to agent if required)

☐ return author's original materials

☐ archive project files

APPENDIX B

A Sales and Marketing Planner

The following planner reflects a composite of models from several Canadian publishers. Not every book requires every blank to be filled, but you should think carefully about those that are not. Of course, new trends and technologies will produce new marketing opportunities— but don't forget the value of the tried-and-true.

Book title and subtitle:

Author:

Warehouse date:

Publication date:

Author questionnaire returned?

Author contact list supplied?

Marketing budget:

Fiction?

Nonfiction? Category:

ARCs?

Review copies?

Author photo on file?

Author website URL:

Blog? Facebook? Twitter? Tumblr? Other?

Author's marketing suggestions:

Will author self-promote?

Potential awards/prizes:

Blurbs/Endorsements: [This point refers to individuals the firm will approach.]

Advance reviews?

Saleable excerpts?

Should sales reps read MS/ARC?

Should author meet sales reps?

Opportunities in author's hometown? Elsewhere?

News release angles (off the book page):

Media kit? Strategy?

Book launch?

Other events?

Book tour?

Bookstore connections?

Other bookseller incentives?

Co-op/Display?

Point-of-purchase?

Advertising?

Direct to consumer?

Non-bookstore sales?

Corporate sales?

Special sales?

Previous strong reviews, awards, distinctions to promote:

APPENDIX C

Standard Markup Symbols

Delete a letter There are extra letters in this example.

Delete a word There are extra ~~extra~~ words in this example.

Insert a character A letter has been omit_t_ed from this sentence.

Insert a word A word has been *inserted* in this sentence.

Change a letter "Practi_s_e" is the preferred Canadian spelling for the verb form.

Change a word A word has been ~~changed~~ *altered* in this sentence.

Close up unwanted space Eye glasses is often, and wrongly, written open. (Close up)

Delete unwanted space This example shows unwanted space.

Insert space This example shows a space being necessary.

Transpose letters Transpositoin is usually less of an issue in manuscripts that have been spell checked. (tr)

Transpose a word or phrase Some of these are in the wrong order (words and phrases). (tr)

Move to the left   This line needs to be left aligned.

Move to the right   This line needs to be indented.

Centre align   This line should be centred in the column.

Move up

This line should be higher on the page.

This line should be lower on the page.

Move down

Align vertically   This line and
    this line and
      this line and
this line should be aligned.

Make a letter upper case   most sentences start with a (uc) capital letter.

Make a letter lower case   This sentence doesn't need all of (lc) its capital letters.

Set a word all upper case   What if you need to capitalize entire words? (uc)

Make a series of letters lower case   What if you don't NEED capital (lc) letters?

Set italic   Use italics on foreign words and (ital) on words used as terms.

Set boldface   The purpose of boldface is to   (bf)
make something stand out in the
sentence.

Set roman   *When something has been set*
in italics in error, use this   (rom)
instruction.

Set in small caps   The purpose of small caps is   (sc)
emphasis.

Correct typeface   When something has been (set in) the   (wf)
wrong font (based on the context),
use this instruction.

Make a character
superscript   This is how to mark 10⁶.   (super)

Make a character
subscript   This is how to mark H₂O.   (sub)

Insert a period   Most sentences ends with terminal   (⊙)
punctuation⊙

Insert a comma   As this sentence shows, some   /,/
sentences contain internal
punctuation, too.

Insert an
apostrophe   I can't remember how to punctuate   /'/
some words correctly.

Insert a question
mark   Should I mark up this sentence as   /?/
a question?

Insert quotation
marks   Put quotation marks around direct   ((/))/
speech, she said.

Insert a hyphen This sentence includes the much /=/
maligned hyphen.

Insert an en dash Use an en dash to indicate a range ¹/ₙ
such as (1939–1945).

Insert an em dash Use an em dash — the punctuation ¹/ₘ
dash — to show interruption.

Insert parentheses Parentheses enclose less important { }
information such as this

Spell out This instruction is useful for
times when ③ or more numbers (sp)
appear in a sentence. Also when
writers forget how to spell (Blvd).

Run in This sentence is intentionally
short. (run in)
Don't let this line start a new
paragraph: run it in.

Start a new Most designers like lines to be
paragraph neatly broken. A new paragraph ¶
should start here.

Don't make the This symbol is important to know. (stet)
change

Query Write the query symbol close to
the line with the query and write (?)
an appropriate query within the
appropriate limits of time, money,
and authority.

APPENDIX D

A Grammar Primer

For those who need it, here's a quick refresher on critical points of grammar and punctuation. Every editor requires a firm sense of grammar and punctuation and should have the vocabulary to explain basic grammar and punctuation decisions. If you're looking for deeper background, I've included a list of resources at the end of this section.

The Parts of Speech

In traditional grammar, there are eight basic parts of speech: *noun, pronoun, verb, adjective, adverb, conjunction, preposition*, and *interjection*. I have also included a few other common terms you may encounter.

- **Noun:** A noun is a word that names a person, place, thing, or concept. Nouns may have specific semantic qualities. For instance, they may be common (e.g., girl) or proper (e.g., Jennifer), singular (e.g., egg) or plural (e.g., eggs), concrete (e.g., table) or abstract (e.g., innocence), count (e.g., people) or mass (e.g., wheat); they may also show possession (see **apostrophe** below). These qualities affect how nouns may appear in sentences (e.g., proper nouns take initial capital letters) and how they interact with other parts of speech (e.g., *a large number of students* but *a large amount of debt*).

  The **teacher** chose his **words** carefully.

  The **incidence** of **rubella** has dropped markedly in the last fifty **years**.

  Pets can teach us **compassion** and **responsibility**.

- **Article:** An article points to a noun—that is, signals that a noun will follow in the sentence. *A* and *an* are called indefinite articles because they refer to generic instances of a noun. *The* is sometimes called the definite article but is more commonly referred to as a **determiner**; it refers to specific instances of a noun.

  I asked Marsha to recommend **a** good book.

  Zak decided to name **the** cat Moustache.

  Humans must eat **a** balanced diet drawn from **the** four food groups.

- **Determiner:** A determiner is a word that points to a specific instance of a noun. *The* is the most common determiner, but many other words can also function as determiners.

  Harris was named **the** head of **the** department.

  I'm interested in **these** shoes.

  We ordered **that** dessert.

- **Pronoun**: A pronoun is a word that stands in place of or refers to a noun. There are two kinds of pronouns in English: personal and indefinite. Personal pronouns may change form according to where they occur in a sentence (called *case*; e.g., *I* versus *me* versus *my*). Indefinite pronouns refer to people, places, and objects in general.

  Andrea bought **her** house in 2009.

  We told James that **he** must collect **his** things and go.

  Someone has left a jacket in the library.

  Children can be **anything they** want as adults.

- **Relative pronoun**: A relative pronoun is a word that introduces a relative (adjectival) clause. There are five relative pronouns: *that, which, who, whom, whose.* (These words can also function as other parts of speech.)

  Where is the dictionary **that** I put on the table this morning?

  Sheila married a man **who** is passionate about sailing.

  We were all a little afraid of Vanji, **whose** reputation for cruelty had far preceded her.

- **Verb**: A verb is a word that expresses action or a state of being. Verbs indicate person (first, second, or third), number (singular or plural), and tense (present or past). The main sentence verb expresses the action of the sentence; it may be supported by auxiliary ("helping") verbs such as *be* and *have* to signal aspect and condition (see also **modal auxiliaries** below).

  Humiliation **hurts**.

  Tim and Donna always **laughed** freely.

  The tide **was dropping** rapidly.

  Robin **has been planning** this party for months.

  A clause contains a subject and a verb or verb phrase. The verb must agree in person and number with the subject. (See **subject–verb disagreement** on page 359.)

- **Modal auxiliary**: A modal auxiliary functions like a verb but lacks the ability to change for person, number, or tense. The modals work with verbs to express aspect and condition. There are ten modal auxiliaries: *can, could, shall, should, will, would, may, might, must,* and *ought* (to).

  Quentin **will** receive the award next month.

  Editors **may** be interested in reading this article.

  I really **ought** to investigate the source of that noise.

- **Infinitive**: An infinitive looks like a two-part verb: *to have, to hold, to love, to go*, and so on. Infinitives do not indicate person, number, or tense because they can never be the main verb in the sentence. Rather, they function like nouns, adjectives, or adverbs, often in the form of infinitive phrases.

  Jimi decided **to buy a new guitar**. (nominal infinitive phrase)

  I made you my promise **to keep**. (adjectival)

  To succeed as an editor, you must commit to lifelong learning. (adverbial infinitive phrase)

- **Gerund**: A gerund is the *-ing* form of a verb, but it functions in a sentence like a noun, often in the form of a gerund phrase. Gerunds can never be the main verb in the sentence.

  Baking is a valuable skill. (subject of sentence)

  I've always enjoyed **hiking**. (direct object of sentence)

  Making you smile is our number-one goal. (gerund phrase as subject)

  Sam likes **listening to children's choirs**. (gerund phrase as direct object)

- **Participle**: A participle is an inflected form of a verb; it may end with *-ing, -ed, -en*, or *-t*. It functions in a sentence like an adjective (or, in rare cases, like an adverb), often in the form of a participle phrase. Participles can never be the main verb in the sentence.

  The professor **standing at the back of the room** is the dean of the college.

  That omission was part of a **calculated** plan to defraud the company.

  The headpiece was one of seven artifacts **stolen from the site**.

  Some people enjoy the taste of **burnt** toast.

- **Adjective**: An adjective is a word that describes a noun, a pronoun, or a word functioning like a noun. Adjectives answer the question *What kind?* and may appear in three forms: the positive (no ending), the comparative (ending in *-er* or preceded by *more*), and the superlative (ending in *-est* or preceded by *most*).

  The **blue** paint in the cellar was **brighter** than I realized.

  Pizza is **delicious**.

  Finn brandished his **sharpest** knife.

- **Adverb:** An adverb is a word that describes a verb, an adjective, another adverb, or a clause. Adverbs answer several questions— *How? How many? How much? When? Where? Why?*—and may appear at various positions within a sentence. Although many adverbs end with *-ly*, many more do not.

  The school closed **permanently** in 2015.

  Here are some points you forgot **yesterday**.

  I am **exuberantly, emphatically, unabashedly** proud of your accomplishments **today**!

- **Conjunction:** A conjunction is a word that connects words, phrases, and clauses. There are two kinds of conjunctions in English: coordinating and subordinating. Coordinating conjunctions connect balanced or equal sentence elements.

  Girls **and** boys should not be separated during these lessons.

  Do you want the chicken **or** the fish?

  I want to go to the dance, **but** I don't have permission.

  Subordinating conjunctions connect unbalanced or unequal sentence elements; the element that begins with the subordinating conjunction is called the dependent clause, and the rest of the sentence is called the independent (main) clause.

  Don't buy a car **until** you can afford insurance.

  Because his colleagues admired him, Mortimer was chosen to lead the new department.

  Trixie was sad all day **after** she heard the ghastly news.

- **Correlative conjunction:** Correlative conjunctions are a small subset of **coordinating conjunctions**. They occur as phrases: *either ... or, neither ... nor, both ... and,* and *not only ... but (also)*. Correlative conjunctions are used in the construction of parallel and balanced structures.

  Pat **not only** enjoys teaching grammar **but** excels at it.

  Christie possesses **both** a vast intelligence **and** a compassionate soul.

- **Conjunctive adverb**: Conjunctive adverbs are a subset of conjunctions. They often cause problems with punctuation because they are used to connect both sentences and topics, and they may appear at various positions within a sentence.

  > You have said that time is money; **therefore**, this meeting is costing the organization a great deal.
  >
  > My preference, **however**, is to go home.
  >
  > Your term has ended; **however**, your influence will linger.
  >
  > She has won the nomination; **thus**, our new plan will go into action tomorrow.

- **Preposition**: A preposition is a word that relates part of a sentence to the rest of the sentence. English has several dozen prepositions, most of them short, common words but some of them phrases (e.g., *apart from* and *with regard to*). Prepositions usually appear in prepositional phrases, made up of a preposition followed by a word or phrase called its object. The object of the preposition will be a noun, a pronoun, or a word functioning like a noun.

  > Mina Loy wrote the poem **about** her former lover.
  >
  > Simon looked distraught **at** the thought **of** leaving town.
  >
  > We put the bat house **under** the eaves **on** the north side **of** our cottage.

  Prepositional phrases function as modifiers like adjectives or adverbs, providing specific detail within sentences.

- **Interjection**: An interjection has no grammatical function in a sentence, but it grabs attention and communicates tone and emotion.

  > **Oh**, that makes me so happy!
  >
  > **Well**, she hasn't made up her mind yet.
  >
  > **Hey!** Did you see that stop sign?

Punctuation Review

Punctuation has two purposes: to indicate the conventional division of phrases and sentences, and to clarify a writer's meaning or tone. Some use of punctuation is grammatical, in the sense that it is related to the structure of communication. Some use of punctuation is stylistic, in the sense that its presence or absence does not impair communication.

- **Period**: A period is used to mark the end of a declarative sentence. It may also be used to mark the end of an abbreviated word.

We are planning to arrive tomorrow.

Arrival time is approx. 1500 hours.

- **Question mark**: A question mark is used to mark the end of a direct question. It may also be used to indicate editorial uncertainty.

    Does anyone know what time it is?

    Christine de Pizan (1364–1430?) was a notable medieval author.

- **Exclamation point**: An exclamation point is used to mark the end of an emphatic statement, indicating strong emotion. Exclamation points are rare in formal writing.

    You love me! You really, really love me!

- **Comma**: A comma is used to separate sentence elements, for instance, in lists, parenthetical constructions, and introductory modifiers.

    Tamsin bought milk, eggs, cheese, and oatmeal.

    Professor Snape, looking bored, rapped Ron on the head.

    Kerry-Ann Keltie, who lived next door to us for years, just won the Giller Prize for her novel.

    In the absence of evidence, the court must assume the accused is innocent.

A serial or series comma (often called an Oxford comma) is the comma that appears before the **coordinating conjunction** in a list. Its presence or absence is a point of style, not of grammar, but must be consistent.

- **Semicolon**: A semicolon is used to join two independent clauses, forming a compound sentence. It may also be used to coordinate the elements of a list if the listed items include commas.

    Virginia Woolf is the best-known woman Modernist writer; nearly a century later, her elegant prose continues to impress readers.

    Our next unit discusses aspects of popular culture, including the changing nature of celebrity; the revival of the women's magazine; the shift from models to celebrities on magazine covers; and the representation of women's work in film and television.

- **Colon**: Like a semicolon, a colon is used to join two independent clauses, forming a compound sentence. However, the second clause explains, exemplifies, or amplifies the first clause. The colon can also form this introductory relationship with single words and with phrases, provided that the structure that precedes the colon is a complete sentence.

> The committee rejected Smith's application: his negative reputation outweighed his skill and talent.
>
> Please wear appropriate seasonal clothing: a heavy (lined) coat, gloves or mitts, a woolen scarf, and a toque.
>
> Derek admires one quality above all others: honesty.

- **Dash**: A dash (em dash) is used to indicate an interruption in the sentence; dashes are often used this way in pairs. A dash may also be used to connect new material loosely to the end of a sentence.

  > This chapter introduces important concepts—royalties, discount structures, and subsidies—that affect editors' acquisition decisions.
  >
  > You might question some of the information in this book— and such questioning is appropriate.

  Dashes affect the pace and tone of sentences, and for that reason tend to be uncommon in formal writing.

- **En dash**: An en dash stands for the word *to*; it is used in ranges and certain noun phrases.

  > Please see *A Room of One's Own*, pages 67–74.
  >
  > This study examines the effect of antidepressants on mother–infant bonding.
  >
  > The Edmonton–Calgary corridor is one of Canada's richest and most industrialized regions.

  An en dash is slightly shorter than a true **dash** and is slightly longer than a **hyphen**.

- **Hyphen**: A hyphen is used to create a compound, such as a compound modifier, or to attach certain prefixes to words.

  > An overflowing bookshelf is a standard feature of today's middle-class home.
  >
  > A high-profile community leader has been arrested in connection with these events.
  >
  > Since 2010, self-publishing has exploded in popularity.
  >
  > Janis and Ian co-own a catering business.

- **Parentheses:** Parentheses are used to set off part of a sentence or paragraph from the rest; they always appear in pairs.

  The provincial flower of Manitoba is the prairie crocus (*Pulsatilla ludoviciana*).

  Most editors love language (although I can think of some who don't) and have great facility with various aspects of English.

Parentheses function in the same way as paired commas or paired dashes, but separate content more distinctly.

- **Brackets:** Brackets (sometimes called editorial brackets) are used to show editorial changes made to quoted text.

  A staffer from the premier's office confirmed that the flooding "[was] under control," although evacuation orders remained in place through Sunday evening.

- **Apostrophe:** An apostrophe has two uses in English: to mark contraction and to show possession. With possession, take care to distinguish whether the possessive noun is singular or plural.

  I **can't** believe he **didn't** recognize me.

  George's younger son was later appointed to the **university's** board of governors.

  The **horses'** stalls **hadn't** been mucked out for days.

- **Quotation marks:** Quotation marks are used to enclose direct speech or exact quotations.

  "Ms. Zuk gave me a lemon," Tom said acidly.

  "If I have the money," Warren leered, "will you make the time?"

  In *A Room of One's Own*, Virginia Woolf says a woman must write "as a woman who has forgotten that she is a woman, so that her pages [are] full of that curious sexual quality which comes only when sex is unconscious of itself."

In Canadian and American print, minor punctuation is enclosed inside the quotation marks, and double quotation marks are the primary style. In British print, minor punctuation appears outside the quotation marks, and single quotation marks are the primary style.

- **Ellipsis points**: Ellipsis points—three periods in a row—indicate that material has been omitted from a quotation or that a thought has trailed off. When ellipsis points occur at the end of a sentence, they may be followed by a period.

> The leader said a solution "is forthcoming ... but not yet ready for discussion."

> My thoughts soon turned to memories of our travels in France ....

Common Errors

While many things may go wrong in composition, most problems fall into a small group of common errors: problems with sentence structure, modifiers, and agreement. Due to limitations of space, this appendix includes only a small sample of common errors; consult the resources in the section that follows for more detail on other grammar problems.

- **Sentence fragment**: A sentence fragment is a group of words that expresses an incomplete thought and lacks a subject, a main verb, or both a subject and a main verb. Fragments may be used stylistically but are not generally accepted in highly formal or stylistically conservative settings. The solution to a fragment is to insert the missing component or components; thus, there are many potential solutions, depending on context.

> **Emerging gradually from the fog and mist.** *versus* Emerging gradually from the fog and mist came the canoe. *or* We recognized the canoe emerging gradually from the fog and mist.

> **A flower modestly nodding its face in the rain.** *versus* I spotted a flower modestly nodding its face in the rain. *or* A flower modestly nodding its face in the rain is the poet's symbol for a woman's shame.

- **Comma splice**: A comma splice is formed when two complete sentences are joined with only a comma, no conjunction or other punctuation. Comma splices are extremely common, but commonness doesn't make them correct, although they are better accepted in fiction and creative nonfiction than in technical or academic prose. A comma splice may be solved in one of three ways: separate the two sentences with a period; replace the comma with a semicolon (or in some cases, a colon); or insert a **coordinating conjunction** after the comma (when the sentence can logically accept one).

> **Jody is a great guy, he's remained modest and still looks out for his teammates.** *versus* Jody is a great guy. He's remained modest

and still looks out for his teammates. *or* Jody is a great guy; he's remained modest and still looks out for his teammates.

- **Run-together sentence**: A run-together sentence (also known as a fused sentence) is formed when two or more complete sentences are joined without punctuation. Run-together sentences may be solved much as comma splices are: by separating the sentences with a period, separating the sentences with a semicolon, or inserting an appropriate **coordinating conjunction** between the sentences. Never turn a run-together sentence into a comma splice as a solution.

  Pamela told her parents the secret they weren't surprised. *versus* Pamela told her parents the secret. They weren't surprised. *or* Pamela told her parents the secret; they weren't surprised. *or* Pamela told her parents the secret, but they weren't surprised.

  The term *run-on sentence* refers to two or more clauses strung together in an uncoordinated way, with or without punctuation. That is, a run-on sentence may be either a comma splice or a run-together sentence. It does not refer to an especially long sentence, however.

- **Dangling modifier**: A dangling modifier occurs when a modifier is appended to a sentence but the word or phrase the modifier modifies is missing from the sentence. Dangling modifiers are thus illogical and confusing, although sometimes funny. Dangling modifiers may be solved in one of two ways: turn the modifier into a dependent clause (with a subject and a verb) or insert a logical word or phrase into the main clause for the modifier to modify.

  The findings are unconvincing even after reading the supporting literature. *versus* The findings are unconvincing even after one reads the supporting literature. *or* Even after reading the supporting literature, we feel the findings are unconvincing.

  After driving for eleven hours, both gas tanks were depleted. *versus* After we had driven for eleven hours, both gas tanks were depleted. *or* After driving for eleven hours, I discovered that both gas tanks were depleted.

  By sharing his story of struggling with self-confidence, it is hoped that you too will overcome this issue. *versus* Since he has shared his story of struggling with self-confidence, it is hoped that you too will overcome this issue. *or* By sharing his story of struggling with depression, he hopes that you too will overcome this issue.

  Using the passive voice is a common way for writers to create dangling modifiers, so watch passive and active voice carefully.

- **Misplaced modifier**: A misplaced modifier occurs when a modifier is appended to a sentence but is too far from the word or phrase it modifies to form a clear, logical relationship. Misplaced modifiers are common and may be solved by moving the modifier close to the word or phrase it modifies.

  Developed from a traditional Polish recipe, you wouldn't guess this tasty spread contains no meat or dairy products. *versus* You wouldn't guess this tasty spread, which was developed from a traditional Polish recipe, contains no meat or dairy products.

  The students protesting in front of the administration building angrily addressed the crowd. *versus* The students protesting angrily in front of the administration building addressed the crowd. *or* The students protesting in front of the administration building addressed the crowd angrily.

- **Pronoun agreement**: A pronoun must have a clear and logical referent with which it agrees in person and number. A relative pronoun must be replaceable by its referent word or phrase. Solve faulty or weak pronoun agreement by changing the pronoun or recasting the sentence.

  What twelve-year-old boy wouldn't love a jar of frosting in their lunch? *versus* What twelve-year-old boy wouldn't love a jar of frosting in his lunch?

  Several articles have been written about the author and their use of religious symbols. *versus* Several articles have been written about the author and her use of religious symbols.

  Some of the cake is missing, which is probably a good sign. *versus* Some of the cake is missing, and its disappearance is probably a good sign.

  The most common pronoun agreement issue occurs between *they* and certain indefinite pronouns (someone/somebody, everyone/ everybody, anyone/anybody, no one/nobody). These pronouns are grammatically singular, while *they* is grammatically plural.

  Almost everyone hopes that one day they will live a life of luxury. *versus* Almost everyone hopes that one day he or she will live a life of luxury. *versus* Most people hope that one day they will live a life of luxury.

In many settings, agreement with *they* is acceptable, but in formal contexts you may have to recast the sentence to eliminate the agreement issue.

- **Subject–verb disagreement:** The subject of a sentence must agree in number and person with the main sentence verb. In English, the verb form that causes most agreement problems is the third-person present tense (*-s*); forms of *be* may also cause trouble. Ensure the verb agrees with the true subject, not a modifier or phrase between subject and verb.

  The Ruffians Rugby Club always seek new recruits. *versus* The Ruffians Rugby Club always seeks new recruits.

  One in nine Canadians are at risk for hemochromatosis. *versus* One in nine Canadians is at risk for hemochromatosis.

  The short list for the Alberta Book Awards have been announced. *versus* The short list for the Alberta Book Awards has been announced.

- **Faulty parallelism:** Parallelism is based on balance. It leans on **conjunctions** to make phrasing stylish and memorable. To solve faulty parallelism, ensure that each element has grammatical parity, flows smoothly from its lead-in, and repeats or omits modifiers and determiners as necessary.

  I have and will always love my country. *versus* I have loved and will always love my country.

  An editor requires a memory for detail, eye for consistency, and instinct for recognizing patterns. *versus* An editor requires a memory for detail, an eye for consistency, and an instinct for recognizing patterns.

  Initially, math was taught through demonstration and rote memorization; today, we use discovery models and application. *versus* Initially, math was taught through demonstration and rote memorization; today, it is taught with discovery models and application. *versus* Initially, we taught math through demonstration and rote memorization; today, we use discovery models and application.

Resources

Here are some common guides to grammar, punctuation, and style, presenting a range in their scope, degree of detail, and seriousness.

C. Beth Burch, *A Writer's Grammar* (New York: Longman, 2003). A textbook, chock full of examples, that explains basic and intermediate concepts in grammar and demonstrates how they apply to writing style and voice.

Roy Peter Clark, *The Glamour of Grammar: A Guide to the Magic and Mystery of Practical English* (New York: Little, Brown and Company, 2010). Clark provides clear-eyed explanations of various elements of grammar and why writers should care about how we use English.

Kitty Burns Florey, *Sister Bernadette's Barking Dog: The Quirky History and Lost Art of Diagramming Sentences* (Hoboken, NJ: Melville House, 2006). If you really enjoy grammar, check out this book, which explains and celebrates traditional sentence diagrams.

Karen Elizabeth Gordon, *The Deluxe Transitive Vampire* (New York: Houghton Mifflin, 1993). An oldie but a goodie, this book provides a thorough introduction to traditional grammar and is whimsically illustrated with gothic-themed woodcuts.

Karen Elizabeth Gordon, *The New Well-Tempered Sentence* (New York: Pantheon Books, 1993). The companion volume to *The Transitive Vampire*, this book deals with matters of punctuation.

Mary Norris, *Between You and Me: Confessions of a Comma Queen* (New York, London: W.W. Norton & Company, 2015). Although this book is primarily the memoir of a copyeditor, it contains clear, succinct explanations of many points of grammar and punctuation.

Patricia T. O'Conner, *Woe Is I: The Grammarphobe's Guide to Better English in Plain English* (New York: Riverhead Books, 2010). An updated edition of a long-time favourite, this book explains basic concepts of grammar as well as punctuation and spelling hints.

Maxine Ruvinsky, *Practical Grammar: A Canadian Writer's Resource*, 3rd ed. (Don Mills, ON: Oxford University Press, 2013). This book is a reliable, meat-and-potatoes presentation of grammar, punctuation, and style written for Canadian post-secondary students.

William Strunk, Jr., and E.B. White, *The Elements of Style*, 4th ed. (New York: Pearson, 1999). A standby in writers' desks throughout the English-speaking world, the venerable Strunk and White provide a brisk discussion of phrases, clauses, and other elements of grammar in aid of developing polished composition.

Lynne Truss, *Eats, Shoots and Leaves: The Zero Tolerance Approach to Punctuation* (New York: Penguin, 2003). You've likely heard about Truss's war on the greengrocer's apostrophe; if you read this book, you'll better understand punctuation marks and why Truss feels their protection is so important.

APPENDIX E

Building an Editing Library

An Idiosyncratic List of Favourite Book-Editing Resources

The following books are by no means the only ones I refer to, but each offers something valuable to the would-be book editor. New books don't arrive in this field very often, so don't be surprised if you must buy some of these titles second-hand. Some of the technical content is frankly out of date, but the discussions of hands-on editing and author–editor relationships remain relevant.

Rick Archbold et al., *Author and Editor: A Working Guide* (Toronto: The Book and Periodical Development Council, 1983). Regrettably, the mechanical information is terribly out of date, but the relationship ideas and the cool-headedness of the discussion in this slim booklet are outstanding.

Robert Bringhurst, *The Elements of Typographic Style,* 4th ed. (Vancouver: Hartley & Marks, 2013). Part textbook, part think piece, part love letter, this book gives anyone who works with type a solid sense of the history, purpose, and application of typography—and it's filled with fascinating details that any editor should appreciate.

The Chicago Manual of Style, 16th edition: If you intend to work in book publishing, you cannot be without this volume. Part style manual, part publishing reference book, *Chicago* holds the answers to most of your editorial questions—and much more.

Betsy Lerner, *The Forest for the Trees: An Editor's Advice to Writers,* revised ed. (New York: Riverhead Books, 2010). Although this book was written for writers, it provides valuable insights for editors. The first section discusses aspects of writers' "types," or personalities, and the habits that may emerge from them. The second section briskly surveys the publication process in the United States from submission to marketing—you might find it useful when you're explaining the process to a first-time author. One of my favourite teaching resources.

Arthur Plotnik, *The Elements of Editing: A Modern Guide for Editors and Journalists* (New York: Macmillan, 1982). Some of the technical content is very dated, but chapter 3 ("Editor and Writer: An Uneasy Alliance") and chapter 4 ("The Agony and the Agony: Line Editors and Their Craft") offer outstanding preparation for anyone who edits text. Plotnik is addressing editors in general, so you'll find references to newspapers and magazines as well as books, but his advice is solid, pertinent, and valuable.

Susan Rabiner and Alfred Fortunato. *Thinking Like Your Editor: How to Write Great Serious Nonfiction and Get It Published* (New York: W.W. Norton & Company, 2002). Anyone who writes or edits serious nonfiction should read this book. Aspects of the business have changed since it was written, but the general advice here is solid—and editors can learn a great deal from reading other editors' perspectives.

Carole Fisher Saller, *The Subversive Copy Editor: Advice from Chicago (or, How to Negotiate Good Relationships with Your Writers, Your Colleagues, and Yourself)* (Chicago: University of Chicago Press, 2009). If you're just beginning your career as an editor and would value the insights of an experienced mentor, this is the resource for you. Saller discusses typical problems editors encounter and processes all editors need to understand, and her writing is personable and witty. I assign this book for proofreading and copyediting courses.

Leslie Sharpe and Irene Gunther, *Editing Fact and Fiction: A Concise Guide to Book Editing* (Cambridge University Press, 1994). Written to provide training for novice editors, this is a brilliant book on book editing. The sections on the editor's senses and editing principles are insightful, and the general overview of the industry and sectors is helpful. The information on electronic editing is out of date, but overall this book should be on every serious editor's shelf. A key text when I'm teaching substantive and structural editing.

Other Books You Might Want or Need

I am an inveterate collector of books of many kinds, but my professional interests have led me to collect books about editing and publishing. Here are a few that you might find interesting and valuable. Again, note that some of these are now out of print, and some of the content may be dated.

Books about writing, editing, and publishing as process
Gerald Gross, *Editors on Editing: What Writers Need to Know About What Editors Do*

Cheryl B. Klein, *Second Sight: An Editor's Talks on Writing, Revising, and Publishing Books for Children and Young Adults*

Marshall Lee, *Bookmaking: Editing/Design/Production*

Judy Mandell, *Book Editors Talk to Writers*

Paul Parsons, *Getting Published: The Acquisition Process at University Presses*

Editors' and publishers' biographies, memoirs, and letters
A. Scott Berg, *Max Perkins: Editor of Genius*

Bennett Cerf, *At Random: The Reminiscences of Bennett Cerf*

Jason Epstein, *Book Business: Publishing Past, Present, and Future*

Douglas Gibson, *Stories about Storytellers: Publishing Alice Munro, Robertson Davies, Alistair MacLeod, Pierre Trudeau, and Others*

Michael Korda, *Another Life: A Memoir of Other People*

Greg Lawrence, *Jackie as Editor: The Literary Life of Jacqueline Kennedy Onassis*

Robert Lecker, *Dr. Delicious: Memoirs of a Life in CanLit*

Stirling Lord, *Lord of Publishing: A Memoir*

Leonard S. Marcus, ed., *Dear Genius: The Letters of Ursula Nordstrom*

Daniel Menaker, *My Mistake: A Memoir*

Sam Solecki, ed., *Imagining Canadian Literature: The Selected Letters of Jack McClelland*

John Hall Wheelock, ed., *Editor to Author: The Letters of Maxwell E. Perkins*

Book culture
Kit Dobson and Smaro Kamboureli, *Producing Canadian Literature: Authors Speak Out on the Literary Marketplace*

Jeff Gomez, *Print Is Dead: Books in Our Digital Age*

Wendy Griswold, *Regionalism and the Reading Class*

Roy MacSkimming, *The Perilous Trade: Publishing Canada's Writers*, 2nd ed.

Laura J. Miller, *Reluctant Capitalists: Bookselling and the Culture of Consumption*

Sherman Young, *The Book Is Dead: Long Live the Book*

Gabriel Zaid, *So Many Books: Reading and Publishing in an Age of Abundance*

Resources for mechanical editing

Susan Bell, *The Artful Edit: On the Practice of Editing Yourself*

Theodore M. Bernstein, *Miss Thistlebottom's Hobgoblins: The Careful Writer's Guide to the Taboos, Bugbears and Outmoded Rules of English Usage*

Jo Billingham, *Editing and Revising Text*

Bruce O. Boston, *Stet! Tricks of the Trade for Writers and Editors*

Bill Bryson, *Troublesome Words*

R.W. Burchfield, ed., *The New Fowler's Modern English Usage* (3rd ed.)

Margery Fee and Janice McAlpine, *Guide to Canadian English Usage*

Constance Hale, *Sin and Syntax: How to Craft Wickedly Effective Prose* and *Vex, Hex, Smash, Smooch: Let Verbs Power Your Writing*

Karen Judd, *Copyediting, A Practical Guide*

Patricia T. O'Conner, *Woe Is I: The Grammarphobe's Guide to Better English in Plain English*

Arthur Plotnik, *Spunk and Bite: A Writer's Guide to Bold, Contemporary Style*

Margaret Shertzer, *The Elements of Grammar*

Elsie Myers Stainton, *The Fine Art of Copyediting*

Mary Stoughton, *Substance and Style: Instruction and Practice in Copyediting*

Marilyn Swartz et al., *Guidelines for Bias-Free Writing*

Bill Walsh, *Lapsing into a Comma*

Specialized editorial resources

Lesley Ellen Harris, *Canadian Copyright Law*

Thomas McCormack, *The Fiction Editor, The Novel, and the Novelist*

Nancy Mulvaney, *Indexing Books*

Scott Norton, *Developmental Editing: A Handbook for Freelancers, Authors, and Publishers*

Sarah Harrison Smith, *The Fact Checker's Bible*

Style manuals

American Psychological Association, *Publication Manual of the American Psychological Association*

Associated Press, *The Associated Press Stylebook and Briefing on Media Law*

Council of Science Editors, *Scientific Style and Format: The CSE Manual for Authors, Editors, and Publishers*

Editors' Association of Canada, *Editing Canadian English*, 3rd ed.

J.A. (Sandy) McFarlane and Warren Clements, *The Globe and Mail Style Book*

Modern Languages Association, *The MLA Style Manual and Guide to Scholarly Publishing*

Public Works and Government Services Canada Translation Bureau, *The Canadian Style: A Guide to Writing and Editing*

The Canadian Press, *The Canadian Press Stylebook: A Guide for Writers and Editors*

Resources for writers

Joni Cole, *Toxic Feedback: Helping Writers Survive and Thrive*

Claire Kehrwald Cook, *Line by Line: How to Edit Your Own Writing*

Karen Elizabeth Gordon, *The New Well-Tempered Sentence: A Punctuation Handbook for the Innocent, the Eager, and the Doomed*

Karen Elizabeth Gordon, *The Deluxe Transitive Vampire: A Handbook of Grammar for the Innocent, the Eager and the Doomed*

Susan Page, *The Shortest Distance Between You and a Published Book*

Bruce Ross-Larson, *Edit Yourself: A Manual for Everyone Who Works with Words*

William Strunk, Jr. and E.B. White, *The Elements of Style*

Pat Walsh, *Seventy-Eight Reasons Why Your Book May Never Be Published and Fourteen Reasons Why It Just Might*

William Zinsser, *On Writing Well*

Glossary: Publishing Lingo

Publishing, like most professional activities, has its own jargon. The following glossary, while by no means comprehensive, attempts to capture terms and concepts that are commonplace among editors working today. Some of the terms are now used infrequently because times and technologies have changed; some are daily vocabulary.

acquisition: the process of putting a manuscript under contract so that it becomes one of the publisher's properties

advance: a sum paid (sometimes in multiple payments) to the author prior to publication, based on the projected first year's royalties

advance reading copy (ARC): an edited but normally unproofread ("uncorrected") version of a book circulated to booksellers, key bloggers, and members of the public prior to publication to generate positive comments, reviews, and buzz; ARCs are usually typeset and bound but are printed at lower resolution than the finished book

agent: a publishing professional, often with a background in editorial or marketing, who represents the author in the relationship with the publisher and others interested in exploiting a manuscript

auction: the process of circulating a manuscript to several editors and soliciting competitive bids in rounds

author copies: a small number of free copies (typically ten) given to an author on the publication date of his/her book

backlist: books that continue to sell year after year; the backlist provides a predictable revenue stream for most publishers

back matter: ancillary materials that follow the body of a text, such as the appendix, glossary, notes, and bibliography

backordered: a book that is in print but is currently not unavailable; books may be (temporarily) backordered when a publisher is shifting to a new format (paperback after the hardcover), preparing a new edition, or evaluating likely sales prior to a reprint decision; recently books have been listed as "backordered" on online bookselling sites during disputes between the bookseller and the publisher

365

beta reading: feedback offered by readers of an early version of a manuscript to assist the author with revision and rewriting; generally refers to online, crowd-sourced feedback

BISAC codes: Book Industry Standards and Communications classification descriptors that help retailers determine where to shelve or categorize a book

bleed: ink coverage that extends beyond the trimmed size of the page

blurb: a short, sales-oriented endorsement of a book offered by a writer or other figure whose opinion may influence a reader's decision to purchase a book

body type: the typeface in which the main reading text of a book is presented (usually a serif font)

book club: a retail mechanism that sells books directly to consumers, often discounted from their published retail price (e.g., Scholastic Books, Book-of-the-Month Club)

book fair: a large-scale publishers' conference at which networking with and selling to international partners are key activities

book group: a local, recurring meeting of readers who come together regularly to discuss previously agreed-upon books

book packager: a supplier who produces outsourced editorial and design materials on behalf of international publishing clients, allowing the nominal publisher to customize the package for its own market

bulk sale: a large, non-returnable sale to a non-traditional outlet (e.g., selling 2,000 copies of a cookbook to a non-profit organization)

callout: an instruction embedded in a digital file that provides design or layout information, or addresses the editor or author

caption: brief text that accompanies visual content

case binding: a specific form of hardcover; see also **cloth binding**

Cataloguing in Publication (CIP): a record of title-related data that helps libraries catalogue and shelve books appropriately

character (in type): a single letter, numeral, or symbol

cloth binding: a hardcover book in which the book boards are wrapped in a durable fabric that is also integral to the spine

CMYK: an initialism that refers to the four inks (cyan, magenta, yellow, and black) of four-colour process printing

coastline: the pattern that letterforms make above or below their x-height

coated: paper that has been finished with a thin veneer of clay that gives it greater weight, opacity, and thickness

colophon: the publisher's logo or insignia; also, a brief statement that appears at the conclusion of a book and discusses the book's design and manufacture

commissioning: the process of approaching a writer or researcher to develop a book-length manuscript on a particular topic, issue, or event (such as hiring a journalist to write a history of the Rotary Club in advance of its hundredth anniversary)

contract proofs: printer's proofs on which the client's signature represents an agreement to accept the print job

co-publication: a process in which two or more publishers share the costs and the income from producing a title in a particular format or language (e.g., a Canadian university press and an American university press co-publish an expensive, full-colour art book, each distributing its edition in its own **territory**)

copyediting: the process of working through text for correctness and consistency, particularly with respect to matters of spelling, grammar, and punctuation; see also **stylistic editing, textual editing**

copy-fitting: removing words and characters to make text fit the space available

copy line: a short piece of sales or marketing information on a book cover

copyright: at its base, the right to copy; for publishers, it refers to the party holding the primary rights in a document

costing sheet: a document generated by a spreadsheet programmed to produce a book budget, breaking down various areas of income and expense

cover: the exterior paper or boards wrapped around the body of a book to give it stability and strength; today, the cover design is integral to positioning a book in the marketplace and communicates, in addition to the title, the author's name, the publisher, and descriptive information about the book's content and intended audience; see also **jacket**

cover stock: paper of a particular basis weight and dimension; also, stiff, heavy-weight paper used to make the jacket of a paperback book

derivative rights: rights that emerge from the existence of a copyrighted text, such as theatrical performance, film adaptation, and translation; also known as *secondary rights* or *subsidiary rights*

design: a set of decisions about the visual presentation of the text: the cover, the page size, the type used for the body, the treatment of illustrative matter, etcetera; see also **layout**

developmental editing: the process of reworking an incomplete or ineffectual manuscript to make it publishable; developmental editing may also involve fitting an idea to a writer or writing team capable of producing a book-length treatment of the idea (such as approaching a well-known science writer to produce a book on Canada's climate change issues); see also **commissioning**

digital rights management (DRM): a software process that permits or restricts access to or reproduction of digital content such as ebooks

discount: the percentage amount deducted from the retail price of a book when that book is sold to the retailer; discounts typically range from twenty to fifty percent

discoverability: a book's success at being found by its ideal readers; also, the mechanisms publishers use to help readers find books

display type: type normally reserved for headings, covers, title pages, and ads; tends to be more ornamented and less legible than body type

distribution: the process of moving books into the supply chain, often undertaken by specialized organizations (distributors) that connect publishers to retailers

dump bins: units (usually made from cardboard) created to display multiple copies of books from the floor of the retail space

earned out: the point at which the royalties derived from sales of a title equal the value of the advance

editing: a comprehensive term used to describe various stages in which text is revised and prepared for publication; normally performed by editors who possess special training in grammar, punctuation, usage, and general matters of language, but who may also possess a specific disciplinary background (e.g., fiction, history, economics); see also **developmental editing, substantive editing, stylistic editing, copyediting,** and **proofreading**

edition: publication of a book whose content or format is distinct from other versions (e.g., a **hardcover versus a mass-market edition**); see also **reprint**

editorial design: collaboration between the editor and the art department to create a particular reading experience or way of using a book

editorial letter: a communication to the author in which the editor collects all reviewers' comments into a single document and directs the author's next steps on the manuscript; see also **transmittal letter**

editorial sensibility: a blend of qualities that an editor brings to work on every manuscript, including problem-solving skills, sensitivity to the author's aims, and method

endpaper: a sheet of paper at the beginning or end of a book that attaches the book block to the hardcover case; it may be plain, coloured, or illustrated

escalating royalty: a royalty percentage that increases when a book meets certain sales goals

flat sheets: unfolded, untrimmed press sheets; normally examined at a **press check** to verify the technical quality of the printing; see also **make-ready**

folios: page numbers (historically, folio referred to a particular paper size); technically, the folio excludes the **footer**

font: type of a particular size and style (e.g., Mrs Eaves Bold Italic 10 point); see also **typeface**

footer: a repeating element that runs at the bottom of a printed page as an orientation device for readers; may display the book title, author name, chapter title, section title, or similar information; may be referred to as a running foot; see also **running head**

foreign rights: a bundle of subsidiary rights that enable a publisher to publish and sell a book outside of its normal territory in its original language or in translation; these rights may be licensed by other publishers

four-colour printing: a process that produces full colour on the printed sheet by applying tiny dots of four standard inks; see also **CMYK, process colour**

Frankfurt Book Fair: arguably the world's most important international rights fair, held annually (normally in October) in Frankfurt, Germany

frontlist: the titles of the current season that are selling now or have been announced and are about to be published

front matter: matter that appears before the body of the text itself, such as the half-title page, the full-title page, the copyright page, the contents page, and the introduction

fulfillment: the supply-chain process that moves books from the publisher to the retailer, often by way of a distributor

galleys: typeset pages used for proofreading; today, with digital typesetting, these are more commonly referred to as *proofs* or **page proofs**

genre fiction: text that is written to conform to certain stylistic and structural conventions; the typical genres include romances, westerns, mysteries, thrillers, science fiction, and fantasy

gratis copies: free copies, generally provided to reviewers or other people with the potential to promote or publicize a book in some way

greeking: nonsense, or dummy, text, used to demonstrate type treatment in design or for copy-fitting; traditional greeking text begins *Lorem ipsum dolor sit amet*

halftone: a photograph or other artwork with continuous tones that has been screened into dots for black-and-white reproduction; see also **line art**

hand-selling: the practice of selling books directly to a reader by asking questions and offering insightful suggestions

hardcover: a book whose body is protected by strong, stiff boards; see also **cloth binding**

imposition: the way in which individual pages of a book are arranged ("imposed") on a printing plate so that the finished printed sheet may be folded into correct book order

imprint: a particular line of books within a larger company or house, often reflecting a specific editor, focus, or audience

ISBN (International Standard Book Number): a thirteen-character (formerly ten-character) string of numbers (and occasionally an X) that uniquely identifies a particular edition of a book in the market

jacket: historically refers to the paper wrapper folded around the boards of a hardcover book, but the term may be used loosely to refer to the **cover** of any book

justified: type that is set in lines of equal length; most books are justified, but some books adopt an unjustified, or ragged, right margin

kerning: the adjustment of space between one letter and another to produce a complementary visual relationship

laminate: a protective coating applied to a book's cover to make it more durable on the shelf and more visually appealing

layout: the process of arranging text and visuals into composed pages; may also refer to the documents created by this process

leading (pronounced *ledding*): the space between one line of type and the next; leading is an important component of legibility

lead title: a publisher's most important book of the season; the title a publisher intends to assign the most time, effort, and money to; not all publishers have a lead title, but it is often easy to identify in a publisher's catalogue from its catalogue space and marketing plan

legal read: the process of having one or more lawyers read a manuscript to ensure both author and publisher are unlikely to be sued for defamation or other legal matters

licensing: the process of granting or acquiring subsidiary rights to a property for a specific time, in a specific territory, in a specific language, or for a specific purpose (e.g., a network might license the film rights for a novel)

ligature: a typographical unit made up from two or more letters, shaped to improve the clarity and readability of the individual characters

line art: artwork that lacks grey tones— that is, an image that is either solid black or white (as opposed to **halftone**)

line editing: see **stylistic editing**

list: all the books a publisher currently has in print and available to sell

make-ready: sheets run through a press in advance of a job to check colour and other aspects of physical printing

marketing collateral: marketing materials produced to promote a particular title, such as book trailers, **shelf talkers**, **dump bins**, and bookmarks

marketing plan: a formal written breakdown of promotion, advertising, and publicity planned for a given title, usually including dates, costs, and staff responsibilities

mass-market edition: a paperback of a particular trim size ($4^1/_4$ by $6^3/_4$ inches), typically printed on low-quality paper; these tend to have flashy covers and are often sold in non-traditional outlets such as convenience stores and groceries as well as in bookstores

mechanical editing: editing for grammar, spelling, punctuation, and mechanics; a synonym for **copyediting**

media kit: an information package sent to a relevant writer, editor, or broadcaster to introduce a book and pitch publicity opportunities; also known (wrongly) as a *press kit*

metadata: data about data; in a publishing context, data about a title or an edition, such as author background, awards won, and age group of intended audience

midlist: books that are unlikely to be bestsellers; titles from previous seasons that have not sold enough to become backlist staples; many authors find being described as "midlist" insulting

moral rights: a bundle of rights, available in British and Commonwealth publishing, that allow the author to control the reputation of text and author; broadly speaking, these rights involve identification, integrity, and association

MS, MSS: manuscript, manuscripts

multiple submission: the process by which an author or agent submits a manuscript to several editors or publishers simultaneously; though generally frowned on by editors, it's a reality of the business because some houses take months to respond

net: the cost of books after discounts have been applied; when used with regard to royalties, net refers to a royalty calculated by the income the publisher received for a book, not the book's retail price

news release: a document, written in the style of a hard-news story, intended to promote a book or some aspect of its publication; the intended audience of a news release is journalists

non-traditional: a retailer whose primary product is not books, such as a gas station with a spinner rack, a big-box hardware store with a small book section, or a women's clothing store

offset lithography: a printing process that uses the chemical properties of ink and water to transfer ink from a **plate** to the printing sheet

on-sale date: the date on which a book is available for retail sale; see also **publication date**

option: the right to reserve the opportunity to exploit a particular right derived from a literary property; most typically used with respect to film rights

orphan: the first line of a paragraph running by itself at the bottom of a page or column, with the rest of the paragraph following on the next page or column; see also **widow**

out of print: a formal decision to stop the printing and distribution of a title; see also **reversion of rights**

over-the-transom submissions: unsolicited submissions, not attached to a particular editor; see also **slush pile**

P&L statement: a financial statement, often produced for an individual book, that outlines overall income and expenses—that is, profit and loss

page proofs: the designed and typeset text, prepared for the author and the proofreader to review; also known as **galleys**

paperback: a book whose body is not bound in stiff board but instead is bound in a heavy-weight paper or card stock; depending on the **trim size**, a paperback may be further classified as a **mass-market edition** or a **trade edition**

paratext: the words and images a publisher adds to the author's text to ready it for publication, such as the cover, the book description, blurbs and excepts from advance reviews, and the title page

peer editing: a process common in writing courses, in which writers at roughly the same level of accomplishment offer an author feedback and suggestions on a manuscript or excerpt; this step normally happens well before a manuscript is submitted to a book editor or publisher

peer review: a process in academic publishing in which a manuscript is read and critiqued by a scholar in the author's discipline to verify the manuscript's quality and currency

perfect binding: a format in which printed pages are folded into signatures and attached to a cover with glue; see also **saddle stitched, sewn binding**

permissions: written statements that allow authors to use copyrighted material in their own work; permissions are issued by whoever holds the rights to the material in question and may require payment of a fee

pica: a unit of type measurement: 1/12 of an inch; see also **point**

plate: in printing, a thin sheet of metal to which ink is applied

point: a unit of type measurement: 1/72 of an inch; see also **pica**

point of sales (POS): materials used to appeal directly to the consumer at the retail level (e.g., **shelf talkers**, posters, bookmarks, display units, **dump bins**)

positioning: the process of making a book identifiable to its audience; making choices in the design, production, pricing, and marketing of a title to help it reach its intended audience

press check: a brief meeting at a printing press at which publishing staff examine flat sheets to verify the tone and saturation of printing ink on the paper; normally done only on full-colour books with specific technical requirements

print on demand (POD): technology that permits in-line rapid printing and binding to produce copies of a book as needed from a standing digital file

print, paper, and binding (PP&B): the basic cost of manufacturing a book, often expressed as a cost per unit

process colour: one of four colours—cyan, magenta, yellow, and black—used in offset colour printing

production: the various processes involved with the physical manufacturing of a printed book; may also refer to various processes associated with design, layout, and pre-publication of paper or digital texts

program: a publisher's areas of interest

project editor: an editor responsible for overseeing the technical editing of a manuscript and coordinating its movement through the production process

promotion: paid mechanisms for drawing attention to a title or an author, such as advertising, an author tour, or contests

proofreading: the process of reviewing a text immediately prior to manufacture to ensure accuracy and consistency in both its verbal and its visual presentation

proofs: see **page proofs**

property: a manuscript under contract

proposal: a well-developed description of a manuscript an author intends to write

publication date: the date on which a book is available for retail sale; see also **on-sale date** publicity: unpaid mechanisms for drawing attention to a title or an author, such as radio and television interviews; stories in newspapers and magazines; outside agents, such as producers and reporters, generating interest

Publishers Weekly: the American-published standard journal of the Western publishing industry; see also *Quill and Quire*

queries: questions or suggestions an editor appends to the manuscript during the editing process

query letter: a pitch letter; a brief communication sent to an editor to solicit interest in a book idea

Quill and Quire: a Canadian periodical published for writers, librarians, booksellers, and the publishing industry; see also *Publishers Weekly*

recto: the right-hand side of a two-page spread

registration: the system that ensures that sequential printing plates align so the content they carry appears where it is intended; most often used in colour printing

remainders: copies of printed books declared excess inventory and sold at a greatly reduced price

reprint: a second or subsequent printing of a strong-selling book; see also **edition**

reserve against returns: withholding a portion of a royalty payment, particularly within the first year of publication, against copies that may still be returned to the publisher

resolution: the amount of data an image contains, usually expressed in terms of dots per inch (dpi) or pixels per inch (ppi)

returns: unsold books returned to the publisher for credit

reversion of rights: a publisher's formal return of the primary right to the author

review copies: gratis copies of a finished book sent to reviewers or media outlets in the hope that it will be reviewed

RGB: red, green, blue, referring to the colour space for computer monitors, digital cameras, and video projectors (as well as the receptors in the human eye)

right of first refusal: contract clause in which the author agrees to offer his/her next manuscript first to the publisher that issued the contract

royalties: a percentage of a book's (net or retail) price that is paid to the author on each original sale (royalties are not paid on the sales of used books)

royalty period: the period for which a publisher calculates royalties to be paid for sales, usually one year

royalty statement: a document that enumerates books sold (minus returns, gratis copies, and damaged inventory) and derivative income received for the preceding period (usually one year), yielding the sum to be paid to the author

running head: a repeating element that appears at the top of a printed page as an orientation device for readers; may display the book title, author name, chapter title, section title, or similar information; see also **footer**

saddle stitched: a format in which staples are punched through the vertical centre of gathered pages and the pages are folded to form a book

sales channel: a retail route through which books reach readers

sales conference: a meeting at which forthcoming books are presented to sales reps

sales handle: a brief statement that communicates the essence of a book, often by referring to another well-known book (e.g., "the Canadian *What to Expect When You're Expecting*" or "the *Anne of Green Gables* for the West Coast")

sales reps: members of the sales and marketing team who represent the publisher and attempt to sell books into retail sales channels (e.g., bookstores, non-traditional outlets, libraries)

sans serif: a typeface that lacks decorative terminal strokes on letters and other characters; see also **serif**

screening: a process of rendering an image as tiny dots to prepare it for printing

season: a period during which a publisher releases a significant number of books (e.g., fall or spring); also, the books planned for release within a given period

sentence case: text styling on titles, heads, and subheads in which only the first word and any proper nouns/adjectives in the phrase take a capital (e.g., Most book publishers avoid sentence case on book jackets); sometimes called *down style*; see also **title case**

serial rights: publication of portions of a book in a magazine or newspaper; prior to the book's publication date we speak of first serial rights; after the book's publication date we speak of second serial rights

serif: a typeface that features decorative terminal strokes on letters and other characters; also, the terminal stroke itself

sewn binding: a format in which printed pages are folded into signatures and sewn through their centres, then sewn into a block, for strength and durability; see also **saddle stitched**, **perfect binding**

sheet-fed press: a printing press that uses large, flat sheets of paper; see also **web press**

shelf talkers: printed cards that can be hung from display shelving in a bookstore to promote a particular author, title, or series

short discount: the discount, usually twenty percent, applied to books sold to college/university bookstores

show-through: the degree to which image or type on one side of a printed sheet shows through on the opposite side

signature: a press sheet, folded into 8, 16, or 32 pages to form a continuous section of a book

slush pile: unsolicited manuscripts; also, manuscripts that are sent speculatively to the house as a whole, not directed to a particular editor; see also **over-the-transom submissions**

soft proofing: the process of reviewing and marking up PDFs rather than printed pages

special sales: a comprehensive term to describe book sales outside the normal retail sales channels, such as a **bulk sale** to a national charity

spot colour: in printing, colour applied with a premixed ink, not one of the four process inks

style sheet: a running list of mechanical decisions compiled as a copyeditor or proofreader reviews a text

stylistic editing: editing a manuscript for clarity, concision, language issues (such as bias or jargon), and flow; also known as *line editing*

subsidiary rights: see **derivative rights**

substantive editing: editing a manuscript to improve its content, structure, reading level, or organization; this stage occurs early in the editorial process

territory: a geographical region in which a publisher has rights to act (e.g., Canada and the United States, Australia and New Zealand, Asia); territory is one of the rights specified in a book contract and is intended to control which publisher may sell a book in a given place (e.g., the British publisher versus the Canadian publisher)

textual editing: a term that includes stylistic editing, copyediting, and proofreading

title case: text styling on titles, heads, and subheads in which all major words take a capital (e.g., Most Publishers Prefer Title Case on Book Jackets); sometimes called *up style*; see also **sentence case**

title-information sheet (TI): a document that identifies a book's key features and is presented to sales reps

trade books: books published for the traditional bookstore and library market; such books are intended for general audiences of adults or children (as distinct from academic, educational, and other kinds of specialized publishing)

trade discount: the discount, generally forty to fifty percent, applied to books sold to booksellers that sell to a general audience

trade edition: refers to paperbacks that are (usually) larger than mass-market size, are printed on better-quality paper, and are sold at a higher price than mass-market books; see also **mass-market edition**

trade publishing: publishing for the commercial book trade; the publication of books intended for the general public rather than for professionals, scholars, or other specialized audiences

transmittal letter: letter to the author that accompanies the copyedited manuscript or proof pages and that gives specific directions about what to do with the materials transmitted and when they are due; see also **editorial letter**

trim size: the finished size of a book, normally measured in inches, width by height (e.g., $5\,^1/_2 \times 8\,^1/_2$)

typeface: the set of a specific design of characters, encompassing all heights, weights, and styles, such as Times New Roman or Garamond

verso: the left-hand side of a two-page spread

vetting: the process of having one or more subject-matter experts read a nonfiction manuscript to ensure it is factually sound and current; see also **legal read**

web press: a printing press that uses large rolls of paper; see also **sheet-fed press**

wholesale discount: the discount, usually sixty percent, applied to books sold to **wholesalers**

wholesaler: a supply-chain business that buys copies of books from publishers and rapidly resells them to retailers

widow: the last line of a paragraph running by itself at the top of a page or column, with the rest of the paragraph appearing on the previous page or column; see also **orphan**

workshopping: the process by which a writer circulates a draft of a manuscript for feedback from other writers; this process happens well prior to the manuscript's submission to a publisher

xerography: a printing process that fuses dry ink to paper using heat

Bibliography

"About [McClelland & Stewart]." *Penguin Random House Canada.* Web. 3 November 2015.

"About Douglas & McIntyre." *Douglas & McIntyre.* Web. 3 November 2015.

Abrams, Dennis. "Random House Raises First Printing of New Dr. Seuss to 1 Million." *Publishing Perspectives* 20 April 2015. Web. 13 October 2015.

Akey, Stephen. "My Book Is Not About Vampires or Childhood Trauma. I'm Doomed. The Problem with Literary Agents." *New Republic* 18 November 2014. Web. 12 November 2015.

Alter, Alexandra. "Dr. Seuss Book: Yes, They Found It in a Box." *New York Times* 21 July 2015. Web. 13 October 2015.

Alter, Alexandra. "'Go Set a Watchman' Sells More Than 1 Million Copies." *New York Times* 20 July 2015. Web. 13 October 2015.

Anderson, Chris. *The Long Tail: Why the Future of Business Is Selling Less of More.* Rev. and updated ed. New York: Hyperion, 2008.

Archbold, Rick, et al. *Author and Editor: A Working Guide.* Toronto: The Book and Periodical Development Council, 1983.

Athill, Diana. *Stet: An Editor's Life.* London: Granta, 2000.

Atwood, Margaret. *Negotiating with the Dead: A Writer on Writing.* Toronto: Anchor Canada, 2002.

Bailey, Neil. "The Right Approach for Editing the Graphic Novel." *Active Voice/Voix active* Spring 2013: 13.

Baker, John F. "Literary Lions Now and Then." *Publishers Weekly* 5 June 1995: 38–40.

Baldassi, Julie. "National Bibliographic." *Quill and Quire* September 2014: 12–13.

Barber, John. "Bertelsmann Takes Full Control of McClelland & Stewart." *Globe and Mail* 10 January 2012. Web. 3 November 2015.

Barber, John. "Where Have All the Book Editors Gone?" *Globe and Mail* 4 February 2011. Web. 12 November 2015.

Barrie, Josh. "Rude Rejection Letters Could Cost You the Next JK Rowling or George Orwell, Publishers Warned." *Independent* 6 December 2015. Web. 9 December 2015.

Bell, Susan. *The Artful Edit: On the Practice of Editing Yourself.* New York, London: W.W. Norton & Company, 2007.

Berg, A. Scott. *Max Perkins, Editor of Genius*. New York: Riverhead Books, 1997.

Bernard, Andrew. *Rotten Rejections: A Literary Companion*. Wainscott, NY: Pushcart Press, 1990.

Bernstein, Theodore M. *Miss Thistlebottom's Hobgoblins: The Careful Writer's Guide to the Taboos, Bugbears and Outmoded Rules of English Usage*. New York: Noonday Press, 1971.

Billingham, Jo. *Editing and Revising Text*. Oxford: Oxford University Press, 2002.

Bloomgarden-Smoke, Kara. "The Taming of the Hue: Ailing Hardcovers Find a Fashion-Fun Niche." *New York Observer* 6 February 2014. Web. 25 January 2016.

Bloxham, Andy. "4M Children in UK Do Not Own a Single Book, Study Finds." *The Telegraph* 5 December 2011. Web. 9 December 2015.

Bond, Gwenda. "The Changing World of Reference: Focus on Reference 2013." *Publishers Weekly* 12 April 2013. Web. 3 November 2015.

Bornstein, David. "A Book in Every Home, and Then Some." *New York Times* 16 May 2011. Web. 9 December 2015.

Boshart, Nic. "Brave New Book World." *Alternatives Journal* 37.3 (2011): 22–23.

Boswell, John. *The Insider's Guide to Getting Published*. New York: Doubleday, 1997.

Bowen, Anna. "Spinning Straw into Gold." *Alternatives Journal* 38.3 (May 2012): 14–15.

Bringhurst, Robert. *The Elements of Typographic Style*. 4th ed. Vancouver: Hartley & Marks, 2013.

Bringhurst, Robert. *The Surface of Meaning: Books and Book Design in Canada*. Vancouver: Canadian Centre for Studies in Publishing, 2009.

Brodie, Deborah, ed. *Writing Changes Everything: The 627 Best Things Anyone Ever Said About Writing*. New York: St. Martin's Press, 1997.

Burnard, Lou, Katherine O'Brien O'Keeffe, and John Unsworth, eds. *Electronic Textual Editing*. New York: The Modern Language Association of America, 2006.

Carver, Jessicah, and Natalie Guidry. *Rethinking Paper and Ink: The Sustainable Publishing Revolution*. Portland, OR: Ooligan Press, 2011.

Cerf, Bennett. *At Random: The Reminiscences of Bennett Cerf*. New York: Random House, 1977.

Chappell, Warren, and Robert Bringhurst. *A Short History of the Printed Word*. Rev. and updated ed. Vancouver: Hartley & Marks, 1999.

Charney, Noah. "The Not-Quite End of the Book Tour." *The Atlantic* 17 October 2015. Web. 9 December 2015.

Cheung, Helen Kwan Yee. *Painted Faces on the Prairies: Cantonese Opera and the Edmonton Chinese Community*. Edmonton: University of Alberta Libraries, 2014.

Cheung, Iva. "Many North American publishers now will take only well-polished manuscripts; they have less time, $ to spend on editing. #commconv2015." *Twitter*, 18 October 2015, 11:32 a.m.

Clark, Alex. "The Lost Art of Editing." *The Guardian* 11 February 2011. Web. 12 November 2015.

Clark, Giles, and Angus Phillips. *Inside Book Publishing*. 5th ed. Oxon, New York: Routledge, 2014.

Cole, Joni B. *Toxic Feedback: Helping Writers Survive and Thrive*. Hanover, London: University Press of New England, 2006.

Colford, Paul D. "New Survey Shows You Really Can Judge a Book Simply by Its Cover." *The Spokesman-Review* 4 May 1997. Web. 16 October 2015.

Cook, Claire Kehrwald. *Line by Line: How to Edit Your Own Writing.* Boston, New York: Houghton Mifflin Harcourt, 1986.

Crawford, Michael G. *The Journalist's Legal Guide.* 5th ed. Scarborough, ON: Thomson Carswell, 2008.

Crawford, Walt. *The Librarian's Guide to Micropublishing: Helping Patrons and Communities Use Free and Low-Cost Publishing Tools to Tell Their Stories.* Medford, NJ: Information Today, Inc., 2012.

Cultural Human Resources Council/Conseil des ressources humaines du secteur culturel. "Culture Statistics Show Strength of Sector" [news release]. 9 September 2014. Web. 3 November 2015.

Cyzewski, Ed. "Can You Promote a Book Without Making Yourself Miserable?" *Jane Friedman* [blog] 9 November 2015. Web. 9 November 2015.

Darbyshire, Peter. "CanLit's $100,000 Controversy: Canadian Writers and Publishers React." *The Province* 9 July 2015. Web. 3 November 2015.

David, Walter. *All Under Heaven: The Chinese World in Maps, Pictures, and Texts from the Collection of Floyd Sully.* Edmonton: University of Alberta Libraries, 2013.

Deahl, Rachel. "Cover Reveal: Harper Lee's 'Go Set a Watchman.'" *Publishers Weekly* 25 March 2015. Web. 13 October 2015.

"Definitions of Editorial Skills." *Editors' Association of Canada.* Web. 18 November 2015.

Denton, Peter. "Where Have All the Readers Gone?" *Globe and Mail* 15 January 2016. Web. 25 January 2016.

Dickerson, Kelly. "The Surprising Story of How Andy Weir's Self-Published Book 'The Martian' Topped Best Seller Lists and Got a Movie Deal." *Business Insider* 22 June 2015. Web. 29 March 2016.

Dinka, Nicholas. "The End (and Beginning) of a CanLit Era." *Quill and Quire* 18 (September 2006): 23.

Dobson, Kit, and Smaro Kamboureli. *Producing Canadian Literature: Authors Speak on the Literary Marketplace.* Waterloo, ON: Wilfrid Laurier University Press, 2013.

Doctorow, Cory. *Information Doesn't Want to Be Free: Laws for the Internet Age.* San Francisco: McSweeney's, 2014.

"Douglas & McIntyre Owner Files for Bankruptcy." *CBC News* 22 October 2012. Web. 3 November 2015.

Driscoll, Molly. "5 Famous Plagiarism and Fraud Accusations in the Book World." *The Christian Science Monitor.* 8 December 2011. Web. 28 October 2015.

Dundas, Deborah. "Giller Prize Short List Shuts Out Penguin Random House." *TheStar.com* 5 October 2015. Web. 16 October 2015.

Dwyer, Colin. "Forget the Book, Have You Read This Irresistible Story on Blurbs?" *NPR Books* [blog] 23 October 2015. Web. 9 November 2015.

The Editorial Eye. *Stet Again! More Tricks of the Trade for Publications People.* Alexandria, VA: EEI Press, 1996.

Editors Canada. *Editing Canadian English: A Guide for Editors, Writers, and Everyone Who Works with Words.* 3rd ed. Toronto: Editors' Association of Canada, 2015.

Editors Canada. *So You Want to Be an Editor.* Toronto: Editors' Association of Canada, 2015.

Einsohn, Amy. *The Copyeditor's Handbook: A Guide for Book Publishing and Corporate Communications*. 3rd ed. Berkeley: University of California Press, 2011.

Ellis, Barbara G. *The Copy-Editing and Headline Handbook*. Cambridge, MA: Perseus Publishing, 2001.

Epstein, Jason. *Book Business: Publishing Past, Present and Future*. New York, London: W.W. Norton & Company, 2002.

Falconer, Tim. "Boys Don't Try." *This Magazine*. March/April 2005: 40–41.

Fallon, Claire. "Did Any Famous Authors Not Have Lost Manuscripts Discovered in 2015?" *Huffington Post* 17 November 2015. Web. 20 November 2015.

Faulder, Liane. "Recipes inspired by Alice in Wonderland." *Edmonton Journal* 13 November 2013: E1.

Fitzsimmons, Rebekah. "Testing the Tastemakers: Children's Literature, Bestseller Lists, and the 'Harry Potter Effect'." *Children's Literature* 40.1 (2012): 78–107. http://dx.doi.org/10.1353/chl.2012.0002.

Flanagan, Padraic. "RIP for OED as World's Finest Dictionary Goes Out of Print." *The Telegraph* 20 April 2014. Web. 13 October 2015.

Flood, Alison. "Author of False Holocaust Memoir Ordered to Return $22.5M to Publisher." *The Guardian* 12 May 2014. Web. 13 October 2015.

Flood, Alison. "Authors' Incomes Collapse to 'Abject' Levels." *The Guardian* 8 July 2014. Web. 22 December 2015.

Flood, Alison. "*Go Set a Watchman* Knocks EL James's *Grey* from Top of UK Book Charts." *The Guardian* 21 July 2015. Web. 13 October 2015.

Flood, Alison. "*Go Set a Watchman* Sells over 1M Copies in the US and Canada." *The Guardian* 20 July 2015. Web. 13 October 2015.

"Fourteen Confessions of a Book Cover Designer." *Mental Floss* n.d. Web. 18 November 2015.

Gardner, Rachelle. "Tips for a Top Book Title." *Book Machine* n.d. Web. 9 December 2015.

Gibson, Douglas. *Stories about Storytellers: Publishing Alice Munro, Robertson Davies, Alistair MacLeod, Pierre Trudeau, and Others*. Toronto: ECW Press, 2011.

"Giller Prize nominations beyond 'wildest dreams' of Windsor's Biblioasis." *CBC News* 10 September 2015. Web. 16 October 2015.

Gomez, Jeff. *Print Is Dead: Books in Our Digital Age*. New York: Palgrave Macmillan, 2008.

Gottlieb, Robert. "Editing Books Versus Editing Magazines." *The Art of Making Magazines: On Being an Editor and Other Views from the Industry*. Eds. Victor S. Navasky and Evan Cornog. New York: Columbia University Press, 2012. 155–64.

Griswold, Wendy. *Regionalism and the Reading Class*. Chicago, London: University of Chicago Press, 2008. http://dx.doi.org/10.7208/chicago/9780226309262.001.0001.

Gross, Gerald. *Editors on Editing: An Inside View of What Editors Really Do*. Rev. ed. New York: Harper & Row, 1985.

Gross, Gerald. *Editors on Editing: What Writers Need to Know About What Editors Do*. 3rd ed. New York: Grove Press, 1993.

Hale, Constance. *Sin and Syntax: How to Craft Wickedly Effective Prose*. New York: Broadway Books, 1999.

Hale, Constance. *Vex, Hex, Smash, Smooch: Let Verbs Power Your Writing*. New York, London: W.W. Norton & Company, 2012.

Harbaugh, Barry. "Yes, Book Editors Edit." *The New Yorker* 12 March 2014. Web. 12 November 2015.

Harnby, Louise. "PDF Proofreading: Essential First-Step Checks." *The Proofreader's Parlour* [blog]. 1 December 2015. Web. 2 December 2015.

"HarperCollins Publishers Sells More Than 1.1 Million Copies of *Go Set a Watchman* in Print, E-Book and Audio Format" [news release]. *HarperCollins*. Web. 13 October 2015.

Harris, Lesley Ellen. *Canadian Copyright Law*. 4th ed. Hoboken, NJ: Wiley, 2014.

Heer, Jeet. "The Life Raft." *The Walrus*. 7 February 2011. Web. 7 February 2011.

Heller, Steven. "Take Off Your Jacket...." *Print* [blog] 25 September 2015. www.printmag.com/daily-heller/take-off-your-jacket. 22 December 2015.

Henderson, Bill, ed. *The Art of Literary Publishing: Editors on Their Craft*. New York: Pushcart Press, 1980.

Henderson, Bill, and André Bernard, eds. *Pushcart's Complete Rotten Reviews and Rejections*. Wainscott, NY: Pushcart Press, 1998.

Henighan, Stephen. "Enemy of Canada's Next Great Book? BookNet." *The Tyee* 4 February 2011. Web. 8 February 2011.

"History – Douglas & McIntyre." Douglas & McIntyre. Web. 3 November 2015.

Houpt, Simon. "Canada's Elastic Policy on Foreign Publishers." *Globe and Mail* 27 June 2013. Web. 3 November 2015.

House of Anansi. "#JaneAusten meets #GoneGirl in @missjanetellis's debut novel 'The Butcher's Hook,' publishing March 2016. #anansipresales." *Twitter*, 28 September 2015, 8:11 a.m.

"How Do We Stop UK Publishing Being So Posh and White?" *The Guardian* 11 December 2015. Web. 22 December 2015.

"Imprinting Change." *Quill and Quire* January/February 2015: 12–14.

Ingram, Matthew. "What Is a Book? The Definition Continues to Blur." *Gigaom Research* 22 April 2011. Web. 9 December 2015.

Italie, Hillel. "Redefining 'Out of Print.'" *Globe and Mail* 19 May 2007.

Janowitz, Brenda. "We Regret to Inform You." *Publishers Weekly* 1 January 2016. Web. 5 January 2016.

Johnson, Tim. "E-Books Are Ugly." *Quill and Quire* April 2010: 28–29.

Judd, Karen. *Copyediting: A Practical Guide*. 2nd ed. Menlo Park, CA: Crisp Publications, 1990.

Kachka, Boris. *Hothouse: The Art of Survival and the Survival of Art at America's Most Celebrated Publishing House, Farrar Straus & Giroux*. New York: Simon & Schuster, 2013.

Kidd, Chip. "Book covers." Grant MacEwan University, Edmonton, AB. 21 January 2014. Lecture.

Kidd, Kenneth. "'Not Censorship but Selection': Censorship and/as Prizing." *Children's Literature in Education* 40.3 (2009): 197–216. http://dx.doi.org/10.1007/s10583-008-9078-4.

Kirkbride, Jasmin. "It's Not You, It's Me: Is It Time to Divorce the Returns System?" *Book Machine*. n.d. Web. 9 December 2015.

Klein, Cheryl B. *Second Sight: An Editor's Talks on Writing, Revising, and Publishing Books for Children and Young Adults*. Brooklyn: Asterisk Books, 2010.

Knight, Sarah. "Dear Authors, I'm Sorry." *Medium*. 1 December 2015. Web.
2 December 2015.

Korda, Michael. *Another Life: A Memoir of Other People*. New York: Random House,
1999.

Korda, Michael. *Making the List: A Cultural History of the American Bestseller 1900–
1999*. New York: Barnes & Noble Books, 2001.

Krissoff, Derek. "University Press Week: We Are What We Acquire." *West Virginia
University Press*. Web. 2 December 2015.

Kwakkel, Erik. "'This Book Looks Weird': Textbooks in the Medieval Classroom."
Distinguished Visitor Lecture Series. University of Alberta, Edmonton. 17 October
2012. Lecture.

Lawrence, Greg. *Jackie as Editor: The Literary Life of Jacqueline Kennedy Onassis*. New
York: St. Martin's Griffin, 2011.

Lecker, Robert. *Dr. Delicious: Memoirs of a Life in CanLit*. Montreal: Véhicule Press,
2006.

Lederman, Marsha. "Book Publisher Douglas & McIntyre Files for Bankruptcy." *Globe
and Mail* 22 October 2012. Web. 3 November 2015.

Lederman, Marsha. "Douglas & McIntyre More Than $6-Million in Debt, Documents
Show." *Globe and Mail* 31 October 2012. Web. 3 November 2015.

Lee, Marshall. *Bookmaking: Editing/Design/Production*. 3rd ed. New York, London:
W.W. Norton & Company, 2004.

Lerner, Betsy. *The Forest for the Trees: An Editor's Advice to Writers*. Rev. ed. New York:
Riverhead Books, 2010.

Lerner, Fred. *The Story of Libraries: From the Invention of Writing to the Computer Age*.
2nd ed. New York, London: Continuum, 2009.

Lewis, Mark. "Doris Kearns Goodwin and the Credibility Gap." *Forbes* 27 February
2002. Web. 28 October 2015.

Lockheed, Gordon. "General Dies in Bed, or, Jack Stoddart's Legacy." *Dooneyscafe.com*
11 September 2002. Web. 24 May 2016.

Low, Jason T. "Where Is the Diversity in Publishing? The 2015 Diversity Baseline
Survey Results." *The Open Book* [blog] 26 January 2016. Web. 31 January 2016.

Lupton, Ellen. *Thinking with Type: A Critical Guide for Designers, Writers, Editors, and
Students*. 2nd ed. New York: Princeton Architectural Press, 2010.

MacDonald, Scott. "Lost in the Shuffle." *Quill and Quire* October 2006: 19–20.

MacDonald, Scott. "The Words Are the Thing." *Quill and Quire* October 2006: 8.

Madrigal, Alexis C. "What Is a Book?" *The Atlantic* 7 May 2014. Web. 9 December
2015.

Magno, Alessandro Marzo. *Bound in Venice: The Serene Republic and the Dawn of the
Book*. New York: Europa Editions, 2013.

Mandell, Judy. *Book Editors Talk to Writers*. New York: John Wiley and Sons, 1995.

Marcus, Leonard S., ed. *Dear Genius: The Letters of Ursula Nordstrom*. New York:
HarperCollins, 2000.

Martin, George R.R. "Editors: The Writer's Natural Enemy." Speech delivered at
Coastcon II, Biloxi, MI, 10 March 1979. Web. 12 November 2015. http://dx.doi.
org/10.1017/rms.2015.67.

Maurer, Rolf. "Brought to the Brink." *Quill and Quire* September 2011: 14.

McGee, Robyn. "The Overwhelming Whiteness of the Publishing Industry." *Bitchmedia* 27 January 2016. Web. 31 January 2016.

Mckinney, Claire. "Publish, Release, Launch: Some of the What and When of Book Publishing." *Claire Mckinney PR* 19 November 2014. Web. 9 December 2015.

McMaster, Geoff. "Jargon Buster Comes to the Aid of Medicine." *Folio* [University of Alberta] 12 February 1999.

Medley, Mark. "Simon & Schuster Canada to Expand." *National Post* 29 May 2013. Web. 3 November 2015.

Medley, Mark. "Will the Newly United Penguin Random House Weaken Canadian Publishing, or Save It?" *Globe and Mail* 26 June 2015. Web. 3 November 2015.

Menaker, Daniel. *My Mistake: A Memoir.* Boston, New York: Houghton Mifflin Harcourt, 2013.

Menaker, Daniel. "Redactor Agonistes." *Barnes and Noble Review* 14 September 2009. Web. 3 November 2015.

Miller, Casey, and Kate Swift. *Words and Women.* Updated ed. Lincoln, NE: iUniverse, 2000.

Milliot, Jim. "'Watchman' Print King of the Digital Era." *Publishers Weekly* 24 July 2015. Web. 13 October 2015.

Milliot, Jim, and Laura Godfrey. "Historic Day One Sales for 'Watchman.'" *Publishers Weekly* 15 July 2015. Web. 13 October 2015.

Mod, Craig. "Books in the Age of the iPad." March 2010. craigmod.com/journal/ipad_and_books. 9 December 2015.

Moore, Georgina. "Ten Tips for Twitter Success in Publishing." *The Bookseller* 23 November 2015. Web. 24 November 2015.

Morais, Betsy. "Has Kindle Killed the Book Cover?" *The Atlantic* 16 April 2012. Web. 9 December 2015.

Moran, Whitney. "The Mysterious Industry." *Atlantic Books Today.* Holiday [Winter], 2012: 26.

Nash, Richard. *What Is the Business of Literature?* Williamsburg, NY: Thought Catalog, 2014.

Neary, Lynn. "'The Martian' Started as a Self-Published Book." *NPR* 27 February 2016. Web. 1 March 2016.

"New Potter Book to Hit U.S. with 12 Million Copies." *Reuters* 14 March 2007. Web. 13 October 2015.

Niles, Elaura. *Some Writers Deserve to Starve! 31 Brutal Truths About the Publishing Industry.* Cincinnati: Writer's Digest Books, 2005.

Norton, Scott. *Developmental Editing: A Handbook for Freelancers, Authors, and Publishers.* Chicago, London: University of Chicago Press, 2009. http://dx.doi.org/10.7208/chicago/9780226595160.001.0001.

"The Not-So-Secret Backdoor to Publishing." *Pubcrawl* 29 May 2012. Web. 3 November 2015.

Owen, Catherine. *The Other 23 & a Half Hours, or, Everything You Wanted to Know That Your MFA Didn't Teach You.* Hamilton, ON: Wolsak and Wynn, 2015.

Parmar, Parmjit. "How to Work with a Publicist." *Quill and Quire* August 2005: 11.

Parsons, Paul. *Getting Published: The Acquisition Process at University Presses.* University of Tennessee, 1989.

Pelley, Chad. "Heads Up: Self-Publishing Is Not Publishing. It's Printing." *Atlantic Books Today* Spring 2012: 20.

Phillips, Angus. *Turning the Page: The Evolution of the Book*. London, New York: Routledge, 2014.

Pilkington, Ed. "Amanda Hocking, the Writer Who Made Millions by Self-Publishing Online." *The Guardian* 12 January 2012. Web. 22 December 2015.

Piper, Andrew. *Book Was There: Reading in Electronic Times*. Chicago, London: University of Chicago Press, 2012.

Plotnik, Arthur. *The Elements of Editing: A Modern Guide for Editors and Journalists*. New York: Macmillan, 1982.

Plotnik, Arthur. *Spunk and Bite: A Writer's Guide to Bold, Contemporary Style*. New York: Random House Reference, 2007.

Plotz, David. "The Plagiarist." *Slate.com* 11 January 2002. Web. 28 October 2015.

Pressick, Jon. "Production Can Get It Done." *Quill and Quire* March 2004: 13.

Pyper, Andrew. "Editing is like giving mouth-to-mouth to a body pulled from the water: out with the bad air, in with the good. Hoping it coughs to life." *Twitter*, 14 September 2015, 6:51 a.m.

Quinn, Robin. "What's in a Name? Ten Plus Tried and True Formulas for Title Success." *PMA Newsletter* June 2000: 37–39.

Rabiner, Susan, and Alfred Fortunato. *Thinking Like Your Editor: How to Write Great Serious Nonfiction and Get It Published*. New York: W.W. Norton & Company, 2002.

Radway, Janice. *A Feeling for Books: The Book-of-the-Month Club, Literary Taste, and Middle-Class Desire*. Chapel Hill, London: University of North Carolina Press, 1997.

Rakoff, Ruth. "Taking It One Stet at a Time." *Quill and Quire* December 2010: 50.

"Random House Becomes Sole Owner of McClelland and Stewart." *CTV News* 11 January 2012. Web. 3 November 2015.

Reynolds, Eileen. "The Entirely Calculable Impact of Terry Gross." *The New Yorker* 26 May 2011. Web. 9 December 2015.

Rich, Motoko, and Joseph Berger. "False Memoir of Holocaust Is Canceled." *New York Times* 28 December 2008. Web. 13 October 2015.

Riggs, Craig. "Follow the Reader: Challenge and Opportunity in the Canadian Book Market." Book Publishers Association of Alberta, Edmonton, AB. 15 July 2009. Workshop.

Robinson, Holly. "Publishing's Unsung Heroes: Copy Editors." *Huffington Post* [blog] 10 September 2010. Web. 12 November 2015.

Ross-Larson, Bruce. *Edit Yourself: A Manual for Everyone Who Works with Words*. Rev. ed. New York, London: W.W. Norton & Company, 1996.

Rowling, J.K. "There is nothing - NOTHING - better to hear than that, so thank you and please send my love to your class!" *Twitter*, 22 November 2015, 8:14 a.m.

"Rules for Good Editing." *Quill and Quire* May 2010: 10.

Rustin, Susanna. "Dan Franklin: 'I am a tart. I am deeply shallow.'" *The Guardian* 14 March 2010. Web. 3 November 2015.

"SalesData." *BookNet Canada*. Web. 10 December 2015.

Saller, Carole Fisher. *The Subversive Copy Editor: Advice from Chicago (or, How to Negotiate Good Relationships with Your Writers, Your Colleagues, and Yourself)*. Chicago: University of Chicago Press, 2009.

Sambuchino, Sam. "How to Make a Book Trailer: Six Tips." *Writers Digest* 3 January 2013. Web. 9 December 2015.

Samson, Natalie. "Self-Publishing Comes of Age." *Quire and Quire* March 2012: 6–7.

Schiffrin, André. *The Business of Books: How International Conglomerates Took Over Publishing and Changed the Way We Read.* London, New York: Verso, 2000.

Schwartz, Marilyn. *Guidelines for Bias-Free Writing.* Bloomington, IN: Indiana University Press, 1995.

Scrivener, Leslie. "The Girl Who Loved Books So Much, She Grew up to Make Them." *The Star* 25 October 2009. Web. 12 November 2015.

Shapiro, Bill. *Other People's Rejection Letters: Relationship Enders, Career Killers, and 150 Other Letters You'll Be Glad You Didn't Receive.* New York: Clarkson/Potter, 2010.

Sharpe, Leslie, and Irene Gunther. *Editing Fact and Fiction: A Concise Guide to Book Editing.* Cambridge University Press, 1994. http://dx.doi.org/10.1017/CBO9780511527111.

Shatzkin, Mike. "What to Watch for in 2013." *The Shatzkin Files* 2 January 2013. Web. 13 October 2015.

"Shelf Awareness for March 26, 2014." *Shelf Awareness.* Web. 3 November 2015.

Sherrett, Monique. "SEO Sucks If All You're Doing Is SEO." *Boxcar Marketing* 4 December 2014. Web. 9 December 2015.

Silverman, Al. *The Time of Their Lives: The Golden Age of Great American Publishers, Their Editors and Authors.* New York: St. Martin's Press, 2008.

Singh, Anita. "*50 Shades of Grey* Is Best-Selling Book of All Time." *The Telegraph* 7 August 2012. Web. 13 October 2015.

Sittenfeld, Curtis. "24 Things No One Tells You About Book Publishing." *Buzz Feed Ideas* 15 January 2015. Web. 20 October 2015.

Smith, Dinitia. "Harvard Novelist Says Copying Was Unintentional." *New York Times* 25 April 2006. Web. 28 October 2015.

Smith, Dinitia. "Novelist Says She Read Copied Books Several Times." *New York Times* 27 April 2006. Web. 28 October 2015.

Smith, Patti. *Just Kids.* New York: Ecco, 2010.

Smith, Russell. "How to Publish a Book in Canada." *Globe and Mail* 3 July 2015. Web. 13 October 2015.

Smith, Sarah Harrison. *The Fact Checker's Bible.* New York: Anchor Books, 2004.

Sobol, John. "The Copyright Wars of 2017." *This Magazine.* May/June 2006: 28–31.

Solecki, Sam, ed. *Imagining Canadian Literature: The Selected Letters of Jack McClelland.* Toronto: Key Porter Books, 1998.

Springen, Karen. "Teenage Tweetland." *Publishers Weekly* 13 May 2013: 30–36.

Stainton, Elsie Myers. *The Fine Art of Copyediting.* 2nd ed. New York: Columbia University Press, 2002.

Steeves, Andrew. *Smoke Proofs: Essays on Literary Publishing, Printing and Typography.* Kentville, NS: Gaspereau Press, 2014.

"Structure of the ISBN." The National Library of Finland. Web. 19 January 2016.

Swanson, Claire. "New Fifty Shades Hits #1, as Vintage Heads to Press for 1.25 Million Copies." *Publishers Weekly* 2 July 2015. Web. 13 October 2015.

Swanson, Claire. "'What Pet Should I Get?' Sells 200K in First Week." *Publishers Weekly* 6 August 2015. Web. 13 October 2015.

Teitel, Emma. "Why Romance Novelists Are the Rock Stars of the Literary World." *Maclean's* 26 April 2015. Web. 9 December 2015.

"Ten Self-Published Authors Who Made It Big." *The Reading Room* 5 November 2015. Web. 17 November 2015.

Think Australian 2015. Books and Publishing: Melbourne, 2015.

"Third Edition of OED Unlikely to Appear in Print Form." *The Guardian* 29 August 2010. Web. 13 October 2015.

Thomson, Graham. "Luck and the Politician." *Edmonton Journal* 21 January 2012: A23.

Thompson, John B. *Merchants of Culture: The Publishing Business in the Twenty-First Century.* 2nd ed. New York: Plume, 2012.

"Torstar Sells Harlequin to News Corp. for $455M." *CBC News* 2 May 2014. Web. 3 November 2015.

"Torstar Sells Harlequin to News Corp. for $455M." *TheStar.com* 2 May 2014. Web. 3 November 2015.

Tuch, Becky. "More Work No Pay: Why I Detest 'Literary Citizenship'." *Slate* 23 April 2014. Web. 9 December 2015.

"'Twelve Years a Slave' and the Oscar Effect." *Publishers Weekly* 27 February 2014. Web. 3 March 2014.

"2015 Giller Prize Short List Includes 2 Books Published at Biblioasis." *CBC News* 5 October 2015. Web. 16 October 2015.

van Herk, Aritha. "Publishing and Perishing with No Parachute." *How Canadians Communicate*, vol. 1. David Taras, Frits Pannekoek, and Maria Bakardjieva, eds. Calgary: University of Calgary Press, 2003. 121–141.

Vanstone, Kay. *Practical Proofreading.* 2nd ed. Toronto: Copp Clark Ltd., 1997.

Walsh, Pat. *78 Reasons Why Your Book May Never Be Published and 14 Reasons Why It Just Might.* New York: Penguin Books, 2005.

Warner, Brooke. "Five Things Every Author Needs to Understand about Book Cover Design." *Huffington Post, The Blog* 14 January 2016. Web. 19 January 2016.

"What Should Editors Read?" *An American Editor* 3 September 2014. Web. 13 October 2015.

Wheelock, John Hall, ed. *Editor to Author: The Letters of Maxwell E. Perkins.* New York: Charles Scribner's Sons, 1979.

Whetter, Darryl. "Feel This Book." *This Magazine.* March/April 2010: 43.

"Why Traditionally Published Authors Are Choosing to Go Indie." *Huffington Post* 19 October 2015. Web. 9 December 2015.

Wilkin, Peter. *The Political Economy of Global Communication: An Introduction.* London: Pluto Press, 2001.

Williams, Joseph M. *Style: Ten Lessons in Clarity and Grace.* 6th ed. New York: Longman, 2000.

Williams, Leigh Anne. "Simon & Schuster to Begin Publishing in Canada." *Publishers Weekly* 30 May 2013. Web. 3 November 2015.

Williams, Leigh Anne. "Winstanley Takes the Lead at Penguin Canada." *Publishers Weekly* 9 July 2012. Web. 12 November 2015.

Williams, Robin. *The Non-Designer's Design Book: Design and Typographic Principles for the Visual Novice.* 4th ed. Berkeley, CA: Peachpit Press, 2014.

Wilson, Ruth. "Copyediting and Proofreading." Simon Fraser University, Vancouver, BC. August 2001. Workshop.

Woods, Stuart. "Making in Canada." *Quill and Quire* December 2013: 20–22.

Woods, Stuart. "Q&Q Salary Survey." *Quill and Quire* September 2013: 18–22.

Woods, Stuart. "Thinking Like a Bookseller." *Quill and Quire* September 2014: 14–17.

"The World's 57 Largest Book Publishers, 2015." *Publishers Weekly* 26 June 2015. Web. 22 December 2015.

The Writers' Union of Canada. "Canadian Writers Working Harder while Earning Less" [news release]. n.d. Web. 22 December 2015.

The Writers' Union of Canada. *Devaluing Creators, Endangering Creativity*. Web. Toronto: The Writers' Union of Canada, 2015.

Young, Sherman. *The Book Is Dead: Long Live the Book*. Sydney: University of New South Wales Press, 2007.

Zaid, Gabriel. *So Many Books: Reading and Publishing in an Age of Abundance*. Philadelphia: Paul Dry Books, 2003.

Zinsser, William. *On Writing Well*. 25th-anniversary ed. New York: Collins Reference, 2001.

Index

About the Author

Leslie Vermeer, PhD, is a writer, editor, reviewer, and professor based in Edmonton, Alberta. She holds master's degrees in English and education. Leslie has worked in publishing for more than twenty-five years, having edited or worked on more than one hundred books to date, and has served as a juror on a number of writing, editing, and publishing awards. She is a former member of the Editors' Association of Canada's Certification Steering Committee and is currently an executive member of the NeWest Press board. Leslie teaches at Grant MacEwan University, where her focus includes editing, grammar, print studies, and communication theory. Her research interests include applied linguistics, censorship, contemporary editing and publishing, and children's and YA publishing.

For information on Leslie's current projects, check out ReadingWithAPencil.com or www.facebook.com/readingwithapencil.